CHILTON'S
REPAIR & TUNE-UP GUIDE

W9-ANG-145

FORD RANGER
1983-84
All models

Vice President and General Manager JOHN P. KUSHNERICK
Managing Editor KERRY A. FREEMAN, S.A.E.
Senior Editor RICHARD J. RIVELE, S.A.E.
Editor W. CALVIN SETTLE JR.

CHILTON BOOK COMPANY
Radnor, Pennsylvania
19089

SAFETY NOTICE

Proper service and repair procedures are vital to the safe, reliable operation of all motor vehicles, as well as the personal safety of those performing repairs. This book outlines procedures for servicing and repairing vehicles using safe, effective methods. The procedures contain many NOTES, CAUTIONS and WARNINGS which should be followed along with standard safety procedures to eliminate the possibility of personal injury or improper service which could damage the vehicle or compromise its safety.

It is important to note that repair procedures and techniques, tools and parts for servicing motor vehicles, as well as the skill and experience of the individual performing the work vary widely. It is not possible to anticipate all of the conceivable ways or conditions under which vehicles may be serviced, or to provide cautions as to all of the possible hazards that may result. Standard and accepted safety precautions and equipment should be used when handling toxic or flammable fluids, and safety goggles or other protection should be used during cutting, grinding, chiseling, prying, or any other process that can cause material removal or projectiles.

Some procedures require the use of tools specially designed for a specific purpose. Before substituting another tool or procedure, you must be completely satisfied that neither your personal safety, nor the performance of the vehicle will be endangered.

Although information in this guide is based on industry sources and is as complete as possible at the time of publication, the possibility exists that the manufacturer made later changes which could not be included here. While striving for total accuracy, Chilton Book Company cannot assume responsibility for any errors, changes, or omissions that may occur in the compilation of this data.

PART NUMBERS

Part numbers listed in this reference are not recommendations by Chilton for any product by brand name. They are references that can be used with interchange manuals and aftermarket supplier catalogs to locate each brand supplier's discrete part number.

SPECIAL TOOLS

Special tools are recommended by the vehicle manufacturer to perform their specific job. Use has been kept to a minimum, but where absolutely necessary, are they referred to in the text by the part number of the tool manufacturer. These tools can be purchased, under the appropriate part number, from Owatonna Tool Company, Owatonna, MN 55060 or an equivalent tool can be purchased locally from a tool supplier or parts outlet. Before substituting any tool for the one recommended, read the SAFETY NOTICE at the top of this page.

ACKNOWLEDGMENTS

The Chilton Book Company expresses its appreciation to the Ford Motor Company, Dearborn, Michigan for their generous assistance.

Copyright © 1984 by Chilton Book Company
All Rights Reserved
Published in Radnor, Pennsylvania 19089, by Chilton Book Company

Manufactured in the United States of America
1234567890   3210987654

Chilton's Repair & Tune-Up Guide: Ford Ranger 1983–84
ISBN 0-8019-7338-4 pbk.
Library of Congress Catalog Card No. 83-72920

CONTENTS

Quick Reference Specifications For Your Vehicle

Fill in this chart with the most commonly used specifications for your vehicle. Specifications can be found in Chapters 1 through 3 or on the tune-up decal under the hood of the vehicle.

Tune-Up

Firing Order_____

Spark Plugs:

    Type_____

    Gap (in.)_____

Point Gap (in.)_____

Dwell Angle (°)_____

Ignition Timing (°)_____

    Vacuum (Connected/Disconnected)_____

Valve Clearance (in.)

    Intake_____   **Exhaust**_____

Capacities

Engine Oil (qts)

    With Filter Change_____

    Without Filter Change_____

Cooling System (qts)_____

Manual Transmission (pts)_____

    Type_____

Automatic Transmission (pts)_____

    Type_____

Front Differential (pts)_____

    Type_____

Rear Differential (pts)_____

    Type_____

Transfer Case (pts)_____

    Type_____

FREQUENTLY REPLACED PARTS

Use these spaces to record the part numbers of frequently replaced parts.

PCV VALVE   **OIL FILTER**   **AIR FILTER**

Manufacturer_____   **Manufacturer**_____   **Manufacturer**_____

Part No._____   **Part No.**_____   **Part No.**_____

General Information and and Maintenance

1

HOW TO USE THIS BOOK

Chilton's Repair & Tune-Up Guide for the Ford Ranger is intended to teach you more about the inner workings of your Ranger and save you money on its upkeep. The first two chapters will be used the most, since they contain maintenance and tune-up information and procedures. The following chapters concern themselves with the more complex systems of your Ranger. Operating systems from engine through brakes are covered to the extent that we feel the average do-it-yourselfer should get involved. This book will not explain such things as rebuilding the differential for the simple reason that the expertise required and the investment in special tools make this task uneconomical. We will tell you how to change your own brake pads and shoes, replace points and plugs, and many more jobs that will save you money, give you personal satisfaction, and help you avoid problems.

A secondary purpose of this book is as a reference for owners who want to understand their Ranger and/or their mechanics better. In this case, no tools at all are required.

Before removing any parts, read through the entire procedure. This will give you the overall view of what tools and supplies will be required.

The sections begin with a brief discussion of the system and what it involves, followed by adjustments, maintenance, removal and installation procedures, and repair or overhaul procedures. When repair is not considered feasible, we tell you how to remove the part and then how to install the new or rebuilt replacement. In this way, you at least save the labor costs. Backyard repair of such components as the alternator is just not practical.

Two basic mechanic's rules should be mentioned here. One, whenever the left side of the Ranger or engine is referred to, it is meant to specify the driver's side of the Ranger. Conversely, the right side of the Ranger means the passenger's side. Secondly, most screws and bolts are removed by turning counterclockwise, and tightened by turning clockwise. Safety is always the most important rule. Constantly be aware of the dangers involved in working on an automobile and take the proper precautions. Use jackstands when working under a raised vehicle. Don't smoke or allow an exposed flame to come near the battery or any part of the fuel system. Always use the proper tool and use it correctly; bruised knuckles and skinned fingers aren't a mechanic's standard equipment. Always take your time and have patience; Once you have some experience, working on your Ranger will become an enjoyable hobby.

TOOLS AND EQUIPMENT

It would be impossible to catalog each and every tool that you may need to perform all the operations included in this book. It would also not be wise for the amateur to rush out and buy an expensive set of tools on the theory that he may need one of them at some time. The best approach is to proceed slowly, gathering together a good quality set of those tools that are used most frequently. Don't be misled by the low cost of bargain tools. It is far better to spend a little more for quality, name brand tools. Forged wrenches, 10 or 12 point sockets and finetooth ratchets are by far preferable to their less expensive counterparts. As any good mechanic can tell you, there are few worse experiences than trying to work on a truck with bad tools. Your monetary savings will be far outweighed by frustration and mangled knuckles.

Begin accumulating those tools that are used most frequently; those associated with routine maintenance and tune-up. In addition to the

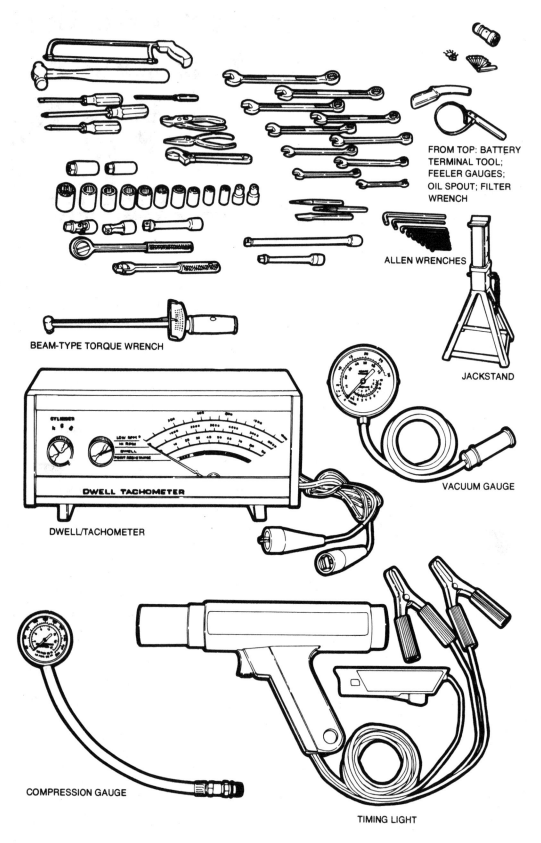

FROM TOP: BATTERY TERMINAL TOOL; FEELER GAUGES; OIL SPOUT; FILTER WRENCH

ALLEN WRENCHES

BEAM-TYPE TORQUE WRENCH

JACKSTAND

DWELL TACHOMETER

DWELL/TACHOMETER

VACUUM GAUGE

COMPRESSION GAUGE

TIMING LIGHT

You need only a basic assortment of hand tools and test instruments for most maintenance and repair jobs normal assortment of screwdrivers and pliers, you should have the following tools for routine maintenance jobs:

1. SAE wrenches, sockets and combination open end/box end wrenches;
2. Jackstands—for support;
3. Oil filter wrench;
4. Oil filler spout or funnel;
5. Grease gun—for chassis lubrication;
6. Hydrometer—for checking the battery;
7. A low flat pan for draining oil;
8. Lots of rags for wiping up the inevitable mess.

In addition to the above items, there are several others that are not absolutely necessary, but are handy to have around. These include oil drying compound, a transmission funnel, and the usual supply of lubricants, antifreeze and fluids, although these can be purchased as needed. This is a basic list for routine maintenance, but only your personal needs can accurately determine your list of tools.

The second list of tools is for tune-ups. While the tools involved here are slightly more sophisticated, they need not be outrageously expensive. There are several inexpensive tach/dwell meters on the market that are every bit as good for the average mechanic as a $100.00 professional model. Just be sure that it goes to at least 1200–1500 rpm on the tach scale, and that it works on 4, 6, and 8 cylinder engines. A basic list of tune-up equipment could include:

1. Tach/dwell meter;
2. Spark plug wrench;
3. Timing light (preferably a DC light that works from the truck's battery);
4. A set of flat feeler gauges;
5. A set of round wire spark plug gauges.

In addition to these basic tools, there are several other tools and gauges you may find useful. These incude:

1. A compression gauge. The screw-in type is slower to use, but eliminates the possibility of a faulty reading due to escaping pressure;
2. A manifold vacuum gauge;
3. A test light;
4. An induction meter. This is used for determining whether or not there is current in a wire. These are handy for use if a wire is broken somewhere in a wiring harness. As a final note, you will probably find a torque wrench necessary for all but the most basic work. The beam type models are perfectly adequate, although the newer click type are more precise.

Special Tools

Normally, the use of special factory tools is avoided for repair procedures, since these are not readily available for the do-it-yourself me-chanic. When it is possible to perform the job with more commonly available tools, it will be pointed out, but occasionally, a special tool was designed to perform a specific function and should be used. Before substituting another tool, you should be convinced that neither your safety nor the performance of the vehicle will be compromised.

Some special tools are available commercially from major tool manufacturers. Others for your Ford Ranger can be purchased from your dealer or from Owatonna Tool CO., Owatonna, Minnesota 55060.

SERVICING YOUR TRUCK SAFELY

It is virtually impossible to anticipate all of the hazards involved with automotive maintenance and service but care and common sense will prevent most accidents.

The rules of safety for mechanics range from "don't smoke around gasoline," to "use the proper tool for the job." The trick to avoid injuries is to develop safe work habits and take every possible precaution.

Do's

• Do keep a fire extinguisher and first aid kit within easy reach.
• Do wear safety glasses or goggles when cutting, drilling, grinding or prying. If you wear glasses for the sake of vision, then they should be made of hardened glass that can serve also as safety glasses, or wear safety goggles over your regular glasses.
• Do shield your eyes whenever you work around the battery. Batteries contain sulphuric acid; in case of contact with the eyes or skin, flush the area with water or a mixture of water and baking soda and get medical attention immediately.
• Do use safety stands for any under-car service. Jacks are for raising vehicles; safety stands are for making sure the vehicle stays raised until you want it to come down. Whenever the vehicle is raised, block the wheels remaining on the ground and set the parking brake.
• Do use adequate ventilation when working with any chemicals. Asbestos dust resulting from brake lining wear can cause cancer.
• Do disconnect the negative battery cable when working on the electrical system. The primary ignition system can contain up to 40,000 volts.
• Do follow manufacturer's directions whenever working with potentially hazardous mate-

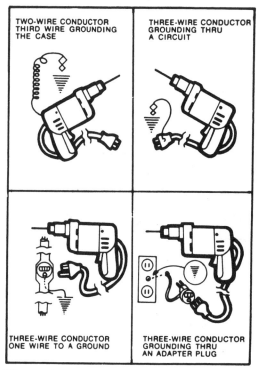

When using electric tools make sure they are properly grounded

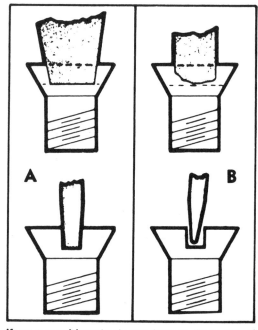

Keep screwdriver tips in good shape. They should fit the slot as shown in "A". If they look like those in "B", they need grinding or replacing

Always use jackstands when working under the truck

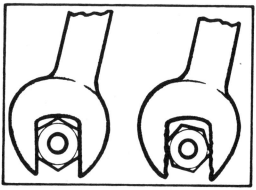

When you're using an open end wrench, use the correct size and position it properly on the flats of the nut or bolt

rials. Both brake fluid and antifreeze are poisonous if taken internally.

• Do properly maintain your tools. Loose hammerheads, mushroomed punches and chisels, frayed or poorly grounded electrical cords, excessively worn screwdrivers, spread wrenches (open end), cracked sockets, slipping ratchets, or faulty droplight sockets can cause accidents.

• Do use the proper size and type of tool for the job being done.

• Do when possible, pull on a wrench handle rather than push on it, and adjust your stance to prevent a fall.

• Do be sure that adjustable wrenches are tightly adjusted on the nut or bolt and pulled so that the face is on the side of the fixed jaw.

• Do select a wrench or socket that fits the nut or bolt. The wrench or socket should sit straight, not cocked.

• Do strike squarely with a hammer to avoid glancing blows.

• Do set the parking brake and block the drive wheels if the work requires that the engine be running.

Don'ts

• Don't run an engine in a garage or anywhere else without proper ventilation—EVER! Carbon monoxide is poisonous; it is absorbed by the body 400 times faster than oxygen; it takes a long time to leave the human body and you can build up a deadly supply of it in your system by simply breathing in a little every day. You may not realize you are slowly poisoning yourself. Always use power vents, windows, fans or open the garage doors.

• Don't work around moving parts while wearing a necktie or other loose clothing. Short sleeves are much safer than long, loose sleeves. Hard-toed shoes with neoprene soles protect your toes and give a better grip on slippery surfaces. Jewelry such as watches, fancy belt buckles, beads or body adornment of any kind is not safe working around a car. Long hair should be hidden under a hat or cap.

• Don't use pockets for toolboxes. A fall or bump can drive a screwdriver deep into your body. Even a wiping cloth hanging from the back pocket can wrap around a spinning shaft or fan.

• Don't smoke when working around gasoline, cleaning solvent or other flammable material.

• Don't smoke when working around the battery. When the battery is being charged, it gives off explosive hydrogen gas.

• Don't use gasoline to wash your hands; there are excellent soaps available. Gasoline may contain lead, and lead can enter the body through a cut, accumulating in the body until you are very ill. Gasoline also removes all the natural oils from the skin so that bone dry hands will suck up oil and grease.

• Don't service the air conditioning system unless you are equipped with the necessary tools and training. The refrigerant, R-12, is extremely cold and when exposed to the air, will instantly freeze any surface it comes in contact with, including your eyes. Although the refrigerant is normally non-toxic, R-12 becomes a deadly poisonous gas in the presence of an open flame. One good whiff of the vapors from burning refrigerant can be fatal.

IDENTIFICATION

Safety Standard Certification Label

The Certification Label is attached to the door latch edge on the driver's door except on the

Safety Standard Certification Labels
Complete Vehicles

(UNITED STATES)

```
MFD. BY FORD MOTOR CO. IN U.S.A.
DATE: 2/83                    GVWR:  3740 LBS/1696 KG
FRONT GAWR:  1910 LBS        REAR GAWR:  2012 LBS
   866 KG          WITH        866 KG            WITH
   P195/75R14SL    TIRES       P195/75R14SL      TIRES
   14x5.0JJ        RIMS        14x5.0JJ          RIMS
AT 35 PSI COLD               AT 35 PSI COLD

THIS VEHICLE CONFORMS TO ALL APPLICABLE FEDERAL MOTOR VEHICLE SAFETY
STANDARDS IN EFFECT ON THE DATE OF MANUFACTURE SHOWN ABOVE

VEHICLE IDENTIFICATION NO.   1FTCR10Z  5DUA00001

TYPE    TRUCK

EXTERIOR PAINT COLORS                          DSO
  WB  | TYPE GVW | BODY | TRANS | AXLE
```

```
         AUX. LABEL
   (Ford)  MFD. BY FORD MOTOR CO. IN U.S.A.
   SNOW PLOW PREP OR MAX. FRONT GAWR OPTION
   FRONT GAWR: 2750 LB/1247 KG
   ONLY WHEN AIR CYLINDER ASSISTED FRONT SPRINGS ARE PRESSURIZED TO
              55 PSI
   FOR COMPLETE INFORMATION, SEE MAIN LABEL
                              E37A-1020472-AA
```

DECAL APPLIED TO ALL
CANADIAN BUILT UNITS AND
ALL U.S.A. BUILT UNITS SOLD
IN CANADA

(QUEBEC)

```
     FABR. AUX E-U PAR LA FORD MOTOR CO.
DATE:                      PNBV:
PNBE AVANT:                PNBE ARRIERE:
                  AVEC
                 ‹PNEUS›
                 ‹JANTES›
A    LB/PO² A FROID        A    LB/PO² A FROID


CE VEHICULE EST CONFORME A TOUTES LES NORMES FEDERALES DE SECURITE
DES V.A. EN VIGUEUR A LA DATE DE FABR. INDIQUEE CI-DESSUS.

N° D'IDENT.
   DU VEHICULE
TYPE
```

FOR VEHICLES MFD IN U.S.A. FOR QUEBEC, CANADA.

INCOMPLETE VEHICLES

THE INCOMPLETE VEHICLE RATING DECAL IS INSTALLED ON THE DRIVER'S DOOR
LOCK PILLAR IN PLACE OF THE SAFETY STANDARD CERTIFICATION LABEL.

VEHICLE RATING DECAL

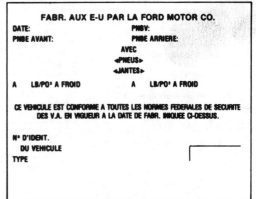

INCOMPLETE VEHICLE MANUFACTURED BY					
GVWR: 4220 LBS/1914 KG					
VEHICLE IDENTIFICATION NUMBER		1FTCR10Z 5DUA00001			
EXTERIOR PAINT COLORS	2H			48	DSO
WB	TYPE-GVW	BODY	TRANS	AXLE	
114	R105	CARS	W	84	2 D

Ford Truck Vehicle Certification Labels

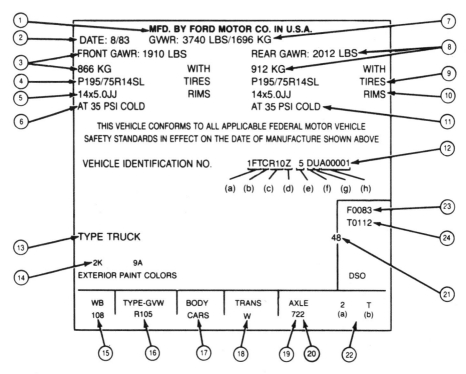

Ford Truck Safety Certification Label

① Name and Location of Manufacturer

② Date of Manufacture

③ Front Gross Axle Weight Ratings in Pounds (LB) and Kilograms (KG)

④ Front Tire Size

⑤ Rim Size

⑥ Front Tire Cold PSI

⑦ Gross Vehicle Weight Rating in Pounds (LB) and Kilograms (KG)

⑧ Rear Gross Axle Weight Rating in Pounds (LB) and Kilograms (KG)

⑨ Rear Tire Size

⑩ Rim Size

⑪ Rear Tire Cold PSI

⑫ Vehicle Identification Number
(a) World Manufacturer Identifier
(b) Brake Type and Gross Vehicle Weight Rating (GVWR) Class
(c) Model or Line, Series, Chassis and Cab Type
(d) Engine Type
(e) Check Digit
(f) Model Year
(g) Assembly Plant Code
(h) Sequential Serial and Model Year

⑬ Type Vehicle

⑭ Exterior Paint Codes (two sets of figures designates a two-tone)

⑮ Wheelbase in Inches

⑯ Model Code and GVW

⑰ Interior Trim, Seat and Body Cab Type

⑱ Transmission Code

⑲ Rear Axle Code

⑳ Front Axle Code if so equipped

㉑ District Special Order Codes

㉒ Suspension Identification Codes
(a) Front Spring Code
(b) Rear Spring Code

㉓ Front Axle Accessory Reserve Capacity in Pounds

㉔ Total Accessory Reserve Capacity in Pounds

SAMPLE VIN NUMBER

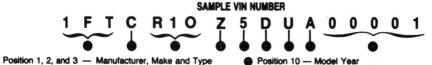

● Position 1, 2, and 3 — Manufacturer, Make and Type (World Manufacturer Identifier)
● Position 4 — Brakes/GVWR
● Position 5, 6, and 7 — Model or Line, Series, Chassis, Cab Type
● Position 8 — Engine Type
● Position 9 — Check Digit
● Position 10 — Model Year
● Position 11 — Assembly Plant
● Position 12 — Constant "A" until sequence number of 99,999 is reached, then changes to a constant "B" and so on
● Position 13 through 17 — Sequence number — begins at 00001

Ford Truck Identification Number (VIN)

Engine Codes

VIN Code	Displacement		Cylinders	Fuel	Manufacturer
	Liter	CID			
C	2.0	122	4	Gas	Ford
A	2.3	140	4	Gas	Ford
S	2.8	173	6	Gas	Ford
P	2.2	134	4	Diesel	Ford

Transmission Codes

Code	Description
V	Automatic-C3
W	Automatic-C5
X	Manual—4 speed
5	Manual—5 Speed Overdrive

Rear Axle Codes and Ratios

Code	Description	# Capacity	Ratio
72	Regular	2200	3.08
74	Regular	2200	3.45
84	Regular	2700	3.45
86	Regular	2700	3.73
F4	Limited Slip	2700	3.45
F6	Limited Slip	2700	3.73

French Certification label which is located on the passenger's side door.

Vehicle Identification Number

The VIN is found on a stamped plate located on the upper left corner of the instrument panel, visible through the windshield.

Engine

The engine can be identified by checking the eighth position on the Vehicle Identification Number Plate.

Transmission

The transmission can be identified by checking the code on the Safety Standard Certification Label attached to the driver's door post.

ROUTINE MAINTENANCE

Air Cleaner

1. Unlock and open the engine compartment cover.

2. Remove the wing nut holding the air cleaner assembly to the top of the carburetor.

3. Disconnect the hoses at the air cleaner and remove the entire air cleaner assembly from the carburetor.

NOTE: *On diesel models the air cleaner assembly must be unbolted from its mounting brackets to be removed.*

4. Remove and discard the old filter element, and inspect the condition of the air cleaner mounting gasket. Replace the gasket as necessary. Thoroughly clean the air cleaner tray.

5. Install the air cleaner body on the carburetor.

6. Place the new filter element in the air cleaner body and install the cover and tighten the wing nut. If the word TOP appears on the element, make sure that the side the word appears on is facing up when the element is in place.

7. Connect the hoses to the air cleaner.

PCV Valve

Check the PCV valve according to the Preventive Maintenance Schedule at the end of this chapter to see if it is free and not gummed up, stuck or blocked. To check the valve, remove it from the engine and work the valve by sticking a screwdriver in the crankcase side of the valve. It should move. It is possible to clean the PCV valve by soaking it in a solvent and blowing it out with compressed air. This can restore the valve to some level of operating order.

This should be used only in emergency situations. Otherwise, the valve should be replaced.

Evaporative Canister

The fuel evaporative emission control canister should be inspected for damage or leaks at the hose fittings. Repair or replace any old or cracked hoses. Replace the canister if it is damaged in any way. The canister is located on the left side radiator support, under the hood.

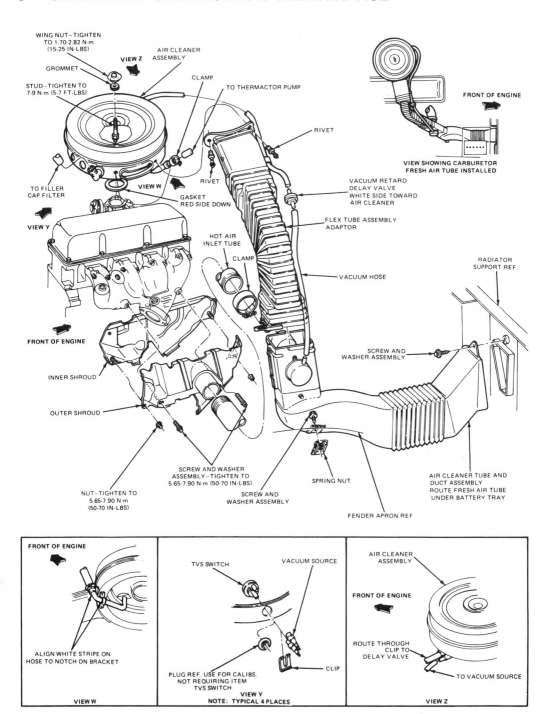

Air cleaner assembly—4-122,140 engines

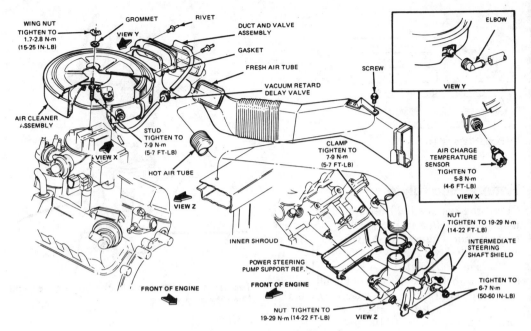

Air cleaner assembly—6-173 engine

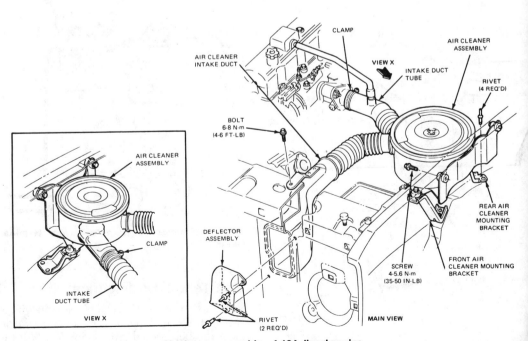

Air cleaner assembly—4-134 diesel engine

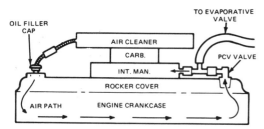

Typical PCV system

Battery Electrolyte

Check the battery fluid level at least once a month; more often in hot weather. Some batteries do not require a fluid level check. These are the sealed type.

Water may be added to a battery when the level drops below the bottom of the filler neck. Add water until the level contacts the bottom of the neck. The water surface will appear distorted upon contact with the neck. Some batteries use a filler cap with a glass rod attached, which will appear to glow when the fluid level in that cell is low. Another brand has a small "eye" in the top of the case, which glows when the electrolyte is low.

The battery should be kept clean and free from corrosion. Corrosion may be removed with a solution of baking soda and water and a stiff wire brush. After assembly, coat the terminals and cable ends with grease. This will prevent a corrosion build up.

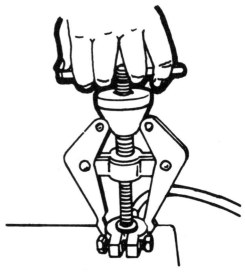

Top terminal battery cable can be removed with this inexpensive tool

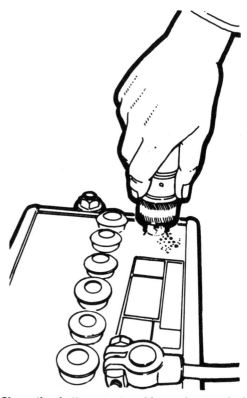

Clean the battery posts with a wire terminal cleaner

Belt Tension Adjustment

Belt tension can be checked by pressing on the belt at the center point of its longest straight run. The belt should give about ¼–½″. If the belt is loose, it will slip. If the belt is too tight

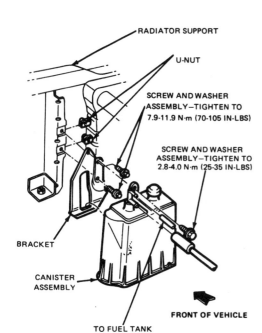

RADIATOR SUPPORT

U-NUT

SCREW AND WASHER ASSEMBLY—TIGHTEN TO 7.9-11.9 N·m (70-105 IN·LBS)

SCREW AND WASHER ASSEMBLY—TIGHTEN TO 2.8-4.0 N·m (25-35 IN·LBS)

BRACKET

CANISTER ASSEMBLY

FRONT OF VEHICLE

TO FUEL TANK

Evaporative Canister

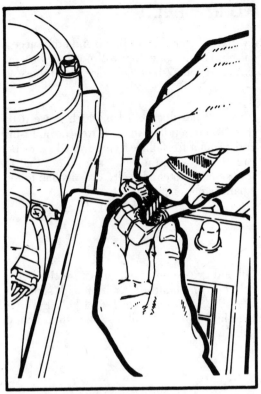

Clean the cable ends with a stiff wire cleaning tool

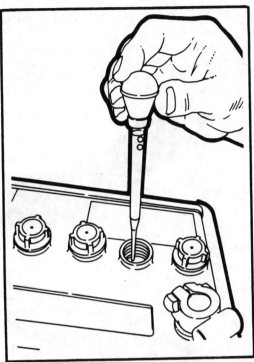

An inexpensive hydrometer will quickly test the battery's state of charge

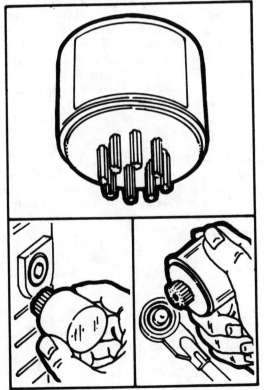

Side terminal batteries require a special wire brush for cleaning

it will damage bearings in the driven unit. Those units being driven, such as the alternator, power steering pump or compressor, have a bolt which when loosened allows the unit to move for belt adjustment. Sometimes it is necessary to loosen the pivot bolt also, to make the adjustment.

Hose Replacement

1. Drain the existing antifreeze and coolant. Open the radiator and engine drain petcocks, or disconnect the bottom radiator hose, at the radiator outlet.

NOTE: *Before opening the radiator petcock, spray it with some penetrating lubricant.*

2. Loosen the clamps on each end of the hose to be removed.

3. Slide the hose off the connections.

4. Position the clamps on each end of the new hose.

5. Slide the hose onto the connections, then tighten the clamps. If the connections have a bead around the edges, make sure the clamps are located beyond the beads.

6. Refill the cooling system with coolant. Run the engine for several minutes, then check the hose connections for leaks.

HOW TO SPOT WORN V-BELTS

V-Belts are vital to efficient engine operation—they drive the fan, water pump and other accessories. They require little maintenance (occasional tightening) but they will not last forever. Slipping or failure of the V-belt will lead to overheating. If your V-belt looks like any of these, it should be replaced.

This belt has deep cracks, which cause it to flex. Too much flexing leads to heat build-up and premature failure. These cracks can be caused by using the belt on a pulley that is too small. Notched belts are available for small diameter pulleys.

Cracking or weathering

Oil and grease on a belt can cause the belt's rubber compounds to soften and separate from the reinforcing cords that hold the belt together. The belt will first slip, then finally fail altogether.

Softening (grease and oil)

Glazing is caused by a belt that is slipping. A slipping belt can cause a run-down battery, erratic power steering, overheating or poor accessory performance. The more the belt slips, the more glazing will be built up on the surface of the belt. The more the belt is glazed, the more it will slip. If the glazing is light, tighten the belt.

Glazing

The cover of this belt is worn off and is peeling away. The reinforcing cords will begin to wear and the belt will shortly break. When the belt cover wears in spots or has a rough jagged appearance, check the pulley grooves for roughness.

Worn cover

This belt is on the verge of breaking and leaving you stranded. The layers of the belt are separating and the reinforcing cords are exposed. It's just a matter of time before it breaks completely.

`paration

HOW TO SPOT BAD HOSES

Both the upper and lower radiator hoses are called upon to perform difficult jobs in an inhospitable environment. They are subject to nearly 18 psi at under hood temperatures often over 280°F., and must circulate nearly 7500 gallons of coolant an hour—3 good reasons to have good hoses.

Swollen hose

A good test for any hose is to feel it for soft or spongy spots. Frequently these will appear as swollen areas of the hose. The most likely cause is oil soaking. This hose could burst at any time, when hot or under pressure.

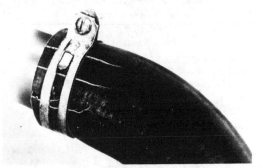

Cracked hose

Cracked hoses can usually be seen but feel the hoses to be sure they have not hardened; a prime cause of cracking. This hose has cracked down to the reinforcing cords and could split at any of the cracks.

Frayed hose end (due to weak clamp)

Weakened clamps frequently are the cause of hose and cooling system failure. The connection between the pipe and hose has deteriorated enough to allow coolant to escape when the engine is hot.

Debris in cooling system

Debris, rust and scale in the cooling system can cause the inside of a hose to weaken. This can usually be felt on the outside of the hose as soft or thinner areas.

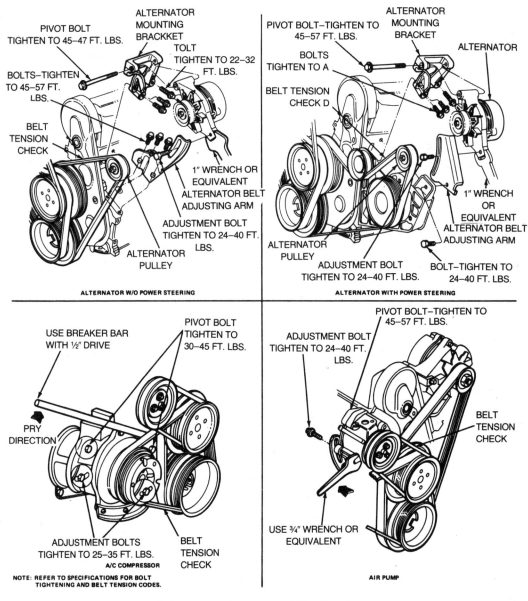

Belt tension adjustment—4-122,140 engines

Air Conditioning

SAFETY PRECAUTIONS

There are two particular hazards associated with air conditioning systems and they both relate to the refrigerant gas.

First, the refrigerant gas is an extremely cold substance. When exposed to air, it will instantly freeze any surface it comes in contact with, including your eyes. The other hazard relates to fire. Although normally non-toxic, refrigerant gas becomes highly poisonous in the presence of an open flame. One good whiff of the vapor formed by burning refrigerant can be fatal. Keep all forms of fire (including cigarettes) well clear of the air conditioning system.

Any repair work to an air conditioning system should be left to a professional. Do not, under any circumstances, attempt to loosen or

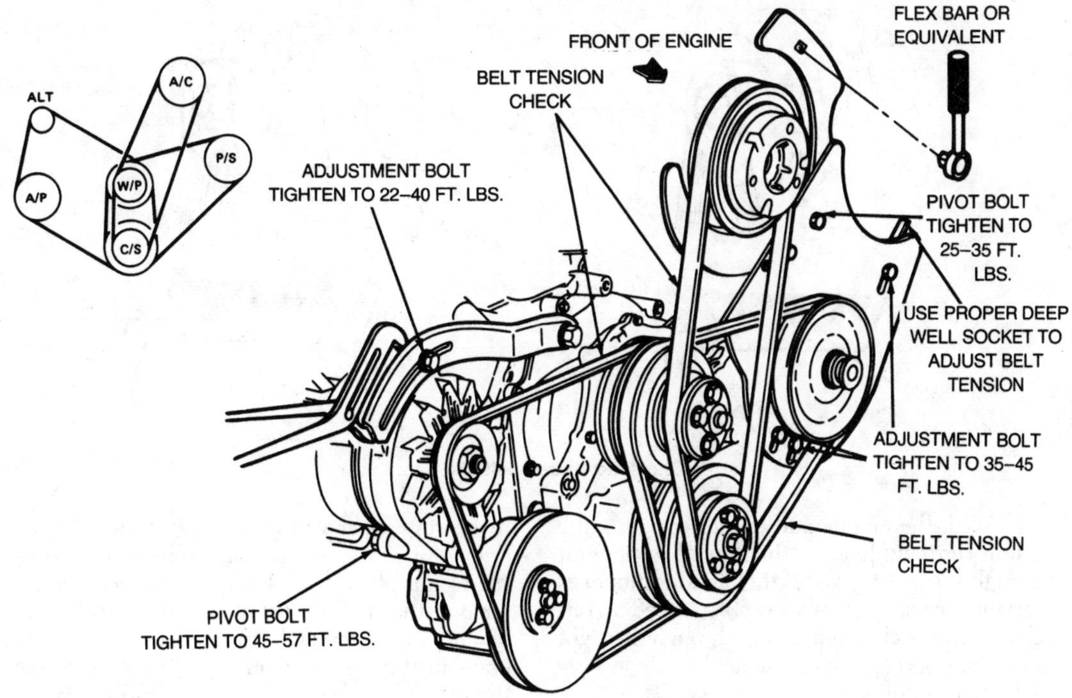
ALT
A/C
P/S
W/P
A/P
C/S
FRONT OF ENGINE
BELT TENSION CHECK
FLEX BAR OR EQUIVALENT
ADJUSTMENT BOLT TIGHTEN TO 22–40 FT. LBS.
PIVOT BOLT TIGHTEN TO 25–35 FT. LBS.
USE PROPER DEEP WELL SOCKET TO ADJUST BELT TENSION
ADJUSTMENT BOLT TIGHTEN TO 35–45 FT. LBS.
BELT TENSION CHECK
PIVOT BOLT TIGHTEN TO 45–57 FT. LBS.

Belt tension adjustments—6-173 engine

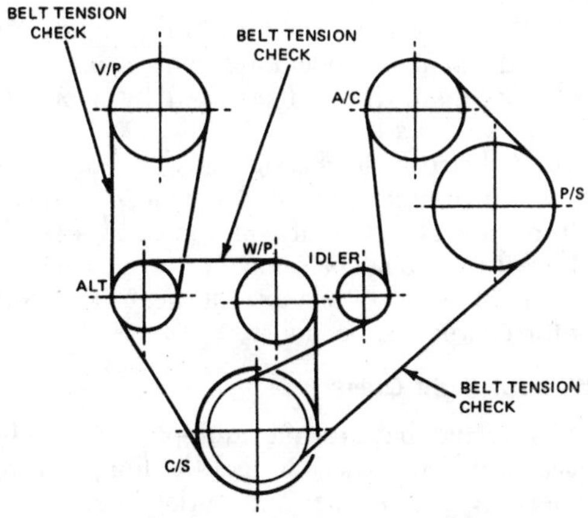
BELT TENSION CHECK
BELT TENSION CHECK
V/P
A/C
P/S
W/P
IDLER
ALT
BELT TENSION CHECK
C/S

Belt tension adjustment—4-134 diesel engine

tighten any fittings or perform any work other than that outlined here.

CHECKING FOR OIL LEAKS

Refrigerant leaks show up as oily areas on the various components because the compressor oil is transported around the entire system along with the refrigerant. Look for oil spots on all the hoses and lines, and especially on the hose and tubing connections. If there are oily deposits, the system may have a leak, and you should have it checked by a qualified repairman.

NOTE: *A small area of oil on the front of the compressor is normal and no cause for alarm.*

KEEP THE CONDENSER CLEAR

Periodically inspect the front of the condenser for bent fins or foreign material (dirt, bugs, leaves, etc.) If any cooling fins are bent, straighten them carefully with needle-nosed pliers. You can remove any debris with a stiff bristle brush or hose.

OPERATE THE A/C SYSTEM PERIODICALLY

A lot of A/C problems can be avoided by simply running the air conditioner at least once a week, regardless of the season. Let the system run for at least 5 minutes a week (even in the winter), and you'll keep the internal parts lubricated as well as preventing the hoses from hardening.

REFRIGERANT LEVEL CHECK

There are two ways to check refrigerant level, depending on how your model is equipped.

With Sight Glass

The first order of business when checking the sight glass is to find the sight glass. It will either be in the head of the receiver/drier, or in one of the metal lines leading from the top of the receiver/drier. Once you've found it, wipe it clean and proceed as follows:

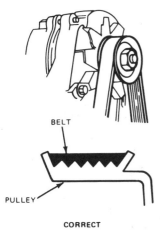 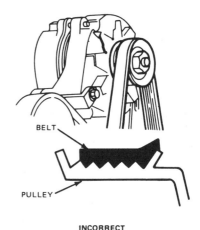

BELT

PULLEY

CORRECT

BELT

PULLEY

INCORRECT

Checking ribbed belt alignment

1. With the engine and the air conditioning system running, look for the flow of refrigerant through the sight glass. If the air conditioner is working properly, you'll be able to see a continuous flow of clear refrigerant through the sight glass, with perhaps an occasional bubble at very high temperatures.

2. Cycle the air conditioner on and off to make sure what you are seeing is clear refrigerant. Since the refrigerant is clear, it is possible to mistake a completely discharged system for one that is fully charged. Turn the system off and watch the sight glass. If there is refrigerant in the system, you'll see bubbles during the off cycle. If you observe no bubbles when the system is running, and the air flow from the unit in the car is delivering cold air, everything is OK.

3. If you observe bubbles in the sight glass while the system is operating, the system is low on refrigerant. Have it checked by a professional.

4. Oil streaks in the sight glass are an indication of trouble. Most of the time, if you see oil in the sight glass, it will appear as a series of streaks, although occasionally it may be a solid stream of oil. In either case, it means that part of the charge has been lost.

Without Sight Glass

On vehicles that are not equipped with sight glasses, it is necessary to feel the temperature difference in the inlet and outlet lines at the receiver/drier to gauge the refrigerant level. Use the following procedure:

1. Locate the receiver/drier. It will generally be up front near the condenser. It is shaped like a small fire extinguisher and will always have two lines connected to it. One line goes to the expansion valve and the other goes to the condenser.

2. With the engine and the air conditioner running, place one hand on the line between the receiver/drier and the expansion valve, and the other on the line from the expansion valve, and the other on the line from the compressor to the condenser. Gauge their relative temperatures. If they are both the same approximate temperature, the system is correctly charged.

3. If the line from the expansion vlave to the

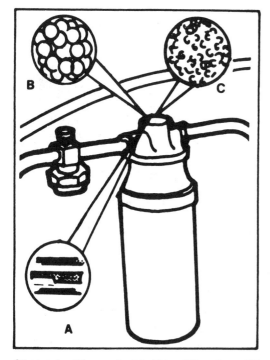

B

C

A

Oil streaks (A), constant bubbles (B) or foam (C) indicate there is not enough refrigerant in the system. Occasional bubbles during initial operation is normal. A clear sight glass indicates a proper charge of refrigerant or no refrigerant at all, which can be determined by the presence of cold air at the outlets in the car. If the glass is clouded with a milky white substance, have the receiver/drier checked professionally

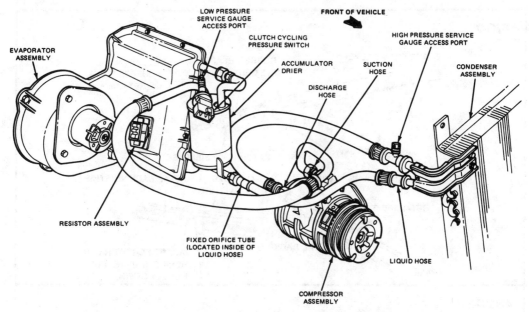

Typical air conditioning system, showing all components

receiver/drier is a lot colder than the line from the condenser to the compressor, then the system is overcharged. It should be noted that this is an extremely rare condition.

4. If the line that leads from the compressor to the condenser is a lot colder than the other line, the system is undercharged.

5. If the system is undercharged or overcharged, have it checked by a professional air conditioning mechanic.

Windshield Wipers

Intense heat from the sun, snow and ice, road oils and the chemicals used in windshield washer solvents combine to deteriorate the rubber wiper refills. The refills should be replaced about twice a year or whenever the blades begin to streak or chatter.

WIPER REFILL REPLACEMENT

Normally, if the wipers are not cleaning the windshield properly, only the refill has to be replaced. The blade and arm usually require replacement only in the event of damage. It is not necessary (except on new Tridon refills) to remove the arm or the blade to replace the refill (rubber part), though you may have to position the arm higher on the glass. You can do this turning the ignition switch on and operating the wipers. When they are positioned where they are accessible, turn the ignition switch off.

There are several types of refills and your vehicle could have any kind, since aftermarket blades and arms may not use exactly the same refill as the original equipment.

Most Anco styles use a release button that is pushed down to allow the refill to slide out of the yoke jaws. The new refills slide in and locks in place. Some Anco refills are removed by locating where the metal backing strip or the refill is wider. Insert a small screwdriver blade between the frame and metal backing strip. Press down to release the refill from the retaining tab.

The Trico style is unlocked at one end by squeezing 2 metal tabs, and the refill is slid out of the frame jaws. When the new refill is installed, the tabs will click into place, locking the refill.

The polycarbonate type is held in place by a locking lever that is pushed downward out of the groove in the arm to free the refill. When the new refill is installed, it will lock in place automatically.

The Tridon refill has a plastic backing strip with a notch about an inch from the end. Hold the blade (frame) on a hard surface so that the frame is tightly bowed. Grip the tip of the backing strip and pull up while twisting counterclockwise. The backing strip will snap out of the retaining tab. Do this for the remaining tabs until the refill is free of the arm. The length of these refills is molded into the end and they should be replaced with identical types.

No matter which type of refill you use, be sure that all of the frame claws engage the refill. Before operating the wipers, be sure that no part of the metal frame is contacting the windshield.

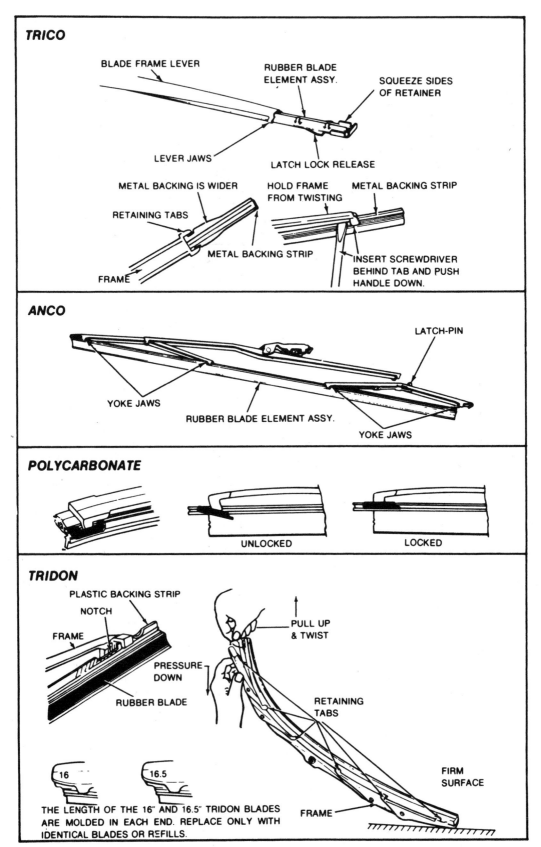

TRICO

BLADE FRAME LEVER

RUBBER BLADE ELEMENT ASSY.

SQUEEZE SIDES OF RETAINER

LEVER JAWS

LATCH LOCK RELEASE

METAL BACKING IS WIDER

HOLD FRAME FROM TWISTING

METAL BACKING STRIP

RETAINING TABS

METAL BACKING STRIP

INSERT SCREWDRIVER BEHIND TAB AND PUSH HANDLE DOWN.

FRAME

ANCO

LATCH-PIN

YOKE JAWS

RUBBER BLADE ELEMENT ASSY.

YOKE JAWS

POLYCARBONATE

UNLOCKED

LOCKED

TRIDON

PLASTIC BACKING STRIP

NOTCH

FRAME

PULL UP & TWIST

PRESSURE DOWN

RUBBER BLADE

RETAINING TABS

16

16.5

FIRM SURFACE

THE LENGTH OF THE 16" AND 16.5" TRIDON BLADES ARE MOLDED IN EACH END. REPLACE ONLY WITH IDENTICAL BLADES OR REFILLS.

FRAME

Popular styles of wiper refills

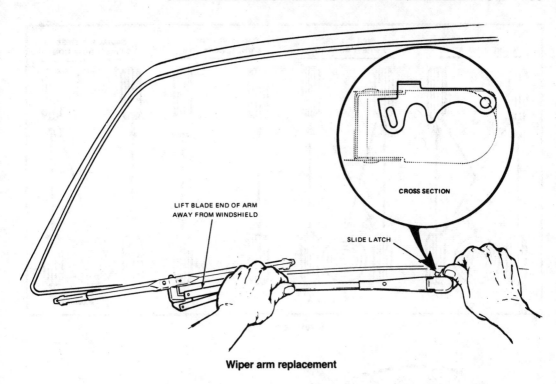

LIFT BLADE END OF ARM
AWAY FROM WINDSHIELD

CROSS SECTION

SLIDE LATCH

Wiper arm replacement

WIPER ARM REPLACEMENT

To remove the arm and blade assembly, raise the blade end of the arm off of the windshield and move the slide latch away from the pivot shaft. The wiper arm can now be removed from the shaft without the use of any tools.

To install, push the main head over the pivot shaft. Be sure the wipers are in the parked position, and the blade assembly is in its correct position. Hold the main arm head onto the pivot shaft while raising the blade end of the wiper arm and push the slide latch into the lock under the pivot shaft head. Then, lower the blade to the windshield. If the blade does not lower to the windshield, the slide latch is not completely in place.

Tires and Wheels

Tires should be rotated periodically. Follow the accompanying diagrams for the proper rotation pattern. Note that radial tires must be kept on the same side of the vehicle on which they were originally installed.

If uneven tire wear occurs before 6,000 miles, rotate the tires sooner and determine the cause of the uneven wear. Uneven wear and abnormal wear patterns may be caused by incorrect front end alignment, uneven tire pressures, unbalanced tires and worn or broken suspension parts. Tire balance should be checked at rotation.

Common sense and good driving habits will prolong the life of any tire. Hard cornering and spinning tires is a waste of money. Overloading and improper inflation also cut tire life.

The tires' air pressure should be checked frequently to be sure they agree with those specified for the tires shown on the safety certification label attached to the driver's side door pillar.

Inspect the tires frequently for cuts, cracks, side wall bubbles or stones. Replace any tire with a deep cut or side wall bubble.

When replacing original equipment tires, remember that the replacement should be in, at least, a set of four. It is a bad idea to mix tire tread patterns or sizes. Tire construction types should never be mixed. The differences in handling characteristics can be hazardous.

When installing oversized tires, make sure that sufficient clearance exists at all points and angles. Oversized flotation tires will require wider rims than those on a stock vehicle. Mud and snow tires should be operated at manufacturer's recommended pressures, and not at sustained high speeds.

In summary, select the type of tire according to the type of driving that will be done most of the time.

Fuel Filter Replacement

It is recommended that the fuel filter be replaced periodically. The filter is of one piece

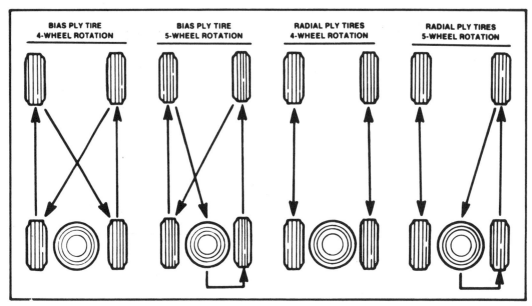

Tire rotation pattern

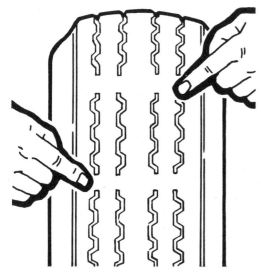

Tread wear indicators are built into tires

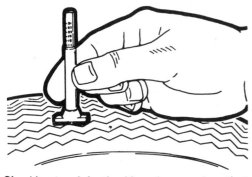

Checking tread depth with an inexpensive depth tester

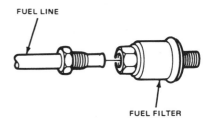

Gasoline fuel filter—Screw-in type

construction and cannot be cleaned, it must be replaced.

GASOLINE ENGINES

1. Remove the air cleaner.
2. Loosen and remove the fuel tube from the filter.
3. Unscrew the filter from the carburetor.
4. Apply Loctite® or equivalent to the external threads of the new filter and screw the filter into the carburetor.
5. Hand start the tube nut into the fuel filter. While holding the filter with a wrench to prevent it from turning, tighten the fuel line tube nut.
6. Start the engine and check for fuel leaks.
7. Replace the air cleaner.

DIESEL ENGINE

1. Remove the spin-on filter by turning counterclockwise with hands or suitable tool, and discard filter.
2. Clean the filter mounting surfaces.
3. Coat the gasket of the new filter with clean diesel fuel.

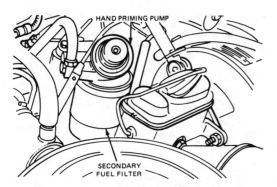

Priming the pump and fuel filter assembly—diesel engine

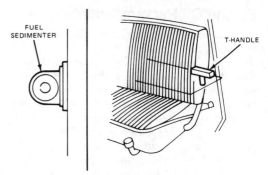

Diesel fuel sedimenter draining

4. Tighten the filter until the gasket touches the filter header, then tighten an additional ½ turn.

5. Air-Bleed the fuel system using the following procedure:

    a. Loosen the fuel filter air vent plug.

    b. Pump the priming pump on the top of the filter adapter.

    c. Continue pumping until clear fuel, free from air bubbles, flows from the air vent plug.

    d. Depress the priming pump and hold down while closing the air vent plug.

Start the engine and check for fuel leaks.

NOTE: *To avoid fuel contamination do not add fuel directly to the new filter.*

Diesel Fuel Sedimenter

Water should be changed from the diesel fuel sedimenter whenever the light on the instrument panel comes on or every 5,000 miles. More frequent drain intervals may be required depending on the quality of the fuel used.

    CAUTION: *The truck must be stopped with the engine off when draining the sedimenter. Fuel may ignite if sedimenter is drained while the engine is running or the truck is moving.*

The instrument panel warning light (WATER IN FUEL) will glow when approximately ½ liter of water has accumulated in the sedimenter. When the warning light glows, shut off the engine as soon as safely possible. A suitable drain pan or container should be placed under the sedimenter, which is mounted inside the frame rail, underneath the driver's side of the cab. To drain the fuel sedimenter, pull up on the T-handle (located on the cab floor behind the driver's seat) until resistance is felt. Turn the ignition switch to the ON position so the warning light glows and hold T-handle up for approximately 45 seconds after light goes out.

To stop draining fuel, release T-handle and inspect sedimenter to verify that draining has stopped. Discard drained fluid suitably.

FLUIDS AND LUBRICANTS

Fuel Recommendations

GASOLINE ENGINES

All trucks equipped with catalytic converters must use *UNLEADED GASOLINE ONLY.* Your truck has been designed to operate using unleaded gasoline with a minimum octane rating of 87.

Use of gasoline with a lower octane rating than 87 can cause persistent, heavy spark knock, which can lead to engine damage. Occasional light spark knock may be noticed when accelerating or driving up hills. This should not be a concern because the maximum fuel economy is obtained under the condition of occasional light spark knock. A higher octane fuel may be used but is not necessary for proper engine operation.

DIESEL ENGINE

The 134cu. in. (2200cc) diesel engine is designed to use number 1-D or 2-D diesel fuel only. At temperatures below 20°F number 2-D fuel may thicken and clog the fuel filter. The engine is equipped with an in-line fuel heater to help prevent the fuel turning to wax as it gets colder and clogging the fuel filter. However, if the engine starts but stalls out after a short time in cold weather and will not restart, the fuel filter may be clogged. For best results in cold weather use number 1-D diesel fuel or a "winterized" number 2-D diesel fuel to prevent waxing in the fuel system

    CAUTION: *DO NOT add gasoline, gasohol, alcohol or cetane improvers to the diesel fuel. Also, DO NOT use starting fluids such as ether in the diesel air intake system. The use of these liquids or fluids will cause damage to the engine and/or fuel system.*

Engine Oil Recommendation

Many factors help to determine the proper oil for your truck. The big question is what viscosity to use and when. The whole question of viscosity revolves around the lowest anticipated ambient temperature to be encountered before your next oil change. The recommended viscosities for sustained temperatures ranging from below 0°F to above 32°F are listed below. Multiviscosity oils are recommended because of their wider range of acceptable temperatures and driving conditions.

NOTE: *Always use detergent oil. Detergent oil does not clean or loosen deposits, it merely prevents or inhibits the formation of deposits.*

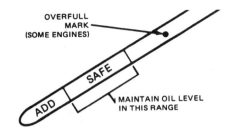

Checking engine oil level

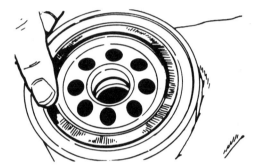

Lubricate the gasket on the new filter with clean engine oil. A dry gasket may not make a good seal and will allow the filter to leak

Lowest Sustained Air Temperature Anticipated	Multiviscosity Engine Oil
Above 32°F	SAE 10W-30, 10W-40 20W-40, or 20W-50
Above 0°F	SAE 10W-30, or 10W-40
Below 0°F	SAE 5W-20, or 5W-30

Gasoline Engine: API category SF
Diesel Engine: API category SF/CC or SF/CD

OIL LEVEL CHECK

Check the engine oil level every time you fill the gas tank. The oil level should be above the ADD mark and not above the FULL mark on the dipstick. Make sure that the dipstick is inserted into the crankcase as far as possible and that the vehicle is resting on level ground.

NOTE: *The engine oil should be checked only when warm (operating temperature).*

CHANGING OIL AND FILTER

NOTE: *The diesel engine has two oil filters, the primary filter is on the bottom left side of the engine and the secondary filter is on the right side.*

Change the oil and filter according to the Preventive Maintenance Schedule at end of this chapter. Always use a good brand of the proper viscosity oil and a known brand of oil filter. If the vehicle is driven in severe climate or heavy dust conditions, a more frequent change schedule is advised. It is a good idea to change the filter every time the oil is changed. If the oil filter is retained, a quart of dirty oil is left in the engine. Before draining the oil, make sure that the engine is at operating temperature. Hot oil will hold more impurities in suspension and will flow better, allowing the removal of more oil and dirt.

Drain the oil into a suitable receptacle. After the drain plug is loosened, unscrew the plug with your fingers, using a rag to shield your fingers from the heat. Push in on the plug as you unscrew it so you can feel when all of the screw threads are out of the hole. You can then remove the plug quickly with the minimum amount of oil running down your arm and you will also have the plug in your hand and not in the bottom of a pan of hot oil. Be careful of the oil. If it is at operating temperatures it is hot enough to burn you.

To change the filter, raise and support the vehicle on jackstands. Place a container under the filter to catch the oil. The use of a filter wrench is highly recommended. Place the wrench over the filter and loosen it. Remove the wrench and unscrew the filter by hand. If for some reason, the filter will not budge, even when using a filter wrench, drive a screwdriver through the filter near the top. Use this to turn the filter.

When installing a new filter, lubricate the gasket with clean engine oil and tighten the filter by hand until it contacts the engine. Turn it one-half turn past this contact point. Overtightening the filter will distort the gasket and cause an oil leak.

Manual Transmission
FLUID RECOMMENDATION

The lubricant in the transmission should be checked and changed periodically, except when the vehicle has been operated in deep water and water has entered the transmission. When this happens, change the lubricant in the transmission as soon as possible. Use Standard Transmission Lube SAE 80 in the manual transmission.

LEVEL CHECK

Before checking the lubricant level in the transmission, make sure that the vehicle is on level ground. Remove the fill plug from the transmission. Remove the plug slowly when it starts to reach the end of the threads on the plug. Hold the plug up against the hole and move it away slowly. This is to minimize the loss of lubricant through the fill hole. The level of the lubricant should be up to the bottom of the fill hole. If lubricant is not present at the bottom of the fill hole, add Standard Transmission Lube SAE 80 until it reaches the proper level. A squeeze bottle or siphon gun is used to fill a manual transmission with lubricant.

DRAIN AND REFILL

Drain and refill the transmission daily if the vehicle has been operating in water. All you have to do is remove the drain plug which is located at the bottom of the transmission. Allow all the lubricant to run out before replacing the plug. Replace the oil with the correct fluid. If you are experiencing hard shifting and the weather is very cold, use a lighter weight fluid in the transmission. If you don't have a pressure gun to install the oil, use a suction gun.

Automatic Transmission
FLUID RECOMMENDATION

Refer to the dipstick to confirm automatic transmission fluid specifications. With a C-5 automatic transmission, add only Type H automatic transmission fluid. With a C-3 automatic transmission, use only Dexron® II automatic transmission fluid.

LEVEL CHECK

The fluid level in an automatic transmission is checked when the transmission is at operating temperatures. If the vehicle has been sitting and is cold, drive it at highway speeds for at least 20 minutes to warm up the transmission. The transmission dipstick is located under the hood, against the firewall, on the right side.

1. With the transmission in Park, the engine running at idle speed, the foot brakes applied and the vehicle resting on level ground, move the transmission gear selector through each of the gear positions, including Reverse, allowing time for the transmission to engage. Return the shift selector to the Park position and apply the parking brake. Do not turn the engine off, but leave it running at idle speed.

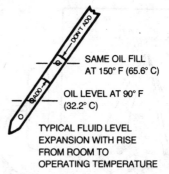

Checking automatic transmission fluid level

2. Clean all dirt from around the transmission dipstick cap and the end of the filler tube.

3. Pull the dipstick out of the tube, wipe it off with a clean cloth, and push it back into the tube all the way, making sure that it seats completely.

4. Pull the dipstick out of the tube again and read the level of the fluid on the stick. The level should be between the ADD and FULL marks. If fluid must be added, add enough fluid through the tube to raise the level up to between the ADD and FULL marks. Do not overfill the transmission because this will cause foaming and loss of fluid through the vent and malfunctioning of the transmission.

DRAIN AND REFILL

The transmission is filled at the factory with a high quality fluid that both transmits power and lubricates and will last a long time. In most cases, the need to change the fluid in the automatic transmission will never arise under normal use. But since this is a truck andmost likely will be subjected to more severe operating conditions than a conventional vehicle, the fluid may have to be replaced. An internal leak in the radiator could develop and contaminate the fluid, necessitating fluid replacement.

The extra load of operating the vehicle in deep sand, towing a heavy trailer, etc., causes the transmission to create more heat due to increased friction. This extra heat is transferred to the transmission fluid and, if the oil is allowed to become too hot, it will change its chemical composition or become scorched. When this occurs, valve bodies become clogged and the transmission doesn't operate as efficiently as it should. Serious damage to the transmission can result.

You can tell if the transmission fluid is scorched by noting a distinctive "burned" smell and discoloration. Scorched transmission fluid is dark brown or black as opposed to its normal bright, clear red color. Since transmission fluid "cooks" in stages, it may develop forms of sludge or varnish. Pull the dip stick out and place the

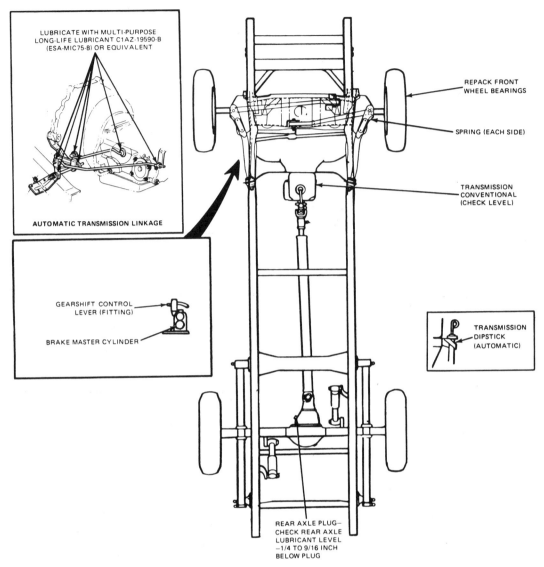

LUBRICATE WITH MULTI-PURPOSE LONG-LIFE LUBRICANT C1AZ-19590-B (ESA-MIC75-B) OR EQUIVALENT

AUTOMATIC TRANSMISSION LINKAGE

GEARSHIFT CONTROL LEVER (FITTING)

BRAKE MASTER CYLINDER

REPACK FRONT WHEEL BEARINGS

SPRING (EACH SIDE)

TRANSMISSION CONVENTIONAL (CHECK LEVEL)

TRANSMISSION DIPSTICK (AUTOMATIC)

REAR AXLE PLUG— CHECK REAR AXLE LUBRICANT LEVEL —1/4 TO 9/16 INCH BELOW PLUG

Lubrication chart—2WD models

end on a tissue or paper towel. Particles of sludge can be seen more easily this way. If any of the above conditions do exist, the transmission fluid should be completely drained, the filtering screens cleaned, the transmission inspected for possible damage and new fluid installed. Refer to Chapter 6 under Automatic Transmission for Pan Removal and Filter Service Procedures.

CAUTION: *Use of a fluid other than those specified could result in transmission malfunction and/or failure.*

NOTE: *If it is necessary to completely drain and refill the transmission, it will be necessary to remove the residual fluid from the torque converter and the cooler lines.*

The procedure for partial drain and refill, for a vehicle that is in service, is as follows:

1. Place a drain pan under the transmission. Loosen the pan bolts and pull one corner down to start the fluid draining. Remove and empty the pan.

2. When all the fluid has drained from the transmission, remove and clean the pan and screen. Make sure not to leave any solvent residue or lint from the rags in the pan.

3. Install the pan with a new gasket and tighten the bolts in a criss-cross pattern.

4. Add three quarts of fluid through the dipstick tube.

With a C-5 automatic transmission, add only fluid meeting Ford Specification ESP-MZC166-H, Type H automatic transmission fluid. With a C-3 automatic transmission, use only DEXRON®-II automatic transmission fluid. The level should be at or below the ADD mark.

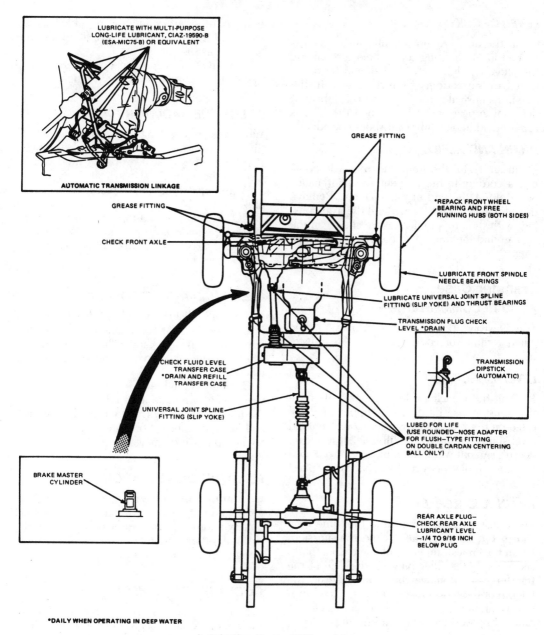

LUBRICATE WITH MULTI-PURPOSE
LONG-LIFE LUBRICANT, C1AZ-19590-B
(ESA-MIC75-B) OR EQUIVALENT

AUTOMATIC TRANSMISSION LINKAGE

GREASE FITTING

GREASE FITTING

CHECK FRONT AXLE

*REPACK FRONT WHEEL
BEARING AND FREE
RUNNING HUBS (BOTH SIDES)

LUBRICATE FRONT SPINDLE
NEEDLE BEARINGS

LUBRICATE UNIVERSAL JOINT SPLINE
FITTING (SLIP YOKE) AND THRUST BEARINGS

TRANSMISSION PLUG CHECK
LEVEL *DRAIN

TRANSMISSION
DIPSTICK
(AUTOMATIC)

CHECK FLUID LEVEL
TRANSFER CASE
*DRAIN AND REFILL
TRANSFER CASE

UNIVERSAL JOINT SPLINE
FITTING (SLIP YOKE)

LUBED FOR LIFE
(USE ROUNDED—NOSE ADAPTER
FOR FLUSH—TYPE FITTING
ON DOUBLE CARDAN CENTERING
BALL ONLY)

BRAKE MASTER
CYLINDER

REAR AXLE PLUG—
CHECK REAR AXLE
LUBRICANT LEVEL
—1/4 TO 9/16 INCH
BELOW PLUG

*DAILY WHEN OPERATING IN DEEP WATER

Lubrication chart—4WD models

5. Check the fluid level as soon as the transmission reaches operating temperature for the first time. Make sure that the level is between ADD and FULL.

To drain the torque converter:

1. Remove the converter housing lower cover.

2. Rotate the torque converter until the drain plug comes into view.

3. Remove the drain plug and allow the transmission fluid to drain.

4. Flush the cooler lines completely.

Front and Rear Axle

FLUID RECOMMENDATION

Use hypoid gear lubricant SAE 80 or 90.

NOTE: *On models with the front locking differential, add 2 oz. of friction modifier Ford part #EST-M2C118-A. On models with the rear locking differential, use only locking differential fluid Ford part #ESP-M2C154-A or its equivalent, and add 4 oz. of friction modifier Ford part #EST-M2C118-A.*

LEVEL CHECK

Clean the area around the fill plug, which is located in the housing cover, before removing the plug. The lubricant level should be maintained to the bottom of the fill hole with the axle in its normal running position. If lubricant does not appear at the hole when the plug is removed additional lubricant should be added.

DRAIN AND REFILL

Drain and refill the front and rear axle housings according to the Preventive Maintenance Schedule at the end of this chapter. Remove the oil with a suction gun. Refill the axle housings with the proper oil. Be sure and clean the area around the drain plug before removing the plug.

Transfer Case

FLUID RECOMMENDATION

Use Dexron® II automatic transmission fluid when refilling or adding fluid to the transfer case.

LEVEL CHECK

Position the vehicle on level ground. Remove the transfer case fill plug (the upper plug) located on the rear of the transfer case. The fluid level should be up to the fill hole. If lubricant doesn't run out when the plug is removed, add lubricant until it does run out and then replace the fill plug.

DRAIN AND REFILL

The transfer case is serviced at the same time and in the same manner as the transmission. Clean the area around the filler and drain plugs and remove the filler plug on the side of the transfer case. Remove the drain plug on the bottom of the transfer case and allow the lubricant to drain completely. Clean and install the drain plug. Add the proper lubricant.

Cooling System

At least once every 2 years, the engine cooling system should be inspected, flushed, and refilled with fresh coolant. If the coolant is left in the system too long, it loses its ability to prevent rust and corrosion. If the coolnat has too much water, it won't protect against freezing.

The pressure cap should be looked at for signs of age or deterioration. Fan belt and other drive belts should be inspected and adjusted to the proper tension.

Hose clamps should be tightened, and soft or cracked hoses replaced. Damp spots, or accumulations of rust or dye near hoses, water pump or other areas, indicate possible leakage, which must be corrected before filling the system with fresh coolant.

> CAUTION: *Never remove the radiator cap under any conditions while the engine is hot.*

CHECK THE RADIATOR CAP

While you are checking the coolant level, check the radiator cap for a worn or cracked gasket. If the cap doesn't seal properly, fluid will be lost and the engine will overheat.

Worn caps should be replaced with a new one.

> NOTE: *The locking-type radiator cap assembly should not be removed to check the coolant level. If necessary, add coolant to the reservoir only.*

CLEAN RADIATOR OF DEBRIS

Periodically clean any debris—leaves, paper, insects, etc.—from the radiator fins. Pick the large pieces off by hand. The smaller pieces can be washed away with water pressure from a hose.

Carefully straighten any bent radiator fins with a pair of needle nose pliers. Be careful—the fins are very soft. Don't wiggle the fins back and forth too much. Straighten them once and try not to move them again.

FLUID RECOMMENDATION

Coolant mixture in the truck is 50–50 ethylene glycol and water for year round use. Use a good quality antifreeze with water pump lubricants, rust inhibitors and other corrosion inhibitors along with acid neutralizers.

COOLANT LEVEL CHECK

When the engine overheats (allowing time for the engine to cool off) or once a month check the engine coolant level when the engine is cool and add coolant as required.

> CAUTION: *Never remove the radiator cap under any circumstances while the engine is hot. Wait until the engine has cooled and even then use extreme care when removing the radiator cap.*

Wrap a thick rag around the cap and turn it slowly to the first stop. Stand back and allow the pressure to be released from the cooling system. After all the pressure has been released from the system, press down again with the rag wrapped around the cap and remove it. Make sure the fluid level is between the filler neck seat and 1½ inches below the filler neck seat. Add coolant is required.

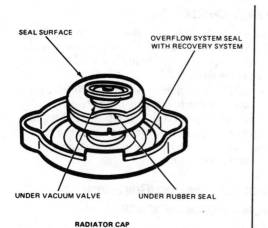

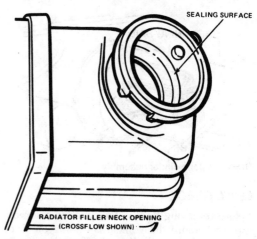

Cleaning and inspecting the radiator cap, and the filler neck opening

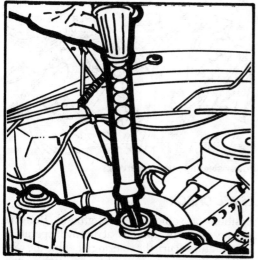

Check anti-freeze protection with an inexpensive tester

MAINTAIN FLUID LEVEL BETWEEN FILLER NECK SEAT AND 38mm (1.5 INCHES) BELOW FILLER NECK SEAT. ADD COOLANT ONLY WHEN FLUID LEVEL IS MORE THAN 38mm (1.5 INCHES) BELOW FILLER NECK SEAT.

Checking the engine coolant level

DRAIN AND REFILL THE COOLING SYSTEM

Completely draining and refilling the cooling system every two years at least will remove accumulated rust, scale and other deposits.

CAUTION: *Never remove the radiator cap under any circumstances while the engine is hot. Wait until the engine has cooled and even then use extreme care when removing the radiator cap.*

1. Remove the radiator cap and drain the existing antifreeze and coolant. Open the radiator and engine drain petcocks, or disconnect the bottom radiator hose, at the radiator outlet.
   NOTE: *Before opening the radiator petcock, spray it with some penetrating lubricant.*

2. Close the petcock or re-connect the lower hose and fill the system with water.

3. Add a can of quality radiator flush.

4. Idle the engine until the upper radiator hose gets hot.

5. Drain the system again.

6. Repeat this process until the drained water is clear and free of scale.

7. Close all petcocks and connect all the hoses.

8. If equipped with a coolant recovery system, flush the reservoir with water and leave empty.

9. Determine the capacity of your cooling system (see capacities specifications). Add a 50/50 mix of quality antifreeze (ethylene glycol) and water to provide the desired protection.

10. Run the engine to operating temperature.

11. Stop the engine and check the coolant level.

12. Check the level ofmprotection with an antifreeze tester, replace the cap and check for leaks.

Brake Master Cylinder

The master cylinder reservoir is located under the hood, on the left side firewall.

FLUID RECOMMENDATION

Fill the master cylinder with a good quality Heavy-Duty Dot 3 Brake Fluid.

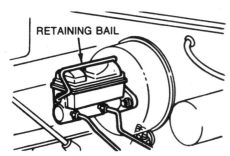

Brake master cylinder assembly

LEVEL CHECK

Before removing the master cylinder reservoir cap, make sure the vehicle is resting on level ground and clean all dirt away from the top of the master cylinder. Pry off the retaining clip and remove the cap. The brake fluid level should be within ¼ in. of the top of the reservoir.

If the level of the brake fluid is less than half the volume of the reservoir, it is advised that you check the brake system for leaks. Leaks in a hydraulic brake system most commonly occur at the wheel cylinder.

There is a rubber diaphragm in the top of the master cylinder cap. As the fluid level lowers in the reservoir due to normal brake shoe wear or leakage, the diaphragm takes up the space. This is to prevent the loss of brake fluid out the vented cap and contamination by dirt. After filling the master cylinder to the proper level with brake fluid, but before replacing the cap, fold the rubber diaphragm up into the cap, then replace the cap on the reservoir and tighten the retaining bolt or snap the retaining clip into place.

Clutch Master Cylinder

The clutch master cylinder reservoir is located under the hood, on the left side firewall.

FLUID RECOMMENDATION

Fill the clutch master cylinder reservoir with a good quality Heavy-Duty Brake Fluid.

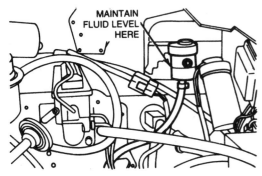

Clutch master cylinder reservoir

LEVEL CHECK

The fluid level in the clutch reservoir should be visible at or above the step in the translucent reservoir body, filling above this point is not necessary.

NOTE: *The fluid level in the clutch reservoir will slowly increase as the clutch wears.*

Before removing the clutch master cylinder reservoir cap, make sure the vehicle is resting on level ground and clean all dirt away from the top of the reservoir.

Power Steering Reservoir

FLUID RECOMMENDATION

Fill the power steering reservoir with a good quality power steering fluid or Auto. Trans. Fluid-Type "F".

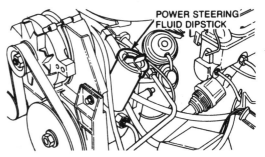

Power steering pump reservoir

LEVEL CHECK

Position the vehicle on level ground. Run the engine until the fluid is at normal operating temperature. Turn the steering wheel all the way to the left and right several times. Position the wheels in the straight ahead position, then shut off the engine. Check the fluid level on the dipstick which is attached to the reservoir cap. The level should be between the ADD and FULL marks on the dipstick. Add fluid accordingly. Do not overfill.

Steering Gear

The steering gear is factory-filled with steering gear grease. Changing of this lubricant should not be performed and the housing should not be drained, lubricant is not required for the life of the steering gear.

Chassis Greasing

The preceding charts indicate where the grease fittings are located on the truck, and other level checks that should be made at the time of the chassis grease job. The vehicle should be greased according to the Preventive Mainte-

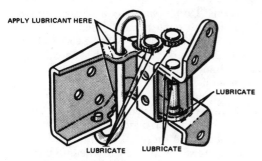

APPLY LUBRICANT HERE

LUBRICATE

LUBRICATE   LUBRICATE

Door hinge lubrication points

nance Schedule at the end of this chapter, and more often if the vehicle is operating in dusty areas or under heavy-duty conditions. If the vehicle is operated in deep water, lubricate the chassis every day.

Body Lubrication

Lubricate the door and tailgate hinges, door locks, door latches, and the hood latch when they become noisy or difficult to operate. A high quality Polyethylene Grease should be used as a lubricant.

Front Hub Assembly

For (4 x 4) vehicles, see Chapter 7.

Wheel Bearings

It is recommended that the front wheel bearings be cleaned, inspected and repacked pe-

riodically and as soon as possible after the front hubs have been submerged in water.

NOTE: *Sodium based grease is not compatible with lithium based grease. Be careful not to mix the two types. The best way to prevent this is to completely clean all of the old grease from the hub assembly before installing any new grease.*

Before handling the bearings there are a few things that you should remember to do and try to avoid. DO the following:

1. Remove all outside dirt from the housing before exposing the bearing.
2. Treat a used bearing as gently as you would a new one.
3. Work with clean tools in clean surroundings.
4 Use clean, dry canvas gloves, or at least clean, dry hands.
5. Clean solvents and flushing fluids are a must.
6. Use clean paper when laying out the bearings to dry.
7. Protect disassembled bearings from rust and dirt. Cover them up.
8. Use clean rags to wipe bearings.
9. Keep the bearings in oil-proof paper when they are to be stored or are not in use.
10. Clean the inside of the housing before replacing the bearing.

Do NOT do the following.

1. Don't work in dirty surroundings.
2. Don't use dirty, chipped, or damaged tools.

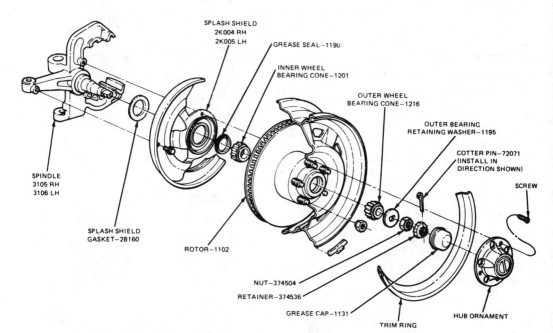

SPLASH SHIELD
2K004 RH
2K005 LH

GREASE SEAL—1190

INNER WHEEL
BEARING CONE—1201

OUTER WHEEL
BEARING CONE—1216

OUTER BEARING
RETAINING WASHER—1195

COTTER PIN—72071
(INSTALL IN
DIRECTION SHOWN)

SCREW

SPINDLE
3105 RH
3106 LH

SPLASH SHIELD
GASKET—2B160

ROTOR—1102

NUT—374504

RETAINER—374536

GREASE CAP—1131

TRIM RING

HUB ORNAMENT

Exploded view of the wheel bearings, grease seal and front hub

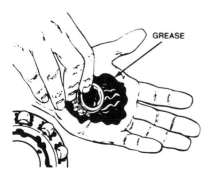

Packing the wheel bearings with grease

3. Try not to work on wooden work benches, or use wooden mallets.

4. Don't handle bearings with dirty or moist hands.

5. Do not use gasoline for cleaning; use a safe solvent.

6. Do not spin-dry bearings with compressed air. They will be damaged.

7. Do not spin unclean bearings.

8. Avoid using cotton waste or dirty clothes to wipe bearings.

9. Try not to scratch or nick bearing surfaces.

10. Do not allow the bearing to come in contact with dirt or rust at any time.

REMOVAL AND INSTALLATION

NOTE: *For (4 x 4) vehicles, see Chapter 7.*

1. Raise the vehicle and support with jackstands. Remove the wheel from the rotor.

2. Remove the caliper and support it from the underbody with a piece of wire.

3. Remove the grease cap from the hub and the cotter pin, nut lock, adjusting nut, and the flatwasher from the spindle. Remove the outer bearing assembly from the hub.

4. Carefully pull the hub and rotor assembly off the spindle.

5. Carefully drive out the inner bearing cone and grease seal from the hub.

6. Clean the inner and outer bearing cups with solvent. Inspect the cups for scratches, pits, excessive wear, and other damage. The cups are removed from the hub by driving them out with a drift pin. They are installed in the same manner.

7. If it is determined that the cups are in satisfactory condition and are to remain in the hub, clean and inspect the cones (bearings). Replace the bearings if necessary. When replacing either the cone or the cup, both parts should be replaced as a unit.

8. Thoroughly clean all components in a suitable solvent and blow them dry with compressed air or allow them to dry while resting on clean paper.

NOTE: *Do not spin the bearings with compressed air while drying them.*

9. Cover the spindle with a clean cloth, and brush all loose dirt from the dust shield. Carefully remove the cloth to prevent dirt from falling from it.

10. Install the inner or outer bearing cups if they were removed. Thoroughly clean the old grease from the surrounding surfaces.

11. Pack the inside of the hub with wheel bearing grease. Add grease to the hub until the grease is flush with the inside diameter of the bearing cup.

12. Pack the bearing cone and roller assembly with wheel bearing grease. A bearing packer is desirable for this operation. If a packer is not available, place a large portion of grease into the palm of your hand and sliding the edge of the roller cage through the grease with your other hand, work as much grease in between the rollers as possible.

13. Position the inner bearing cone and roller assembly in the inner cup. Apply a light film of grease to the lips of a new grease seal and install the seal into the hub.

14. Carefully position the hub and rotor assembly onto the spindle. Be careful not to damage the grease seal.

15. Place the outer bearing into position on the spindle and into the bearing cup. Install the adjusting nut finger tight.

16. Adjust the wheel bearings as shown in the illustration. Install the grease cap.

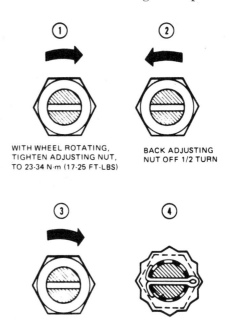

Front wheel bearing adjustment procedure

17. Install the caliper to the spindle and the wheel to the hub.

18. Remove the jackstands and lower the vehicle. Torque the lug nuts to 85–115 ft. lbs.

PUSHING AND TOWING

To push-start your vehicle, (manual transmissions only) follow the procedures below. Check to make sure that the bumpers of both vehicles are aligned so neither will be damaged. Be sure that all electrical system components are turned off (headlights, heater, blower, etc.). Turn on the ignition switch. Place the shift lever in Third or Fourth and push in the clutch pedal. At about 15 mph, signal the driver of the pushing vehicle to fall back, depress the accelerator pedal, and release the clutch pedal slowly. The engine should start.

When you are doing the pushing or pulling, make sure that the two bumpers match so you won't damage the vehicle you are to push. Another good idea is to put an old tire between the two vehicles. If the bumpers don't match, perhaps you should tow the other vehicle. If the other vehicle is just stuck, use First gear to slowly push it out. Tell the driver of the other vehicle to go slowly too. Try to keep your truck right up against the other vehicle while you are pushing. If the two vehicles do separate, stop and start over again instead of trying to catch up and ramming the other vehicle. Also try, as much as possible, to avoid riding or slipping the clutch. When the other vehicle gains enough traction, it should pull away from your vehicle.

If you have to tow the other vehicle, make sure that the two chain or rope is sufficiently long and strong, and that it is attached securely to both vehicles at a strong place. Attach the chain at a point on the frame or as close to it as possible. Once again, go slowly and tell the other driver to do the same. Warn the other driver not to allow too much slack in the line when he gains traction and can move under his own power. Otherwise he may run over the tow line and damage both vehicles. If your truck has to be towed by a tow truck, it can be towed forward for any distance with the driveshaft connected as long as it is done fairly slowly. If your truck has to be towed backward and is a (4 x 4) model, unlock the front axle driving hubs, to prevent the front differential from rotating and place the transfer case in neutral. Also clamp the steering wheel on all models, in the straight ahead position with a clamping device designed for towing service.

JACKING AND HOSTING

It is very important to be careful about running the engine, on vehicles equipped with limited slip differentials, while the vehicle is up on a jack. This is because if the drive train is engaged, power is transmitted to the wheel with the best traction and the vehicle will drive off the jack, resulting in possible damage or injury.

Jack the truck from under the axles, radius arms, or spring hangers and the frame. Be sure and block the diagonally opposite wheel to prevent the vehicle from moving. Place jackstands under the vehicle at the points mentioned above when you are going to work under the vehicle.

CAUTION: *On models equipped with an under chassis mounted spare tire, remove the tire, wheel or tire carrier from the vehicle before it is placed in a high lift position in order to avoid sudden weight release from the chassis.*

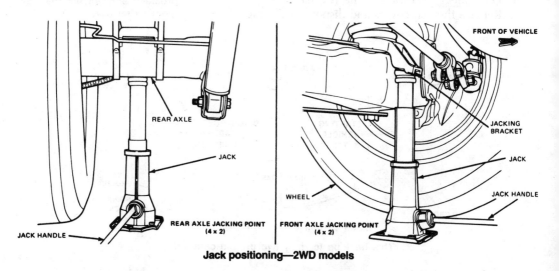

Jack positioning—2WD models

JUMP STARTING A DEAD BATTERY

The chemical reaction in a battery produces explosive hydrogen gas. This is the safe way to jump start a dead battery, reducing the chances of an accidental spark that could cause an explosion.

Jump Starting Precautions

1. Be sure both batteries are of the same voltage.
2. Be sure both batteries are of the same polarity (have the same grounded terminal).
3. Be sure the vehicles are not touching.
4. Be sure the vent cap holes are not obstructed.
5. Do not smoke or allow sparks around the battery.
6. In cold weather, check for frozen electrolyte in the battery.
7. Do not allow electrolyte on your skin or clothing.
8. Be sure the electrolyte is not frozen.

Jump Starting Procedure

1. Determine voltages of the two batteries; they must be the same.
2. Bring the starting vehicle close (they must not touch) so that the batteries can be reached easily.
3. Turn off all accessories and both engines. Put both cars in Neutral or Park and set the handbrake.
4. Cover the cell caps with a rag—do not cover terminals.
5. If the terminals on the run-down battery are heavily corroded, clean them.
6. Identify the positive and negative posts on both batteries and connect the cables in the order shown.
7. Start the engine of the starting vehicle and run it at fast idle. Try to start the car with the dead battery. Crank it for no more than 10 seconds at a time and let it cool off for 20 seconds in between tries.
8. If it doesn't start in 3 tries, there is something else wrong.
9. Disconnect the cables in the reverse order.
10. Replace the cell covers and dispose of the rags.

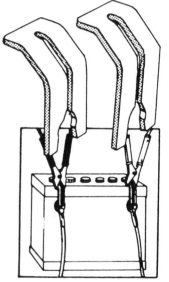

Side terminal batteries occasionally pose a problem when connecting jumper cables. There frequently isn't enough room to clamp the cables without touching sheet metal. Side terminal adaptors are available to alleviate this problem and should be removed after use.

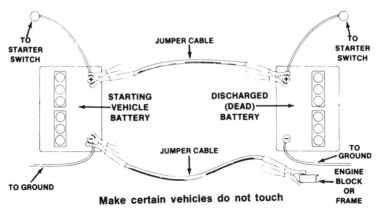

TO STARTER SWITCH

JUMPER CABLE

TO STARTER SWITCH

STARTING VEHICLE BATTERY

DISCHARGED (DEAD) BATTERY

JUMPER CABLE

TO GROUND

TO GROUND

ENGINE BLOCK OR FRAME

Make certain vehicles do not touch

This hook-up for negative ground cars only

When raising the vehicle on a hoist, position the front end adapters under the center of the lower suspension arm or the spring supports as near to the wheels as practical. The rear hoist adapters should be placed under the spring mounting pads or the rear axle housing. Be careful not to touch the rear shock absorber mounting brackets.

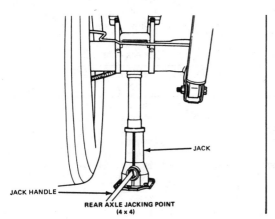 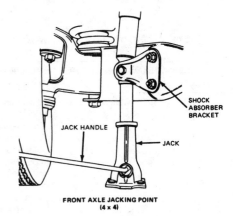

Jack positioning—4WD models

Preventive Maintenance Schedule

Interval	Item	Service
Perform at each month or distance shown, whichever comes first.		
Gasoline Engine		
7½ mos/7,500 miles	engine oil & filter	change
	drive belts	check tension & condition
	idle speed (2.0L & 2.3L only)	check
	valve clearance (2.8L only)	check
	wheel lug nuts	torque
	u-joints	lubricate
	double cardin joint	lubricate
12 mos/12,000 miles	cooling system	check & inspect
30 mos/30,000 miles	spark plugs	replace
	air cleaner filter	replace
	PCV valve	replace
	crankcase emission filter	replace
	choke linkage	clean
	clutch reservoir	check fluid level
	disc brake system	inspect
	front wheel bearings (4x2)	inspect & lubricate
	spindle needle bearings (4x4)	inspect & lubricate
	thrust bearings (4x4)	inspect & lubricate
	hub lock (4x4)	inspect & lubricate
	driveshaft output slip yokes	lubricate
	exhaust system	inspect
	drive axle R.H. axle shaft slip yoke	lubricate
	steering gear	inspect

NOTE: *When operating under severe conditions, cut maintenance schedules in half. When operating daily in water, repack hubs daily and change axle, transmission and transfer case fluids every 1,000 miles.*

Preventive Maintenance Schedule

Interval	Item	Service
Perform at each month or distance shown, whichever comes first.		
Diesel Engines		
5 mos/5,000 miles	engine oil & filter fuel sedimenter wheel lug nuts	change drain water torque
12 mos/12,000 miles	bypass oil filter cooling system	change check & inspect
15 mos/15,000 miles	drive belts valve clearance	check tension & condition check
30 mos/30,000 miles	air cleaner filter air cleaner hoses secondary fuel filter disc brake system clutch reservoir front wheel bearings driveshaft slip yoke u-joints exhaust system steering gear	replace inspect replace inspect check fluid level inspect & lubricate lubricate lubricate inspect inspect
36 mos/36,000 miles	coolant	replace

NOTE: *When operating under severe conditions, cut maintenance schedules in half. When operating daily in water, repack hubs daily and change axle, transmission and transfer case fluids every 1,000 miles.*

Capacities Chart

Year	Engine No. Cyl Displacement	Crankcase With Filter (qts)	Transmission		Transfer Case (pts)	Axle (pts)		Cooling System (qts)	
			Manual (pts)	Auto- matic (qts)		Front	Rear	wo-A/C	w-A/C
1983–84	4-122 (2.0L)	5	3 ②	8 ③	2	1	5	6.5	—
	4-140 (2.3L)	6	3 ②	8 ③	2	1	5	6.5	7.2
	6-173 (2.8L)	5	3 ②	8 ③	2	1	5	7.2	7.8
	4-134 (2.2L) ①	7	3 ②	8 ③	2	1	5	10.0	10.7

① Diesel Engine
② 5-speed overdrive trans.: 3.6
③ C-5 trans. (4x2): 7.5
wo-A/C: without Air Conditioning
w-A/C: with Air Conditioning

Tune-Up and Performance Maintenance

2

GASOLINE ENGINE TUNE-UP PROCEDURES

Spark Plugs

REPLACING SPARK PLUGS

A set of spark plugs usually requires replacement after 30,000 miles on trucks with electronic ignition. In normal operation, plug gap increases about 0.001 in. for every 1,000–2,500 miles. As the gap increases, the plug's voltage requirement also increases. It requires a greater voltage to jump the wider gap and about two to three times as much voltage to fire a plug at high speeds than at idle.

When you're removing spark plugs, you should work on one at a time. Don't start by removing the plug wires all at once, because unless you number them, they may become mixed up. Take a minute before you begin and number the wires with tape. The best location for numbering is near where the wires come out of the cap.

1. Twist the spark plug boot and remove the boot and wire from the plug. Do not pull on the wire itself as this will ruin the wire.

2. If possible, use a brush or rag to clean the area around the spark plug. Make sure that all the dirt is removed so that none will enter the cylinder after the plug is removed.

3. Remove the spark plug using the proper size socket. Turn the socket counterclockwise to remove the plug. Be sure to hold the socket straight on the plug to avoid breaking the plug, or rounding off the hex on the plug.

4. Once the plug is out, check it against the plugs shown in this section to determine engine condition. This is crucial since plug readings are vital signs of engine condition.

5. Use a round wire feeler gauge to check the plug gap. The correct size gauge should pass through the electrode gap with a slight drag. If

you're in doubt, try one size smaller and one larger. The smaller gauge should go through easily while the larger one shouldn't go through at all. If the gap is incorrect, use the electrode bending tool on the end of the gauge to adjust the gap. When adjusting the gap, always bend the side electrode. The center electrode is non-adjustable.

6. Squirt a drop of penetrating oil on the threads of the new plug and install it. Don't oil the threads too heavily. Turn the plug in cockwise by hand until it is snug.

7. When the plug is finger tight, tighten it with a wrench.

NOTE: *Whenever a high tension wire is removed for any reason from a spark plug, coil or distributor terminal housing, silicone grease must be applied to the boot before it is reconnected. Using a small clean tool, coat the entire interior surface of the boot with Ford silicone grease D7AZ 19A331-A or equivalent.*

8. Install the plug boot firmly over the plug. Proceed to the next plug.

SPARK PLUG ANALYSIS

Spark plugs ignite the air and fuel mixture in the cylinder as the piston reaches the top of the compression stroke. The controlled explosion that results forces the piston down, turning the crankshaft and the rest of the drive train.

Ford recommends that spark plugs be changed every 30,000 miles with electronic ignition systems. Under severe driving conditions, those intervals should be halved. Severe driving conditions are:

1. Extended periods of idling or low speed operation, such as off-road or door-to-door delivery.

2. Driving short distances (less than 10 miles) when the average temperature is below 10°F for 60 days or more.

Tune-Up Specifications

Year	Engine No. Cyl Displacement cu. in. (c.c.)	Spark Plugs		Distributor		Ignition Timing		Fuel Pump Pressure (psi)	Compression Pressure (psi)	Idle Speed		Clearance (in.)	
		Type	Gap (in.)	Point Dwell (deg)	Point Gap (in.)	Manual Trans	Auto Trans			Manual Trans	Auto Trans	Intake	Exhaust
1983–84	4-122(2000)	①	①	Electronic		①	①	5–7	②	①	①	Hyd.	Hyd.
	4-140(2300)	①	①	Electronic		①	①	5–7	②	①	①	Hyd.	Hyd.
	6-173(2800)	AWSF-42	.045	Electronic		10	10	4½–6½	②	①	①	.014	.016

① See underhood specifications sticker.
② The lowest compression reading should be within 75 percent of the highest reading.
NOTE: The underhood specifications sticker often reflects tune-up specification changes made in production. Sticker figures must be used, if they conflict with those in this chart.
† Spark plugs shown are original equipment. Part numbers in this reference are not recommendations by Chilton for any product by brand name.

Diesel Tune-Up Specifications

| Year | Engine No. Cyl Displacement | Valve Clearance (warm) | | Injection Timing (ATDC) | Injection Nozzle Pressure (psi) | Idle Speed (rpm) | Cranking Compression Pressure (psi) |
		Intake (in.)	Exhaust (in.)				
1983–84	4-134(2200)	.012	.012	2°	1957	700	427 ①

① At 200 rpm

3. Excessive dust or blowing dirt conditions.

When you remove the spark plugs, check their condition. They are a good indicator of the condition of the engine. It is a good idea to remove the spark plugs at regular intervals, such as every 3,000 or 4,000 miles, just so you can keep an eye on the mechanical state of the engine.

A small deposit of light tan or gray material on a spark plug that has been used for any period of time is considered normal. Any other color, or abnormal amounts of deposit, indicate that there is something amiss in the engine.

A small deposit of light tan or gray material on a spark plug that has been used for any period of time is considered normal. Any other color, or abnormal amounts of deposit, indicate that there is something amiss in the engine.

The gap between the center electrode and the side or ground electrode can be expected to increase not more than 0.001 in. every 1,000 miles under normal conditions. When, and if, a plug fouls and begins to misfire, you will have to investigate, correct the cause of the fouling and either clean or replace the plug.

There are several reasons why a spark plug will foul and you can learn which reason is at fault by just looking at the plug. A few of the most common reasons for plug fouling and a description of fouled plug appearance are listed in the "Color Insert" section, which also offers solution to the fouling causes.

CHECKING AND REPLACING SPARK PLUG CABLES

Visually inspect the spark plug cables for burns, cuts, or breaks in the insulation. Check the spark plug boots and the nipples on the distributor cap and coil. Replace any damaged wiring. If no physical damage is obvious, the wires can be checked with an ohmmeter for excessive resistance. (See the Tuneup and Troubleshooting section.)

When installing a new set of spark plug cables, replace the cables one at a time so there will be no mixup. Start by replacing the longest cable first. Install the boot firmly over the spark plug. Route the wire exactly the same as the original. Insert the nipple firmly into the tower on the distributor cap. Repeat the process for each cable.

Removal

When removing spark plug wires, use great care. Grasp and twist the insulator back and forth on the spark plug to free the insulator. Do not pull on the wire directly as it may become separated from the connector inside the insulator.

Installation

NOTE: *Whenever a high tension wire is removed for any reason form a spark plug, coil or distributor terminal housing, silicone grease must be applied to the boot before it is reconnected. Using a small clean tool, coat the entire interior surface of the boot with Ford silicone grease D7AZ 19A331-A or equivalent.*

1. Install each wire in or on the proper terminal of the distributor cap. Be sure the terminal connector inside the insulator is fully seated. The No. 1 terminal is identified on the cap.

2. Remove wire separators from old wire set and install them on new set in approximately same position.

3. Connect wires to proper spark plugs. Install ignition coil wire. Be certain all wires are fully seated on terminals.

FIRING ORDER

NOTE: *To avoid confusion, replace spark plugs and wires one at a time.*

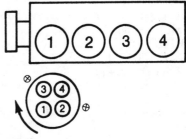

4-122,140 engine
Firing order: 1-3-4-2
Distributor rotation: clockwise

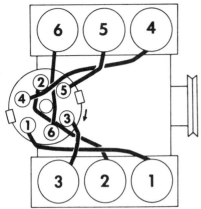

6-173 cu. in. engine firing order: 1-4-2-5-3-6 Distributor rotation: clockwise

Electronic Ignition

For all repair and adjustment procedures, please refer to Chapter 3, Engine Electrical section.

Ignition Timing

Ignition timing is the measurement, in degrees of crankshaft rotation, of the point at which the spark plugs fire in each of the cylinders. It is measured in degrees before or after Top Dead Center (TDC) of the compression stroke. Ignition timing is controlled by turning the distributor body in the engine.

Ideally, the air/fuel mixture in the cylinder will be ignited by the spark plug just as the piston passes TDC of the compression stroke. If this happens, the piston will be beginning the power stroke just as the compressed and ignited air/fuel mixture starts to expand. The expansion of the air/fuel mixture then forces the piston down on the power stroke and turns the crankshaft.

Because it takes a fraction of a second for the spark plug to ignite the mixture in the cylinder, the spark plug must fire a little before the piston reaches TDC. Otherwise, the mixture will not be completely ignited as the piston passes TDC and the full power of the explosion will not be used by the engine.

The timing measurement is given in degrees of crankshaft rotation before the piston reaches TDC (BTDC). If the setting for the ignition timing is 5° BTDC, the spark plug must fire 5° before each piston reaches TDC. This only holds true, however, when, the engine is at idle speed.

As the engine speed increases, the pistons go faster. The spark plugs have to ignite the fuel even sooner if it is to be completely ignited when the piston reaches TDC. To do this, the electronic control module has a means to ad-

vance the timing of the spark as the engine speed increases.

If the ignition is set too far advanced (BTDC), the ignition and expansion of the fuel in the cylinder will occur too soon and tend to force the piston down while it is still traveling up. This causes engine ping. If the ignition spark is set too far retarded after TDC (ATDC), the piston will have already passed TDC and started on its way down when the fuel is ignited. This will cause the piston to be forced down for only a portion of its travel. This will result in poor engine performance and lack of power.

The timing is best checked with a timing light. This device is connected in series with the No. 1 spark plug. The current that fires the spark plug also causes the timing light to flash.

There is a notch on the crankshaft pulley on the 6 cylinder engines. A scale of degrees of crankshaft rotation is attached to the engine block in such a position that the notch will pass close by the scale. When the engine is running, the timing light is aimed at the mark on the crankshaft pulley and the scale.

IGNITION TIMING ADJUSTMENT

NOTE: *Check the underhood Vehicle Emission Control Information decal for specifications and any special instructions.*

1. Locate the timing marks on the crankshaft pulley and the front of the engine.

2. Clean off the timing marks so that you can see them.

3. Mark the timing marks with a piece of chalk or with paint. Color the mark on the scale that will indicate the correct timing when it is aligned with the mark on the pulley or the pointer. It is also helpful to mark the notch in the pulley or the tip of the pointer with a small dab of color.

4. Attach a tachometer to the engine.

5. Attach a timing light according to the manufacturer's instructions.

6. Check to make sure that all of the wires clear the fan and then start the engine.

7. Adjust the idle to the correct setting.

8. Aim the timing light at the timing marks. If the marks that you put on the pulley and the engine are aligned when the light flashes, the timing is correct. Turn off the engine and remove the tachometer and the timing light. If the marks are not in alignment, proceed with the following steps.

9. Loosen the distributor lockbolt just enough so that the distributor can be turned with a little effort.

NOTE: *Some engines may be equipped with a security-type hold-down bolt. Use Distributor Hold-Down Wrench, Tool T82L-12270-A, or equivalent, to loosen the hold-down bolt.*

10. With the timing light aimed at the pulley and the marks on the engine, turn the distributor in the direction of rotor rotation to retard the spark, and in the opposite direction of rotor rotation to advance the spark. Align the marks on the pulley and the engine with the flashes of the timing light.

11. When the marks are aligned, tighten the distributor lockbolt and recheck the timing with the timing light to make sure that the distributor did not move when you tightened the lockbolt.

12. Turn off the engine and remove the timing light.

Valve Lash

Valve adjustment determines how far the valves enter the cylinder and how long they stay open and closed.

If the valve clearance is too large, part of the life of the camshaft will be used to removing the excessive clearance. Consequently, the valve will not be opening as far as it should. This condition has two effects: the valve train components will emit a tapping sound as they take up the excessive clearance and the engine will perform poorly because the valves don't open fully and allow the proper amount of gases to flow into and out of the engine.

If the valve clearance is too small, the intake valve and the exhaust valves will open too far and they will not fully seat on the cylinder head when they close. When a valve seats itself on the cylinder head, it does two things: it seals the combustion chamber so that none of the gases in the cylinder escape and it cools itself by transferring some of the heat it absorbs from the combustion in the cylinder to the cylinder head and to the engine's cooling system. If the valve clearance is too small, the engine will run poorly because of the gases escaping from the combustion chamber. The valves will also become overheated and will warp, since they cannot transfer heat unless they are touching the valve seat in the cylinder head.

NOTE: *While all valve adjustments must be made as accurately as possible, it is better to have the valve adjustment slightly loose than slightly tight as a burned valve may result from overly tight adjustments.*

ADJUSTMENT

4-122, 140 Engines

NOTE: *The 4 cylinder gasoline engines in this vehicle are equipped with hydraulic valve lash adjusters. Adjustment is not necessary as a tune up procedure. To check the valve lash use the following procedure.*

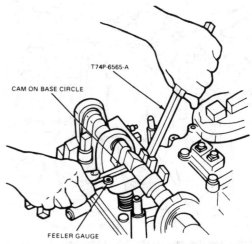

Checking the valve lash—4-122,140 engines

1. Disconnect the battery ground cable.
2. Remove the rocker arm cover following the procedure in Chapter 3.
3. Position the camshaft so that the base circle of the lobe is facing the cam follower of the valve to be checked.
4. Using tool T74P-6565-A, slowly apply pressure to the cam follower until the lash adjuster is completely collapsed. Hold the follower in this position and insert the proper size feeler gauge between the base circle of the cam and the follower.
5. If the clearance is excessive, remove the cam follower and inspect for damage.
6. If the cam follower appears to be intact, and not excessively worn, measure the valve spring damper assembly assembled height to be sure the valve is not sticking.
7. If the valve spring damper spring assembled height is correct, check the dimensions of the camshaft following the procedure in Chapter 3.
8. If the camshaft dimensions are to specifications, remove, clean and test the lash adjuster.
9. Reinstall the lash adjuster and check the clearance. Replace damaged or worn parts as necessary.

6-173 Engine

NOTE: *The following procedure should be performed on a cold engine.*

1. Disconnect the battery ground cable.
2. Remove the rocker arm cover following the procedure in Chapter 3.
3. Place your finger on the adjusting screw of the intake valve rocker arm for the number 5 cylinder. You should be able to feel any movement in the rocker arm.
4. Using a remote starter switch, "bump" the engine over until the intake valve for the

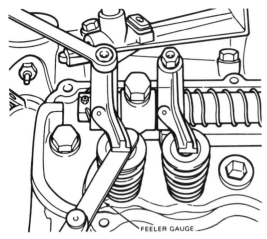

Adjusting the valve lash—6-173 engine

To adjust both valves for cylinder number	1	4	2	5	3	6
The intake valve must be opening for cylinder number	5	3	6	1	4	2

Valve adjusting arrangement—6-173 engine

number 5 cylinder just begins to open. The valves on the number 1 cylinder may now be adjusted.

5. Adjust the number 1 intake valve so that a .014 in. feeler gauge has a light drag and a .015 in. feeler gauge is very tight. Turn the adjusting screw clockwise to decrease the gap and counterclockwise to increase the gap. The adjusting screws are self-locking and will stay in position once they are set.

NOTE: *When checking the valve lash, be sure to insert the feeler gauge between the rocker arm and the valve tip at the front or (rear) edge of the valve and move it toward the opposite edge with a rearward or (foreward) motion. DO NOT insert the feeler gauge at the outer edge and move toward the inner edge (inward toward the carburetor), this will produce an incorrect reading which will result in overly tight valves.*

6. Using the same method, adjust the number 1 exhaust valve lash so that a .016 in. feeler gauge has a light drag and a .017 in. feeler gauge is very tight.

7. Adjust the remaining valves in the same manner, in the firing order (1-4-2-5-3-6) by positioning the camshaft according to the chart below.

8. Install the rocker arm covers following the procedure in Chapter 3 under "Engine Mechanical".

9. Reconnect the battery ground cable.

10. Start the engine and check for oil and vacuum leaks.

Carburetor

This section contains only tune-up adjustment procedures for the carburetor. Descriptions, adjustments and overhaul procedures for the carburetor can be found in the "Fuel System" section of this book.

When the engine in your Ranger is running, the air/fuel mixture from the carburetor is being drawn into the engine by a partial vacuum created by the downward movement of the pistons on the intake stroke. The amount of air/fuel mixture that enters the engine is controlled by the throttle plate(s) in the bottom of the carburetor. When the engine is not running, the throttle plates are closed, completely blocking off the air/fuel passage(s) at the bottom of the carburetor. The throttle plates are connected by the throttle linkage to the accelerator pedal in the passenger compartment of the truck. When you depress the pedal, you open the throttle plates in the carburetor to admit more air/fuel mixture to the engine.

When the engine is idling, it is necessary to have the throttle plates open slightly. To prevent having to hold your foot on the pedal, an idle speed adjusting screw is located on the carburetor linkage.

The idle adjusting screw contacts a lever (throttle lever) on the outside of the carburetor. When the screw is turned, it opens or closes the throttle plates of the carburetor, raising or lowering the idle speed of the engine. This screw is called the curb idle adjusting screw. There are three different types of carburetors used on the Ford Ranger. The 4-122,140 engines use the Carter model YFA 1-bbl. carburetor except on the California and High Altitude models which are equipped with the Carter model YFA 1-bbl. Feedback carburetor. The 6-173 engine is equipped with a Motorcraft model 2150 2-bbl. carburetor.

IDLE SPEED ADJUSTMENTS

4-122,140 Engines with Carter YFA-1V & YFA-1V Feedback Carburetors

1. Block the wheels and apply the parking brake.

2. Place the transmission in Neutral or Park.

3. Bring engine to normal operating temperature.

4. Place the air conditioning selector in the Off position.

5. Place transmission in specified position as referred to on the emissions decal.

6. Check/adjust curb idle RPM. If adjustment is required, turn the hex head adjustment at the rear of the TSP (throttle solenoid positioner) housing.

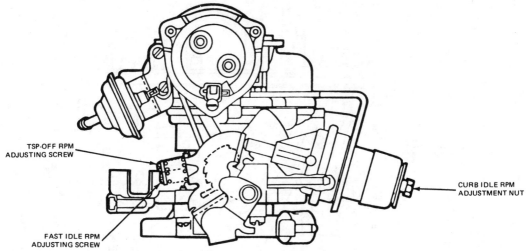

TSP-OFF RPM
ADJUSTING SCREW

CURB IDLE RPM
ADJUSTMENT NUT

FAST IDLE RPM
ADJUSTING SCREW

Carter YFA-1V & YFA-1V Feedback carburetor—Idle speed adjustment

7. Place the transmission in Neutral or Park. Rev the engine momentarily. Place transmission in specified position and recheck curb idle RPM. Readjust if required.

8. Turn the ignition key to the Off position.

9. If a curb idle RPM adjustment was required and the carburetor is equipped with a dashpot, adjust the dashpot clearance to specification as follows:

    a. Turn key to On position. Open throttle to allow TSP solenoid plunger to extend to the curb idle position.

    b. Collapse dashpot plunger to maximum extent. Measure clearance between tip of plunger and extension pad on throttle vent lever. If required, adjust to specification. Tighten dashpot locknut. Recheck clearance. Turn key to Off position.

10. If curb idle adjustment was required:
Check/adjust the bowl vent setting as follows:

    a. Turn ignition key to the On position to activate the TSP (engine not running). Open throttle to allow the TSP solenoid plunger to extend to the curb idle position.

    b. Secure the choke plate in the wide open position.

    c. Open throttle so that the throttle vent lever does not touch the bowl vent rod. Close the throttle to the idle set position and measure the travel of the fuel bowl vent rod from the open throttle position.

    d. Travel of the bowl vent rod should be within specification (.100 to .150 inches).

    e. If out of specification, bend the throttle vent lever at notch to obtain required travel.

11. Remove all test equipment and reinstall air cleaner assembly. Tighten the holddown bolt to specification.

6-173 Engine with Motorcraft 2150A-2V Carburetor

NOTE: *On models equipped with air conditioning, the A/C-On RPM speed must be set prior to setting the Curb Idle Speed adjustment. This adjustment is made with the vacuum operated throttle modulator (VOTM) on.*

AC-ON RPM ADJUSTMENT

1. Remove the air cleaner and disconnect and plug the vacuum lines.

2. Block the wheels, apply the parking brake, turn off all accessories, start the engine and run it to normalize underhood temperatures.

3. Check that the choke plate is fully open and connect a tachometer according to the manufacturer's instructions.

4. Disconnect the A/C clutch wire at the compressor.

5. Place the the heater control selector to maximum cooling and set the blower switch in the high position.

6. Place the manual transmission in neutral; the automatic transmission in drive.

7. Using the saddle bracket adjusting screw, adjust the A/C-ON RPM to the specifications shown on the under hood emission sticker.

8. Reconnect the A/C compressor clutch wire.

9. Proceed to step 4 below and set the Curb Idle Speed adjustment.

CURB IDLE SPEED ADJUSTMENT

1. Remove the air cleaner and disconnect and plug the vacuum lines.

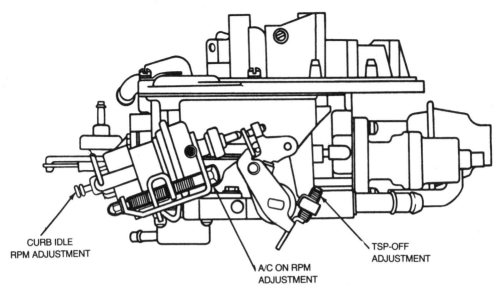

Motorcraft 2150A-2V carburetor—Idle speed adjustments w/AC

2. Block the wheels, apply the parking brake, turn off all accessories, start the engine and run it to normalize underhood temperatures.

3. Check that the choke plate is fully open and connect a tachometer according to the manufacturer's instructions.

4. Place the manual transmission in neutral; the automatic transmission in drive and make certain the (TSP) throttle stop positioner plunger is extended.

5. Turn the saddle bracket adjustment screw (non-A/C), or the hex head protruding from the rear of the TSP diaphram assembly (A/C models) until the specified idle speed is obtained.

6. Check the TSP-off speed as follows:
   a. disconnect the TSP wire.
   b. place the transmission in neutral and check the RPM. If necessary, adjust to the specified TSP-off speed with the throttle adjusting screw. Check the underhood sticker for specifications.

7. Install the air cleaner and connect the vacuum lines. Recheck the idle speed. Adjust, if necessary, with the air cleaner on.

IDLE MIXTURE ADJUSTMENT

NOTE: *For this procedure, Ford recommends a propane enrichment procedure. This*

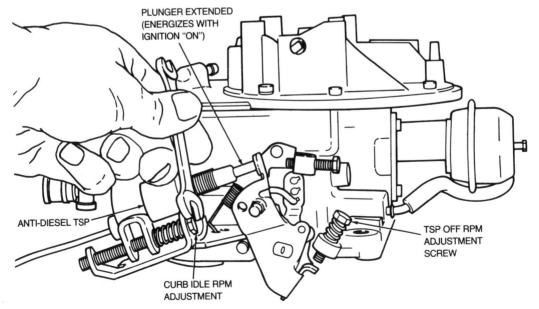

Motorcraft 2150A-2V carburetor—Idle speed adjustments wo/AC

requires special equipment not available to the general public. In lieu of this equipment the following procedure may be followed to obtain a satisfactory idle mixture.

Removing Limiter Plugs

4-122,140 ENGINES WITH CARTER YFA-1V 9 YFA-1V FEEDBACK CARBURETORS

1. Remove the carburetor from the engine as described in Chapter 4 under "Fuel Systems."

2. Drain the fuel from the carburetor into a suitable container.

3. Invert the carburetor and cover all vacuum and fuel connection openings with tape. With a hack saw, carefully saw a slot lengthwise through the metal thickness of the cup. Use care to prevent contact between the saw blade and throttle body. Insert a screwdriver in the slot just cut, and twist, spreading the outer cup sufficiently to allow removal of the inner cap. After removing cap, count the number of turns required to seat the mixture screw needle lightly. This information will be used in assembly. Remove the screw and cup. After cleaning the metal shavings from the carburetor, remove the tape from the openings.

4. Install the idle mixture screw and spring, and a new adjustment limiting cup. Set the screw to the same number of turns out from the lightly seated position as noted during disassembly.

5. Install the carburetor on the vehicle and perform the idle mixture setting procedure.

6. After making the mixture adjustment, install the mixture limiting cap.

6-173 ENGINE WITH MOTORCRAFT 2150A-2V CARBURETOR

The idle mixture adjusting screws are covered with a two-piece tamper-resistant limiter plugs. To adjust the idle mixture the plugs must be removed using the following procedure:

1. Remove and drain the carburetor using the procedure in Chapter 4 under "Fuel Systems".

2. Turn the carburetor over and locate the locking tab on each locking cap.

3. Using a blunt punch and a light hammer, tap the locking cap until the locking tab has cleared the detent in the locking plug.

NOTE: *Support the area under the limiter plug when removing it to prevent the adjusting screw from bending.*

4. Remove the locking cap from the locking plug and remove the support from under the locking cap.

5. Repeat steps 3 and 4 for the other locking cap.

6. Install the carburetor on the engine and perform the idle mixture adjustment.

7. To install the cap, align with the detent in the plug and press the cap into the plug.

Mixture Adjustment

1. Block the wheels, set the parking brake and run the engine to bring it to normal operating temperature.

2. Disconnect the hose between the emission canister and the air cleaner.

3. On engines equipped with the Thermactor air injection system, the routing of the vacuum lines connected to the dump valve will

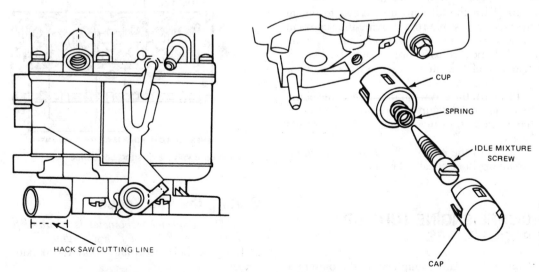

Mixture screw locking caps—Carter YFA-1V & YFA-1V Feedback carburetor

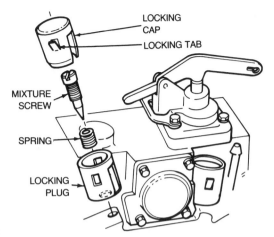

Mixture screw locking caps—Motorcraft 2150-2V

(labels in figure: LOCKING CAP, LOCKING TAB, MIXTURE SCREW, SPRING, LOCKING PLUG)

have to be temporarily changed. Mark them for reconnection before switching them.

4. For valves with one or two vacuum lines at the side, disconnect and plug the lines.

5. For valves with one vacuum line at the top, check the line to see if it is connected to the intake manifold or an intake manifold source such as the carburetor or distributor vacuum line. If not, remove and plug the line at the dump valve and connect a temporary length of vacuum hose from the dump valve fitting to a source of intake manifold vacuum.

6. Remove the limiter caps from the mixture screws by CAREFULLY cutting them with a sharp knife.

7. Place the transmission in neutral and run the engine at 2500 rpm for 15 seconds.

8. Place the automatic transmission in Drive; the manual in neutral.

9. Adjust the idle speed to the higher of the two figures given on the underhood sticker.

10. Turn the idle mixture screws to obtain the highest possible rpm, leaving the screws in the leanest position that will maintain this rpm.

11. Repeat steps 7 thru 10 until further adjustment of the mixture screws does not increase the rpm.

12. Turn the screws in until the lower of the two idle speed figures is reached. Turn the screws in ¼ turn increments each to insure a balance.

13. Turn the engine off and remove the tachometer. Reinstall all equipment.

DIESEL ENGINE TUNE-UP PROCEDURES

Due to the relative simplicity of the diesel engien as compared to the gasoline engine, tune-

up procedures consist of adjusting the valves and adjusting the engine idle speed.

Valve Lash

ADJUSTMENT

1. Warm the engine until normal operating temperature is reached.

2. Remove the valve cover. Check the head bolt torque in sequence. Refer to Chapter 3 under "Cylinder Head" for this procedure.

3. Turn the engien to bring the No. 1 piston to TDC (top dead center) of the compression stroke.

4. Adjust the following valves:
   No. 1 Intake
   No. 1 Exhaust
   No. 2 Intake
   No. 3 Exhaust

5. Rotate the crankshaft 360° and bring No. 4 piston to TDC of the compression stroke.

6. Adjust the following valves:
   No. 2 Exhaust
   No. 3 Intake
   No. 4 Intake
   No. 4 Exhaust

7. To adjust the valves, loosen the locknut on the rocker arm. Rotate the adjusting screw clockwise to reduce clearance, counterclockwise to increase clearance. Clearance is checked with a flat feeler gauge that is passed between the rocker arm and valve stem.

8. After adjustments are made, be sure the locknuts are tight. Be sure mounting surfaces are clean. Install the valve cover and new valve cover gasket.

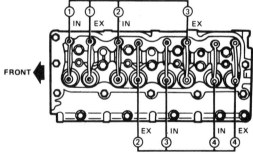

Diesel engine valve adjusting sequence

(figure labels: WHEN NO. 1 CYLINDER IS AT TOP DEAD ENTER; FRONT; WHEN NO. 4 CYLINDER IS AT TOP DEAD ENTER)

Setting the Idle Speed

NOTE: *A special tachometer is required to check engine RPM on a diesel engine.*

1. Block the wheels and apply the parking brake.

2. Start and run engine until the normal op-

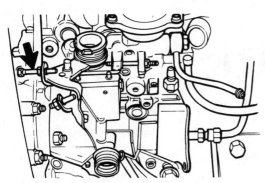

Diesel engine idle speed adjustment location

erating temperature is reached. Shut off engine.

3. Connect diesel engine tachometer.
4. Start engine and check RPM. Refer to emissions decal for latest specifications. RPM is usually adjusted in Neutral for manual transmissions and Drive for automatic models.

5. The adjustment bolt is located on the bell crank at the top of the injector pump. The upper bolt is for curb idle, the lower for max speed.

6. Loosen the locknut. Turn the adjustment screw clockwise to increase RPM, counterclockwise to lower the RPM.

7. Tighten the locknut. Increase engine speed several times and recheck idle. Readjust if necessary.

Injection Timing

NOTE: *For injection pump timing please refer to Chapter 4 under Diesel Fuel Systems.*

Engine and Engine Rebuilding

3

ENGINE ELECTRICAL

The 4-122,140 engines, found in the Ford Ranger, are equipped with Dura Spark II ignition system. However, depending on engine calibration, the Dura Spark II system may use a standard module or a "Universal Ignition Module." The Universal Ignition Module (UIM) is capable of providing spark timing retard in response to barometric or engine sensors, or MCU signal.

The Ranger truck equipped with the 6-173 engine uses a universal distributor design which incorporates an integrally mounted TFI-IV module. The distributor uses a "Hall Effect" vane switch stator assembly and has provision for fixed octane adjustment. A new cap, adapter and rotor are designed for use on the Universal Distributor. The Thick Film Integrated (TFI) module is contained in moulded thermo-plastic and is mounted on the distributor base. The TFI-IV features a "push start" mode which allows push starting of the vehicle, if necessary.

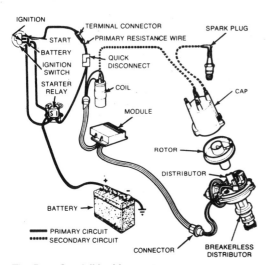

The Dura Spark II Ignition system

The TFI-IV system uses an "E-Core" ignition coil, which replaces the oil-filled coil found on other systems.

DUAL MODE TIMING IGNITION MODULE

On some applications, a special Dura Spark II ignition module is used with altitude compensation. This special module plus the barometric pressure switch, allows the base engine timing to be modified to suit altitude conditions. All other elements and performance characteristics of this module are identical in both modes of operation to the basic Dura Spark II system. All Dura Spark II modules equipped with altitude features, have three connectors instead of the normal two. A barometric switch provides an automatic retard signal to the module at different altitudes, giving appropriate advanced timing at higher altitude and retard mode for spark knock control at lower altitudes.

DISTRIBUTOR

The distributors are equipped with both vacuum and centrifugal spark advances which operate the same regardless of the type of ignition system used. A dual vacuum advance is used on certain engines to provide ignition retard during engine closed throttle operation, to help control engine exhaust emissions.

CIRCUIT OPERATION

All systems consist of a primary (low voltage) and a secondary (high voltage) circuit.

The Primary Circuit—The components involved in the primary circuit are:
1. Battery
2. Ignition switch
3. Integral primary circuit resistance wire
4. Primary windings of the ignition coil
5. Magnetic pickup coil assembly in the distributor
6. Ignition module.

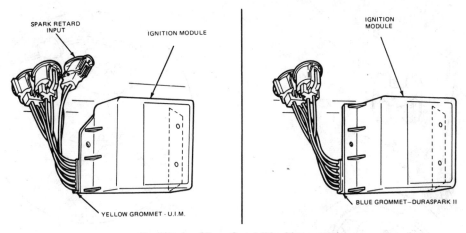

SPARK RETARD
INPUT

IGNITION MODULE

IGNITION
MODULE

YELLOW GROMMET - U.I.M.

BLUE GROMMET—DURASPARK II

Two types of Dura Spark II ignition modules

The Secondary Circuit—The components of the secondary circuit are:

1. Secondary windings of the ignition coil
2. Distributor rotor
3. Distributor cap and adapter
4. Secondary spark plug wires
5. Spark plugs

Operation

With the ignition switch in the "ON" position, the primary circuit is energized and the magnetic field is built up by the current flowing through the primary windings of the ignition coil. When the armature spokes align with the center of the magnetic pickup coil, the module turns off the coil primary current and the high voltage is produced in the secondary circuit by the collapsing magnetic field. High voltage is produced each time the magnetic field is caused to collapse due to a timing circuit in the module, which starts and stops the primary circuit through the coil. The high voltage flows through the coil secondary lead to the distributor cap, where the rotor distributes the spark to the proper spark plug terminal in the distributor cap. The secondary current then flows through the secondary wire to the spark plug.

System Adjustments

No adjustments are made to the Dura Spark II ignition system except the initial timing and spark plug gap.

SECONDARY WIRE USAGE

Spark plug wires that are used with the Dura Spark II system are 8mm in size, to contain the

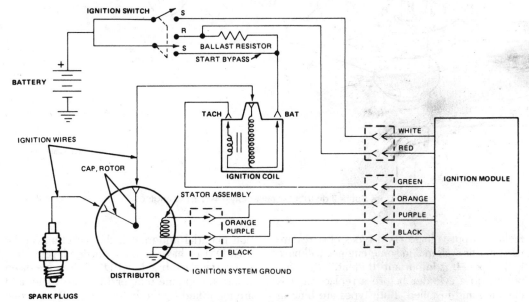

IGNITION SWITCH

BALLAST RESISTOR
START BYPASS

BATTERY

TACH   BAT

IGNITION WIRES

CAP, ROTOR

IGNITION COIL

STATOR ASSEMBLY

ORANGE
PURPLE

BLACK

DISTRIBUTOR

IGNITION SYSTEM GROUND

SPARK PLUGS

WHITE
RED

GREEN
ORANGE
PURPLE
BLACK

IGNITION MODULE

Dura Spark II circuit operation

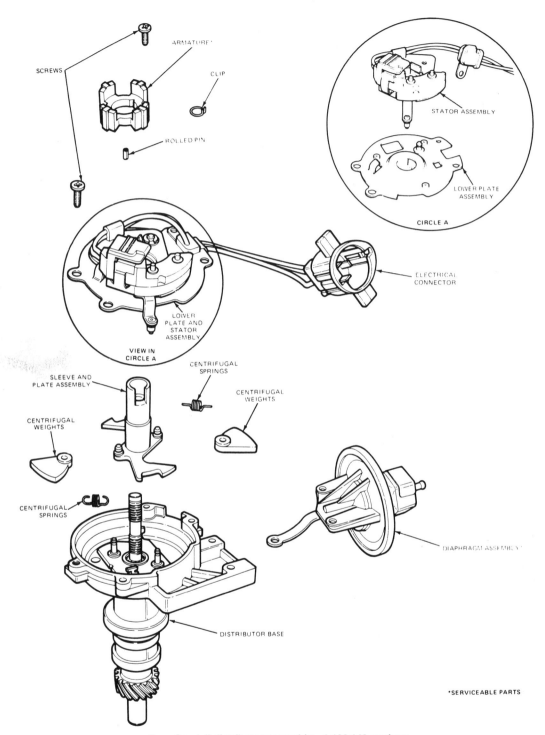

Dura Spark II distributor assembly—4-122,140 engines

higher output voltage. Two types of wires are used in this system and some engines will have both types. It is important to identify the type of wire to a cylinder before a replacement is obtained and installed. Both types are blue in color and have silicone jacketing. The insula-

tion material underneath the jacketing can be a EPDM or have another silicone layer, separated by glass braid. EPDM wires are used where the engine temperatures are cooler and are identified by the letters "SE". The silicone jacket type are used where the engine temperatures are high and are identified by the letters "SS".

NOTE: *Whenever a Dura Spark II high tension wire is removed for any purpose from a spark plug, coil or distributor cap, silicone grease must be applied to the boot before it is recommended.*

The spark plug wires are marked with the cylinder number, model year and date of cable manufacture (quarter and year). Service replacement wires do not have this information.

TROUBLESHOOTING

To properly diagnose the ignition system, a starting place must be established and an order of inspection followed until the fault is found and repaired. A recheck should be made, again in its order of inspection, to verify the repairs and to assure trouble-free operation.

Run Mode Test

1. If no spark is available at the spark plug, remove the coil high tension lead at the distributor and either place it ¼ inch from the engine block or place a modified spark plug into the coil wire and ground the spark plug body.

2. Turn the ignition switch to the "RUN" position and tap the distributor body with a screwdriver type tool handle. Check for spark while tapping.

3. If spark is available, crank the engine with the starter and check for spark. If spark occurs, the primary ignition system is OK.

4. If no spark occurs, turn the key to the "OFF" position and crank the engine to align the engine timing pointer with the initial timing degree line on the damper pulley. Turn the key to the "RUN" position and again tap the distributor and check for spark.

5. If no spark occurs, measure battery voltage and measure the battery voltage on the module's red wire without disconnecting any connectors. The voltage in the red wire should equal battery voltage.

6. If battery voltage is not present in the module red wire, repair the circuit between the battery and the module connector. Recheck the voltage supply.

7. With the voltage present in the module's red wire, cycle the ignition switch between the "RUN" and "OFF" position. A spark should be seen each time the switch is turned to the "OFF" position.

8. If no spark occurs, measure the voltage on the battery side of the coil.

   a. Less than 6 volts—Repair the wire carrying current to the battery terminal of the coil and repeat test.

   b. If voltage is 6–8 volts—Substitute, but do not install, a known good module and re-

peat the test. If spark then occurs, reconnect the original module to verify its being defective. Replace as required. Refer to step 10 if the battery voltage is present.

9. If a spark occurs from step 7, substitute, but do not install, and ground a good distributor of any calibration 4, 6 or 8 cylinder. Spin the distributor shaft and check for high tension spark.

   a. If a spark occurs, reconnect the old distributor and verify its being defective. Replace as required.

   b. If no spark occurs, disconnect the distributor connector and 4 post connector at the module. Check the harness wires that mate with the module and distributor orange and purple wires for continuity between the module and distributor end of the harness. Check to be sure there is no short between the two wires and there is an open circuit to ground. If not OK, repair the wiring and repeat the test to verify repairs.

   c. If no spark occurs after completing step 9b, reconnect the distributor connector and substitute, but do not install, a known good module and repeat the test. If a spark occurs, reconnect the original module and verify it is defective. Repair as required.

10. If battery voltage is present at the battery terminal of the coil,

   a. Disconnect the 4 wire connector at the module. Insert a paper clip between the green and black wires of the module and remeasure the voltage at the battery terminal of the coil.

   b. If the voltage is between 6 to 8 volts, substitute, but do not install, a known good module and repeat the tests. If spark occurs, reconnect the old module and verify its being defective. Replace as required.

   c. If battery voltage is still present at the battery terminal of the coil, be sure the coil connector remains in place on the coil and ground the negative terminal of the coil. Remeasure the voltage on the coil battery terminal. If battery voltage still is present, remove the paper clip from the 4 wire connector and reconnect the module. Substitute, but do not install, a known good coil and repeat the test. If a spark does not occur, connect the original coil and substitute a known good module, but do not install, and repeat the test. If a spark occurs, replace the module as required. If 4 to 7 volts is measured at the coil positive terminal, remove the ground from the coil negative terminal and ground from the paper clip connector in the 4 wire connector. Remeasure the voltage at the coil battery terminal. The voltage should be 4 to 7 volts. If the 4 to 7 volts are present, repair the ground circuit mating with the module black wire. Remove the paper clip from the 4 wire connector and reconnect the module. Repeat the test. If no voltage is present, repair the module to coil wire that mates with the module green wire. Remove the paper clip from the connector and reconnect the module. Repeat the test.

Cranking Test

1. Measure the voltage at the battery terminal of the ignition coil while cranking the engine. The reading should be within 1.0 volt of battery voltage. If not with-in specifications, repair the wire or circuit to the coil terminal.
2. While cranking the engine, check for spark from the high tension leads.
3. If no spark occurs, check the battery voltage on the white wire, while cranking the engine without disconnecting the module's two wire connectors. The voltage should be within 1.0 volt of battery voltage. If not, repair the white feed wire to the module.
4. Substitute, but do not install, a known good module and repeat the test. If a spark occurs, reconnect the original module and verify its being defective. Replace as required.

INTERMITTENT OPERATION DIAGNOSIS

Should the ingition system become operative during the tests and a repair has not been made to the system, it is likely an intermittent connection or component has become functional. Try to duplicate the problem with the engine running, by wiggling the wires at the coil, module, distributor and other harness connections, preferrably the connections that have been disturbed during the test proceedings. Check all ground connections, especially with-in the distributor. Disconnecting and connecting connectors may also help.

Heating Components for Tests

Pick-up Coil

Using a 250 watt heat lamp, approximately 1 to 2 inches from the pick-up coil, apply heat for 4 to 6 minutes while monitoring the pick-up coil continuity between the parallel blades of the disconnected distributor connector. The resistance should be 400 to 1000 ohms. Tapping with a screwdriver type handle may also be helpful to locate problem. If specifications cannot be met or held, replace the pick-up coil.

IGNITION MODULE

With the engine running, heat the module by placing a 250 watt heat lamp bulb approximately 1 to 2 inches from the module top surface.

CAUTION: *This procedure should not heat the module over 212 degrees F. After the first 10 minutes of heating, check the temperature by applying a few drops of water on the module housing. Repeat the check every one to two minutes until the water droplets boil.* Tapping the module may be helpful, but do not tap hard enough to damage or distort the housing. If this procedure results in an ignition malfunction, substitute, but do not install, a known good module. If the ignition malfunction is corrected by the substitution, reinstall the original module and recheck. Replace the module as required.

EEC-IV Electronic Engine Control

The EEC-IV system utilizes microprocessor technology for instantaneous detection and response to the engine operation conditions. A significant advantage of the EEC-IV system over the earlier electronic-control systems is the capacity to process almost a million control commands a second through two microcircuits which are integrated into one semiconductor chip about a quarter-inch square. Some of the most important functions of the EEC-IV system are the following:

- Sensing the amount of free oxygen remaining in the exhaust gas (an indication of the efficiency of combustion in the cylinders) to modify the system's control of the fuel-air mixture delivered by the carburetor.
- Control of the spark advance of the universal design ignition distributor which has an integral thick film electronic ignition module.
- A memory bank function that stores engine operation information and gradually adjusts the control functions to maintain maximum performance as the engine gradually "breaks in", reducing internal friction.
- Actuation of an automatic air-conditioner cut-off when the throttle is wide-open to eliminate the power drag of the compressor when full power is needed for maximum acceleration.
- Control of the exhaust-gas recirculation system which reduces nitrous oxide emissions to the legislated levels.
- Engine idle speed control which compensates for items like power steering, air-conditioning, and engine internal friction before complete "break-in".
- A self-test feature stores any malfunction in the memory for later readout by a technician using the proper test equipment.

The operation of the universal distributor is accomplished through the "Hall Effect" vane switch assembly, causing the ignition coil to be switched on and off by the EEC-IV and the TFI-IV modules. The vane switch is an encap-

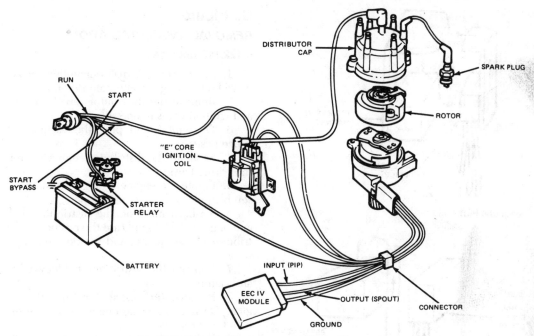

The EEC-IV Thick Film Integrated (TFI) Ignition system

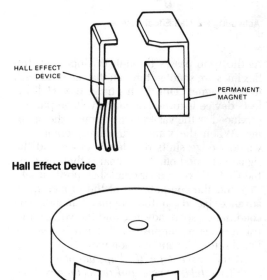

Hall Effect Device

Rotary Vane Cap

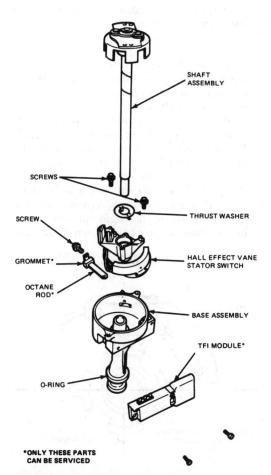

*ONLY THESE PARTS
CAN BE SERVICED

Exploded view of the EEC-IV distributor

suled package consisting of a plastic vane with a Hall sensor on one side and a permanent magnet on the other side.

A rotary vane cup, made of ferrous metal, is used to turn the coil on and off. When the window of the vane cup is between the magnet and the 'Hall Effect' device, a magnetic flux field is completed from the magnet through the "Hall Effect" device and back to the magnet.

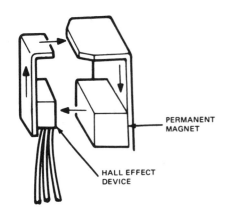

Magnetic Flux Field

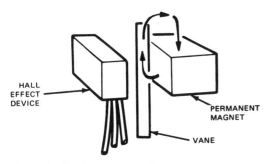

Activating the Hall Effect Device

As the vane passes through this opening, the flux lines are shunted through the vane and back to the magnet. During this time, the "Hall Effect" device is turned on and a voltage pulse is produced as the vane passes through the opening. When the vane clears the opening, the window edge shuts the device down and the signal is turned off. The signal is then used by the EEC-IV system for crankshaft position sensing and the computation of the proper spark advance based on the engine demand. The conditioned spark advance and the voltage distribution is accomplished through a conventional rotor, cap and ignition wires.

NOTE: *Except for the cap, adapter, rotor, TFI module, O-ring and the octane rod, no other distributor parts are replaceable. There is no calibration required with the universal distributor.*

TROUBLESHOOTING THE FORD EEC-IV IGNITION SYSTEM

Ford has substantially complicated their test procedure for the EEC-IV electronic ignition system. Due to the sensitive nature of the system and the complexity of the test procedures, it is recommended that you refer to your dealer if you suspect a problem in your electronic ignition system.

Distributor
REMOVAL AND INSTALLATION
4-122,140 Engines

1. Remove one alternator mounting bolt and drive belt. Swing the alternator to one side.
2. Remove the distributor cap. Position it and ignition wires to one side.
3. Disconnect and plug the vacuum advance hose.
4. Separate the distributor connector from the wiring harness.
5. Rotate the engine to align the stator assembly pole and any armature pole.
6. Scribe a mark on the distributor body and engine block to indicate the position of distributor in the engine, and the position of the rotor.
7. Remvoe the distributor holddown bolt and clamp.
8. Remove the distributor from the engine. Do not rotate the engine while the distributor is removed.
9. If the engine was rotated while the distributor was removed:
   a. Rotate the engine until number 1 piston is on the compression stroke.
   b. Align the timing marks for correct initial timing.
   c. Install the distributor with rotor pointing at number one terminal position in the cap, and the armature and the stator assembly poles aligned.
   d. Make sure the oil pump intermediate shaft properly engages the distributor shaft. It may be necessary to crank the engine after the distributor gear is partially engaged in order to engage the oil pump intermediate shaft and fully seat the distributor in the block.
   e. If it was necessary to crank the engine, again rotate the engine until the number 1 piston is on compression stroke and

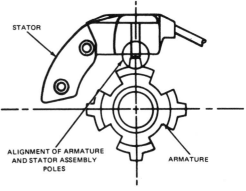

Dura Spark II armature-stator assembly alignment

align the timing marks for the correct initial timing.

f. Rotate the distributor in the block to align the armature and the stator assembly poles, and verify the rotor is pointing at the number one cap terminal.

g. Install the distributor holddown bolt and clamp; do not tighten.

10. If the engine was not rotated while the distributor was removed and the original distributor is being replaced:

a. Position the distributor in the engine with the rotor and distributor aligning with the previously scribed mark. The armature and stator assembly poles should also align, fif the distributor is fully seated in the block and properly installed. Crank the engine if necessary to fully seat the distributor in block.

b. Install the distributor holddown bolt and clamp; do not tighten.

11. If the engine was not rotated while distributor was removed and the new distributor is being installed:

a. Position the distributor in the engine with the rotor aligned with the previously scribed mark. If necessary, crank the engine to fully seat the distributor.

b. Rotate the engine until the timing marks for the correct initial timing align and the rotor is pointing at the number one cap terminal.

c. Rotate the distributor in the block to align the armature and stator assembly poles.

d. Install the distributor holddown bolt and clamp; do not tighten.

12. If in steps 9–11 above, the armature and stator assembly poles cannot be aligned by rotating the distributor in the block, pull the distributor out of the block enough to disengage the distributor gear and rotate the distributor shaft to engage a different distributor gear tooth and re-install the distributor. Repeat steps 9–11 as necessary.

13. Connect the distributor wiring harness.

14. Install the distributor cap and ignition wires. Check that the ignition wires are securely connected to the distributor cap and spark plugs.

15. Reinstall the alternator mounting bolt and drive belt. Adjust to Specification. Refer to Belt Tension Adjustment, described later in this chapter.

16. Set the initial timing per specification on the Vehicle Emission Control Information Decal.

17. Tighten the distributor holddown bolt to 17–25 ft.lbs.

18. Recheck the initial timing. Readjust if necessary.

19. Connect the vacuum advance hose.

6-173 Engine

1. Remove the air cleaner assembly, taking note of the hose locations.

2. Disconnect the primary wiring connector from the distributor.

NOTE: *Before removing the distributor cap, mark the position of the No. 1 wire tower on the distributor base for future reference.*

3. Using a screwdriver, remove the distributor cap and adapter and position it and the attached wires out of the way.

4. Remove the rotor and place it out of the way to avoid damage.

5. Remove the Thick Film Integrated module connector.

6. Remove the distributor hold-down bolt and clamp and remove the distributor.

NOTE: *Some engines may be equipped with a security-type hold-down bolt. Use Distributor Hold-Down Wrench, Tool T82L-12270-A, or equivalent, to remove the hold-down bolt.*

7. Rotate the ngine until the No. 1 piston is on the compression stroke.

8. Align the timing marks for the correct initial timing.

9. Rotate the distributor shaft so that the rotor tip is pointing toward the mark previously made on the distributor base.

10. Continue rotating slightly so that the leading edge of the vane is centered in the vane switch stator assembly.

11. Rotate the distributor in the engine block to align the leading edge of the vane and the vane switch and verify that the rotor is pointing at No. 1 cap terminal.

NOTE: *If the vane and vane switch stator cannot be aligned by rotating the distributor out of the block, pull the distributor out of the block enough to disengage the distributor and rotate the distributor to engage a different distributor gear tooth. Repeat Steps 8, 9 and 10 as necessary.*

12. Install the distributor hold-down bolt and clamp. Do not tighten at this time.

13. Connect the distributor Thick Film Integrated (TFI) and the primary wiring harnesses.

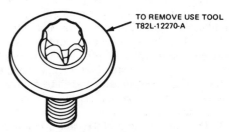

TO REMOVE USE TOOL T82L-12270-A

Security-type hold-down bolt

14. Install the distributor rotor and tighten the attaching screws.

15. Install the distributor cap adapter and tighten the attaching screws.

16. Install the distributor cap and wires. Check that the ignition wires are securely attached to the cap and spark plugs.

NOTE: *Before installing the plug wires, coat the inside of each boot with silicone lubricant.*

17. Set the initial timing, with a timing light, to specification. Refer to the underhood Vehicle Emission Control Information Decal.

18. Tighten the distributor hold-down bolt to 17–25 ft. lbs.

19. Recheck and adjust the timing, if necessary.

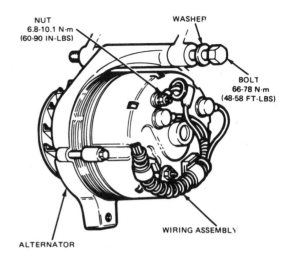

Rear terminal alternator contact locations

Alternator

The alternator charging system is a negative (−) ground system which consists of an alternator, a regulator, a charge indicator, a storage battery and wiring connecting the components.

The alternator is belt-driven from the engine. Energy is supplied from the alternator regulator system to the rotating field through two brushes to two slip rings. The slip rings are mounted on the rotor shaft and are connected to the field coil. This energy supplied to the rotating field from the battery is called excitation current and is used to initially energize the field to begin the generation of electricity. Once the alternator starts to generate electricity, the excitation current comes from its own output rather than the battery.

The alternator produces power in the form of alternating current. The alternating current is rectified to direct current by 6 diodes. The direct current is used to charge the battery and power the rest of the electrical system.

ALTERNATOR PRECAUTIONS

To prevent damage to the alternator and regulator, the following precautionary measures must be taken when working with the electrical system.

1. Never reverse battery connections. Always check the battery polarity visually. This should be done before any connections are made to be sure that all of the connections correspond to the battery ground polarity of the truck.

2. Booster batteries for starting must be connected properly. Make sure that the positive cable of the booster battery is connected to the positive terminal of the battery that is getting the boost. The same applies to the negative cables.

3. Disconnect the battery cables before using a fast charger; the charger has a tendency

to force current through the diodes in the opposite direction for which they were designed. This burns out the diodes.

4. Never use a fast charger as a booster for starting the vehicle.

5. Never disconnect the voltage regulator while the engine is running.

6. Do not ground the alternator output terminal.

7. Do not operate the alternator on an open circuit with the field energized.

8. Do not attempt to polarize an alternator.

REMOVAL AND INSTALLATION

1. Open the hood and disconnect the battery ground cable.

2. Remove the adjusting arm bolt and loosen the pivot bolt.

3. Remove the drive belt from the alternator pulley

4. Label all the leads to the alternator so that they can be reinstalled correctly and remove the leads from the alternator.

5. Remove the alternator pivot bolt and remove the alternator from the truck.

6. To install, reverse the above procedure.

BELT TENSION ADJUSTMENT

The fan belt drives the alternator and water pump. If the belt is too loose, it will slip and the alternator will not be able to produce its rated current.

Also, the water pump will not operate efficiently and the engine could overheat. Check the tension of the fan belt by pushing your thumb down on the longest span of the belt, midway between the pulleys. Belt deflection should be approximately ½ in.

1. Loosen the alternator mounting bolt and the adjusting arm bolts.

2. Apply pressure on the alternator front housing only, moving the alternator away from the engine to tighten the belt. Do not apply pressure to the rear of the cast aluminum housing of an alternator; damage to the housing could result.

3. Tighten the alternator mounting bolt and the adjusting arm bolts when the correct tension is reached.

Regulator

The alternator regulator has been designed to control the charging system's rate of charge and to compensate for seasonal temperature changes. This regulator is 100 percent solid state, consisting of transistors, diodes, and resistors. The operating functions are achieved in basically four circuits: The output stage, the voltage control stage, the solid state relay, and the field circuit overload protection stage. There are two different regulators used on your Ford truck. The units both look alike, but are not interchangeable due to the different wiring connector plugs. One unit is used on trucks equipped with an ammeter and the other is used on alternator warning-light equipped trucks. The regulators are calibrated by the manufacturer and no adjustment is required or possible on these units.

REMOVAL AND INSTALLATION

1. Disconnect the positive terminal of the battery.

2. Disconnect all of the electrical leads at the regulator. Label them as removed, so you can replace them in the correct order on the replacement unit.

3. Remove all of the hold-down screws, then remove the unit from the vehicle.

4. Install the new voltage regulator using the hold-down screws from the old one, or new ones if they are provided with the replacement regulator. Tighten the hold-down screws.

5. Connect all the leads to the new regulator.

Starter Motor
REMOVAL AND INSTALLATION
Gasoline Engines

1. Disconnect the positive battery terminal.

2. Raise the vehicle and disconnect the starter cable at the starter terminal and remove the starter ground cable.

3. Remove all of the starter attaching bolts that attach the starter to the bellhousing.

4. Remove the starter from the engine.

5. Install the starter in the reverse order of removal.

Diesel Engine

1. Disconnect the battery ground cables from both batteries.

2. Remove the air intake hose between the air cleaner and the intake manifold.

3. Remove the No. 1 glow plug relay from the starter and position it out of the way.

4. Disconnect the starter solenoid wiring.

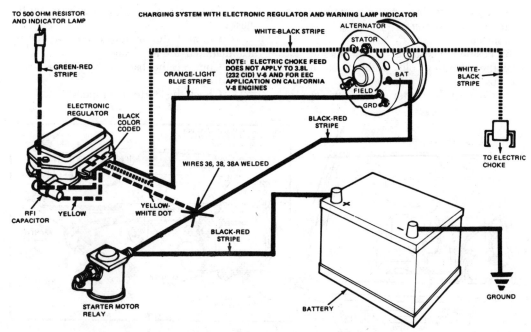

Electronic regulator with warning lamp charging system

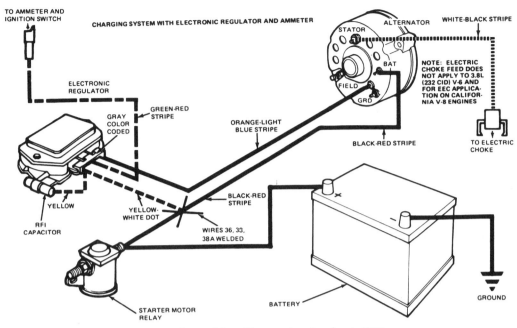

Electronic regulator with ammeter charging system

Alternator Specifications

Year	Color Code	Output		Field Current Amps	Cut-In rpm	Brush Length Inches	
		Amps	Watts			New	Limit
1983–84	Orange	40	600	4.0	900	½	¼
	Green	60	900	4.0	1025	½	¼

5. Remove the three starter mounting bolts, and remove the starter.

To install:

6. Position the starter on the engine and install the mounting bolts. Tighten bolts to 48–65 ft. lbs.

7. Connect the starter solenoid wiring.

8. Install the No. 1 glow plug relay on the starter.

9. Connect the air intake hose to the intake manifold and air cleaner.

10. Connect the battery ground cables to both batteries.

11. Check the starter operation.

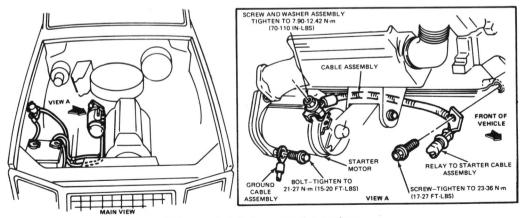

Stater, exploded view—gasoline engines

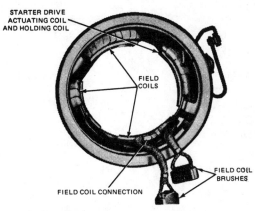

Starter motor field coil assembly with brushes

STARTER OVERHAUL

Brush Replacement

GASOLINE ENGINE

Replacement of the starter brushes should be made when they are worn to a length of ¼ inch or less.

NOTE: *This procedure requires the use of a 300-watt soldering iron and rosin core solder. If you are unfamiliar with the use of this tool, do not attempt this procedure.*

1. Remove the two through bolts from the starter frame.

2. Remove the brush end plate, brush springs and brushes from the holder.

3. Remove the ground brush attaching screws from the frame and remove the brushes.

4. Cut the insulated brush leads from the field coils, as close to the field connection point as possible.

5. Check the plastic brush holder for cracks or broken mounting pads. Replace it if necessary.

6. Position the new insulated field brushes lead on the field coil connection. Position and crimp the clip provided with the brushes to hold the brush lead to the connection. Solder the lead, clip, and connection together.

7. Install the ground brush leads to the frame with the attaching screws.

8. Install the brush holder and insert the brushes in the holder and install the brush springs. Positive brush leads should be positioned in their respective slots in the brush holder to prevent potential grounding.

9. Install the brush end plate. Be sure end plate insulator is positioned properly on the end plate.

10. Install the two through bolts to the starter frame and tighten.

11. Connect the starter to a battery to check its operation.

DIESEL ENGINE

Replacement of the starter brushes should be made when they are worn to a length of ⁷⁄₁₆ inch or less.

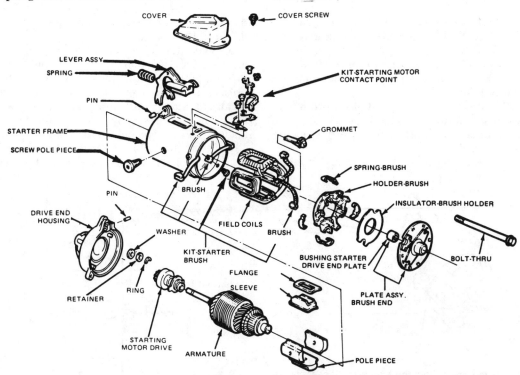

Starter, exploded view

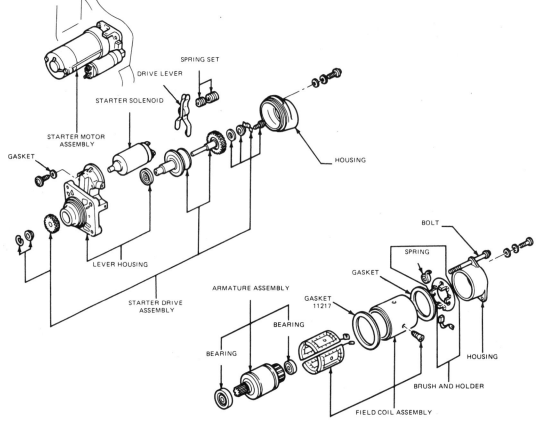

Starter, exploded view—diesel engine

NOTE: *This procedure requires the use of a 300-watt soldering iron and rosin core solder. If you are unfamiliar with the use of this tool, do not attempt this procedure.*

1. Remove the two through bolts from the starter frame.

2. Remove the brush end plate, brush lead wires and brushes from the holder.

3. Break the brush to remove it from the lead wire.

4. Clean the brush lead wire and position the new brush on the brush lead wire, through the small taper side.

5. Solder the brush and brush lead wire using rosin core solder and a 300-watt iron.

6. Install the brush holder and insert the brushes in the holder and install the brush springs. Positive brush leads should be positioned in their respective slots in the brush holder to prevent potential grounding.

7. Install the brush end plate. Be sure end plate insulator is positioned properly on the end plate.

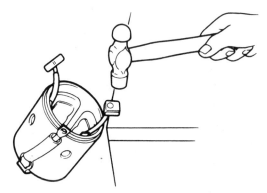

Removing brush from the lead wire—diesel engine starter

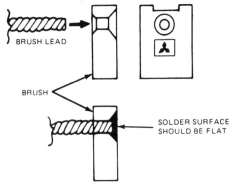

Installing brush to the lead wire—diesel engine starter

8. Install the two through bolts to the starter frame and tighten.

9. Connect the starter to a battery to check its operation.

Starter Drive Replacement

GASOLINE ENGINES

1. Remove the cover of the starter drive's plunger lever arm. Remove the through-bolts, starter drive gear housing and the return spring of the driver gear's actuating lever.

2. Remove the pivot pin which retains the starter gear plunger level and remove the lever.

3. Remove the stop-ring retainer. Remove and discard the stop-ring which holds the drive gear to the armature shaft and then remove the drive gear assembly.

To install the drive gear assembly:

4. Lightly Lubriplate® the armature shaft splines and install the starter drive gear assembly on the shaft. Install a new stop-ring and stop-ring retainer.

5. Position the starter drive gear plunger lever to the frame and starter drive assembly.

6. Install the pivot pin.

7. Position the drive plunger lever return spring and the drive gear housing to the frame, then install and tighten the throughbolts. Be sure that the stop-ring retainer is properly seated in the drive housing.

8. Position the starter drive plunger lever cover with its gasket, on the starter. Tighten the cover retaining screw.

DIESEL ENGINES

NOTE: *The starter used on diesel engines requires disassembly to repair or replace the starter drive. The procedure is as follows.*

1. Remove the starter solenoid.

2. Remove the through bolts and separate the rear cover and the armature assembly from the starter drive assembly. Remove and discard the gasket.

3. Remove the screws attaching the rear housing to the brush holder assembly and remove the housing. Remove and discard the gasket.

4. Remove the armature assembly from the field coil assembly.

5. Remove the end cap from center housing.

6. Remove the C-clip and washer from the driveshaft assembly.

7. Remove the bolt attaching the center housing to the starter drive assembly, and remove the center housing, if necessary.

8. Using a suitable tool and arbor press, remove bearings from armature assembly, if necessary.

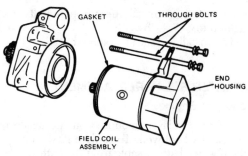

Removing the starter through bolts

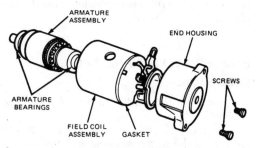

Removing the armature from the starter

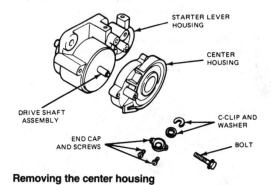

Removing the center housing

9. Clean, inspect, repair and replace parts as necessary.

To assemble:

10. Using a suitable tool and arbor press, install new armature assembly bearings, if they were removed.

11. Position the center housing on the starter drive assembly and install the attaching bolt. Tighten bolt to 5–7 ft. lbs.

12. Install the washer and C-clip on the driveshaft assembly.

13. Install end cap on the center housing.

14. Install armature assembly in the field coil assembly, making sure the brushes are positioned correctly on the commutator.

15. Using a new gasket, position the rear housing and install the bolts attaching the housing to the brush holder. Tighten bolts to 5–7 ft. lbs.

16. Using a new gasket, position the rear housing and armature assembly on the starter

drive housing. Install the through bolts and tighten to 5–7 ft. lbs.

17. Install the starter solenoid.

STARTER RELAY REPLACEMENT

Gasoline Engine

The starter relay is mounted on the inside of the right wheel well. To replace it, disconnect the positive battery cable from the battery, disconnect all of the electrical leads from the relay and remove the relay from the fender well. Replace in the reverse order of removal.

STARTER SOLENOID REPLACEMENT

Diesel Engine

1. Remove the starter as described in this chapter.

2. Remove the nut and washer from the M terminal of the starter solenoid and position the field strap out of the way.

3. Position the solenoid on the starter and install the attaching screws. Tighten to 5–7 ft. lbs.

4. Position the strap to the M terminal on the solenoid and install the nut and washer. Tighten to 80–120 in. lbs.

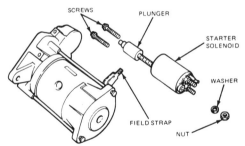

Removing the starter solenoid

5. Install the starter as described in this chapter.

Battery

REMOVAL AND INSTALLATION

1. Loosen the nuts that secure the cable ends to the battery terminals. Lift the battery cables from the terminals with a twisting motion.

2. If there is a battery cable puller available, make use of it.

3. Remove the hold-down nuts from the battery hold-down bracket and remove the bracket and the battery. Lift the battery straight up and out of the vehicle, being sure to keep the battery level so as to not spill out any of the battery acid.

4. Before installing the battery in the vehicle, make sure that the battery terminals are clean and free from corrosion. Use a battery terminal cleaner on the terminals and on the inside of the battery cable ends. If a cleaner is not available, use coarse grade sandpaper to remove the corrosion. A mixture of baking soda and water poured over the terminals and cable ends will help remove and neutralize any acid build up. Before installing the cables onto the terminals, cut a piece of felt cloth or something similar into a circle about 3 in. across. Cut a hole in the middle about the size of the battery terminals at their base. Push the cloth pieces over the terminals so they lie flat on the top of the battery. Soak the pieces of cloth with oil. This will keep the formation of oxidized acid to a minimum. Place the battery in the vehicle. Install the cables onto the terminals. Tighten the nuts on the cable ends. Smear a light coating of grease on the cable ends and tops of the terminals. This will further prevent the build up of oxidized acid on the terminals and the cable ends. Install and tighten the nuts of the battery hold bracket.

Battery and Starter Specifications

Year	Engine	Battery Ampere/ Hour Capacity	Volts	Ground	Lock Test Amps	Volts	No Load Test Amps	Volts	Cranking Speed RPM	Brush Spring Tension (oz)
1983–84	Gas	45	12	Neg.	200	12	70	12	180–250	40
	Gas	63	12	Neg.	180	12	80	12	150–290	80
	Diesel	54	12	Neg.	500	12	180	12	150–220	

General Engine Specifications

Year	Engine No. Cyl Displacement cu. in. (c.c.)	Carburetor Type	Advertised Horsepower @ rpm	Advertised Torque @ rpm (ft. lbs.)	Bore x Stroke (in.)	Advertised Compression Ratio	Oil Pressure @ 2000 rpm (psi)
1983–84	4-122(2000)	1 bbl.	73 @ 4000	107 @ 2400	3.52 x 3.13	9.0	40–60
	4-140(2300)	1 bbl.	79 @ 3800 ①	124 @ 2200 ②	3.78 x 3.13	9.0	40–60
	6-173(2800)	2 bbl.	115 @ 4600	150 @ 2600	3.66 x 2.70	8.7	40–60
	4-134(2200) Diesel	F.I.	59 @ 4000	90 @ 2500	3.50 x 3.50	22:1	51 ③

① Auto trans: 82 @ 4200
② Auto trans: 126 @ 2200
③ @ 3600 rpm

Valve Specifications

Year	Engine No. Cyl Displacement cu. in. (c.c.)	Seat Angle (deg)	Face Angle (deg)	Spring Test Pressure (lbs @ in.)	Spring Installed Height (in.)	Stem-to-Guide Clearance (in.) Intake	Stem-to-Guide Clearance (in.) Exhaust	Stem Diameter (in.) Intake	Stem Diameter (in.) Exhaust
1983–84	4-122(2000)	45°	44°	149 @ 1.12	1.49–1.55	.0010–.0027	.0015–.0032	.3416–.3423	.3411–.3418
	4-140(2300)	45°	44°	149 @ 1.12	1.53–1.59	.0010–.0027	.0015–.0032	.3416–.3423	.3411–.3418
	6-173(2800)	45°	44°	143 @ 1.22	1.58–1.61	.0008–.0025	.0018–.0035	.3159–.3167	.3149–.3156
	4-134(2200) Diesel	①	①	②	③	.0015–.0046	.0020–.0051	.3150	.3150

① Intake: 45° Exhaust: 30°
② Outer: 40 @ 1.59 in.
   Inner: 28 @ 1.49 in.
③ Outer: 1.587 in.
   Inner: 1.488 in.

Crankshaft and Connecting Rod Specifications
(All measurements given in in.)

Year	Engine No Cyl Displacement cu. in. (c.c.)	Crankshaft Main Brg Journal Dia	Crankshaft Main Brg Oil Clearance	Crankshaft Shaft End-play	Crankshaft Thrust on No	Connecting Rod Journal Diameter	Connecting Rod Oil Clearance	Connecting Rod Side Clearance
1983–84	4-122(2000)	2.399–2.398	.0008–.0015	.004–.008	3	2.0462–2.0472	.0008–.0015	.0035–.0105
	4-140(2300)	2.399–2.398	.0008–.0015	.004–.008	3	2.0462–2.0472	.0008–.0015	.0035–.0105
	6-173(2800)	2.2433–2.2441	.0008–.0015	.004–.008	3	2.1252–2.1260	.0006–.0016	.004–.011
	4-134(2200) Diesel	2.5591	.0016–.0036	.0055–.0154	3	2.0866	.0014–.0030	.0094–.0134

Piston and Ring Specifications
(All measurements in inches)

Year	Engine	Piston to Bore Clearance	Ring Side Clearance			Ring Gap		
			Top Compression	Bottom Compression	Oil Control	Top Compression	Bottom Compression	Oil Control
1983–84	4-122(2000)	.0014–.0022	.0020–.0040	.0020–.0040	Snug	.010–.020	.010–.020	.015–.055
	4-140(2300)	.0014–.0022	.0020–.0040	.0020–.0040	Snug	.010–.020	.010–.020	.015–.055
	6-173(2800)	.0011–.0019	.0020–.0033	.0020–.0033	Snug	.015–.023	.015–.023	.015–.055
	4-134(2200) Diesel	.0021–.0031	.0020–.0035	.0016–.0031	.0012–.0028	.0157–.0217	.0118–.0157	.0138–.0217

Camshaft Specifications
(All measurements in inches)

Engine	Journal Diameter				Bearing Clearance	Lobe Lift		Camshaft End Play
	1	2	3	4		Intake	Exhaust	
4-122(2000)	All 1.7713–1.7720				.001–.003	.2381	.2381	.001–.007
4-140(2300)	All 1.7713–1.7720				.001–.003	.2381	.2381	.001–.007
6-173(2800)	1.7285–1.7293	1.7135–1.7143	1.6985–1.6992	1.6835–1.6842	.001–.003	.2555	.2555	.0008–.0040
4-134(2200) Diesel	2.0472	2.0374	2.0177	—	.0024–.0047	.257	.257	.0008–.0071

Torque Specifications
(All readings in ft. lbs.)

Year	Engine	Cylinder Head Bolts	Rod Bearing Bolts	Main Bearing Bolts	Crankshaft Pulley Bolt	Flywheel-to-Crankshaft Bolts	Manifold	
							Intake	Exhaust
1983–84	4-122(2000)	80–90 ①	30–36 ②	80–90 ①	100–120	56–64	14–21 ③	16–23 ④
	4-140(2300)	80–90 ①	30–36 ②	80–90 ①	100–120	56–64	14–21 ③	16–23 ④
	6-173(2800)	70–85 ⑤	19–24	65–75	85–96	47–52	15–18 ⑥	20–30
	4-134(2200) Diesel	80–85	50–54	80–85	253–289	95–137	12–17	17–20 ⑦

① Torque in two steps: 1 50–60 ft. lbs., 2 80–90 ft. lbs.
② Torque in two steps: 1 25–30 ft. lbs., 2 30–36 ft. lbs.
③ Torque in two steps: 1 5–7 ft. lbs., 2 14–21 ft. lbs.
④ Torque in two steps: 1 5–7 ft. lbs., 2 16–23 ft. lbs.
⑤ Torque in three steps: 1 29–40 ft. lbs., 2 40–51 ft. lbs., 3 70–85 ft. lbs.
⑥ Torque in five steps: 1 Hand start and snug nuts, 2 3–6 ft. lbs., 3 6–11 ft. lbs., 4 11–15 ft. lbs., 5 15–18 ft. lbs. Repeat step 5 after warm up.
⑦ Retorque after warm up.

ENGINE MECHANICAL

Design

4 CYLINDER GASOLINE ENGINES

The 4-122,140 overhead cam engines are of lightweight iron construction. The crankshaft is supported on five main bearings and the camshaft by four. Main, connecting rod, camshaft and auxiliary shaft bearings are all replaceable.

The camshaft is driven from the crankshaft by a cogged belt, which also operates the auxiliary shaft, and through this shaft, the oil pump, fuel pump and the distributor. Tension on the cam drive belt is maintained by a locked idler pulley bearing on the outside of the belt.

Water pump and fan are separately driven from the crankshaft by a 6-ribbed belt which also drives the alternator.

Hydraulic valve lash adjusters are used in the valve train. These units are placed at the fulcrum point of the cam followers (or rocker arms). Their action is similar to the hydraulic tappets used in push-rod engines and they are constructed and serviced in the same manner. The cylinder head has drilled oil passages to provide engine oil pressure to the lash adjusters.

A set of metric wrenches is required to service the 4-122,140 engine.

V6 GASOLINE ENGINE

The V6 engine is of the standard, two-bank, V-design with the banks of cylinders opposed to each other at a 60° angle.

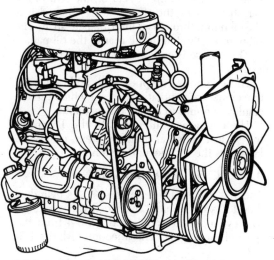

6-173 engine with Thermactor emission system

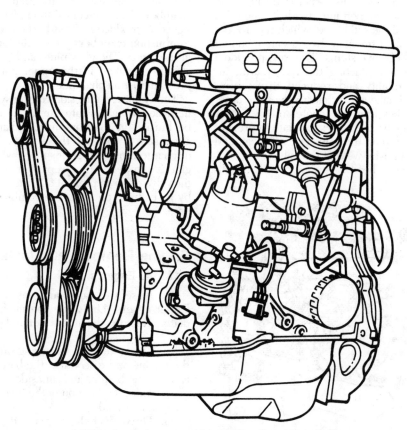

4-140 cu.in. engine assembly—4-122 cu.in. engine similar

The crankshaft is supported by 4 main bearings, with crankshaft end thrust controlled by the flanged No. 3 bearing.

The camshaft, which is located in the center of the V design of the engine, is mounted on 4 bearings and is gear driven by the crankshaft. An eccentric on the front of the camshaft operates the fuel pump. A gear on the rear of the camshaft drives the distributor, which drives the oil pump through an intermediate shaft. The oil pump is located in the rear of the oil pan.

The engine is equipped with solid valve lifters.

The engine is equipped with a closed positive crankcase ventilation system which directs crankcase fumes to the intake manifold.

The engine is equipped with the Thermactor exhaust emission control system, otherwise known as the air injection system.

4 CYLINDER DIESEL ENGINE

The 134 cu. in. Diesel engine is a 4-cylinder, 4-cycle, water cooled, overhead valve engine. The cylinders are numbered 1-2-3-4 from the front of the engine. The injection order is 1-3-4-2.

The valve mechanism is of the overhead valve type. The rocker arm shaft is prevented from rotating by a taper pin installed through the first rocker arm support into the shaft. The valve tappets are of the solid type, which require periodic valve adjustment. Valve caps are mounted on the end of valve stems. The caps provide a large area for contacting the rocker arm, increased durability and reduced thrust pressure. Both intake and exhaust valves are offset by 0.04 inches from the center of the rocker arm. This allows the valves to rotate to prevent carbon buildup on the valve face and seat, and to prevent uneven wear of the valves.

The cylinder head is designed with the intake ports on the left side and exhaust ports on the right side. This crossflow design provides high intake/exhaust efficiency.

The cylinder block is of thin, ductile, cast iron, with dry-type, pressed in, cylinder liners made of heat-resistant cast iron.

The crankshaft is supported by five main bearings. The bearing caps are not interchangeable with each other. The No. 1 and No. 2 main caps are numbered, and the No. 4 cap is identical to the No. 1 and No. 2 caps, but is not marked. The No. 3 and No. 5 caps are unique and not marked. The crank pins and main journals are hardened for high wear resistance.

The camshaft is supported by bores in the cylinder block, and is held in place by a thrust plate. There are no bearing inserts in the camshaft bore.

The aluminum alloy pistons are fitted with two compression rings and one oil ring. The top compression ring and the oil ring are plated. A nickle alloy insert is cast in the top compression ring groove to reduce wear due to heat. To reduce piston slap, a steel strut is cast into the piston skirt to help control expansion rates. There are no oversize pistons available.

A heat-resisting alloy pre-combustion chamber insert is installed in each combustion chamber. The pre-combustion chamber is designed to produce fuel swirl. The pre- and main combustion chambers are connected by a port in the insert. The glow plugs and injection nozzles are installed in the upper portion of the pre-combustion chamber.

The crankcase emission control system channels blow-by gases into the intake manifold to be burned in the combustion chamber. It is also used to prevent these gases from being discharged into the atmosphere when the engine is stopped. An oil separator is installed in the valve cover to prevent oil mixed in the blow-by gases from entering the combustion chamber.

Engine Removal and Installation
4-122,140 Engines

1. Raise the hood and install protective fender covers. Drain the coolant from the radiator. Remove the air cleaner and duct assembly.

2. Disconnect the battery ground cable at the engine and disconnect the battery positive cable at the battery and set aside.

3. Mark the location of the hood hinges and remove the hood.

4. Disconnect the upper and lower radiator hoses from the engine. Remove the radia-

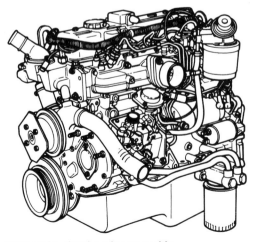
4-134 cu.in. diesel engine assembly

tor shroud screws. Remove the radiator upper supports.

5. Remove engine fan and shroud assembly. Then remove the radiator. Remove the oil fill cap.

6. Disconnect the coil primary wire at the coil. Disconnect the oil pressure and the water temperature sending unit wires from the sending units.

7. Disconnect the alternator wire from the alternator, the starter cable from the starter and the accelerator cable from the carburetor. If so equipped, disconnect the transmission kickdown rod.

8. If so equipped, remove the A/C compressor from the mounting bracket and position it out of the way, leaving the refrigerant lines attached.

9. Disconnect the power brake vacuum hose. Disconnect the chassis fuel line from the fuel pump. Disconnect the heater hoses from the engine.

10. Remove the engine mount nuts. Raise the vehicle and safely support on jackstands.

11. Drain engine oil from the crankcase. Remove the starter motor.

12. Disconnect the muffler exhaust inlet pipe at the exhaust manifold.

13. Remove the dust cover (manual transmission) or converter inspection plate (automatic transmission).

14. On vehicles with a manual transmission, remove the flywheel housing cover lower attaching bolts. On vehicles with automatic transmissions, remove the converter-to-flywheel bolts, then remove the converter housing lower attaching bolts.

15. Remove clutch slave cylinder (manual transmission). Lower the vehicle.

16. Support the transmission and flywheel or converter housing with a jack.

17. Remove the flywheel housing or converter housing upper attaching bolts.

18. Attach the engine lifting hooks to the existing lifting brackets. Carefully, so as not to damage any components, lift the engine out of the vehicle.

19. To install the engine: If clutch was removed, reinstall. Carefully lower the engine into the engine compartment. On a vehicle with automatic transmission, start the converter pilot into the crankshaft. On a vehicle with a manual

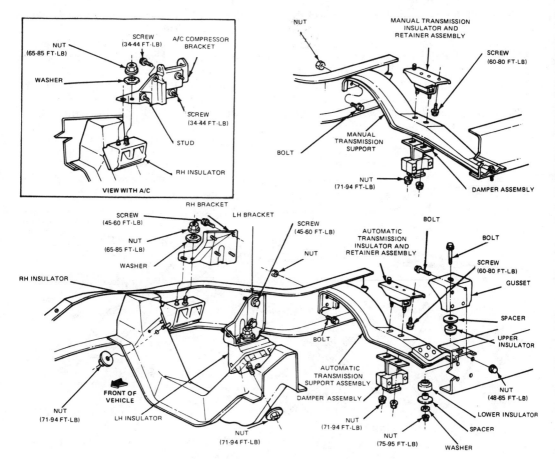

Engine mounting supports for the 4-122,140 engines

transmission, start the transmission main drive gear into the clutch disc. It may be necessary to adjust the position of the transmission in relation to the engine if the input shaft will not enter the clutch disc. If the engine hangs up after the shaft enters, turn the crankshaft in the clockwise direction slowly (transmission in gear), until the shaft splines mesh with the clutch disc splines.

20. Install the flywheel or converter housing upper attaching bolts. Remove the engine lifting hooks from the lifting brackets.

21. Remove the jack from under the transmission. Raise the vehicle and safely support on jackstands.

22. On a vehicle with a manual transmission, install the flywheel lower housing bolts and tighten to specifications. On a vehicle with an automatic transmission, attach the converter to the flywheel bolts and tighten to specifications. Install the converter housing-to-engine bolts and tighten to specifications.

23. Install clutch slave cylinder.

24. Install the dust cover (manual transmission) or converter inspection plate (automatic transmission). Correct the exhaust inlet pipe to the exhaust manifold.

25. Install the starter motor and connect the starter cables.

26. Lower the vehicle. Install the engine mount nuts and tighten to 65–85 ft. lbs.

27. Connect the heater hoses to the engine. Connect the chassis fuel line to the fuel pump. Connect the power brake vacuum hose.

28. Connect the alternator wire to the alternator, connect the accelerator cable to the car-buretor. If so equipped, connect the transmission kickdown rod. If so equipped, install the A/C compressor to the mounting bracket.

29. Connect the coil primary wire at the coil. Connect the oil pressure and water temperature sending unit wires. Install oil fill cap.

30. Install the radiator and secure with upper support brackets. Install the fan and shroud assembly. Connect upper and lower radiator hoses.

31. Install the hood and align.

32. Install the air cleaner assembly. Fill and bleed the cooling system.

33. Fill the crankcase with specified oil. Connect battery ground cable to engine and battery positive cable to battery.

34. Start the engine and check for leaks.

6-173 Engine

Remove or disconnect the Thermactor system parts that will interfere with the removal or installation of the engine.

1. Disconnect the battery ground cable and drain the cooling system.

2. Remove the hood.

3. Remove the air cleaner and intake duct assembly.

4. Disconnect the radiator upper and lower hoses at the radiator.

5. Remove the fan shroud attaching bolts and position the shroud over the fan. Remove the radiator and shroud.

6. Remove the alternator and bracket. Position the alternator out of the way. Disconnect the alternator ground wire from the cylinder block.

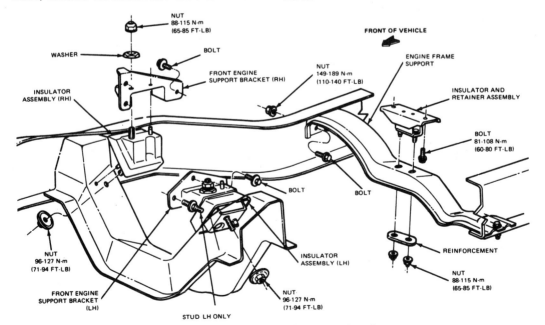

Engine mounting supports for the 6-173 engine

7. Remove A/C compressor and power steering and position them out of the way, if so equipped. DO NOT disconnect the A/C refrigerant lines.

8. Disconnect the heater hoses at the block and water pump.

9. Remove the ground wires from the cylinder block.

10. Disconnect the fuel tank to fuel pump fuel line at the fuel pump. Plug the fuel tank line.

11. Disconnect the throttle cable linkage at the carburetor and intake manifold.

12. Label and disconnect the primary wires from the ignition coil. Disconnect the brake booster vacuum hose. Label and disconnect the wiring from the oil pressure and engine coolant temperature senders.

13. Raise the vehicle and secure with jackstands.

14. Disconnect the muffler inlet pipes at the exhaust manifolds.

15. Disconnect the starter cable and remove the starter.

16. Remove the engine front support to crossmember attaching nuts or through bolts.

17. If equipped with automatic transmission, remove the converter inspection cover and disconnect the flywheel from the converter.

Remove the kickdown rod.

Remove the converter housing-to-cylinder block bolts and the adapter plate-to-converter housing bolt.

On vehicles equipped with a manual transmission, remove the clutch linkage.

18. Lower the vehicle.

19. Attach an engine lifting sling and hoist to the lifting brackets at the exhaust manifolds.

20. Position a jack under the transmission.

21. Raise the engine slightly and carefully pull it from the transmission. Carefully lift the engine out of the engine compartment. Install the engine on a work stand.

To install:

If clutch pressure plate and disc have been removed, install by following procedures in Chapter 6.

22. Attach an engine lifting sling and hoist to the lifting brackets at the exhaust manifolds. Remove the engine from the work stand.

23. Lower the engine carefully into the engine compartment. Make sure the exhaust manifolds are properly aligned with the muffler inlet pipes.

On a vehicle with a manual transmission, start the transmission main shaft into the clutch disc. It may be necessary to adjust the position of the transmission in relation to the engine if the input shaft will not enter the clutch disc. **If the engine hangs up after the shaft enters, turn the crankshaft slowly (transmission in gear) until the shaft splines mesh with the clutch disc splines.** On a vehicle with an automatic transmission, start the converter pilot into the crankshaft.

24. Install the clutch housing or converter housing upper bolts, making sure that the dowels in the cylinder block engage the flywheel housing. Remove the jack from under the transmission.

25. Remove the lifting sling from the engine.

26. On a vehicle with an automatic transmission, position the kickdown rod on the transmission and engine.

27. Raise the vehicle and secure with jackstands.

28. On a vehicle with an automatic transmission, position the transmission linkage bracket and install the remaining converter housing bolts. Install the adapter plate-to-converter housing bolt. Install the converter-to-flywheel nuts and install the inspection cover. Connect the kickdown rod on the transmission.

29. Install the starter and connect the cable.

30. Connect the muffler inlet pipes at the exhaust manifolds.

31. Install the engine front support nuts and washer attaching it to the crossmember or through bolts.

32. Lower the vehicle.

33. Install the battery ground cable.

34. Connect the ignition coil primary wires, then connect the coolant temperature sending unit and oil pressure sending unit. Connect the brake booster vacuum hose.

35. Install the throttle linkage.

36. Connect the fuel tank line at the fuel pump.

37. Connect the ground cable at the cylinder block.

38. Connect the heater hoses to the water pump and cylinder block.

39. Install the alternator and bracket. Connect the alternator ground wire to the cylinder block. Install the drive belt and adjust the belt tension, refer to Chapter 1 "Belt Tension Adjustment."

40. Install A/C compressor and power steering pump, if so equipped.

41. Position the fan shroud over the fan. Install the radiator and connect the radiator upper and lower hoses. Install the fan shroud attaching bolts.

42. Fill and bleed the cooling system. Fill the crankcase with the proper grade and quantity of oil.

43. Reconnect the battery ground cable.

44. Operate the engine at fast idle until it

reaches normal operating temperature and check all gaskets and hose connections for leaks. Adjust the ignition timing and the idle speed.

45. Install the air cleaner and intake duct. Install and align the hood.

4-134 Diesel Engine

1. Open hood and install protective fender covers. Mark location of hood hinges and remove hood.

2. Disconnect battery ground cables from both batteries. Disconnect battery ground cables at engine.

3. Drain coolant from radiator.

4. Disconnect air intake hose from air cleaner and intake manifold.

5. Disconnect upper and lower radiator hoses from engine. Remove engine cooling fan. Remove radiator shroud screws. Remove radiator upper supports and remove radiator and shroud.

6. Disconnect radio ground strap, if so equipped.

7. Remove No. 2 glow plug relay from firewall, with harness attached, and lay on engine.

8. Disconnect engine wiring harness at main connector located on left fender apron. Disconnect starter cable from starter.

9. Disconnect accelerator cable and speed control cable, if so equipped, from injection pump.

10. Remove cold start cable from injection pump.

CAUTION: *Do not disconnect air conditioning lines or discharge the system unless the proper equipment is on hand and you are familiar with the procedure. Have the system discharged by a qualified mechanic prior to start of engine removal.*

11. Discharge A/C system and remove A/C refrigerant lines and position out of the way.

12. Remove pressure and return hoses from power steering pump, if so equipped.

13. Disconnect vacuum fitting from vacuum pump and position fitting and vacuum hoses out of the way.

14. Disconnect and cap fuel inlet line at fuel line heater and fuel return line at injection pump.

15. Disconnect heater hoses from engine.

16. Loosen engine insulator nuts. Raise vehicle and safely support on jackstands.

17. Drain engine oil from oil pan and remove primary oil filter.

18. Disconnect oil pressure sender hose from oil filter mounting adapter.

19. Disconnect muffler inlet pipe at exhaust manifold.

20. Remove bottom engine insulator nuts. Remove transmission bolts. Lower vehicle. At-

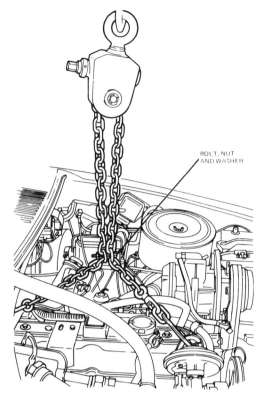

BOLT, NUT AND WASHER

Removing the 4-134 diesel engine

tach engine lifting sling and chain hoist.

21. Carefully lift engine out of vehicle to avoid damage to components.

22. Install engine on work stand, if necessary.

23. When installing the engine; Carefully lower engine into engine compartment to avoid damage to components.

24. Install two top transmission-to-engine attaching bolts. Remove engine lifting sling.

25. Raise vehicle and safely support on jackstands.

26. Install engine insulator nuts and tighten to specification.

27. Install remaining transmission-to-engine attaching bolts and tighten all bolts to specification.

28. Connect muffler inlet pipe to exhaust manifold and tighten to specification.

29. Install oil pressure sender hose and install new oil filter as described in this Section.

30. Lower vehicle.

31. Tighten upper engine insulator nuts to specification.

32. Connect heater hoses to engine. Connect fuel inlet line to fuel line heater and fuel return line to injection pump. Connect vacuum fitting and hoses to vacuum pump. Connect pressure and return hoses to power steer-

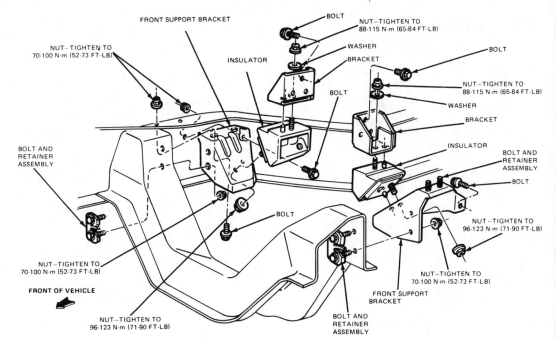

Engine mounting supports for the 4-134 diesel engine

ing pump, if so equipped. Check and add power steering fluid.

33. Install A/C refrigerant lines and charge system, if so equipped.

NOTE: *System can be charged after engine installation is complete.*

Install A/C drive belt, and tighten to specification.

34. Connect cold start cable to injection pump. Connect accelerator cable and speed control cable, if so equipped, to injection pump.

35. Connect engine wiring harness to main wiring harness at left fender apron. Connect radio ground strap, if so equipped.

36. Position radiator in vehicle, install radiator upper support brackets and tighten to specification. Install radiator fan shroud and tighten to specification. Install radiator fan and tighten to specification.

37. Connect upper and lower radiator hoses to engine and tighten clamps to specification. Connect air intake hose to air cleaner and intake manifold.

38. Fill and bleed cooling system.

39. Fill crankcase with specified quantity and quality of oil.

40. Connect battery ground cables to engine. Connect battery ground cables to both batteries.

41. Run engine and check for oil, fuel and coolant leaks. Close hood.

Valve Rocker Arm Cover

REMOVAL AND INSTALLATION

1. Remove the air cleaner and attaching parts.

NOTE: *Label each spark plug wire prior to its removal in order to ease the installation of the wires on the correct spark plugs.*

2. Remove the spark plug wires.

3. Remove the PCV valve and hose.

4. Remove the carburetor choke air deflector plate (shield).

5. Remove the rocker arm cover attaching screws and the load distribution washers (patch pieces). Be sure the washers are installed in their original position.

6. Remove the transmission fluid level indicator tube and bracket, which is attached to rocker arm cover.

7. Disconnect the kickdown linkage and the carburetor (automatic transmission only).

8. Position the thermactor air hose and the wiring harness away from the right hand rocker arm cover.

9. Remove the engine oil fill cap.

10. Disconnect the vacuum line at the canister purge solenoid and disconnect the line routed from the canister to the purge solenoid (disconnect the power brake booster hose, if so equipped).

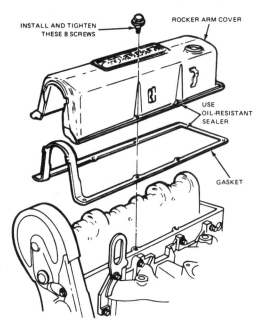

Typical 4 cylinder rocker arm cover installation

11. With a light plastic hammer, tap the rocker arm covers to break the seal.

12. Remove the rocker arm covers.

To install:

13. Clean all gasket material from the cylinder heads and rocker arm cover gasket surfaces.

14. Install the rocker arm covers, using new gaskets and install the attaching screw and rocker arm cover reinforcement pieces.

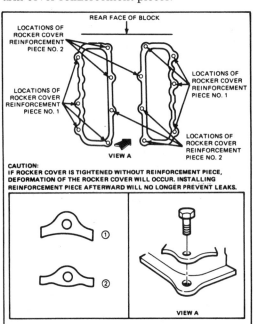

Rocker arm cover reinforcement washer locations—6-173 engine

15. Install the transmission fluid level indicator tube and the brackt (attaches to rocker arm cover).

16. Connect the kickdown linkage (automatic transmission only).

17. After ensuring all rocker arm cover reinforcement washers are installed in their original position, tighten the rocker arm cover screws.

18. Install the spark plug wires.

19. Install the PCV valve and hose.

20. Install the carburetor choke air deflector plate (shield).

21. Reposition the thermactor air hose and the wiring harness in their original places.

22. Install the engine oil fill cap.

23. Connect the vacuum line at the canister purge (connect power brake hose, if so equipped) solenoid and connect the line routed from canister to the purge solenoid.

24. Install the air cleaner and the attaching parts.

25. Start the engine and check for oil leaks.

Rocker Arms

REMOVAL AND INSTALLATION

4-122,140 Engines

NOTE: *A special tool is required to compress the lash adjuster.*

1. Remove the valve cover and associated parts as required.

2. Rotate the camshaft so that the base circle of the cam is against the cam follower you intend to remove.

3. Remove the retaining spring from the cam follower, if so equipped.

4. Using special tool T74P-6565-B or a valve spring compressor tool, collapse the lash adjuster and/or depress the valve spring, as neces-

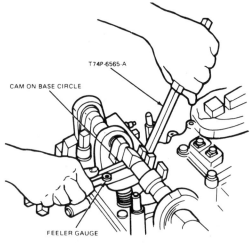

Using the special tool to collapse the lash adjuster

sary, and slide the cam follower over the lash adjuster and out from under the camshaft.

5. Install the cam follower in the reverse order of removal. Make sure that the lash adjuster is collapsed and released before rotating the cam shaft.

Rocker Arm Shaft Assembly

REMOVAL AND INSTALLATION

4-134 Diesel Engine

1. Remove the valve cover.
2. Remove the bolts attaching the rocker shaft to the cylinder head and remove the rocker shaft.
3. Remove the push rods, if necessry.
NOTE: *Note position of push rods so they may be returned to their original positions.*
To install:
4. Install the push rods, if removed.
NOTE: *Ball end goes toward tappet.*
5. Position the rocker shaft on the cylinder head and install the retaining bolts.
NOTE: *Before tightening rocker shaft bolts, make sure the rocker arms are fully seated in the push rod cups.*
6. Tighten the rocker shaft bolts alternately, two to three turns at a time, working from the center to the ends until all rocker shaft brackets are seated. Then tighten cylinder head to specification in sequence shown in this chapter under Cylinder Head.
7. Adjust valve rocker arms as described in Chapter 2 under Valve Lash Adjustment.

8. Install the valve cover.
9. Connect the heater tube assembly to valve cover.
10. Run the engine and check for oil leaks.

6-173 Engine

1. Remove the valve rocker arm covers following the procedure given above.
2. Remove the rocker arm shaft stand attaching bolts by loosening the bolts two turns at a time, in sequence.
3. Lift off the rocker arm and shaft assembly and the oil baffle.
To install:
4. Loosen the valve lash adjusting screws a few turns. Apply the engine oil to the assembly to provide the initial lubrication.
5. Install the oil baffle and rocker arm shaft assembly to the cylinder head and guide adjusting screws on to the push rods.
6. Install and tighten rocker arm stand attaching bolts to 43–50 ft. lbs., two turns at a time, in sequence. Adjust valve lash to cold specified setting.
7. Adjust the valve lash to the cold specified setting. Refer to Chapter 2 under "Valve Lash Adjustment" for adjustment procedures.
8. Install the valve rocker arm covers following the proceure given above.

DISASSEMBLY AND REASSEMBLY

1. Remove the spring washer and pin from each end of the valve ocker arm shaft.
2. Slide the rocker arms, springs and rocker arm shaft supports off the shaft. Be sure to mark the parts for re-assembly in the same locations.
3. If it is necessary to remove the plugs from

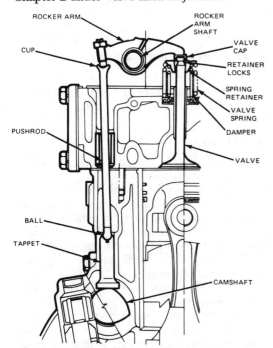

4-134 diesel engine valve train assembly

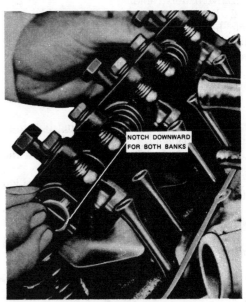

Rocker arm shaft assembly—6-173 engine

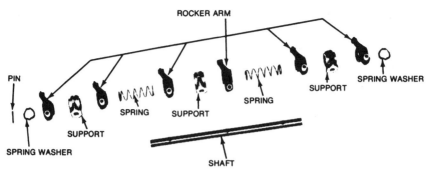

Rocker arm shaft assembly disassembled—6-173 engine

each end of the shaft, drill or pierce the plug on one end. Use a steel ro to knock out the plug on the opposite end. Working from the open end, knock out the remaining plug.

4. The oil holes in the rocker arm shaft must point down when the shaft is installed. This position of the shaft can be recognized by a notch on the front face of the shaft.

5. If the plugs were removed from the shaft, use a blunt tool and install a plug, cup side out, in each end of the shaft.

6. Install a spring washer and pin on one end of the shaft, coat the rocker arm shaft with heavy engine oil and install the parts in the same sequence they were removed.

Intake Manifold

REMOVAL AND INSTALLATION

4-122,140 Engines

1. Drain the cooling system. Remove the air cleaner and duct assembly. Disconnect the negative battery cable.

2. Disconnect the accelerator cable, vacuum hoses (as required) and the hot water hose at the manifold fitting. Be sure to identify all vacuum hoses for proper reinstallation.

3. Remove the engine oil dipstick. Disconnect the heat tube at the EGR (exhaust gas recirculation) valve. Disconnect the fuel line at the carburetor fuel fitting.

4. Remove the dipstick retaining bolt from the intake manifold.

5. Disconnect and remove the PCV at the engine and intake manifold.

6. Remove the distributor cap and position the cap and wires out of the way, after removing the plastic plug connector from the valve cover.

7. Remove the intake manifold retaining bolts. Remove the manifold from the engine.

8. Clean all gasket mounting surfaces.

9. Install a new mounting gasket and intake manifold on the engine. Torque the bolts in proper sequence in two steps, first 5–7 ft. lbs.,

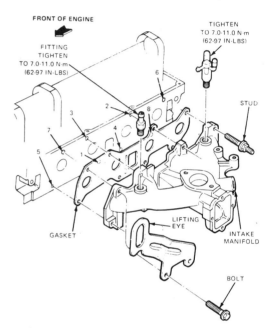

4-122,140 engines, intake manifold installation

then 14–21 ft. lbs. The rest of the installation is in the reverse order of removal.

6-173 Engine

1. Disconnect the negative battery cable.

2. Remove the air cleaner.

3. Disconnect the throttle cable.

4. Drain the coolant. Disconnect and remove the hose from the water outlet to the radiator and bypass hose from the intake manifold to the thermostat housing rear cover.

5. Remove the distributor cap and spark plug wires as an assembly.

NOTE: *Mark each plug wire with its cylinder number.*

Disconnect distributor wiring harness.

6. Observe and mark the location of the distributor rotor and housing so ignition timing can be maintained at reassembly. Remove dis-

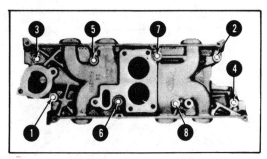

6-173 engine intake manifold torque sequence

tributor hold-down screw and clamp and lift out distributor.

NOTE: *Some engines may be eqipped with a security-type hold-down bolt. Use Distributor Hold-Down Wrench, Tool T82L-12270-A, or equivalent, to remove the hold-down bolt.*

7. Remove the rocker arm covers.

8. Remove the fuel line and filter.

9. Remove the intake manifold attaching bolts and nuts. Tap manifold lightly with a plastic mallet to break the gasket seal. Lift off the manifold.

10. Remove all the old gasket material and sealing compound.

To install:

11. Apply silicone sealer to the joining surfaces. Place the intake manifold gasket in position. Make sure that the tab on the right bank cylinder head gasket fits into the cutout of the manifold gasket.

12. Apply silicone sealer to the attaching bolt bosses on the intake manifold and position the intake manifold. Follow the torque sequence and torque the bolts to specifications.

13. Install the distributor so that the rotor and housing are in the same position marked at removal.

14. Install the distributor clamp and attaching bolt. Connect distributor wires.

15. Install the fuel line.

16. Replace the rocker arm cover gaskets, and reinstall the rocker arm valve covers using the procedure given under Rocker Arm Cover removal and installation.

17. Install the distributor cap. Coat the inside of each spark plug wire connector with silicone grease with a small screwdriver, and install the wires. Connect the distributor wiring harness.

18. Install and adjust the throttle linkage.

19. Install the air cleaner and the air cleaner tube at carburetor.

20. Connect the negative batter cable.

21. Connect the hoses from the wate outlet to the radiator and the bypass hose from the

thermostat housing rear cover to the intake manifold.

22. Refill and bleed the cooling system.

23. Recheck the ignition timing and reset the engine idle speed to specification.

Run the engine at fast idle and check for coolant and oil leaks.

4-134 Diesel Engine

1. Disconnect the battery ground cables from both batteries.

2. Disconnect the air inlet hose from the air cleaner and intake manifold. Disconnect and remove the fuel injection lines from the nozzles and injection pump. Cap all lines and fittings to prevent dirt pickup.

3. Remove the nut attaching the lower fuel return line brace to the intake manifold.

4. Disconnect and remove the lower fuel line from the injector pump and upper fuel return line.

5. Remove the air conditioner compressor with the lines attached and position out of the way. Remove the power steering pump and rear support with the lines still attached and position out of the way.

6. Remove the air inlet adapter, dropping resistor (electrical measuring device) and the gaskets.

7. Disconnect the fuel filter inlet line, remove the fuel filter mounting bracket from the cylinder head and position the filter assembly out of the way.

8. Remove the mounting nuts for the fuel line heater assembly to intake manifold and position the heater out of the way.

9. Remove the nuts that attach the intake manifold to the cylinder head. Remove the intake manifold and gasket.

10. Clean all gasket mounting surfaces.

11. Use a new intake manifold mounting gasket. Install the intake manifold in the reverse order of removal.

12. Do not tighten the mounting nuts until No. 3 lower nut that holds the fuel return line bracket is installed. After installation of the No. 3 nut, tighten all of the mounting nuts to 12-17 ft. lbs.

Exhaust Manifold

REMOVAL AND INSTALLATION

4-122,140 Engines

1. Remove the air cleaner and duct assembly. Disconnect the negative battery cable.

2. Remove the EGR line at the exhaust manifold. Loosen the EGR tube. Remove the check valve at the exhaust manifold and disconnect the hose at the end of the air by-pass valve.

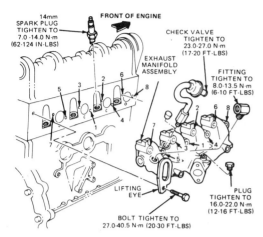

4-122,140 engines, exhaust manifold installation

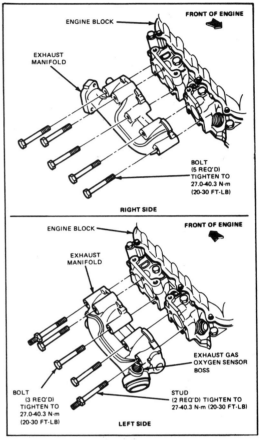

6-173 engine exhaust manifold torque sequence

3. Remove the bracket attaching the heater hoses to the valve cover. Disconnect the exhaust pipe from the exhaust manifold.

4. Remove the exhaust manifold mounting bolts/nuts and remove the manifold.

5. Install the exhaust manifold in the reverse order. Torque the manifold in sequence in two steps, first 5–7 ft. lbs. and then 16–23 ft. lbs.

6-173 Engine

1. Remove the carburetor air cleaner.

2. Remove the attaching nuts from the exhaust manifold shroud (left side).

3. Disconnect the attaching nuts from the muffler inlet pipe. Remove thermactor components as necessary to allow the removal of the exhaust manifold(s).

4. Disconnect the choke heat tubes at the carburetor.

5. Remove the manifold attaching bolts.

6. Lift the manifold from the cylinder head. To install:

7. Position the manifold on the heads and install and tighten the attaching bolts to specification.

8. Install a new inlet pipe gasket. Install and tighten the inlet pipe attaching nuts.

9. Position the exhaust manifold shroud on the manifold and install and tighten the attaching nuts to specification (left side). Install the thermactor components that had been removed.

10. Install the carburetor air cleaner. Reinstall the choke heat tube.

4-134 Diesel Engine

1. Disconnect the ground cables from both batteries.

2. Disconnect the exhaust pipe from the manifold.

3. Remove the heater hose bracket from the valve cover and exhaust manifold studs.

4. Remove the vacuum pump support brace and bracket. Remove the bolt that attaches the engine oil dipstick tube support bracket to the exhaust manifold.

5. Remove the nuts that attach the exhaust manifold to the engine and remove the manifold.

6. Clean all gasket mounting surfaces. Install a new mounting gasket and install the exhaust manifold and components in the reverse order of removal. Torque the mounting bolts to 17–20 ft. lbs. After warming up engine retighten to the same torque specification.

Cylinder Head

REMOVAL AND INSTALLATION

4-122,140 Engine

1. Drain the cooling system. Disconnect the negative battery cable.

2. Remove the air cleaner.

3. Remove the valve cover.

NOTE: *On models with air conditioning, remove the mounting bolts and the drive belt,* and position the compressor out of the way. Remove the compressor upper mounting bracket from the cylinder head.

CAUTION: *If the compressor refrigerant lines do not have enough slack to permit repositioning of the compressor without first disconnecting the refrigerant lines, the air conditioning system will have to be evacuated by a trained air conditioning serviceman. Under no circumstances should an untrained person attempt to disconnect the air conditioning refrigerant lines.*

4. Remove the intake and exhaust manifolds from the head.

5. Remove the camshaft drive belt cover. Note the location of the belt cover attaching screws that have rubber grommets.

6. Loosen the drive belt tensioner and remove the belt.

7. Remove the water outlet elbow from the cylinder head with the hose attached.

8. Remove the cylinder head attaching bolts.

9. Remove the cylinder head from the engine.

10. Clean all gasket material and carbon from the top of the cylinder block and pistons and from the bottom of the cylinder head.

11. Position a new cyliner head gasket on the engine and place the head on the engine.

NOTE: *If you encounter difficulty in positioning the cylinder head on the engine block, it may be necessary to install guide studs in*

the block to correctly align the head and the block. To fabricate guide studs, obtain two new cylinder head bolts and cut their heads off with a hack saw. Install the bolts in the holes in the engine block which correspond with cylinder head bolt holes nos. 3 and 4, as identified in the cylinder head bolt tightening sequence illustration. Then, install the head gasket and head over the bolts. Install the cylinder head attaching bolts, replacing the studs with the original head bolts.

12. Using a torque wrench, tighten the head bolts in the sequence in two steps, first 50–60 ft. lbs., then 80–90 ft. lbs.

13. Install the camshaft drive belt.

14. Install the camshaft drive belt cover and its attaching bolts. Make sure the rubber grommets are installed on the bolts. Tighten the bolts to 6–13 ft. lbs.

15. Install the water outlet elbow and a new gasket on the engine and tighten the attaching bolts to 12–15 ft. lbs.

16. Install the intake and exhaust manifolds.

17. Assemble the rest of the components in reverse order of removal.

6-173 Engine

1. Disconnect the battery ground cable.

2. Drain the radiator coolant.

3. Remove the air cleaner from the carburetor and disconnect the throttle linkage.

4. Remove the distributor. Refer to Distributor, Removal and Installation as described earlier in this Chapter.

5. Remove the radiator hose and the bypass hose from the thermostat housing and intake manifold.

6. Remove the rocker arm covers and the rocker arm shafts as described in this Chapter.

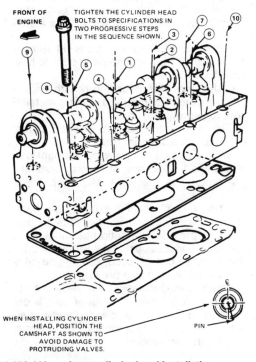

4-122,140 engines, cylinder head installation

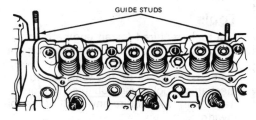

Cylinder head alignment studs—6-173 engine

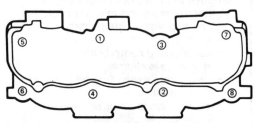

Cylinder head torque sequence—6-173 engine

ENGINE OVERHAUL

Most engine overhaul procedures are fairly standard. In addition to specific parts replacement procedures and complete specifications for your individual engine, this chapter also is a guide to accepted rebuilding procedures. Examples of standard rebuilding practice are shown and should be used along with specific details concerning your particular engine.

Competent and accurate machine shop services will ensure maximum performance, reliability and engine life. Procedures marked with the symbol shown above should be performed by a competent machine shop, and are provided so that you will be familiar with the procedures necessary to a successful overhaul.

In most instances it is more profitable for the do-it-yourself mechanic to remove, clean and inspect the component, buy the necessary parts and deliver these to a shop for actual machine work.

On the other hand, much of the rebuilding work (crankshaft, block, bearings, pistons, rods, and other components) is well within the scope of the do-it-yourself mechanic.

Tools

The tools required for an engine overhaul or parts replacement will depend on the depth of your involvement. With a few exceptions, they will be the tools found in a mechanic's tool kit (see Chapter 1). More indepth work will require any or all of the following:
• a dial indicator (reading in thousandths) mounted on a universal base
  • micrometers and telescope gauges
  • jaw and screw-type pullers
  • scraper
  • valve spring compressor
  • ring groove cleaner
  • piston ring expander and compressor
  • ridge reamer
  • cylinder hone or glaze breaker

• Plastigage®
• engine stand

Use of most of these tools is illustrated in this chapter. Many can be rented for a one-time use from a local parts jobber or tool supply house specializing in automotive work.

Occasionally, the use of special tools is called for. See the information on Special Tools and the Safety Notice in the front of this book before substituting another tool.

Inspection Techniques

Procedures and specifications are given in this chapter for inspecting, cleaning and assessing the wear limits of most major components. Other procedures such as Magnaflux and Zyglo can be used to locate material flaws and stress cracks. Magnaflux is a magnetic process applicable only to ferrous materials. The Zyglo process coats the material with a flourescent dye penetrant and can be used on any material. Check for suspected surface cracks can be more readily made using spot check dye. The dye is sprayed onto the suspected area, wiped off and the area sprayed with a developer. Cracks will show up brightly.

Overhaul Tips

Aluminum has become extremely popular for use in engines, due to its low weight. Observe the following precautions when handling aluminum parts:
• Never hot tank aluminum parts (the caustic hot-tank solution will eat the aluminum)
• Remove all aluminum parts (identification tag, etc.) from engine parts prior to hot-tanking.
• Always coat threads lightly with engine oil or anti-seize compounds before installation, to prevent seizure.
• Never over-torque bolts or spark plugs, especially in aluminum threads.

Stripped threads in any component can be repaired using any of several commercial repair kits (Heli-Coil, Microdot, Keen-serts, etc.)

When assembling the engine, any parts that will be in frictional contact must be pre-lubed to provide lubrication at initial start-up. Any product specifically formulated for this purpose can be used, but engine oil is not recommended as a pre-lube.

When semi-permanent (locked, but removable) installation of bolts or nuts is desired, threads should be cleaned and coated with Loctite® or other similar, commercial non-hardening sealant.

Repairing Damaged Threads

Several methods of repairing damaged threads are available. Heli-Coil® (shown here), Keenserts® and Microdot® are among the most widely used. All involve basically the same principle—drilling out stripped threads, tapping the hole and installing a prewound insert—making welding, plugging and oversize fasteners unnecessary.

Two types of thread repair inserts are usually supplied—a standard type for most Inch Coarse, Inch Fine, Metric Coarse and Metric Fine thread sizes and a spark plug type to fit most spark plug port sizes. Consult the individual manufacturer's catalog to determine exact applications. Typical thread repair kits will contain a selection of prewound threaded inserts, a tap (corresponding to the outside diameter threads of the insert) and an installation tool. Spark plug inserts usually differ because they require a tap equipped with pilot threads and a combined reamer/tap section. Most manufacturers also supply blister-packed thread repair inserts separately in addition to a master kit containing a variety of taps and inserts plus installation tools.

Before effecting a repair to a threaded hole, remove any snapped, broken or damaged bolts or studs. Penetrating oil can be used to free frozen threads; the offending item can be removed with locking pliers or with a screw or stud extractor. After the hole is clear, the thread can be repaired, as follows:

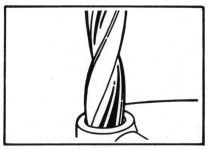

Drill out the damaged threads with specified drill. Drill completely through the hole or to the bottom of a blind hole

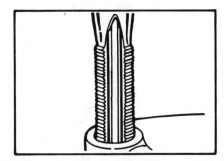

With the tap supplied, tap the hole to receive the thread insert. Keep the tap well oiled and back it out frequently to avoid clogging the threads

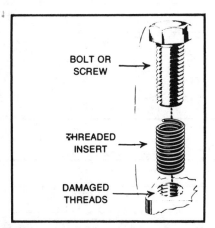

Damaged bolt holes can be repaired with thread repair inserts

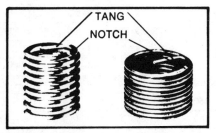

Standard thread repair insert (left) and spark plug thread insert (right)

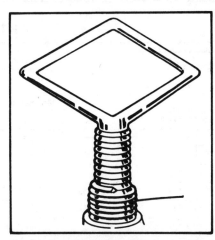

Screw the threaded insert onto the installation tool until the tang engages the slot. Screw the insert into the tapped hole until it is ¼–½ turn below the top surface, After installation break off the tang with a hammer and punch

Standard Torque Specifications and Fastener Markings

In the absence of specific torques, the following chart can be used as a guide to the maximum safe torque of a particular size/grade of fastener.

- There is no torque difference for fine or coarse threads.
- Torque values are based on clean, dry threads. Reduce the value by 10% if threads are oiled prior to assembly.
- The torque required for aluminum components or fasteners is considerably less.

U.S. Bolts

SAE Grade Number	1 or 2			5			6 or 7		
Number of lines always 2 less than the grade number.									
Bolt Size (Inches)—(Thread)	Maximum Torque			Maximum Torque			Maximum Torque		
	Ft./Lbs.	Kgm	Nm	Ft./Lbs.	Kgm	Nm	Ft./Lbs.	Kgm	Nm
¼ — 20	5	0.7	6.8	8	1.1	10.8	10	1.4	13.5
— 28	6	0.8	8.1	10	1.4	13.6			
⁵⁄₁₆ — 18	11	1.5	14.9	17	2.3	23.0	19	2.6	25.8
— 24	13	1.8	17.6	19	2.6	25.7			
⅜ — 16	18	2.5	24.4	31	4.3	42.0	34	4.7	46.0
— 24	20	2.75	27.1	35	4.8	47.5			
⁷⁄₁₆ — 14	28	3.8	37.0	49	6.8	66.4	55	7.6	74.5
— 20	30	4.2	40.7	55	7.6	74.5			
½ — 13	39	5.4	52.8	75	10.4	101.7	85	11.75	115.2
— 20	41	5.7	55.6	85	11.7	115.2			
⁹⁄₁₆ — 12	51	7.0	69.2	110	15.2	149.1	120	16.6	162.7
— 18	55	7.6	74.5	120	16.6	162.7			
⅝ — 11	83	11.5	112.5	150	20.7	203.3	167	23.0	226.5
— 18	95	13.1	128.8	170	23.5	230.5			
¾ — 10	105	14.5	142.3	270	37.3	366.0	280	38.7	379.6
— 16	115	15.9	155.9	295	40.8	400.0			
⅞ — 9	160	22.1	216.9	395	54.6	535.5	440	60.9	596.5
— 14	175	24.2	237.2	435	60.1	589.7			
1 — 8	236	32.5	318.6	590	81.6	799.9	660	91.3	894.8
— 14	250	34.6	338.9	660	91.3	849.8			

Metric Bolts

Relative Strength Marking	4.6, 4.8			8.8		
Bolt Markings						
Bolt Size Thread Size x Pitch (mm)	Maximum Torque			Maximum Torque		
	Ft./Lbs.	Kgm	Nm	Ft./Lbs.	Kgm	Nm
6 x 1.0	2–3	.2–.4	3–4	3–6	.4–.8	5–8
8 x 1.25	6–8	.8–1	8–12	9–14	1.2–1.9	13–19
10 x 1.25	12–17	1.5–2.3	16–23	20–29	2.7–4.0	27–39
12 x 1.25	21–32	2.9–4.4	29–43	35–53	4.8–7.3	47–72
14 x 1.5	35–52	4.8–7.1	48–70	57–85	7.8–11.7	77–110
16 x 1.5	51–77	7.0–10.6	67–100	90–120	12.4–16.5	130–160
18 x 1.5	74–110	10.2–15.1	100–150	130–170	17.9–23.4	180–230
20 x 1.5	110–140	15.1–19.3	150–190	190–240	26.2–46.9	160–320
22 x 1.5	150–190	22.0–26.2	200–260	250–320	34.5–44.1	340–430
24 x 1.5	190–240	26.2–46.9	260–320	310–410	42.7–56.5	420–550

7. Remove the fuel line from carburetor and remove the carburetor.

8. Remove the intake manifold as described in this Chapter.

9. Remove and label the pushrods in order to keep them in sequence for proper assembly.

10. Remove the exhause manifolds as described in this Chapter.

11. Remove the cylinder head attaching bolts. Remove the cylinder heads and discard the head gaskets.

To install:

12. Clean the cylinder heads, intake manifold, valve rocker arm cover and cylinder block gasket surfaces.

13. Place the cylinder head gaskets in position on the cylinder block.

NOTE: *Gaskets are marked with the words "front" and "top" for correct positioning. Left and right cylinder head gaskets are not interchangeable.*

14. Install the fabricated alignment dowels in the cylinder block and install the cylinder head assemblies on the cylinder block, one at a time.

15. Remove the alignment dowels and install the cylinder head attaching bolts. Tighten the bolts to specification following the torque sequence.

16. Install the intake manifold as described in this Chapter.

17. Install the exhaust manifolds as described in this Chapter.

18. Apply Lubriplate, or equivalent, to both ends of the push rods and install the push rods.

19. Install oil baffles and rocker arms as described in this Chapter under Rocker Arm Shaft Assembly.

20. Install the distributor as described under Distributor Removal and Installation in this Chapter.

21. Adjust the valves as described in Chapter 2 under Valve Lash adjustment.

22. Install the rocker arm covers.

23. Install the carburetor. Connect the fuel line to the carburetor.

24. Install the distributor cap with spark plug wires attached. Coat the inside of each spark plug boot with silicone lubricant and install them on the spark plugs.

25. Install the throttle linkage and the air cleaner.

26. Fill the cooling system according to instructions on the underhood decal and bleed the cooling system.

27. Connect the battery ground cable.

28. Operate the engine at fast idle and check for oil, fuel and coolant leaks.

29. Check and adjust, if necessary the ignition timing and idle speed.

4-134 Diesel Engine

1. Disconnect the ground cables from both batteries.

2. Mark the hood hinges for realignment on installation and remove the hood. Drain the cooling system.

3. Disconnect the breather hose from the valve cover and remove the intake hose and breather hose from the air cleaner and intake manifold.

4. Remove the heater hose bracket from the valve cover and exhaust manifold. Disconnect the heater hoses from the water pump and thermostat housing and position tube assembly out of the way.

5. Remove the vacuum pump support brace from the pump bracket and cylinder head.

6. Loosen and remove the alternator and vacuum pump drive belts. Loosen and remove the A/C compressor and/or power steering drive belt.

7. Disconnect the brake booster vacuum hose and remove the vacuum pump.

8. Disconnect the exhaust pipe from the exhaust manifold. Disconnect the coolant thermoswitch and coolant temperature sender wiring harness.

9. Disconnect and remove the fuel injection lines from the injector nozzles and pump. Cap all lines and fittings to prevent dirt from entering the system.

10. Disconnect the engine wire harness from the alternator, the glow plug harness and dropping resistor and position the harness out of the way.

11. Disconnect the fuel lines from both sides of the fuel heater. Remove the fuel filter assembly from the mounting bracket and position out of the way with the fuel line attached.

12. Loosen the lower No. 3 intake port nut and the bolt on the injection pump; disconnect the lower fuel return line from the intake manifold stud and the upper fuel return line.

13. If equipped with power steering, remove the bolt that attaches the pump rear support bracket to the cylinder head.

14. Remove the upper radiator hose. Disconnect the by-pass hose from the thermostat housing.

15. Remove the A/C compressor and position out of the way with the lines still attached.

CAUTION: *Do not disconnect the compressor lines unless the proper tools are on hand to discharge the system and you are familiar with the procedure.*

16. Remove the valve cover, rocker arm shaft assembly and the pushrods. Identify the pushrods and keep them in order for return to their original position.

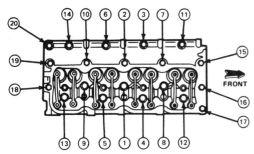

4-134 diesel engine, head bolt torque sequence

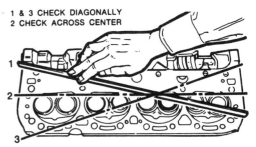

1 & 3 CHECK DIAGONALLY
2 CHECK ACROSS CENTER

Check the cylinder head for warpage

17. Remove the cylinder head attaching bolts, starting at the ends of the head, working alternately toward the center. Remove the cylinder head from the truck.

18. Clean all gasket mounting surfaces. Install the cylinder head in the reverse order of removal. Torque the cylinder head bolts in the proper sequence to 80–85 ft. lbs.

CLEANING AND INSPECTION

1. With the valves installed to protect the valve seats, remove deposits from the combustion chambers and valve heads with a scraper and a wire brush. Be careful not to damage the cylinder head gasket surface. After the valves are removed, clean the valve guide bores with a valve guide cleaning tool. Using cleaning solvent to remove dirt, grease and other deposits, clean all bolt holes; be sure the oil passage is clean.

2. Remove all deposits from the valves with a fine wire brush or buffing wheel.

3. Inspect the cylinder heads for cracks or excessively burned areas in the exhaust outlet ports.

4. Check the cylinder head for cracks and inspect the gasket surface for burrs and nicks. Replace the head if it is cracked.

5. On cylinder heads that incorporate valve seat inserts, check the inserts for excessive wear, cracks or looseness.

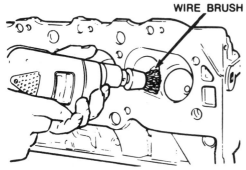

WIRE BRUSH

Remove the carbon from the cylinder head with a wire brush and electric drill

RESURFACING

Cylinder Head Flatness

When a cylinder head is removed because of gasket leaks, check the flatness of the cylinder head gasket surface.

1. Place a straight-edge across the gasket surface of the cylinder head. Using feeler gauges, determine the clearance at the center of the straight-edge.

2. If warpage exceeds .003″ in a 6″ span, or .006″ over the total length, the cylinder head must be resurfaced.

3. If necessary to refinish the cylinder head gasket surface, do not plane or grind off more than .254 mm (0.010 inch) from the original gasket surface.

NOTE: *When milling the cylinder heads of V-6 engines, the intake manifold mounting position is altered, and must be corrected by milling the manifold flange a proportionate amount.*

Valves and Springs

VALVE LASH ADJUSTMENT

Refer to Chapter 2 under Tune-Up Procedures for the Valve Lash Adjustment procedure.

Valve Spring, Retainer and Seal

REMOVAL AND INSTALLATION

Broken valve springs or damaged valve stem seals and retainers may be replaced without removing the cylinder head, provided damage to the valve or valve seat has not occurred.

NOTE: *The following procedure requires the use of special tools: air compressor, air line adapter tool to fit the spark plug hole, and a valve spring compressor tool designed to be used with the head on the engine. If the head has been removed from the engine the procedure will only require the use of a valve spring compressor tool designed to be used with the head off.*

Gasoline Engines

1. Remove the valve rocker arm cover.

2. Remove the applicable spark plug wire and spark plug.

3. Remove the valve rocker arm or shaft as described under Rocker Arm or Rocker Arm Shaft removal and installation.

4. Remove both the valve push rods from the cylinder being serviced. Remove the cam follower on overhead cam engines.

5. Install an air line with an adapter in the spark plug hole and apply air pressure to hold the valve(s) in the closed position. Failure to hold the valve(s) closed is an indication of valve seat damage and requires removal of the cylinder head.

6. Install the valve spring compressor tool T74P-6565-A & B or equivalent. Compress the valve spring and remove the retainer locks, spring retainer and valve spring.

7. Remove and discard the valve stem seal.

8. If air pressure has forced the piston to the bottom of the cylinder, any removal of air pressure will allow the valve(s) to fall into the cylinder. A rubber band wrapped around the end of the valve stem will prevent this condition and will still allow enough travel to check the valve for binds.

9. Inspect the valve stem for damage. Rotate the valve and check the valve stem tip for

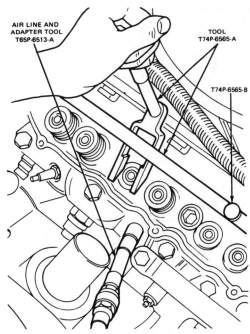

Compressing the valve spring with the cylinder head on the 6-173 engine

eccentric movement during rotation. Move the valve up and down through normal travel in the valve guide and check the stem for binds.

NOTE: *If the valve has been damaged, it will be necessary to remove the cylinder head.*

10. If the valve condition proves satisfactory, lubricate the valve stem with engine oil. Hold the valve in the closed position and apply air pressure within the cylinder.

11. Install a new valve stem seal. Place the spring in position over the valve and install the valve spring retainer. Compress the valve spring and install the valve spring retainer locks. Remove the valve spring compressor tools.

12. Lubricate the push rod ends with Lubriplate® or equivalent and install the push rod. Apply Lubriplate® or equivalent to the tip of the valve stem and to both ends of the rocker arm.

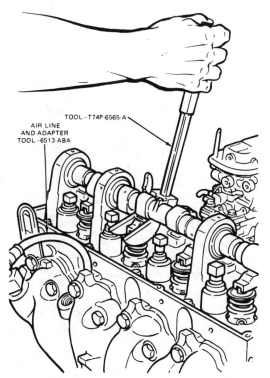

Compressing the valve spring on the 4-122,140 engines

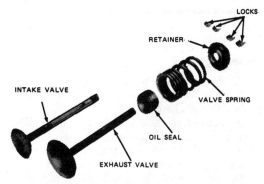

Valve train components—6-173 engine

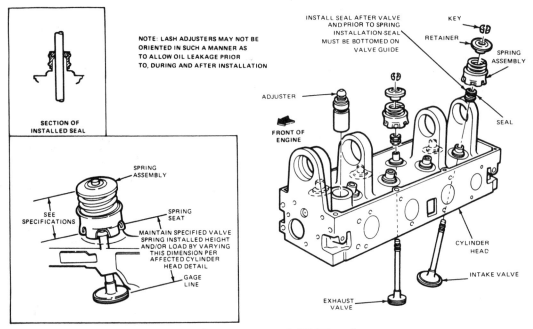

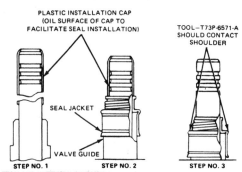

Valve train components—4-122,140 engines

STEP NO. 1 STEP NO. 2 STEP NO. 3

STEP NO. 1– WITH VALVES IN HEAD, PLACE PLASTIC INSTALLATION CAP OVER END OF VALVE STEM.
STEP NO. 2– START VALVE STEM SEAL CAREFULLY OVER CAP. PUSH SEAL DOWN UNTIL JACKET TOUCHES TOP OF GUIDE.
STEP NO. 3– REMOVE PLASTIC INSTALLATION CAP. USE INSTALLA TOOL–T73P-6571-A OR SCREWDRIVERS TO BOTTOM SEAL ON VALVE GUIDE.

Installing the valve stem seals—4-122,140 engines

13. Turn off the air and remove the air line and adapter. Install the spark plug and connect the spark plug wire.

14. Clean and install the remaining valve train components and the rocker arm cover.

Diesel Engine

1. Remove valve rocker arm cover.

2. Remove the rocker arm shaft as described in this chapter.

3. Remove the glow plug harness from glow plugs and remove glow plugs.

4. Install the adapter from the compression Test kit, Rotunda 19-6001 or equivalent, in the glow plug hole, attach an airline, and turn on the air supply.

NOTE: *An alternate method of holding the valves up, is to rotate the crankshaft until the affected piston is at TDC.*

5. Install the valve spring compressor bar, Tool T83T-6513-B, and using Valve Spring compressor Tool T74P-6565-A or equivalent, compress valve the spring and remove retainer locks, spring retainer, valve spring and damper.

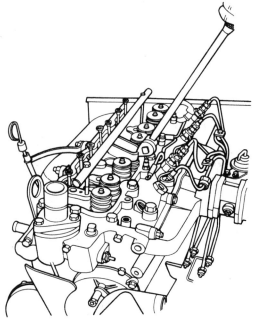

Compressing the valve spring assembly—4-134 diesel engine

6. Remove valve stem seal(s).

To Install:

7. Install new valve stem seal(s).

8. Install damper, valve spring and valve spring retainer over the valve stem. Using Tool T74P-6565-A or equivalent, compress the valve spring assembly and install the retainer locks.

CAUTION: *Make sure retainer locks are fully seated in groove on valve stem.*

9. Repeat the procedure for each valve spring assembly as necessary.

10. Disconnect the air supply line and remove the adapter from glow plug hole.

11. Install the glow plugs and tighten to 11–15 ft. lbs.

12. Install glow plug harness.

13. Install the rocker arm shaft as described in this chapter.

14. Adjust the valves as described in Chapter 2 under Diesel Engine Tune Up Procedures.

15. Install valve cover, with a new gasket.

16. Connect the heater hose tube assembly to the valve cover.

17. Run the engine and check for oil leaks.

INSPECTION

Valves

Minor pits, grooves, etc., may be removed. Discard valves that are severely damaged, or if the face runout cannot be corrected by refinishing or if the stem clearance exceeds specifications. Discard any worn or damaged valve train parts.

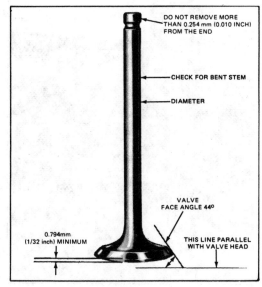

Critical valve dimensions

REFACING VALVES

NOTE: *The valve seat refacing operation should be coordinated with the valve refacing operations so that the finished angles of the valve seat and valve face will be to specifications and provide a compression tight fit.*

If the valve face runout is excessive and/or to remove pits and grooves, reface the valves to a true 44 degree angle. Remove only enough stock to correct the runout or to clean up the grooves and pits.

If the edge of the head is less than 0.794mm (1/32 inch) thick after grinding, replace the valve because the valve will run too hot for the engine. The interference fit of the valve and seat should not be lapped out.

Remove all grooves or score marks from the end of the valve stem, and chamfer it as necessary. Do not remove more than 0.254mm (0.010 inch) from the end of the valve stem.

If the valve and/or valve seat has been refaced, it will be necessary to check the clearance between the rocker arm pad and the valve stem tip with the valve train assembly installed in the engine.

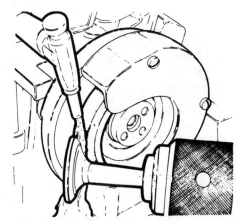

Valve grinding by machine

CHECK SPRINGS

Check the valve spring for proper pressure at the specified spring lengths using valve spring pressure tool. Weak valve springs cause poor performance; therefore, if the pressure of any spring is lower than the service limit, replace the spring. Springs should be ±5 lbs of all other springs.

Check each valve spring for squareness. Stand the spring on a flat surface next to a square. Measure the height of the spring, and rotate the spring slowly and observe the space between the top coil of the spring and the square. If the spring is out of square more than 5/64 inch or the height varies (by comparison) by more than 1/16 inch, replace the spring.

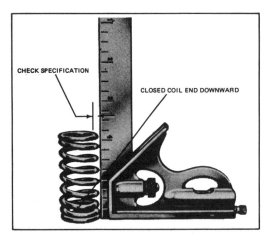

Checking the valve spring for squareness

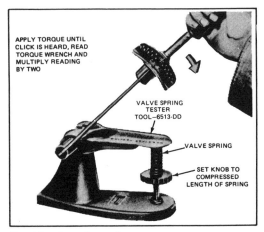

Checking the valve spring pressure

Valve Seats

CUTTING THE SEATS

NOTE: *The valve refacing operation should be coordinated with the refacing of the valve seats so that the finished angles of the valve seat and valve face will be to specifications and provide a compression tight fit.*

Grind the valve seats of all engines to a true 45 degree angle. Remove only enough stock to clean up pits and grooves or to correct the valve seat runout.

The finished valve seat should contact the approximate center of the valve face. It is good practice to determine where the valve seat contacts the valve face. To do this, coat the seat with Prussian blue and set the valve in place. Rotate the valve with light pressure. If the blue is transferred to the top edge of the valve face, lower the valve seat. If the blue is transferred to the bottom edge of the valve face, raise the valve seat.

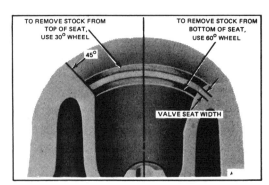

Refacing the valve seats

Valve Guides

REAMING VALVE GUIDES

If it becomes necessary to ream a valve guide to install a valve with an oversize stem, a reaming kit is available which contains oversize reamers and pilot tools.

When replacing a standard size valve with an oversize valve always use the reamer in sequence (smallest oversize first, then next smallest, etc.) so as not to overload the reamers. Always re-face the valve seat after the valve

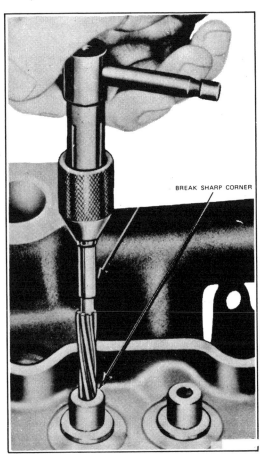

Reaming the valve guides

guide has been reamed, and use a suitable scraper to break the sharp corner at the top of the valve guide.

Camshaft Drive Belt and Cover

4-140 cu. in. Engine

The correct installation and adjustment of the camshaft drive belt is mandatory if the engine is to run properly. The camshaft controls the opening of the camshaft and the crankshaft. When any given piston is on the intake stroke the corresponding intake valve must be open to admit air/fuel mixture into the cylinder. When the same piston is on the compression and power strokes, both valves in that cylinder must be closed. When the piston is on the exhaust stroke, the exhaust valve for that cylinder must be open. If the opening and closing of the valves is not coordinated with the movements of the pistons, the engine will run very poorly, if at all.

The camshaft drive belt also turns the engine auxiliary shaft. The distributor is driven by the engine auxiliary shaft. Since the distributor controls ignition timing, the auxiliary shaft must be coordinated with the camshaft and the crankshaft, since both valves in any given cylinder must be closed and the piston in that cylinder near the top of the compression stroke when the spark plug fires.

Due to this complex interrelationship between the camshaft, the crankshaft and the auxiliary shaft, the cogged pulleys on each component must be aligned when the camshaft drive belt is installed.

TROUBLESHOOTING

Should the camshaft drive belt jump timing by a tooth or two, the engine could still run; but very poorly. To visually check for correct timing of the crankshaft, auxiliary shaft, and the camshaft follow this procedure:

NOTE: *There is an access plug provided in the cam drive belt cover so that the camshaft timing can be checked without moving the drive belt cover.*

1. Remove the access plug.

2. Turn the crankshaft until the timing marks on the crankshaft indicate TDC.

3. Make sure that the timing mark on the camshaft drive sprocket is aligned with the pointer on the inner belt cover. Also, the rotor of the distributor must align with the No. 1 cylinder firing position.

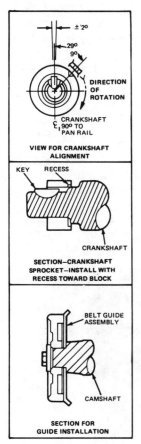

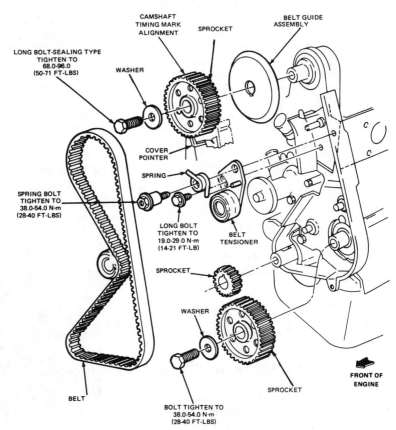

4-122,140 engine camshaft drivetrain installation

NOTE: *Never turn the crankshaft of any of the overhead cam engines in the opposite direction of normal rotation. Backward rotation of the crankshaft may cause the timing belt to slip and alter the timing.*

REMOVAL AND INSTALLATION

1. Set the engine to TDC as described in the troubleshooting section. The crankshaft and camshaft timing marks should align with their respective pointers and the distributor rotor should point to the No. 1 plug tower.

2. Loosen the adjustment bolts on the alternator and acessories and remove the drive belts. To provide clearance for removing the camshaft belt, remove the fan and pulley.

3. Remove the belt outer cover.

4. Remove the distributor cap from the distributor and position it out of the way.

5. Loosen the belt tensioner adjustment and pivot bolts. Lever the tensioner away from the belt and retighten the adjustment bolt to hold it away.

6. Remove the crankshaft bolt and pulley. Remove the belt guide behind the pulley.

7. Remove the camshaft drive belt.

8. Install the new belt over the crankshaft pulley first, then counter-clockwise over the auxiliary shaft sprocket and the camshaft sprocket. Adjust the belt fore and aft so that it is centered on the sprockets.

9. Loosen the tensioner adjustment bolt, allowing it to spring back against the belt.

10. Rotate the crankshaft two complete turns in the normal rotation direction to remove any belt slack. Turn the crankshaft until the timing check marks are lined up. If the timing has slipped, remove the belt and repeat the procedure.

11. Tighten the tensioner adjustment bolt to 14–21 ft. lbs., and the pivot bolt to 28–40 ft. lbs.

12. Replace the belt guide and crankshaft pulley, distributor cap, belt outer cover, fan and pulley, drive belts and accessories. Adjust the accessory drive belt tension. Start the engine and check the ignition timing.

Timing Gear Cover & Oil Seal
REMOVAL AND INSTALLATION
6-173 Engine

1. Remove the oil pan as described under Oil Pan removal and installation.

2. Drain the coolant. Remove the radiator.

3. Remove the A/C compressor and the power steering bracket, if so equipped, and position then out of the way. DO NOT disconnect the A/C refrigerant lines.

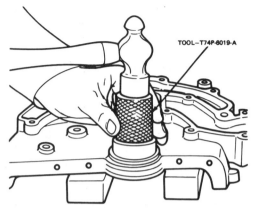

TOOL–T74P-6019-A

Installing the front cover seal

4. Remove the alternator, thermactor pump and drive belt(s).

5. Remove the fan.

6. Remove the water pump and the heater and radiator hoses.

7. Remove the drive pulley from the crankshaft.

8. Remove the front cover retaining bolts. If necessary, tap the cover lightly with a plastic hammer to break the gasket seal. Remove the front cover. If the front cover plate gasket needs replacement, remove the two screws and remove the plate. If necessary, remove the guide sleeves from the cylinder block.

9. If the front cover oil seal needs replacement use the following procedure:

   A. Support the front cover to prevent damage while driving out the seal.

   B. Drive out the seal from front cover with Front Cover Aligner, T74P-6019-A, or equivalent.

   C. Support the front cover to prevent damage while installing the seal.

   D. Coat the new front cover oil seal with

Installing the guide sleeves

Installing the front cover plate

Aligning the front cover

Lubriplate or equivalent. Install the new seal in the front cover.

10. Clean the front cover mating surfaces of gasket material. Apply sealer to the gasket surfaces on the cylinder block and back side of the front cover plate. Install the guide sleeves, with new seal rings, with the chamfered end toward the front cover, if removed. Position the gasket and the front cover plate on the cylinder block. Temporarily install the four front cover screws to position the gasket and cover plate in place. Install and tighten the two cover plate attaching bolts, then remove the four screws that were temporarily installed.

11. Apply gasket sealer to the front cover gasket surface. Place the gasket in position on the front cover.

12. Place the front cover on the engine and start all the retaining screws two or three turns. Center the cover by inserting Front Cover Aligner, Tool T74P-6019-A, or equivalent in oil seal.

13. Torque the front cover attaching screws to 13–16 ft. lbs.

14. Install the belt drive pulley.

15. Install the oil pan as described under Oil Pan removal and installation.

16. Install the water pump, heater hose, A/C compressor, alternator, themactor pump and drive belt(s). Adjust drive belt tension.

17. Fill and bleed the cooling system.

18. Operate the engine at fast idle speed and check for coolant and oil leaks.

Timing Gears
REMOVAL AND INSTALLATION
6-173 Engine

1. Drain the cooling system and crankcase. Remove the oil pan and radiator.

2. Remove the cylinder front cover and water pump, drive belt, and camshaft timing gear.

3. Use the gear puller T71P-19703-B and Shaft Protector T71P-7137-H or equivalent and remove the crankshaft gear.

To install:

4. Align the keyway in the gear with the

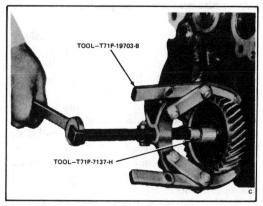

Removing the crankshaft gear

Installing the crankshaft gear

Correct alignment of the timing marks

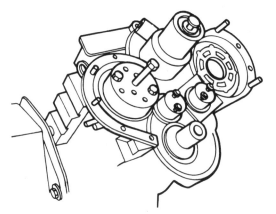

Removing the camshaft gear—4-134 diesel engine

key, then slide the gear onto the shaft, making sure that it seats tight against the spacer.

5. Check the camshaft end play. Refer to checking Camshaft. If not within specifications, replace the thrust plate.

6. Align the keyway in the crankshaft gear with key in the crankshaft, and align the timing marks. Install the gear, using the Crankshaft Sprocket Replacer Tool.

7. Install the cylinder front cover following the procedures in this section. Install the oil pan and radiator.

8. Fill and bleed the cooling system and crankcase.

9. Start the engine and adjust the ignition timing.

10. Operate the engine at fast idle and check all hose connections and gaskets for leaks.

Timing Cover/Seal and Timing Chain/Gears

REMOVAL & INSTALLATION

4-134 Diesel Engine

1. Bring the engine to No. 1 piston at TDC on the compression stroke.

2. Disconnect the ground cables from the batteries. Drain the cooling system.

3. Remove the radiator fan shroud and cooling fan. Drain the engine oil from the crankcase.

4. Loosen the idler pulley and remove the A/C compressor belt. Remove the power steering belt. Remove the power steering pump and

mounting bracket, position out of the way with the hoses attached.

5. Loosen and remove the alternator and vacuum pump drive belts.

6. Remove the water pump. Using a suitable puller, remove the crankshaft pulley.

7. Remove the nuts and bolts retaining the timing case cover to the engine block. Remove the timing case cover.

8. Remove the engine oil pan.

9. Verify that all timing marks are aligned. Rotate the engine, if necessary, to align marks.

10. Remove the bolt attaching the camshaft gear and remove the washer and friction gear.

11. Remove the bolt attaching the injection pump gear and remove the washer and friction gear.

12. Install Ford tool T83T6306A or equivalent on to the camshaft drive gear and remove the gear. Attach the puller to the injection pump drive gear and remove the gear.

13. Remove the nuts attaching the idler gears after marking reference points on the idler gears for reinstallation position. Remove the idler gear assemblies.

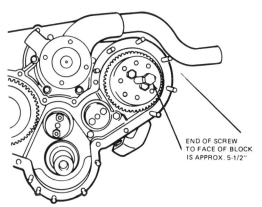

Removing the injection pump gear—4-134 diesel engine

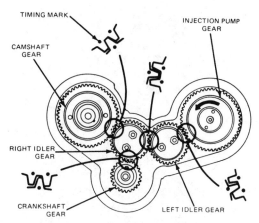

TIMING MARK

CAMSHAFT GEAR

INJECTION PUMP GEAR

RIGHT IDLER GEAR

CRANKSHAFT GEAR

LEFT IDLER GEAR

Timing gear alignment—4-134 diesel engine

14. Remove the nuts attaching the injection pump to the timing gear case. Support the injection pump in position.

15. Remove the bolts that attaching the timing gear case to the engine block and remove the case if necessary.

16. Clean all gasket mounting surfaces. Clean all parts, replace as necessary.

17. Remove the old oil seal from the front cover and replace.

18. Position the timing gear cover case with a new mounting gasket and install.

19. Install the timing gears as follows;

a. Verify that the crankshaft and right idler pulley timing marks align and install the right idler gear assembly.

b. Install the camshaft gear so that the timing marks align with the timing mark on the right idler gear.

c. Install the left idler gear assembly so that the timing marks align with the timing mark on the right idler gear.

d. Install the injection pump gear so that the timing marks align with the timing mark on the left idler gear.

e. Install all friction gears, washers, nuts and bolts on the gears.

20. Install the timing case covers using a new mounting gasket.

21. Install the remaining components in the reverse order of removal.

Camshaft

REMOVAL AND INSTALLATION

4-122,140 Engine

NOTE: *The following procedure covers camshaft removal and installation with the cylinder head on or off the engine. If the cylinder head has been removed start at Step 9.*

1. Drain the cooling system. Remove the air cleaner assembly and disconnect the negative battery cable.

2. Remove the spark plug wires from the plugs, disconnect the retainer from the valve cover and position the wires out of the way. Disconnect rubber vacuum lines as necessary.

3. Remove all drive belts. Remove the alternator mounting bracket-to-cylinder head mounting bolts, position bracket and alternator out of the way.

4. Disconnect and remove the upper radiator hose. Disconnect the radiator shroud.

5. Remove the fan blades and water pump pulley and fan shroud. Remove cam belt and valve covers.

6. Align engine timing marks at TDC for No. 1 cylinder. Remove cam drive belt.

7. Jack up the front of the vehicle and support on jackstands. Remove the front motor mount bolts. Disconnect the lower radiator hose from the radiator. Disconnect and plug the automatic transmission cooler lines.

8. Position a piece of wood on a floor jack and raise the engine carefully as far as it will go. Place blocks of wood between the engine mounts and crossmember pedestals.

9. Remove the rocker arms.

10. Remove the camshaft drive gear and belt guide using a suitable puller. Remove the front oil seal with a sheet metal screw and slide hammer.

11. Remove the camshaft retainer located on the rear mounting stand by unbolting the two bolts.

12. Remove the camshaft by carefully withdrawing toward the front of the engine. Caution should be used to prevent damage to cam bearings, lobes and journals.

13. Check the camshaft journals and lobes for wear. Inspect the cam bearings, if worn (unless the proper bearing installing tool is on hand), the cylinder head must be removed for new bearings to be installed by a machine shop.

14. Cam installation is in the reverse order of removal. See following notes.

NOTE: *Coat the camshaft with heavy SF oil before sliding it into the cylinder head. Install a new front seal. Apply a coat of sealer or teflon tape to the cam drive gear bolt before installation.*

NOTE: *After any procedure requiring removal of the rocker arms, each lash adjuster must be fully collapsed after assembly, then released. This must be done before the camshaft is turned.*

6-173 Engine

1. Disconnect the battery ground cable from the battery.

2. Drain the oil from the crankcase.

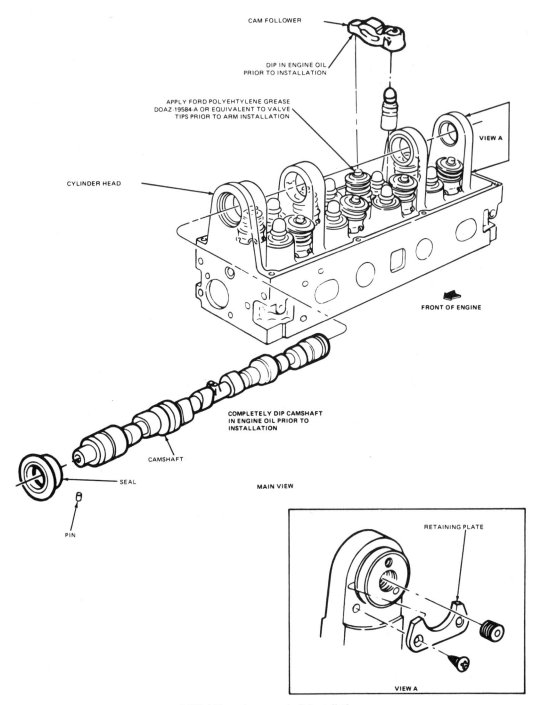

CAM FOLLOWER

DIP IN ENGINE OIL
PRIOR TO INSTALLATION

APPLY FORD POLYEHTYLENE GREASE
DOAZ-19584-A OR EQUIVALENT TO VALVE
TIPS PRIOR TO ARM INSTALLATION

VIEW A

CYLINDER HEAD

FRONT OF ENGINE

COMPLETELY DIP CAMSHAFT
IN ENGINE OIL PRIOR TO
INSTALLATION

CAMSHAFT

MAIN VIEW

SEAL

PIN

RETAINING PLATE

VIEW A

4-122,140 engine camshaft installation

3. Remove the radiator, fan and spacer, drive belt and pulley.

4. Label and remove the spark plug wires from the spark plugs.

5. Remove the distributor cap with spark plug wires as an assembly.

6. Disconnect the distributor wiring harness and remove the distributor.

7. Remove the alternator.

8. Remove the thermactor pump.

9. Remove the fuel lines, fuel filter and carburetor.

10. Remove the intake manifold as described earlier.

11. Remove the rocker arm covers and rocker arm and shaft assemblies as described in this

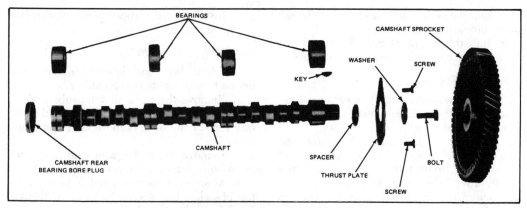

Camshaft and related parts—6-173 engine

Chapter. Label and remove the push rods and the tappets, so they can be reinstalled in the same location.

12. Remove the oil pan as described in this Chapter.

13. Remove the crankshaft damper.

14. Remove the engine front cover and water pump as an assembly.

15. Remove the camshaft gear attaching bolt and washer, and slide gear off camshaft.

16. Remove the camshaft thrust plate.

17. Carefully remove the camshaft from the block, avoiding any damage to the camshaft bearings.

18. Remove the camshaft drive gear and spacer ring.

To install:

19. Oil the camshaft journals with heavy SF grade engine oil and apply Lubriplate® or equivalent lubricant to the cam lobes. Install the spacer ring with the chamfered side toward the camshaft. Insert the camshaft key.

20. Install the camshaft in the block, carefully avoiding damage to the bearing surfaces.

21. Install the thrust plate so that it covers the main oil gallery.

22. Check the camshaft end play. The spacer

ring and thrust plate are available in two thicknesses to permit adjusting the end play.

23. Install camshaft gear as described under Timing Gear removal and installation.

24. Install the engine front cover and water pump as an assembly.

25. Install the crankshaft pulley and secure with washer and attaching bolt. Torque the bolt to 85–96 ft. lbs.

26. Install the oil pan, as described in this chapter.

27. Position the tappets in their original locations. Apply Lubriplate or equivalent to both ends of the push rods.

NOTE: *Install the push rods in same location as removed.*

28. Install the intake manifold, as described earlier.

29. Install the oil baffles and rocker arm and shaft assemblies. Tighten the rocker arm stand bolts to 43–50 ft. lbs. Adjust the valves and install the valve rocker arm covers.

30. Install the water pump pulley, fan spacer, fan, and drive belt. Adjust the belt tension.

31. Install the carburetor, fuel filter and fuel line.

32. Install the thermactor pump and the alternator.

33. Install the distributor, distributor wiring harness and distributor cap and plug wires. Connect the plug wires to the spark plugs. Refer to Distributer Removal and Installation earlier in this chapter.

NOTE: *Before installing plug wires, coat inside of each boot with silicone lubricant using a small screwdriver.*

34. Install the radiator.

35. Fill the cooling system to the proper level with a 50-50 mix of antifreeze and bleed cooling system.

36. Fill the crankcase with oil.

37. Connect the battery ground cable to the battery.

Camshaft thrust plate

38. Run the engine and check and adjust the engine timing and idle speed.

39. Run the engine at fast idle speed and check for coolant, fuel, vacuum and oil leaks.

4-134 Diesel Engine

1. Ford recommends that the engine be removed from the vehicle when camshaft replacement is necessary.

2. With the engine removed; remove the valve cover, rocker arms and shaft assembly and the pushrods. Remove the lifters, identify and keep in order if they are to be reused.

3. Remove the front timing case cover and camshaft gear.

4. Remove the engine oil pan and oil pump.

5. Remove the camshaft thrust plate and the camshaft. Take care when removing the camshaft not to damage lobes or bearings.

6. Apply oil to the camshaft bearings and bearing journals. Apply Polyethylene grease to the camshaft lobes and install the camshaft into the engine.

7. Reinstall components in the reverse order of removal.

CHECKING CAMSHAFT

Camshaft Lobe Lift

4-122,140 ENGINE

Check the lift of each lobe in consecutive order and make a note of the readings.

1. Remove the air cleaner and the valve rocker arm cover.

2. Measure the distance between the major (A—A) and minor (B—B) diameters of each cam lobe with a Vernier caliper and record the readings. The difference in the readings on each cam diameter is the lobe lift.

3. If the readings do not meet specifications, replace the camshaft and all rocker arms.

4. Install the valve rocker arm cover and the air cleaner.

6-173 AND 4-134 ENGINES

Check the lift of each lobe in consecutive order and make a note of the reading.

1. Remove the fresh air inlet tube and the air cleaner. Remove the heater hose and crankcase ventilation hoses. Remove valve rocker arm cover(s).

2. Remove the rocker arm stud nut or fulcrum bolts, fulcrum seat and rocker arm.

3. Make sure the push rod is in the valve tappet socket. Install a dial indicator D78P-4201-B (or equivalent) so that the actuating point of the indicator is in the push rod socket (or the indicator ball socket adapter Tool 6565-AB is on the end of the push rod) and in the same plane as the push rod movement.

4. Disconnect the I terminal and the S terminal at the stater relay. Install an auxiliary stater switch between the battery and S terminals of the starter relay. Crank the engine with the ignition switch off. Turn the crankshaft over until the tappet is on the base circle of the camshaft lobe. At this position, the push rod will be in its lowest position.

5. Zero the dial indicator. Continue to rotate the crankshaft slowly until the push rod is in the fully raised position.

6. Compare the total lift recorded on the dial indicator with the specification shown on the "Camshaft Specification" chart.

To check the accuracy of the original indica-

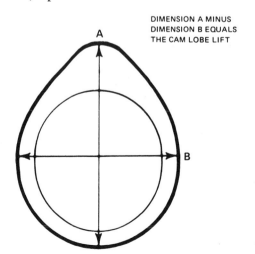

DIMENSION A MINUS DIMENSION B EQUALS THE CAM LOBE LIFT

Checking OHC camshaft lobe lift

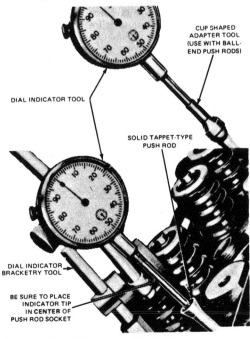

CUP SHAPED ADAPTER TOOL (USE WITH BALL-END PUSH RODS)

DIAL INDICATOR TOOL

SOLID TAPPET-TYPE PUSH ROD

DIAL INDICATOR BRACKETRY TOOL

BE SURE TO PLACE INDICATOR TIP IN CENTER OF PUSH ROD SOCKET

Checking the OHV camshaft lobe lift

tor reading, continue to rotate the crankshaft until the indicator reads zero. If the lift on any lobe is below specified wear limits listed, the camshaft and the valve tappet operating on the worn lobe(s) must be replaced.

7. Remove the dial indicator and auxiliary starter switch.

8. Install the rocker arm, fulcrum seat and stud nut or fulcrum bolts. Check the valve clearance. Adjust if required (refer to procedure in Chapter 2).

9. Install the valve rocker arm covers and the air cleaner.

Camshaft End Play

4-122,140 ENGINES

Remove the camshaft drive belt cover. Push the camshaft toward the rear of the engine. Install a dial indicator so that the indicator point is on the camshaft sprocket attaching screw or gear hub. Zero the dial indicator. Position a prybar between the camshaft sprocket or gear and the cylinder head. Pull the camshaft forward and release it. Compare the dial indicator reading with specifications. If the end play is excessive, replace the thrust plate at the rear of the cylinder head. Remove the dial indicator and install the camshaft drive belt cover.

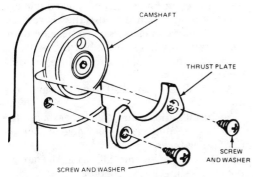

Camshaft thrust plate installation—4-122,140 engines

6-173 ENGINE

1. Push the camshaft toward the rear of the engine. Install a dial indicator (Tools D78P-4201-C or equivalent so that the indicator point is on the camshaft sprocket attaching screw.

2. Zero the dial indicator. Position a prybar between the camshaft gear and the block. Pull the camshaft forward and release it. Compare the dial indicator reading with the "Camshaft Specification Chart."

3. If the end play is excessive, check the spacer for correct installation before it is removed. If the spacer is correctly installed, replace the thrust plate.

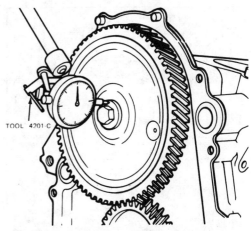

Checking the camshaft end play—6-173 engine

NOTE: *The spacer ring and thrust plate are available in two thicknesses to permit adjusting the end play.*

4. Remove the dial indicator.

4-134 DIESEL ENGINE

1. Remove the camshaft as described earlier in this chapter.

2. Mount the thrust plate. Camshaft gear and the friction gear on the camshaft.

3. Install and tighten the lock bolt.

4. Measure the end play by inserting a feeler gauge between the thrust plate and the cam gear.

5. If the end play exceeds specification shown in "Camshaft Specification Chart," replace the thrust plate.

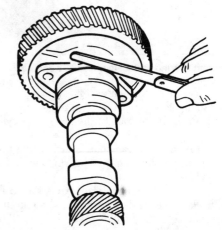

Checking the camshaft end play—4-134 diesel engine

CAMSHAFT BEARING REPLACEMENT

1. Remove the engine following the procedures in this chapter and install it on a work stand.

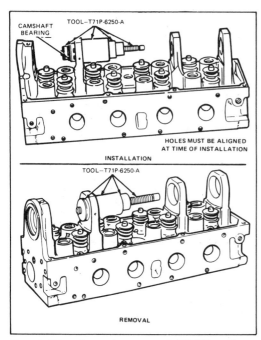

Camshaft bearing replacement—4-122,140 engines

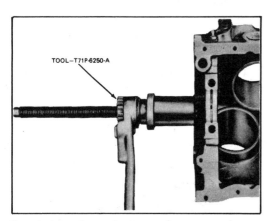

Camshaft bearing replacement—6-173 engine

2. Remove the camshaft, flywheel and crankshaft, following the appropriate procedures. Push the pistons to the top of the cylinders.

3. Remove the camshaft rear bearing bore plug. Remove the camshaft bearings with Tool T71P-6250-A or equivalent.

4. Select the proper size expanding collet and back-up nut and assemble on the mandrel. With the expanding collet collapsed, install the collet assembly in the camshaft bearing and tighten the back-up nut on the expanding mandrel until the collet fits the camshaft bearing.

5. Assemble the puller screw and extension (if necessary) and install on the expanding mandrel. Wrap a cloth around the threads of the puller screw to protect the front bearing or journal. Tighten the pulling nut against the

Checking the oil hole alignment in the no. 2 and 3 camshaft bearings—6-173 engine

thrust bearing and pulling plate to remove the camshaft bearing. Be sure to hold a wrench on the end of the puller screw to prevent it from turning.

6. To remove the front and rear bearings, install the special adapter tube Tool T72C-6250 or equivalent.

7. Position the new bearings at the bearing bores, and press them in place with Tool T71P-6250-A or equivalent. Be sure to center the pulling plate and puller screw to avoid damage to the bearing. **Failure to use the correct expanding collet can cause severe bearing damage.** Align the oil holes in the bearings with the oil holes in the cylinder block before pressing bearings into place.

8. Install the camshaft rear bearing bore plug.

9. Install the camshaft, crankshaft, flywheel and related parts, following the appropriate procedures.

10. Install the engine following the appropriate procedure in this chapter.

Auxiliary Shaft

REMOVAL AND INSTALLATION

4-140,122 Engine

1. Remove the camshaft drive belt cover.

2. Remove the drive belt. Remove the auxiliary shaft sprocket. A puller may be necessary to remove the sprocket.

3. Remove the distributor and fuel pump.

4. Remove the auxiliary shaft cover and thrust plate.

5. Withdraw the auxiliary shaft from the block.

NOTE: *The distributor drive gear and the fuel pump eccentric on the auxiliary shaft must not be allowed to touch the auxiliary*

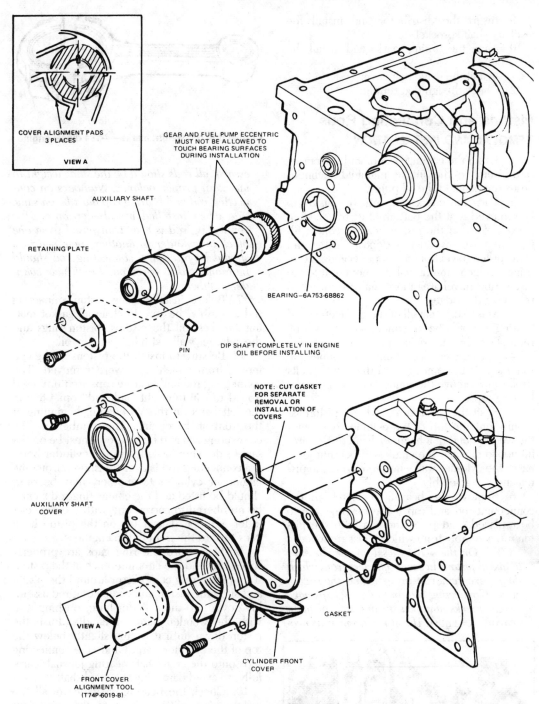

COVER ALIGNMENT PADS
3 PLACES

VIEW A

GEAR AND FUEL PUMP ECCENTRIC
MUST NOT BE ALLOWED TO
TOUCH BEARING SURFACES
DURING INSTALLATION

AUXILIARY SHAFT

RETAINING PLATE

BEARING—6A753-6B862

PIN

DIP SHAFT COMPLETELY IN ENGINE
OIL BEFORE INSTALLING

NOTE: CUT GASKET
FOR SEPARATE
REMOVAL OR
INSTALLATION OF
COVERS

AUXILIARY SHAFT
COVER

GASKET

VIEW A

CYLINDER FRONT
COVER

FRONT COVER
ALIGNMENT TOOL
(T74P-6019-B)

Auxiliary shaft installation—4-122,140 engines

shaft bearings during removal and installation. Completely coat the shaft with oil before sliding it into place.

6. Slide the auxiliary shaft into the housing and insert the thrust plate to hold the shaft.

7. Install a new gasket and auxiliary shaft cover.

NOTE: *The auxiliary shaft cover and cylinder front cover share a gasket. Cut off the old gasket around the cylinder cover and use half of the new gasket on the auxiliary shaft cover.*

8. Fit a new gasket into the fuel pump and install the pump.

9. Insert the distributor and install the auxiliary shaft sprocket.

10. Align the timing marks and install the drive belt.

11. Install the drive belt cover.

12. Check the ignition timing.

Pistons and Connecting Rods

REMOVAL AND INSTALLATION

1. Drain the cooling system and the crankcase. Remove the intake manifold, cylinder heads, oil pan and the oil pump.

2. Turn the crankshaft until the piston to be removed is at the bottom of its travel, then place a cloth on the piston head to collect filings. Remove any ridge of deposits at the end of the piston travel from the upper cylinder bore, using a ridge reaming tool. Do not cut into the piston ring travel area more than $\frac{1}{33}$ in. when removing the ridge.

3. Make sure that all of the connecting rod bearing caps can be identified, so they will be reinstalled in their original positions.

4. Turn the crankshaft until the connecting rod that is to be removed is at the bottom of its stroke and remove the connecting rod nuts and bearing cap.

5. Push the connecting rod and piston assebmly out the top of the cylinder bore with the wooden end of a hammer handle. Be careful not to damage the crankshaft bearing journal or the cylinder wall when removing the piston and rod assembly.

6. Remove the bearing inserts from the connecting rod and cap if the bearings are to be replaced, and place the cap onto the piston/rod assembly from which it was removed.

NOTE: *On the 4-134 diesel engine, be sure to install pistons in same cylinders from which they were removed or to which they were fitted. Connecting rod and bearing caps have weight marks stamped on one side of main bearing bore boss. If rod replacement is nec-*

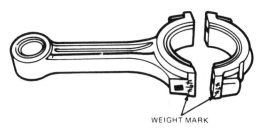

WEIGHT MARK

Connecting rod weight marks—4-134 diesel engine

essary, all rods should be the same weight to maintain proper balance. Numbers on connecting rod and bearing cap must be on same side when installed in cylinder bore. If a connecting rod is ever transposed from one block or cylinder to another, new bearings should be fitted and connecting rod should be numbered to correspond with new cylinder number.

7. Before installing the piston/connecting rod assembly, be sure to clean all gasket mating surfaces, oil the pistons, piston rings and the cylinder walls with light engine oil.

8. Be sure to install the pistons in the cylinders from which they were removed. The connecting rod and bearing caps are numbered from 1 to 3 in the right bank and from 4 to 6 in the left bank on the V6 engine, beginning at the front of the engine. The numbers on the connecting rod and bearing cap must be on the same side when installed in the cylinder bore. If a connecting rod is ever transposed from one engine or cylinder to another, new bearings should be fitted and the connecting rod should be numbered to correspond with the new cylinder number. The notch on the piston head goes toward the front of the engine.

9. Make sure the ring gaps are properly spaced around the circumference of the piston. Fit a piston ring compressor around the piston and slide the piston and connecting rod assembly down into the cylinder bore, pushing it in with the wooden hammer handle. Push the piston down until it is only slightly below the top of the cylinder bore. Guide the connecting rods onto the crankshaft bearing journals carefully, to avoid damaging the crankshaft.

10. Check the bearing clearance of all the rod bearings, fitting them to the crankshaft bearing journals.

11. After the bearings have been fitted, apply a light coating of engine oil to the journals and bearings.

12. Turn the crankshaft until the appropriate bearing journal is at the bottom of its stroke, then push the piston assembly all the way down until the connecting rod bearing seats on the crankshaft journal. Be careful not to allow the bearing cap screws to strike the crank-

Connecting rod and bearing cap numbering

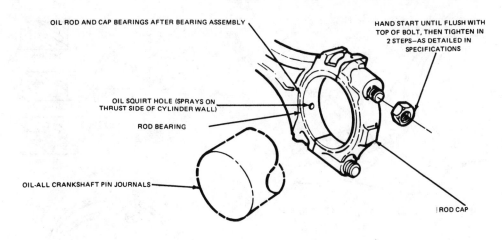

OIL ROD AND CAP BEARINGS AFTER BEARING ASSEMBLY

HAND START UNTIL FLUSH WITH
TOP OF BOLT, THEN TIGHTEN IN
2 STEPS—AS DETAILED IN
SPECIFICATIONS

OIL SQUIRT HOLE (SPRAYS ON
THRUST SIDE OF CYLINDER WALL)

ROD BEARING

OIL-ALL CRANKSHAFT PIN JOURNALS

ROD CAP

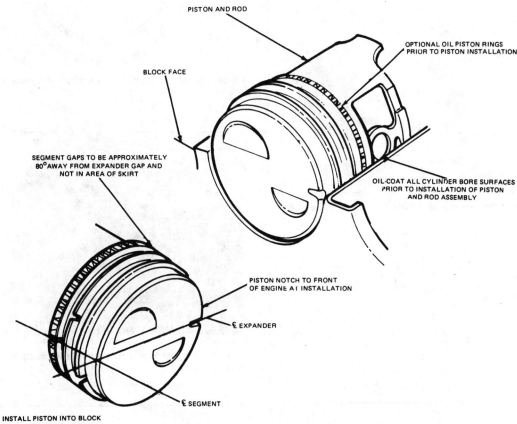

PISTON AND ROD

OPTIONAL OIL PISTON RINGS
PRIOR TO PISTON INSTALLATION

BLOCK FACE

SEGMENT GAPS TO BE APPROXIMATELY
80°AWAY FROM EXPANDER GAP AND
NOT IN AREA OF SKIRT

OIL-COAT ALL CYLINDER BORE SURFACES
PRIOR TO INSTALLATION OF PISTON
AND ROD ASSEMBLY

PISTON NOTCH TO FRONT
OF ENGINE AT INSTALLATION

₵ EXPANDER

₵ SEGMENT

INSTALL PISTON INTO BLOCK
WITH RING GAPS AS FOLLOWS
EXPANDER—TO FRONT OF PISTON
SEGMENT—TO REAR OF PISTON

Connecting rod, piston and ring installation—4-122,140 engines

shaft bearing journals and damage them.

13. After the piston and connecting rod assemblies have been installed, check the connecting rod side clearance on each crankshaft journal.

14. Prime and install the oil pump and the oil pump intake tube, then install the oil pan.

15. Reassemble the rest of the engine in the reverse order of disassembly.

PISTON RING REPLACEMENT

1. Select the proper ring set for the size cylinder bore.

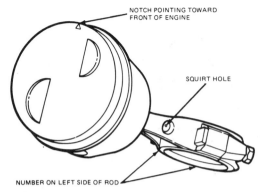

Correct piston and rod positioning—4-122,140 engines

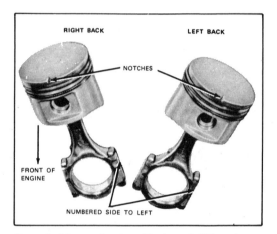

Correct piston and rod positioning—6-173 engine

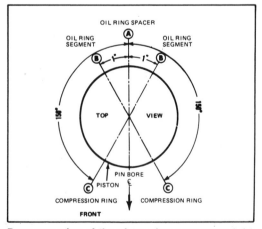

Proper spacing of the piston ring gaps around the circumference of the piston—gasoline engines

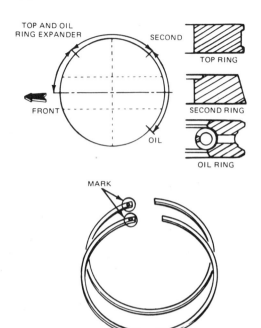

Proper spacing of the piston ring gaps—4-134 diesel engine

Installing the piston and connecting rod assembly—gasoline engines

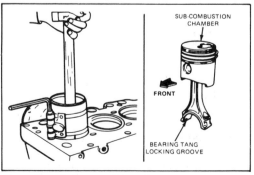

Piston installation—4-134 engines

2. Position the ring in the bore in which it is going to be used.

3. Push the ring down into the bore area where normal ring wear is not encountered.

4. Use the head of the piston to position the ring in the bore so that the ring is square with

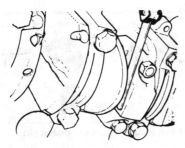
Checking the connecting rod side clearance on the crankshaft bearing journal

the cylinder wall. Use caution to avoid damage to the ring or cylinder bore.

5. Measure the gap between the ends of the ring with a feeler gauge. Ring gap in a worn cylinder is normally greater than specification. If the ring gap is greater than the specified limits, try an oversize ring set.

6. Check the ring side clearance of the compression rings with a feeler gauge inserted between the ring and its lower land according to specification. The gauge should slide freely around the entire ring circumference without binding. Any wear that occurs will form a step at the inner portion of the lower land. If the lower lands have high steps, the piston should be replaced.

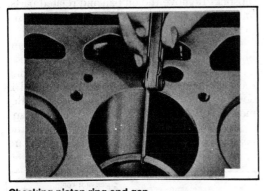
Checking piston ring end gap

Checking piston ring side clearance

CLEANING AND INSPECTION

Connecting Rods

1. Remove the bearings from the rod and cap. Identify the bearings if they are to be used again. Clean the connecting rod in solvent, including the rod bore and the back of the bearing inserts. Do not use a caustic cleaning solution. Blow out all passages with compressed air.

2. The connecting rods and related parts should be carefully inspected and checked for conformance to specifications. Various forms of engine wear caused by these parts can be readily identified.

3. A shiny surface on the pin boss side of the piston usually indicates that a connecting rod is bent or the piston pin hole is not in proper relation to the piston skirt and ring grooves.

4. Abnormal connecting rod bearing wear can be caused by either a bent connecting rod, an improperly machined journal, or a tapered connecting rod bore.

5. Twisted connecting rods will not create an easily identifiable wear pattern, but badly twisted rods will disturb the action of the entire piston, rings, and connecting rod assembly and may be the cause of excessive oil consumption.

6. Inspect the connecting rods for signs of fractures and the bearing bores for out-of-round and taper. If the bore exceeds the maximum limit and/or if the rod is fractured, it should be replaced.

7. Check the ID of the connecting rod piston pin bore. Install oversize piston pin if the pin bore is not within specifications. Replace worn or damaged connecting rod nuts and bolts.

8. After the connecting rods are assembled to the piston, check the rods for bends or twists on a suitable alignment fixture. Follow the instructions of the fixture manufacturer. If the bend and/or twist exceeds specifications, the rod must be straightened or replaced.

Pistons, Pins and Rings

1. Remove deposits from the piston surfaces. Clean gum or varnish from the piston skirt, piston pins and rings with solvent. **Do not use a caustic cleaning solution or a wire brush to clean pistons.** Clean the ring groove with a ring groove cleaner. Make sure the oil ring slots (or holes) are clean.

2. Carefully inspect the pistons for fractures at the ring lands, skirts, and pin bosses, and for scuffed, rough, or scored skirts. If the lower inner portion of the ring grooves have high steps, replace the piston. The step will interfere with ring operation and cause excessive ring side clearance.

3. Spongy, eroded areas near the edge of the

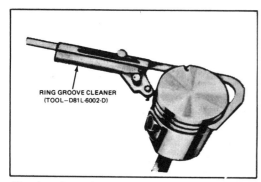

Cleaning piston ring grooves

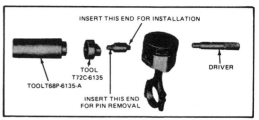

Removal and installation of the piston pin

piston top are usually caused by detonation or pre-ignition. A shiny surface on the thrust surface of the piston, offset from the centerline between the piston pin holes, can be caused by a bent connecting rod. Replace pistons that show signs of excessive wear, wavy ring lands or fractures, or damage from detonation or pre-ignition.

4. Check the piston to cylinder bore clearance by measuring the piston and bore diameters. **Measure the OD of the piston with micrometers at the centerline of the piston pin bore and at 90 degrees to the pin bore axis. Check the ring side clearance following the procedure under Piston Ring Replacement in this chapter.**

5. Replace piston pins showing signs of fracture, etching or wear. Check the piston pin fit in the piston and rod.

6. Check the OD of the piston pin and the ID of the pin bore in the piston. Replace any piston pin or piston that is not within specifications.

7. Replace all rings that are scored, chipped or cracked. Check the end gap and side clearance. It is good practice to always install new rings when overhauling an engine. Rings should not be transferred from one piston to another regardless of mileage.

PISTON PIN REPLACEMENT

1. Remove the bearing inserts from the connecting rod and cap.

2. Mark the pistons to assure assembly with the same rod, rod position and installation in the same cylinders from which they were removed.

3. Using an Arbor press and tool T68P-6135-A or equivalent, press the piston pin from the piston and connecting rod. Remove the piston rings if they are to be replaced.

NOTE: *Check the fit of a new piston in the cylinder bore before assembling the piston and piston pin to the connecting rod.*

4. Apply a light coat of engine oil to all parts.

Assemble the piston to the connecting rod with the indentation or notch in the original position.

5. Start the piston pin in the connecting rod (this may require a very light tap with a mallet). Using an Arbor press and tool T68P-6135-A or equivalent, press the piston pin through the piston and connecting rod until the pin is centered in the piston.

6. Install the piston rings using a piston ring installation tool of the proper size (refer to "Piston Ring Replacement" in this chapter).

7. Be sure the bearing inserts and the bearing bore in the connecting rod and cap are clean. Foreign material under the inserts will distort the bearing and cause it to fail.

ROD BEARING REPLACEMENT

1. Drain the crankcase. Remove the oil level dipstick. Remove the oil pan and related parts, following the procedure under "Oil Pan removal and installation" in this chapter.

2. Remove the oil pump inlet tube assembly and the oil pump.

3. Turn the crankshaft until the connecting rod to which new bearings are to be fitted is down. Remove the connecting rod cap. Remove the bearing inserts from the rod and cap.

4. Be sure the bearing inserts and the bearing bore in the connecting rod and cap are

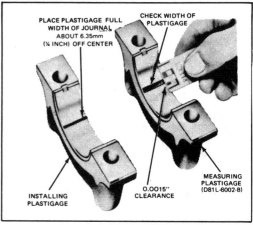

Measuring with Plastigage® to determine bearing clearance

clean. Foreign material under the inserts will distort the bearing and cause failure.

5. Clean the crankshaft journal. Inspect journals for nicks, burrs or bearing pick-up that would cause premature bearing wear.

6. Install the bearing inserts in the connecting rod and cap with the tangs fitting in slots provided.

7. Pull the connecting rod assembly down firmly on the crankshaft journal.

8. Select fit the bearing using the following procedures:

   a. Place a piece of Plastigage® or it's equivalent, on the bearing surface across the full width of the bearing cap and about 6.35mm (¼ inch) off center.

   b. Install cap and tighten bolts to specifications. Do not turn crankshaft while Plastigage® is in place.

   c. Remove cap. Using Plastigage® scale, check width of Plastigage® at widest point to get minimum clearance. Check at narrowest point to get maximum clearance. Difference between readings is taper of journal.

   d. If clearance exceeds specified limits, try a 0.001 or 0.002 inch undersize bearing in combination with the standard bearing. Bearing clearance must be within specified limits. If standard and 0.002 inch undersize bearing does not bring clearance within desired limits, refinish crankshaft journal, then use undersize bearings.

9. After bearing has been fitted, apply light coat of engine oil to journal and bearings. Install bearing cap. Tighten cap bolts to specifications.

10. Repeat procedures for remaining bearings that require replacement.

11. Clean the oil pump inlet tube screen. Prime the oil pump by filling the inlet opening with oil and rotating the pump shaft until oil emerges from the outlet opening. Install the oil pump and inlet tube assembly.

12. Install the oil pan and related parts, following the procedure under "Oil Pan removal and installation" in this chapter. Install the oil level dipstick.

13. Fill the crankcase with engine oil. Start the engine and check for oil pressure. Operate the engine at fast idle and check for oil leaks.

Crankshaft and Main Bearings
REMOVAL AND INSTALLATION
Gasoline Engines

1. With the engine removed from the vehicle and placed in a work stand, disconnect the spark plug wires from the spark plugs and remove the wires and bracket assembly from the attaching stud on the valve rocker arm

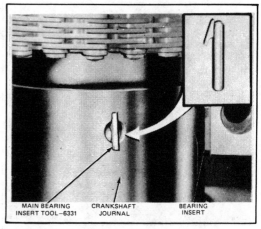

MAIN BEARING   CRANKSHAFT   BEARING
INSERT TOOL–6331   JOURNAL   INSERT

Installing the upper main bearing inserts

cover(s) if so equipped. Disconnect the oil to distributor high-tension lead at the coil. Remove the distributor cap and spark plug wires as an assembly. Remove the spark plugs to allow easy rotation of the crankshaft.

2. Remove the fuel pump and oil filter. Remove the alternator and mounting brackets.

3. Remove the crankshaft pulley from the crankshaft vibration damper. Remove the capscrew and washer from the end of the crankshaft. Install a universal puller, Tool T58P-6316-D or equivalent on the crankshaft vibration damper and remove the damper.

4. Remove the cylinder front cover and crankshaft gear, refer to "Timing Gear Cover" or "Camshaft Drive Belt and Cover" in this chapter.

5. Invert the engine on the work stand. Remove the clutch pressure plate and disc (manual-shift trans.). Remove the flywheel and engine rear cover plate Remove the oil pan and gasket. Remove the oil pump.

6. Make sure all bearing caps (main and connecting rod) are marked so that they can be installed in their original locations. Turn the crankshaft until the connecting rod from which the cap is being removed is down, and remove the bearing cap. Push the connecting rod and piston assembly up into the cylinder. Repeat this procedure until all the connecting rod bearing caps are removed.

7. Remove the main bearing caps.

8. Carefully lift the crankshaft out of the block so that the thrust bearing surfaces are not damaged. Handle the crankshaft with care to avoid possible fracture to the finished surfaces.

9. Remove the rear journal oil seal from the block and rear main bearing cap.

10. Remove the main bearing inserts from the block and bearing caps.

11. Remove the connecting rod bearing inserts from the connecting rods and caps.

Applying RTV sealer to the rear main bearing cap—6-173 engine

12. If the crankshaft main bearing journals have been refinished to a definite undersize, install the correct undersize bearings. Be sure the bearing inserts and bearing bores are clean. Foreign material under the inserts will distort the bearing and cause a failure.

13. Install the upper main bearings lubricate the bearings with engine oil, then place the end of the bearing over the shaft on the locking tang side of the block and partially install the bearing so that Tool 6331-E can be inserted in the journal oil hole. With Tool 6331-E installed, rotate the crankshaft slowly in the opposite direction of engine rotation until the bearing tang is seated. Remove the bearing tool

14. Install the lower main bearing inserts in the bearing caps.

15. Clean the rear journal oil seal groove and the mating surfaces of the block and rear main bearing cap.

16. Carefully lower the crankshaft into place. Be careful not to damage the bearing surfaces.

17. Check the clearance of each main bearing by using the following procedure:

a. Place a piece of Plastigage® or equivalent, on bearing surface across full width of bearing cap and about ¼ inch off center.

b. Install cap and tighten bolts to specifications. Do not turn crankshaft while plastigage® is in place.

c. Remove the cap. Using Plastigage® scale, check width of Plastigage® at widest point to get maximum clearance. Difference between readings is taper of journal.

d. If clearance exceeds specified limits, try a 0.001 or 0.002 inch undersize bearing in combination with the standard bearing. Bearing clearance must be within specified limits. If standard and 0.002 inch undersize bearing does not bring clearance within desired limits, refinish crankshaft journal, then install undersize bearings.

18. Apply engine oil to the journals and bearings.

19. Install all the bearing caps except the center thrust bearing cap. Be sure the main bearing caps are installed in their original locations. Tighten the bearing cap bolts to specifications.

NOTE: *Apply RTV sealer to the rear main bearing cap before installing.*

20. Install the thrust bearing cap with the bolts finger tight.

21. Pry the crankshaft forward against the thrust surface of the upper half of the bearing.

22. Hold the crankshaft forward and pry the thrust bearing cap to the rear. This will align the thrust surfaces of both halves of the bearing.

23. Retain the forward pressure on the crankshaft. Tighten the cap bolts to specifications.

24. Check the crankshaft end play using the following procedures:

a. Force the crankshaft toward the rear of the engine.

b. Install a dial indicator (tools D78P-4201-F, -G or equivalent) so that the contact point rests against the crankshaft flange and the indicator axis is parallel to the crankshaft axis.

c. Zero the dial indicator. Push the crankshaft forward and note the reading on the dial.

d. If the end play exceeds the wear limit

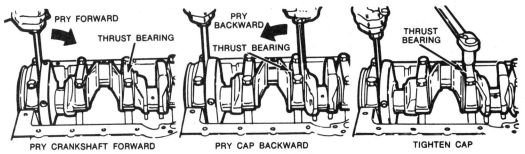

PRY CRANKSHAFT FORWARD   PRY CAP BACKWARD   TIGHTEN CAP

Aligning the thrust bearing

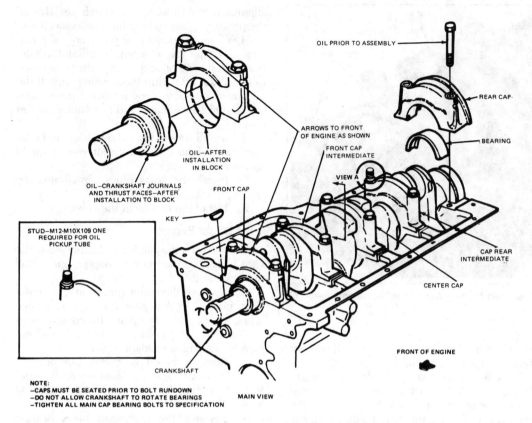

STUD-M12-M10X109 ONE
REQUIRED FOR OIL
PICKUP TUBE

OIL PRIOR TO ASSEMBLY

REAR CAP·

BEARING

ARROWS TO FRONT
OF ENGINE AS SHOWN

FRONT CAP
INTERMEDIATE

VIEW A

CAP REAR
INTERMEDIATE

CENTER CAP

OIL—AFTER
INSTALLATION
IN BLOCK

OIL-CRANKSHAFT JOURNALS
AND THRUST FACES-AFTER
INSTALLATION TO BLOCK

FRONT CAP

KEY

CRANKSHAFT

FRONT OF ENGINE

MAIN VIEW

NOTE:
-CAPS MUST BE SEATED PRIOR TO BOLT RUNDOWN
-DO NOT ALLOW CRANKSHAFT TO ROTATE BEARINGS
-TIGHTEN ALL MAIN CAP BEARING BOLTS TO SPECIFICATION

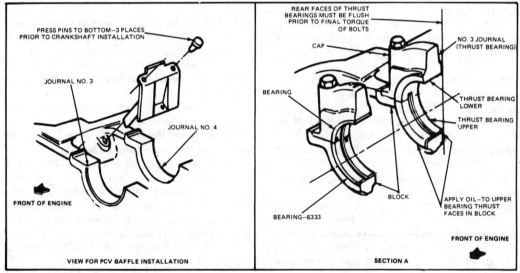

PRESS PINS TO BOTTOM-3 PLACES
PRIOR TO CRANKSHAFT INSTALLATION

JOURNAL NO. 3

JOURNAL NO. 4

FRONT OF ENGINE

VIEW FOR PCV BAFFLE INSTALLATION

REAR FACES OF THRUST
BEARINGS MUST BE FLUSH
PRIOR TO FINAL TORQUE
OF BOLTS

CAP

NO. 3 JOURNAL
(THRUST BEARING)

BEARING

THRUST BEARING
LOWER

THRUST BEARING
UPPER

BLOCK

BEARING-6333

APPLY OIL—TO UPPER
BEARING THRUST
FACES IN BLOCK

FRONT OF ENGINE

SECTION A

Crankshaft and main bearing installation—4-122,140 engines

listed in the "Crankshaft and Connecting Rod Specifications" chart, replace the thrust bearing. If the end play is less than the minimum limit, inspect the thrust bearing faces for scratches, burrs, nicks, or dirt. If the thrust faces are not damaged or dirty, then they probably were not aligned properly. Lubricate and install the new thrust bearing and align the faces following procedures 20 thru 23.

25. Coat a new crankshaft rear oil seal with oil and install, refer to Rear Main Oil Seal in-

WEDGE SEALS

Rear main bearing wedge seal replacement—6-173 engine

stallation. Inspect the seal to be sure it was not damaged during installation.

26. Using a flat tool, push the two wedge-shaped seals between the cylinder block and rear main bearing cap on the 6-173 engine. Position the seals with the round side facing the main bearing cap.

27. Install new bearing inserts in the connecting rods and caps. Check the clearance of each bearing, following the procedure (17a thru d).

28. After the connecting rod bearings have been fitted, apply a light coat of engine oil to the journals and bearings.

29. Turn the crankshaft throw to the bottom of its stroke. Push the piston all the way down until the rod bearing seats on the crankshaft journal.

30. Install the connecting rod cap. Tighten the nuts to specifications.

31. After the piston and connecting rod assemblies have been installed, check the side clearance with a feeler gauge between the connecting rods on each connecting rod crankshaft journal. Refer to "Crankshaft and Connecting Rod Specifications" chart in this chapter.

32. Install the timing gears or belt, cylinder front cover and crankshaft pulley and adapter, following steps under Timing Gear Cover or Camshaft Drive Belt and Cover in this chapter.

33. Coat the threads of the flywheel attaching bolts with Loctite® or equivalent. Position the flywheel on the crankshaft flange. Install and tighten the bolts to specifications. On a flywheel for manual-shift transmission, use a clutch

alignment tool to locate the clutch disc. Install the pressure plate and tighten to specifications.

34. Clean the oil pan, oil pump and oil pump screen. Prime the oil pump by filling the inlet port with engine oil and rotating the pump shaft to distribute oil within the housing. Install the oil pump and oil pan by following procedures under "Oil Pan removal and installation" in this chapter.

35. Install the oil filter, fuel pump and connect the fuel lines. Install the alternator, shield and mounting bracket.

36. Install the spark plugs, distributor cap and spark plug wires.

37. Install the engine in the vehicle.

4-134 Diesel Engine

1. Remove the engine assembly from the vehicle as described in this chapter, and install in work stand.

2. Remove the water pump pulley, crankshaft pulley, timing gear case cover, timing gears, fuel injection pump and timing gear case.

3. Remove the starter, flywheel, and engine-to-transmission adapter plate.

4. Remove the oil pan and oil pump.

5. Remove the rear oil seal assembly as described in this chapter under Rear Main Oil Seal.

6. Remove the crankshaft main bearing caps.

NOTE: *Main bearing caps are numbered 1 through 5, front to rear, and must be returned to their original positions.*

7. Carefully lift the crankshaft out of block so the thrust bearing surfaces are not damaged. To install:

8. Remove the main bearing inserts from the block and bearing caps.

9. Remove the connecting rod bearing inserts from the connecting rods and caps.

10. If the crankshaft main bearing journals have been refinished to a definite undersize, install the correct undersize bearing. Be sure that the bearing inserts and bearing bores are clean. Foreign material under inserts will distort bearing and cause failure.

11. Place the upper main bearing inserts in bores with tang in slot.

NOTE: *The oil holes in the bearing inserts must be aligned with the oil holes in the cylinder block.*

12. Install the lower main bearing inserts in bearing caps.

13. Clean the mating surfaces of block and rear main bearing cap.

14. Carefully lower the crankshaft into place. **Be careful not to damage bearing surfaces.**

15. Check the clearance of each main bearing by using the following procedure:

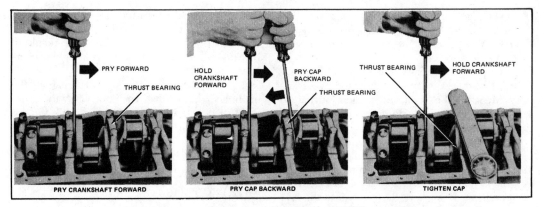

PRY FORWARD · THRUST BEARING · HOLD CRANKSHAFT FORWARD · PRY CAP BACKWARD · THRUST BEARING · THRUST BEARING · HOLD CRANKSHAFT FORWARD

PRY CRANKSHAFT FORWARD · PRY CAP BACKWARD · TIGHTEN CAP

Aligning the crankshaft thrust bearings—4-134 diesel engine

a. Place a piece of Plastigage® or it's equivalent, on bearing surface across full width of bearing cap and about ¼ inch off center.

b. Install cap and tighten bolts to specifications. Do not turn crankshaft while plastigage® is in place.

c. Remove the cap. Using Plastigage® scale, check width of Plastigage® at widest point to get maximum clearance. Difference between readings is taper of journal.

d. If clearance exceeds specified limits, try a 0.001 or 0.002 inch undersize bearing in combination with the standard bearing. Bearing clearance must be within specified limits. If standard and 0.002 inch undersize bearing does not bring clearance within desired limits, refinish crankshaft journal, then install undersize bearings.

16. After the bearings have been fitted, apply a light coat of engine oil to the journals and bearings. Install the rear main bearing cap. Install all bearing caps except the thrust bearing cap (No. 3 bearing). **Be sure that main bearing caps are installed in original locations.** Tighten the bearing cap bolts to 80–85 ft. lb.

17. Install the thrust bearing cap with bolts fingertight.

18. Pry the crankshaft forward against the thrust surface of upper half of bearing.

19. Hold the crankshaft forward and pry the thrust bearing cap to the rear. This aligns the thrust surfaces of both halves of the bearing.

20. Retain the forward pressure on the crankshaft. Tighten the cap bolts to 80–85 ft. lbs.

21. Force the crankshaft toward the rear of engine.

22. Install new bearing inserts in the connecting rods and caps. Check the clearance of each bearing, following procedure described under step 15.

23. After the connecting rod bearings have been fitted, apply light coat of engine oil to the journals and bearings.

24. Turn the crankshaft throw to bottom of its stroke. Push the piston all the way down until the rod bearing seats on crankshaft journal.

25. Install the connecting rod cap. Be sure that the connecting rod bolt heads are properly seated in the connecting rod. Tighten nuts to 50–54 ft. lbs.

26. After piston and connecting rod assemblies have been installed, check side clearance (refer to "Crankshaft and Connecting Rod Specifications") between connecting rods on each connecting rod crankshaft journal.

27. Install a new rear main oil seal in oil seal adapter as described in this chapter under "Rear Main Oil Seal."

28. Install rear main oil seal adapter.

29. Install the oil pump and oil pan.

30. Install the engine-to-transmission adapter plate, flywheel and starter.

31. Install the timing gear case, fuel injection pump, timing gears, timing gear case cover, new crankshaft front oil seal, and crankshaft pulley.

32. Install the engine assembly in vehicle as described in this chapter.

CLEANING AND INSPECTION
Crankshaft

NOTE: *Handle the crankshaft carefully to avoid damage to the finished surfaces.*

1. Clean the crankshaft with solvent, and blow out all oil passages with compressed air. Clean the oil seal contact surface at the rear of the crankshaft with solvent to remove any corrosion, sludge or varnish deposits.

2. Use crocus cloth to remove any sharp edges, burrs or other imperfections which might damage the oil seal during installation or cause premature seal wear.

NOTE: *Do not use crocus cloth to polish the seal surfaces. A finely polished surface many produce poor sealing or cause premature seal wear.*

3. Inspect the main and connecting rod journals for cracks, scratches, grooves or scores.

4. Measure the diameter of each journal at least four places to determine out-of-round, taper or undersize condition.

5. On an engine with a manual transmission, check the fit of the clutch pilot bearing in the bore of the crankshaft. A needle roller bearing and adapter assembly is used as a clutch pilot bearing. It is inserted directly into the engine crankshaft. The bearing and adapter assembly cannot be serviced separately. A new bearing must be installed whenever a bearing is removed.

6. Inspect the pilot bearing, when used, for roughness, evidence of overheating or loss of lubricant. Replace if any of these conditions are found.

7. Inspect the rear oil seal surface of the crankshaft for deep grooves, nicks, burrs, porosity, or scratches which could damage the oil seal lip during installation. Remove all nicks and burrs with crocus cloth.

Main Bearings

1. Clean the bearing inserts and caps thoroughly in solvent, and dry them with compressed air.

NOTE: *Do not scrape varnish or gum deposits from the bearing shells.*

2. Inspect each bearing carefully. Bearings that have a scored, chipped, or worn surface should be replaced.

3. The copper-lead bearing base may be visible through the bearing overlay in small localized areas. This may not mean that the bearing is excessively worn. It is not necessary to replace the bearing if the bearing clearance is within recommended specifications.

4. Check the clearance of bearings that appear to be satisfactory with Plastigage® or it's equivalent. Fit the new bearings following the procedure "Crankshaft and Main Bearings removal and installation" in this chapter.

REGRINDING JOURNALS

1. Dress minor scores with an oil stone. If the journals are severely marred or exceed the service limit, they should be reground to size for the next undersize bearing.

2. Regrind the journals to give the proper clearance with the next undersize bearing. If the journal will not clean up to maximum undersize bearing available, replace the crankshaft.

3. Always reproduce the same journal shoulder radius that existed originally. Too small a radius will result in fatigue failure of the crankshaft. Too large a radius will result in bearing failure due to radius ride of the bearing.

4. After regrinding the journals, chamfer the oil holes; then polish the journals with a no. 320 grit polishing cloth and engine oil. Crocus cloth may also be used as a polishing agent.

Oil Pan

REMOVAL AND INSTALLATION

4-122,140 Engine

1. Disconnect the negative battery cable.

2. Remove the air cleaner assembly. Remove the oil dipstick. Remove the engine mount retaining nuts.

3. Remove the oil cooler lines at the radiator, if so equipped. Remove the (2) bolts retaining the fan shroud to the radiator and remove shroud.

4. Remove the radiator retaining bolts (automatic only). Position radiator upward and wire to the hood (automatic only).

5. Raise the vehicle and safely support on jackstands.

6. Drain the oil from crankcase.

7. Remove the starter cable from starter and remove the starter.

8. Disconnect the exhaust manifold tube to the inlet pipe bracket at the thermactor check valve.

9. Remove the transmission mount retaining nuts to the crossmember.

10. Remove the bellcrank from the converter housing (automatic only).

11. Remove the oil cooler lines from retainer at the block (automatic only).

12. Remove the front crossmember (automatic only).

13. Disconnect the right front lower shock absorber mount (manual only).

14. Position the jack under the engine, raise and block with a piece of wood approximately 2½" high. Remove the jack.

15. Position the jack under the transmission and raise slightly (automatic only).

16. Remove the oil pan retaining bolts, lower the pan to the chassis. Remove the oil pump drive and pick-up tube assembly.

17. Remove the oil pan (out the front—automatic only) (out the rear—manual only).

18. Clean the oil pan and inspect for damage. Clean the oil pan gasket surface at the cylinder block. Clean the oil pump exterior and oil pump pick-up tube screen.

19. Position the oil pan gasket and end seals to the cylinder block (use contact cement to retain).

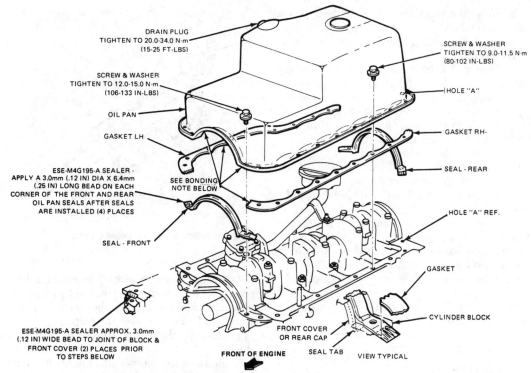

DRAIN PLUG
TIGHTEN TO 20.0-34.0 N·m
(15-25 FT-LBS)

SCREW & WASHER
TIGHTEN TO 9.0-11.5 N·m
(80-102 IN-LBS)

SCREW & WASHER
TIGHTEN TO 12.0-15.0 N·m
(106-133 IN-LBS)

HOLE "A"

OIL PAN

GASKET RH·

GASKET LH

SEAL - REAR

ESE-M4G195-A SEALER -
APPLY A 3.0mm (.12 IN) DIA X 6.4mm
(.25 IN) LONG BEAD ON EACH
CORNER OF THE FRONT AND REAR
OIL PAN SEALS AFTER SEALS
ARE INSTALLED (4) PLACES

SEE BONDING
NOTE BELOW

HOLE "A" REF.

SEAL - FRONT

GASKET

CYLINDER BLOCK

ESE-M4G195-A SEALER APPROX. 3.0mm
(.12 IN) WIDE BEAD TO JOINT OF BLOCK &
FRONT COVER (2) PLACES PRIOR
TO STEPS BELOW

FRONT COVER
OR REAR CAP

SEAL TAB

FRONT OF ENGINE

VIEW TYPICAL

THERMAL BONDING INSTRUCTIONS - OIL PAN GASKETS TO BE BONDED SECURELY TO OIL PAN
USING A THERMAL PROCESS MEETING THE REQUIREMENTS OF THE (ES-DOAE-6584-A OR EQUIVALENT)
ADHESIVE COATING SPECIFICATION - IF NECESSARY IN PLACE OF THERMAL BONDING USE ADHESIVE
(ESE-M2G52-A OR B OR EQUIVALENT) APPLY EVENLY TO OIL PAN FLANGE & TO PAN SIDE OF GASKETS -
ALLOW ADHESIVE TO DRY PAST "WET" STAGE THEN INSTALL GASKETS TO OIL PAN.

1. APPLY SEALER AS NOTED ABOVE
2. INSTALL SEALS TO FRONT COVER & REAR BEARING CAP - PRESS SEAL TABS FIRMLY INTO BLOCK
3. INSTALL (2) GUIDE PINS
4. INSTALL OIL PAN OVER GUIDE PINS & SECURE WITH (4) BOLTS
5. INSTALL (18) BOLTS
6. TORQUE ALL BOLTS IN SEQUENCE CLOCKWISE FROM HOLE "A" AS NOTED ABOVE

Oil pan installation—4-122,140 engines

20. Position the oil pan to the crossmember.

21. Install the oil pump and pick-up tube assembly. Install the oil pan to cylinder block with retaining bolts.

22. Lower the jack under transmission (automatic only).

23. Position the jack under the engine, raise slightly, and remove the wood spacer block.

24. Replace the oil filter.

25. Connect the exhaust manifold tube to the inlet pipe bracket at the thermactor check valve.

26. Install the transmission mount to the crossmember.

27. Install the oil cooler lines to the retainer at the block (automatic only).

28. Install the bellcrank to the converter housing (automatic only).

29. Install the right front lower shock absorber mount (manual only). Install the front crossmember (automatic only).

30. Install the starter and connect the cable. Lower vehicle.

31. Install the engine mount bolts.

32. Locate the radiator to the supports and install the (2) retaining bracket bolts (automatic only). Install the fan shroud on the radiator.

33. Connect the oil cooler lines to the radiator (automatic only).

34. Install the air cleaner assembly.

35. Install the oil dipstick. Fill the crankcase with oil.

36. Start the engine and check for leaks.

6-173 Engine

1. Disconnect the battery ground cable.

2. Remove the carburetor air cleaner assembly.

3. Remove the fan shroud and position it over the fan.

4. Remove the distributor cap with the wires still attached, and position it forward of the dash panel.

5. Remove the distributor and cover the opening with a clean rag.

6. Remove the nuts attaching the front engine mounts to the cross member.

7. Remove the engine oil dipstick tube.

8. Raise the truck on a hoist and support with jackstands.

9. Drain the engine crankcase and remove the oil filter.

10. Remove the transmission fluid filler tube and plug the hole in the pan. (On automatic transmission models.)

11. Disconnect the muffler inlet pipes.

12. If equipped with an oil cooler, disconnect the bracket and lower the cooler.

13. Remove the starter motor.

14. On automatic transmission models, position the cooler lines out of the way.

15. Disconnect the front stabilizer bar and position it foreward.

16. Position a jack under the engine and raise the engine until it touches the dash panel. Install wooden blocks between the front motor mounts and the no. 2 crossmember.

17. Lower the engine onto the blocks and remove the jack.

18. Remove the oil pan attaching bolts and lowr the pan assembly.

19. Installation is the reverse of the removal procedure.

4-134 Diesel Engine

1. Disconnect the ground battery cables from both batteries.

2. Remove the engine oil dipstick. Disconnect the air intake hose from the air cleaner and the intake manifold.

3. Drain the coolant and remove the fan and fan shroud.

4. Disconnect the radiator hoses. Remove the radiator upper support brackets and remove radiator and fan shroud.

5. Disconnect and cap the fuel inlet and outlet lines at the fuel filter and the return line at the injection pump.

6. Remove the fuel filter assembly from the mounting bracket. Remove the fuel filter mounting bracket from the cylinder head.

7. Remove the nuts and washers attaching the engine brackets to the insulators.

8. Raise the vehicle and safely support on jackstands.

9. Loosen the transmission insulator bolts at the rear of the transmission. Remove the bottom engine insulator bolts.

10. Drain the engine oil from the crankcase. Remove the primary oil filter from the left side of engine.

11. Remove the by-pass filter mounting bracket and hoses.

12. Lower the vehicle.

13. Attach an engine lifting sling and hoist. Raise the engine until the insulator studs clear the insulators. Slide the engine forward, then raise the engine approximately 3 inches.

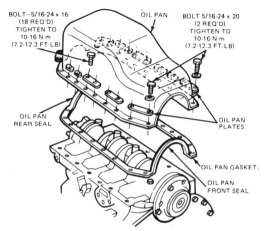

Oil pan installation—4-134 diesel engine

14. Install a wooden block 3 inches high between the left mount and bracket. Install a wooden block 4¼ inches high between the right mount and bracket. Lower the engine.

15. Remove the lifting sling and raise the vehicle.

16. Remove the oil pan attaching bolts, and lower the oil pan onto the cross member.

17. Disconnect the oil pickup from the oil pump and bearing cap, and lay in the oil pan.

18. Move the oil pan forward and up between the front of engine and the front body sheet metal.

NOTE: *If additional clearance is needed, move the A/C condensor forward.*

19. Clean the gasket mating surfaces of the oil pan and engine block with a suitable solvent and dry thoroughly. Apply ⅛ inch bead of Silicone Sealer on the split line between the engine block and the engine front cover and along the side rails.

20. Locate the oil pan gaskets in position with Gasket Cement and make sure that the gasket tabs are seated in seal cap grooves.

21. Press the front and rear oil pan seals in the seal cap grooves with both ends of the seals contacting oil pan gaskets.

22. Apply the ⅛ inch bead of sealer at the ends of the oil pan seals where they meet the oil pan gaskets.

23. Position the oil pan with the pickup tube on the No. 1 corssmember.

24. Install the oil pickup tube, with a new gasket, and tighten bolts to 6–9 ft. lbs. Install the oil pan with attaching bolts and plates. Tighten bolts to 7–12 ft. lbs.

25. Lower the vehicle.

26. Install a lifting sling, raise the engine and remove the wooden blocks.

27. Lower the engine onto the insulators and install and tighten the nuts and washers.

28. Raise the vehicle and safely support on jackstands.

29. Install the transmission mount nuts.

30. Install the by-pass filter bracket and hoses. Install the by-pass oil filter.

31. Install the oil pan drain plug. Install the new primary oil filter.

32. Lower the vehicle.

33. Install the fuel filter bracket on engine.

34. Install the fuel filter and adapter on mounting bracket.

35. Install the fuel return line on the injection pump and the fuel lines on fuel filter.

36. Position the radiator in the vehicle, install the radiator hoses and upper support brackets.

37. Install the radiator fan shroud. Install the radiator fan and tighten.

38. Fill and bleed the cooling system.

39. Fill the crankcase with the specified quantity and quality of oil.

40. Install the engine oil dipstick.

41. Install the air intake hose on the air cleaner and intake manifold.

42. Connect the battery ground cables to both batteries.

42. Run the engine and check for oil, fuel and coolant leaks.

Oil Pump

REMOVAL AND INSTALLATION

Gasoline Engines

1. Remove the oil pan.

2. Remove the oil pump inlet tube and screen assembly.

3. Remove the oil pump attaching bolts and remove the oil pump gasket and intermediate driveshaft.

4. Before installing the oil pump, prime it by filling the inlet and outlet port with engine

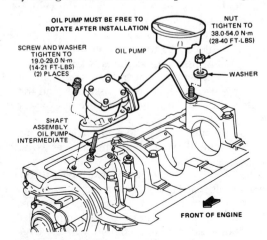

Oil pump installation—4-122,140 engines

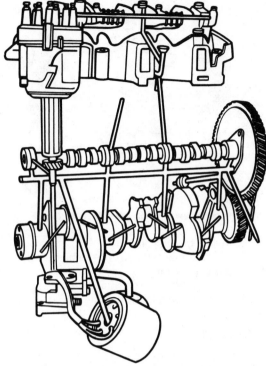

Oil pump and full pressure lubrication system—6-173 engine

oil and rotating the shaft of the pump to distribute it.

5. Position the intermediate drive shaft into the distributor socket.

6. Position the new gasket on the pump body and insert the intermediate driveshaft into the pumpbody.

7. Install the pump and intermediate driveshaft as an assembly. Do not force the pump if it does not seat readily. The driveshaft may be misaligned with the distributor shaft. To align it, rotate the intermediate driveshaft into a new position.

8. Install the oil pump attaching bolts and torque them to 6–10 ft. lbs.

9. Install the oil pan.

4-134 Diesel Engine

1. Disconnect the battery ground cables from both batteries.

2. Remove the oil pan.

3. Disconnect the oil pump outlet tube from cylinder block.

4. Remove the oil pump set screw and remove oil pump.

5. Install the oil pump.

6. Apply teflon tape, or equivalent, to the threads of the oil pump set screw. Install the set screw and tighten.

7. Install a new gasket on the oil pump outlet tube and tighten the bolts to 6–9 ft. lbs.

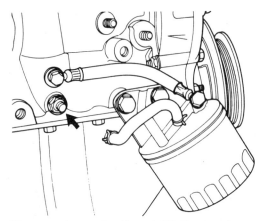

Oil pump set screw location—4-134 diesel engine

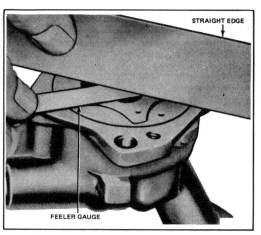

Checking the rotor end play

8. Install the oil pan.

9. Fill the crankcase with specified quantity and quality of oil.

10. Fill and bleed the cooling system.

11. Connect the battery ground cables to both batteries.

OVERHAUL

1. Wash all parts in a solvent and dry them thoroughly with compressed air. Use a brush to clean the inside of the pump housing and the pressure relief valve chamber. Be sure all dirt and metal particles are removed.

2. Check the inside of the pump housing and the outer race and rotor for damage or excessive wear or scoring.

3. Check the mating surface of the pump cover for wear. If the cover mating surface is worn, scored or grooved, replace the pump.

4. Measure the inner rotor tip clearance.

5. With the rotor assembly installed in the housing, place a straight edge over the rotor assembly and the housing. Measure the clearance (motor end play) between the straight edge and the rotor and the outer race.

6. Check the driveshaft to housing bearing clearance by measuring the OD of the shaft and the ID of the housing bearing.

7. Components of the oil pump are not serviced. If any part of the oil pump requires replacement, replace the complete pump assembly.

8. Inspect the relief valve spring to see if it is collapsed or worn.

9. Check the relief valve piston for scores and free operation in the bore.

Rear Main Oil Seal

REMOVAL AND INSTALLATION

Gasoline Engines

If the crankshaft rear oil seal replacement is the only operation being performed, it can be done in the vehicle as detailed in the following procedure. If the oil seal is being replaced in conjunction with a rear main bearing replacement, the engine must be removed from the vehicle and installed on a work stand.

1. Remove the starter.

2. Remove the transmission from the vehicle, following the procedures in Chapter 6.

3. On a manual-shift transmission, remove the pressure plate and cover assembly and the clutch disc following the procedure in Chapter 6.

4. Remove the flywheel attaching bolts and remove the flywheel and engine rear cover plate.

5. Use an awl to punch two holes in the crankshaft rear oil seal. Punch the holes on opposite sides of the crankshaft and just above the bearing cap to cylinder block split line. Install a sheet metal screw in each hole. Use two large screwdrivers or small pry bars and pry against

NOTE:
WITH ROTOR ASSEMBLY REMOVED FROM
THE PUMP AND RESTING ON A FLAT
SURFACE, THE INNER AND OUTER ROTOR
TIP CLEARANCE MUST NOT EXCEED 0.30mm
(0.012 IN) WITH FEELER GAUGE INSERTED
13mm (0.5 IN) MINIMUM.

Checking the inner rotor tip clearance

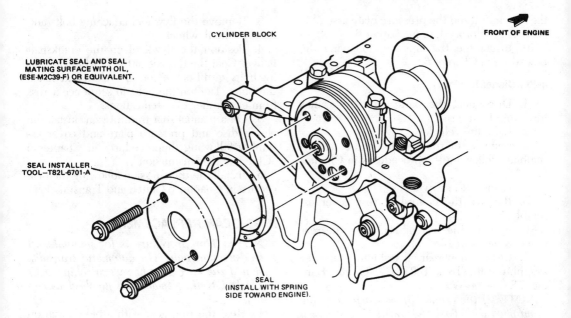

CYLINDER BLOCK

FRONT OF ENGINE

LUBRICATE SEAL AND SEAL
MATING SURFACE WITH OIL,
(ESE-M2C39-F) OR EQUIVALENT.

SEAL INSTALLER
TOOL—T82L-6701-A

SEAL
(INSTALL WITH SPRING
SIDE TOWARD ENGINE).

NOTE: REAR FACE OF SEAL MUST BE WITHIN 0.127mm (0.005-INCH) OF THE REAR FACE OF THE BLOCK.

Installing the crankshaft rear oil seal—4-122,140 engines

both screws at the same time to remove the crankshaft rear oil seal. It may be necessary to place small blocks of wood against the cylinder block to provide a fulcrum point for the pry bars. **Use caution throughout this procedure to avoid scratching or otherwise damaging the crankshaft oil seal surface.**

6. Clean the oil seal recess in the cylinder block and main bearing cap.

7. Clean, inspect and polish the rear oil seal rubbing surface on the crankshaft. Coat a new oil seal and the crankshaft with a light film of engine oil. Start the seal in the recess with the seal lip facing forward and install it with a seal driver. Keep the tool, T82L-6701-A (4-cyl. engines) or T72C-6165 (6-cyl. engine) straight with the centerline of the crankshaft and install the seal until the tool contacts the cylinder block surface. Remove the tool and inspect the seal to be sure it was not damaged during installation.

8. Install the engine rear cover plate. Position the flywheel on the crankshaft flange. Coat the threads of the flywheel attaching bolts with oil-resistant sealer and install the bolts. Tighten the bolts in sequence across from each other to the specifications listed in the Torque chart at the beginning of this chapter.

9. On a manual-shift transmission, install

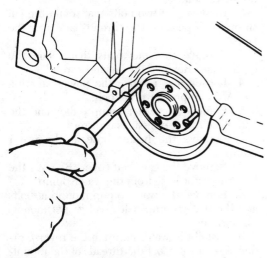

Removing the rear main oil seal

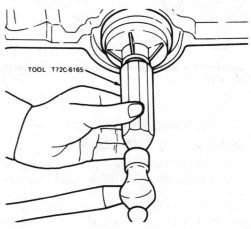

TOOL T72C-6165

Installing the crankshaft rear main oil seal—6-173 engine

the clutch disc and the pressure plate assembly following the procedure in chapter 6.

10. Install the transmission, following the procedure in Chapter 6.

4-134 Diesel Engine

1. Disconnect the battery ground cables from both batteries.

2. Raise the vehicle.

3. Remove the transmission and clutch assemblies, following the procedures in Chapter 6.

4. Remove the flywheel.

5. Remove the crankshaft rear cover assembly.

6. Remove the rear oil seal from the rear cover using a suitable tool.

7. Install a new rear oil seal into rear cover assembly using Tool, T83T-6701-C, and Handle, T80T-4000-W.

NOTE: *If the crankshaft is worn, use ring supplied with Tool T83T-6701-C to seat seal over a new wear area.*

8. Install the crankshaft rear cover assembly and tighten bolts to 11–15 ft. lbs.

9. Install the flywheel and tighten to 95–137 ft. lbs.

10. Install the clutch and transmission, following the procedures in Chapter 6.

11. Lower the vehicle.

12. Connect the battery ground cables to both batteries.

13. Start the engine and check for oil leaks.

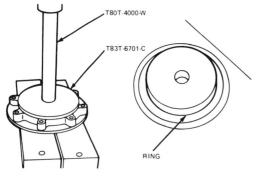

Installing the crankshaft rear main oil seal—4-134 diesel engine

Flywheel and Ring Gear
REMOVAL AND INSTALLATION

1. Remove the transmission, following the procedures in chapter 6 "Clutch and Transmission".

2. On a manual-shift transmission, remove the clutch pressure plate and cover assembly and clutch disc, following the procedures in chapter 6 "Clutch and Transmission".

3. Remove the flywheel attaching bolts and remove the flywheel.

4. Position the flywheel on the crankshaft flange. Coat the threads of the flywheel attaching bolts with Loctite® or equivalent and install the bolts. Tighten the bolts in sequence across from each other to specifications.

5. On a manual shift transmission, install the clutch disc and pressure plate and cover assembly following theprocedures in Chapter 6 "Clutch and Transmission".

6. Install the transmission following the procedure in Chapter 6 Clutch and Transmission.

RING GEAR REPLACEMENT

NOTE: *This procedure is for manual-shift transmission only. On automatic transmission if the ring gear has worn, chipped or cracked teeth, replace the flywheel assembly.*

1. Heat the ring gear with a blow torch on the engine side of the gear, and knock it off the flywheel. Do not hit the flywheel when removing the ring gear.

2. Heat the new ring gear evenly until the gear expands enough to slip onto the flywheel. Make sure the gear is properly seated against the shoulder. Do not heat any part of the gear more than 500 degrees F. If this limit is exceeded, the hardness will be removed from the ring gear teeth.

Water Pump
REMOVAL AND INSTALLATION
4-122,140 Engines

1. Disconnect the negative battery cable. Drain the cooling system. Loosen and remove the drive belt.

2. Remove the two bolts that retain the fan shroud and position the shroud back over the fan.

3. Remove the four bolts that retain the cooling fan. Remove the fan and shroud.

4. Loosen and remove the power steering and A/C compressor drive belts.

5. Remove the water pump pulley and the vent hose to the emissions canister.

6. Remove the heater hose at the water pump.

7. Remove the cam belt cover. Remove the lower radiator hose from the water pump.

8. Remove the water pump mounting bolts and the water pump. Clean all gasket mounting surfaces.

9. Install the water pump in the reverse order of removal. Coat the threads of the mounting bolts with sealer before installation.

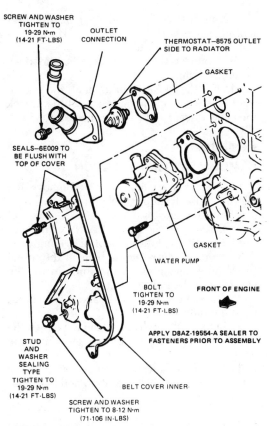

SCREW AND WASHER TIGHTEN TO 19-29 N·m (14-21 FT-LBS)

OUTLET CONNECTION

THERMOSTAT—8575 OUTLET SIDE TO RADIATOR

GASKET

SEALS—6E009 TO BE FLUSH WITH TOP OF COVER

GASKET

WATER PUMP

BOLT TIGHTEN TO 19-29 N·m (14-21 FT-LBS)

FRONT OF ENGINE

APPLY D8AZ-19554-A SEALER TO FASTENERS PRIOR TO ASSEMBLY

STUD AND WASHER SEALING TYPE TIGHTEN TO 19-29 N·m (14-21 FT-LBS)

BELT COVER INNER

SCREW AND WASHER TIGHTEN TO 8-12 N·m (71-106 IN-LBS)

Water pump and thermostat installation—4-122,140 engines

6-173 Engine

1. Drain the coolant from the radiator and remove the lower hose and the return hose from the water inlet housing.

2. Using Tools T83T-6312-A and B remove the fan and clutch assembly from the front of the water pump.

NOTE: *The fan clutch assembly uses a left*

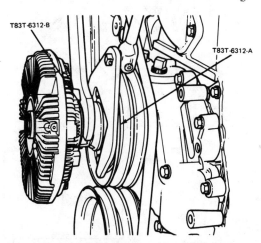

T83T-6312-B

T83T-6312-A

Removing the fan clutch assembly—6-173 engine

hand thread, remove by turning the nut counterclockwise.

3. Loosen the alternator mounting bolts and remove the alternator belt.

4. Remove the water pump pulley.

5. Remove the bolts retaining the water pump assembly and remove the water pump, water inlet housing, and the thermostat from the front cover.

6. Before installing the water pump, clean the gasket surfaces on the front cover and on the water pump assembly. Apply gasket sealer to both sides of the new gasket and install the water pump in the reverse order of removal.

4-134 Diesel Engine

1. Disconnect the ground cables from both batteries. Drain the cooling system.

2. Remove all drive belts.

3. Remove the radiator fan shroud, cooling fan and pump pulley.

Disconnect the heater hose, by-pass hose and radiator hose from the water pump.

4. Remove the nuts and bolts that mount the water pump to the engine.

5. Clean all gasket mounting surfaces.

6. Install water pump in the reverse order of removal.

Thermostat

REMOVAL AND INSTALLATION

1. Drain the cooling system below the level of the coolant outlet housing.

2. Disconnect the heater return hose at the thermostat housing located on the left front lower side of engine.

3. Remove the coolant outlet housing retaining bolts and slide the housing with the hose attached to one side.

4. Turn the thermostat counterclockwise to unlock it from the outlet.

5. Remove the gasket from the engine block and clean both mating surfaces.

NOTE: *It is a good practice to check the operation of a new thermostat before it is installed in an engine. Place the thermostat in*

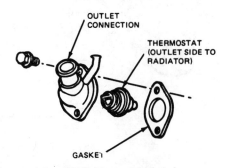

OUTLET CONNECTION

THERMOSTAT (OUTLET SIDE TO RADIATOR)

GASKET

Thermostat and housing—exploded view

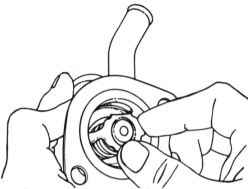

Installing the thermostat in the thermostat housing

a pan of boiling water. If it does not open more than ¼ in., do not install it in the engine.

6. To install the thermostat, coat a new gasket with water resistant sealer and position it on the outlet of the engine. The gasket must be in place before the thermostat is installed.

7. Install the thermostat with the bridge (opposite end from the spring) inside the elbow connection and turn it clockwise to lock it in position, with the bridge against the flats cast into the elbow connection.

8. Position the elbow connection onto the mounting surface of the outlet, so that the thermostat flange is resting on the gasket and install the retaining bolts.

9. Connect the heater hose to the thermostat housing.

10. Fill the radiator and operate the engine until it reaches operating temperature. Check the coolant level and adjust as necessary.

Radiator

REMOVAL AND INSTALLATION

1. Drain the cooling system. Remove the overflow tube from the coolant recovery bottle and from the radiator.

2. Disconnect the transmission cooling lines from the bottom of the radiator, if so equipped.

3. Remove the retaining bolts at the top of the shroud, and position the shroud over the fan, clear of the radiator.

4. Disconnect the upper and lower hoses from the radiator.

5. Remove the radiator retaining bolts or the upper supports and lift the radiator from vehicle.

6. Install the radiator in the reverse order of removal. Fill the cooling system and check for leaks.

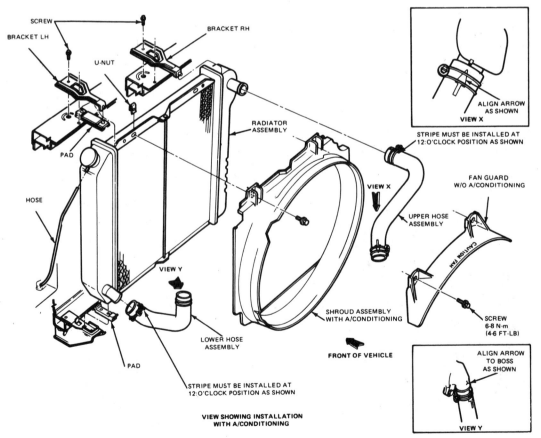

Radiator assembly—6-173 engine

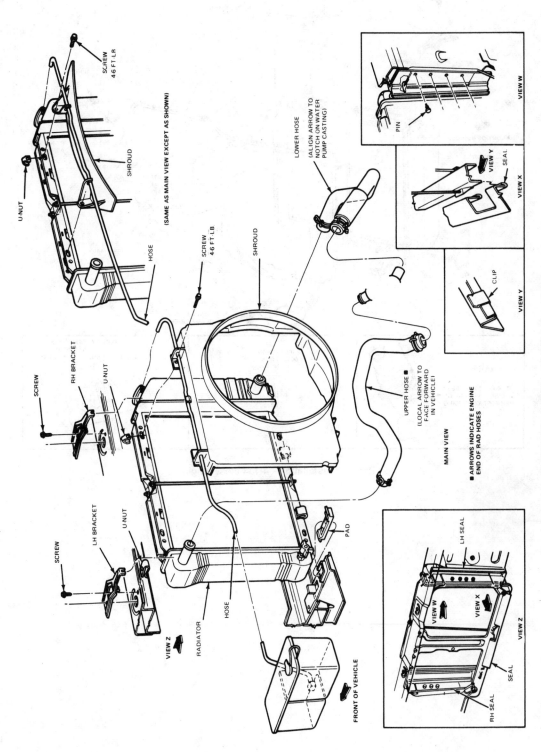

Radiator installation—4-122, 140 engines

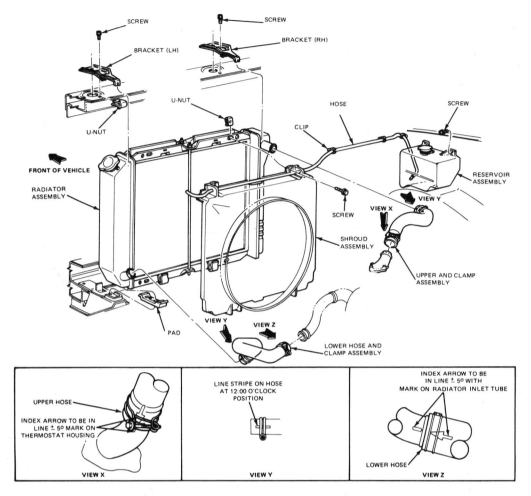

Radiator installation—4-134 diesel engine

Emission Controls and Fuel System

4

EMISSION CONTROLS

There are three types of automobile pollutants that concern automotive engineers: crankcase fumes, exhaust gases and gasoline vapors from evaporation. The devices and systems used to limit these pollutants are commonly called emission control equipment.

Crankcase Emission Controls

The crankcase emission control equipment consists of a positive crankcase ventilation (PCV) valve, a closed oil filler cap and the hoses that connect this equipment.

When the engine is running, a small portion of the gases which are formed in the combustion chamber leak by the piston rings and enter the crankcase. Since these gases are under pressure they tend to escape from the crankcase and enter into the atmosphere. If these gases were allowed to remain in the crankcase

for any length of time, they would contaminate the engine oil and cause sludge to build up. If the gases are allowed to escape into the atmosphere, they would pollute the air, as they contain unburned hydrocarbons. The crankcase emission control equipment recycles these gases back into the engine combustion chamber, where they are burned.

Crankcase gases are recycled in the following manner. While the engine is running, clean filtered air is drawn into the crankcase either directly through the oil filler cap or through the carburetor air filter and then through a hose leading to the oil filler cap. As the air passes through the crankcase it picks up the combustion gases and carries them out of the crankcase up through the PCV valve and into the intake manifold. After they enter the intake manifold they are drawn into the combustion chamber and are burned.

The most critical component of the system is the PCV valve. This vacuum-controlled valve regulates the amount of gases which are recy-

FROM CRANKCASE AND/OR ROCKER ARM COVER → TO INTAKE MANIFOLD

LOW SPEED OPERATION—HIGH MANIFOLD VACUUM

HIGH SPEED OPERATION—LOW MANIFOLD VACUUM

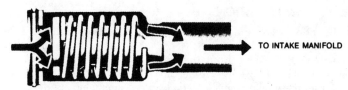

FROM CRANKCASE AND/OR ROCKER ARM COVER → TO INTAKE MANIFOLD

A cutaway of a PCV valve showing its operation

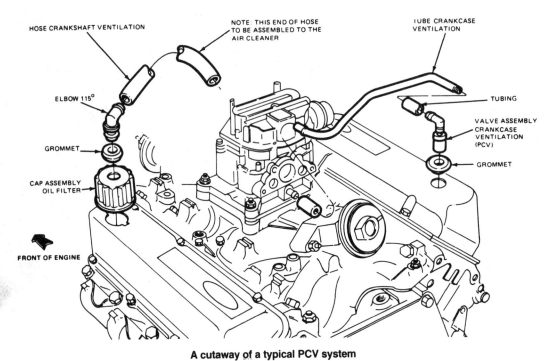

HOSE CRANKSHAFT VENTILATION

NOTE: THIS END OF HOSE
TO BE ASSEMBLED TO THE
AIR CLEANER

IUBE CRANKCASE
VENTILATION

ELBOW 115°

TUBING

GROMMET

VALVE ASSEMBLY
CRANKCASE
VENTILATION
(PCV)

CAP ASSEMBLY
OIL FILTER

GROMMET

FRONT OF ENGINE

A cutaway of a typical PCV system

cled into the combustion chamber. At low engine speeds the valve is partially closed, limiting the flow of gases into the intake manifold. As engine speed increases, the valve opens to admit greater quantities of the gases into the intake manifold. If the valve should become blocked or plugged, the gases will be prevented from escaping the crankcase by the normal route. Since these gases are under pressure, they will find their own way out of the crankcase. This alternate route is usually a weak oil seal or gasket in the engine. As the gas escapes by the gasket, it also creates an oil leak. Besides causing oil leaks, a clogged PCV valve also allows these gases to remain in the crankcase for an extended period of time, promoting the formation of sludge in the engine.

TROUBLESHOOTING

With the engine running, pull the PCV valve and hose from the valve rocker cover rubber grommet. Block off the end of the valve with your finger. A strong vacuum should be felt. Shake the valve; a clicking noise indicates it is free. Replace the valve if it is suspected of being blocked.

REMOVAL AND INSTALLATION

1. Pull the PCV valve and hose from the rubber grommet in the rocker cover.
2. Remove the PCV valve from the hose. Inspect the inside of the PCV valve. If it is dirty, disconnect it from the intake manifold and clean it in a suitable, safe solvent.

To install, proceed as follows:
1. If the PCV valve hose was removed, connect it to the intake manifold.
2. Connect the PCV valve to its hose.
3. Install the PCV valve into the rubber grommet in the valve rocker cover.

Evaporative Emission Controls

All gasoline powered Ranger vehicles are equipped with fuel evaporative emission control. The system is designed to limit fuel vapors released into the atmosphere.

Changes in atmospheric temperature cause fuel tanks to "breathe"; that is, the air within the tank expands and condenses with outside temperature changes. As the temperature rises, air escapes through the tank vent tube or the vent in the tank cap. The air which escapes contains gasoline vapors. In a similar manner, the gasoline which fills the carburetor float bowl expands when the engine is stopped. Engine heat causes this expansion. The vapors escape through the carburetor and air cleaner.

The Evaporative Emission Control System provides a sealed fuel system with the capability to store and condense fuel vapors. The system has three parts: a fill control vent system; a vapor vent and storage system; and a pressure and vacuum relief system (special fill cap).

The fill control vent system is a modification to the fuel tank. It uses an air space within the tank which is 10–12% of the tank's volume. The air space is sufficient to provide for the thermal

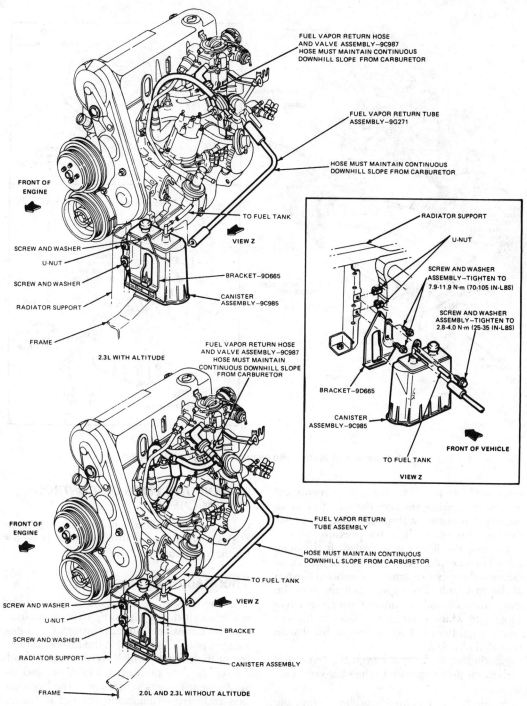

Carburetor and evaporative canister venting—4-122,140 engines

expansion of the fuel. The space also serves as part of the in-tank vapor vent system.

The in-tank vent system consists of the air space previously described and a vapor separator assembly. The separator assembly is mounted to the top of the fuel tank and is secured by a cam-lockring, similar to the one which secures the fuel sending unit. Foam ma-

terial fills the vapor separator assembly. The foam material separates raw fuel and vapors, thus retarding the entrance of fuel into the vapor line.

The sealed filler cap has a pressure vacuum relief valve. Under normal operating conditions, the filler cap operates as a check valve, allowing air to enter the tank to replace the fuel

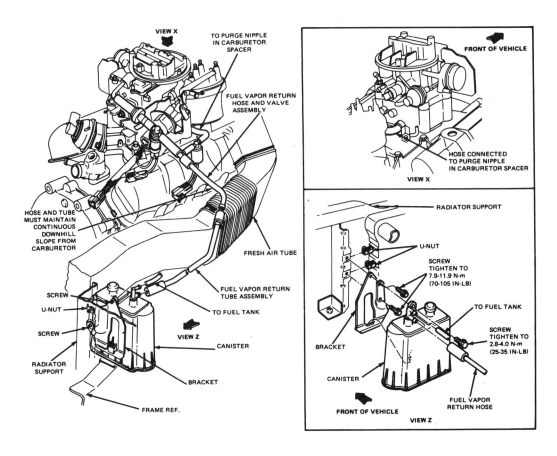

Carburetor and evaporative canister venting—6-173 engine

consumed. At the same time, it prevents vapors from escaping through the cap. In case of excessive pressure within the tank, the filler cap valve opens to relieve the pressure.

Because the filler cap is sealed, fuel vapors have but one place through which they may escape—the vapor separator assembly at the top of the fuel tank. The vapors pass through the foam material and continue through a single vapor line which leads to a canister in the engine compartment. The canister is filled with activated charcoal.

Another vapor line runs from the top of the carburetor float chamber to the charcoal canister.

As the fuel vapors (hydrocarbons), enter the charcoal canister, they are absorbed by the charcoal. The air is dispelled through the open bottom of the charcoal canister, leaving the hydrocarbons trapped within the charcoal. When the engine is started, vacuum causes fresh air to be drawn into the canister from its open bottom. The fresh air passes through the charcoal picking up the hydrocarbons which are trapped there and feeding them into the carburetor for burning with the fuel mixture.

EVAPORATIVE EMISSION CONTROL SYSTEM CHECK

Other than a visual check to determine that none of the vapor lines are broken, there is no test for this equipment.

Thermactor System

The Thermactor emission control system makes use of a belt-driven air pump to inject fresh air into the hot exhaust stream through the engine exhaust ports. The result is the extended burning of those fumes which were not completely ignited in the combustion chamber, and the subsequent reduction of some of the hydrocarbon and carbon monoxide content of the exhaust emissions into harmless carbon dioxide and water.

The Thermactor system is composed ot the following components:

1. Air supply pump (belt-driven)
2. Air by pass valve
3. Check valves
4. Air manifolds (internal or external)
5. Air supply tubes (on external manifolds only).

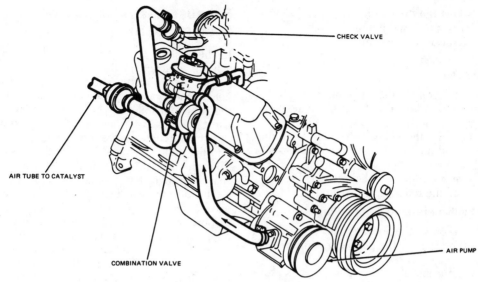

CHECK VALVE

AIR TUBE TO CATALYST

COMBINATION VALVE

AIR PUMP

Typical Thermactor system

Air for the Thermactor system is cleaned by means of a centrifugal filter fan mounted on the air pump driveshaft. The air filter does not require a replaceable element.

To prevent excessive pressure, the air pump is equipped with a pressure relief valve which uses a replaceable plastic plug to control the pressure setting.

The Thermactor air pump has sealed bearings which are lubricated for the life of the unit, and pre-set rotor vane and bearing clearances, which do not require any periodic adjustments.

The air supply from the pump is controlled by the air by-pass valve, sometimes called a dump valve. During deceleration, the air by-pass valve opens, momentarily diverting the air supply through a silencer and into the atmosphere, thus preventing backfires within the exhaust system.

A check valve is incorporated in the air inlet side of the air manifolds. Its purpose is to prevent exhaust gases from backing up into the Thermactor system. This valve is especially important in the event of drive belt failure, and during deceleration, when the air by-pass valve is dumping the air supply.

The air manifolds and air supply tubes channel the air from the Thermactor air pump into the exhaust ports of each cylinder, thus completing the cycle of the Thermactor system.

REPLACEMENT

Air By-Pass Valve

1. Disconnect the air and vacuum hoses at the air by-pass valve body.

2. Position the air by-pass valve and connect the respective hoses.

Check Valve

1. Disconnect the air supply hose at the valve. Use 1¼ in. crowfoot wrench. The valve has a standard, right-hand pipe thread.

2. Clean the threads on the air supply tube with a wire brush. Do not blow compressed air through the check valve in either direction.

3. Install the check valve and tighten.

4. Connect the air supply hose.

Air Pump and Filter Fan

1. Loosen the air pump attaching bolts.

2. Remove the drive pulley attaching bolts and pull the pulley off the air pump shaft.

3. Pry the outer disc loose, then remove the centrifugal filter fan. Care must be used to prevent foreign matter from entering the air intake hole, especially if the fan breaks during removal. Do not attempt to remove the metal drive hub.

4. Install the new filter fan by drawing it into position with the pulley bolts.

Air Pump

1. Disconnect the air outlet hose at the air pump.

2. Loosen the pump belt tension adjuster.

3. Disengage the drive belt.

4. Remove the mounting bolt and air pump.

5. Position the air pump on the mounting bracket and install the mounting bolt.

6. Place the drive belt in the pulley and attach the adjusting arm to the air pump.

7. Adjust the drive belt tension and tighten the adjusting arm and mounting bolts.

8. Connect the air outlet hose to the air pump.

Relief Valve

Do not disassemble the air pump on the truck to replace the relief valve, but remove the pump from the engine.

1. Remove the relief valve on the pump housing and hold it in position with a block of wood.

2. Use a hammer to lightly tap the wood block until the relief valve is seated.

Relief Valve Pressure-Setting Plug

1. Compress the locking tabs inward (together) and remove the plastic pressure-setting plug.

2. Before installing the new plug, be sure that the plug is the correct one. The plugs are color-coded.

3. Insert the plug in the relief valve hole and push in until it snaps into place.

Catalytic Converter

The converter is in the exhaust system ahead of the muffler. It contains a catalytic agent made of platinum and palladium, used to oxidize hydrocarbons (HC) and carbon monoxide (CO). The catalyst is expected to function without service of any kind for at least 50,000 miles. Use of leaded fuel would quickly cause catalyst failure; for this reason, a tank filler restriction prevents the entry of service station leaded fuel nozzles.

Exhaust Gas Recirculation System (EGR)

In this system, a vacuum-operated EGR flow valve is attached to the carburetor spacer. A passage in the carburetor spacer mates with a hole in the mounting face of the EGR valve or the intake manifold. This system allows exhaust gases to flow from the exhaust crossover, through the control valve and through the spacer into the intake manifold below the carburetor. The exhaust gases are routed to the carburetor spacer through steel tubing.

The vacuum signal which operates the EGR valve originates at the EGR vacuum port in the carburetor. This signal is controlled by at least one, and sometimes two, series of valves.

The position of the EGR vacuum port in the carburetor and calibration of the EGR valve can be varied to give the required modulation of EGR during acceleration and low speed cruise conditions. However, a more complicated system using an exhaust valve position sensor mounted on top of the valve is sometimes needed to provide control of EGR for engine operation.

The EVP sensor is used on vehicles having electronic engine control. This sensor sends out a signal to the control assembly that tells how far the valve is open. The control assembly also receives other signals, such as temperature, rpm, throttle opening, etc. The electronic control assembly then signals the EGR control solenoids to maintain or alter the EGR flow depending on the engine operating conditions.

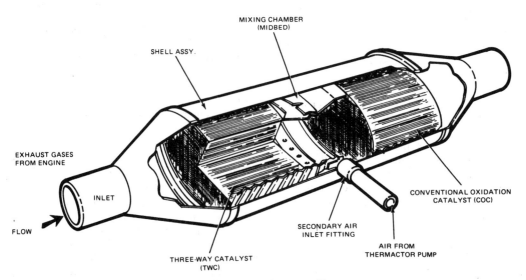

Catalytic converter assembly

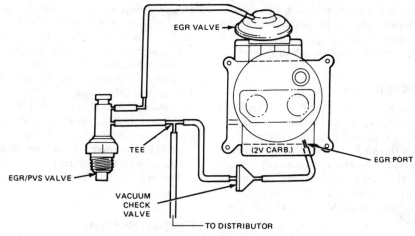

Typical EGR system

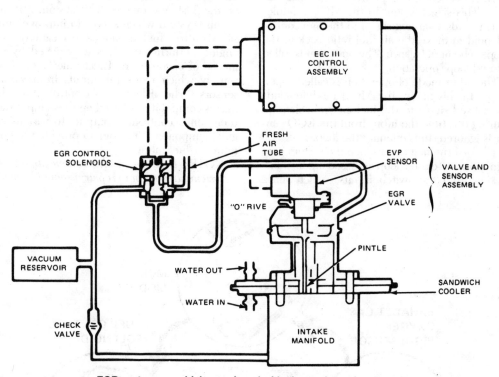

EGR system on vehicles equipped with electronic engine control

EGR VALVE CLEANING

Valves Which Cannot Be Disassembled

Valves which are riveted or otherwise permanently assembled should be replaced if highly contaminated; they cannot be cleaned.

EGR SUPPLY PASSAGES AND CARBURETOR SPACE CLEANING

Remove the carburetor and carburetor spacer on engines so equipped. Clean the supply tube with a small power-driven rotary type wire brush or blast cleaning equipment. Clean the exhaust gas passages in the spacer using a suitable wire brush and/or scraper. The machined holes in the spacer can be cleaned by using a suitable round wire brush. Hard encrusted material should be probed loose first, then brushed out.

EGR EXHAUST GAS CHANNEL CLEANING

Clean the exhaust gas channel, where applicable, in the intake manifold, using a suitable carbon scraper. Clean the exhaust gas entry port in the intake manifold by hand passing a suitable drill bit thru the holes to auger out the deposits. Do not use a wire brush. The manifold riser bore(s) should be suitably plugged during the above action to prevent any of the residue from entering the induction system.

MCU System

The MCU system is used on the 122 and 140 in-line 4-cylinder engines. The heart of the system is the fuel control system. This is necessary to keep the air-fuel ratio at proper chemical balance (14.7) to obtain maximum catalyst efficiency. The fuel control "Loop" consists of an Exhaust Gas Oxygen (EGO) sensor, Microprocessor Control Unit (MCU), and Fuel Control Solenoid.

The EGO sensor senses whether the exhaust gas is rich or lean of proper chemical balance. This signal is sent to the MCU module, which sends a varying signal to the fuel control solenoid to move the air-fuel ratio back to the proper chemical balance. The operation is called "closed loop" operation.

The other mode of operation is called "open loop." In this mode, the MCU module sends out a fixed signal to the fuel control solenoid. During this time the input from the EGO sensor is ignored, thus opening the loop.

The determining factor when the system goes into open or closed loop is based upon information from the switch inputs, which sense coolant temperature, manifold vacuum, and throttle position. Generally, the vehicle will be in closed loop when the vehicle is at operating temperature and at a steady part throttle cruise.

Other functions controlled by the MCU module, by means of vacuum solenoids, are the Thermactor Air Bypass (TAB) valve and the Thermactor Air Diverter (TAD) valve. Also controlled, but not on all calibrations, are Canister Purge and the Spark Retard Solenoid.

NOTE: *Because of the complexity of this system no attempt to repair it should be made. It should only be serivced by a qualified mechanic.*

EEC-IV System

The electronic engine control IV system is used on the 2.8L V-6 engine. This system is a controlling system which serves to improve emission control, fuel economy, driveability, and engine performance. This is achieved by the means of an on-board Electronic Control Assembly which reads the inputs from various sensors. The Electronic Control Assembly makes computations based on these inputs and then sends controlling outputs to various engine components in order to provide the optimum air/fuel ratio.

NOTE: *Because of the complexity of this system no attempt to repair it should be made.*

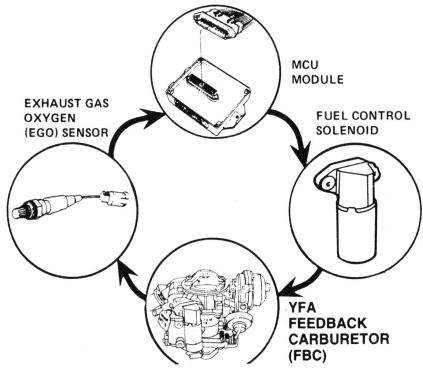

EXHAUST GAS OXYGEN (EGO) SENSOR

MCU MODULE

FUEL CONTROL SOLENOID

YFA FEEDBACK CARBURETOR (FBC)

4-122,140 engines, fuel control loop—MCU system

ELECTRONIC CONTROL
ASSEMBLY (ECA)
(PASSENGER
COMPARTMENT
RH KICK PANEL)

EEC
POWER
RELAY
(PASSENGER
COMPARTMENT
RH KICK PANEL)

THROTTLE
POSITION
SENSOR
(TPS)

PROFILE
IGNITION
PICK-UP
(PIP)
(IN
DISTRIBUTOR)

IDLE
TRACKING
SWITCH (ITS)
(INTEGRAL
WITH IDLE
SPEED CONTROL
DC MOTOR)

EXHAUST
GAS O₂
SENSOR (EGO)
(ON EXHAUST
MANIFOLD)

AIR CHARGE
TEMPERATURE
SENSOR (ACT)
(PLUGS INTO
AIR CLEANER)

EGR VALVE
POSITION
SENSOR

ENGINE
COOLANT
TEMPERATURE
SENSOR (ECT)

KNOCK
SENSOR (KS)
(BELOW
EXHAUST
MANIFOLD)

MANIFOLD
ABSOLUTE
PRESSURE
SENSOR (MAP)

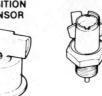

A/C
COMPRESSOR
CLUTCH
SIGNAL
(ACC)

EEC IV system inputs

UPSHIFT LIGHT
AND
SELF-TEST
CONNECTOR

THERMACTOR
AIR DIVERTER
VALVE (TAD)

VARIABLE
VOLTAGE
CHOKE (VVC)

FEEDBACK
CONTROL
SOLENOID
(ON REAR OF
CARBURETOR)

TFI-IV
IGNITION
MODULE
(ON REAR OF
DISTRIBUTOR)

EGR VALVE

THERMACTOR
AIR BYPASS
VALVE (TAB)
(BELOW TAD)

TEMPERATURE
COMPENSATED
ACCELERATOR
PUMP (TCP)

IDLE SPEED
CONTROL
DC MOTOR
(ISC)

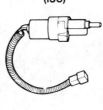

CANISTER
PURGE
VALVE
(CANP)

EEC IV system outputs

It should only be serviced by a qualified mechanic.

GASOLINE ENGINE FUEL SYSTEM

Fuel Pump

The Ford Ranger engines use a camshaft eccentric-actuated combination fuel pump located on the lower left-side of the engine block.

REMOVAL

1. Disconnect the fuel inlet and outlet lines at the fuel pump. Discard the fuel inlet retaining clamp.
2. Remove the pump retaining bolts then remove the pump assembly and gasket from the engine. Discard the gasket.

INSTALLATION

1. If a new pump is to be installed, remove the fuel line connector fitting from the old pump and install it in the new pump (if so equipped).
2. Remove all gasket material from the mounting pad and pump flange. Apply oil resistant sealer to both sides of a new gasket.
3. Position the new gasket on the pump flange and hold the pump in position against the mounting pad. Make sure that the rocker arm is riding on the camshaft eccentric.
4. Press the pump tight against the pad, install the retaining bolts and alternately torque them to 14–21 ft. lbs. Connect the fuel lines. Use a new clamp on the fuel inlet line.
5. Operate the engine and check for leaks.

TESTING

Incorrect fuel pump pressure and low volume (flow rate) are the two most likely fuel pump troubles that will affect engine performance.

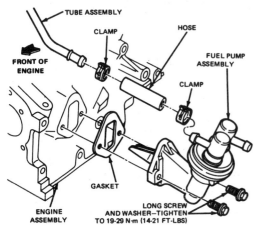

Fuel pump installation—typical

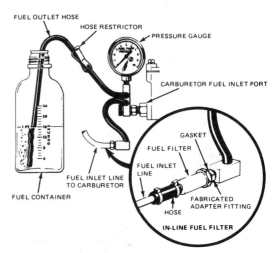

Fuel pump volume and pressure test equipment

Low pressure will cause a lean mixture and fuel starvation at high speeds and excessive pressure will cause high fuel consumption and carburetor flooding.

To determine that the fuel pump is in satisfactory operating condition, tests for both fuel pump pressure and volume should be performed.

The tests are performed with the fuel pump installed on the engine and the engine at normal operating temperature and at idle speed.

Before the test, make sure that the replaceable fuel filter has been changed at the proper mileage interval. If in doubt, install a new filter.

Pressure Test

1. Remove the air cleaner assembly. Disconnect the fuel inlet line of the fuel filter at the carburetor. Use care to prevent fire, due to fuel spillage. Place an absorbent cloth under the connection before removing the line to catch any fuel that might flow out of the line.
2. Connect a pressure gauge, a restrictor and a flexible hose between the fuel filter and the carburetor.
3. Position the flexible hose and the restrictor so that the fuel can be discharged into a suitable, graduated container.
4. Before taking a pressure reading, operate the engine at the specified idle rpm and vent the system into the container by opening the hose restrictor momentarily.
5. Close the hose restrictor, allow the pressure to stabilize and note the reading.

If the pump pressure is not within 4.5–6.5 psi and the fuel lines and filter are in satisfactory condition, the pump is defective and should be replaced.

If the pump pressure is within the proper range, perform the test for fuel volume.

Volume Test

1. Operate the engine at the specified idle rpm.

2. Open the hose restrictor and catch the fuel in the container while observing the time it takes to pump 1 pint. It should take 30 seconds for 1 pint to be expelled. If the pump does not pump to specifications, check for proper fuel tank venting or a restriction in the fuel line leading from the fuel tank to the carburetor before replacing the fuel pump.

Carburetors

The carburetor identification tag is attached to the carburetor. The basic part number for all carburetors is 9510. To obtain replacement parts, it is necessary to know the part number prefix, suffix and, in some cases, the design change code. If the carburetor is ever replaced by a new unit, make sure that the identification tag stays with the new carburetor and the vehicle.

REMOVAL AND INSTALLATION

1. Remove the air cleaner.

2. Remove the throttle cable and transmission linkage from the throttle lever. Disconnect all vacuum lines, emission hoses, the fuel line and electrical connections.

3. Remove the carburetor retaining nuts then remove the carburetor. Remove the carburetor mounting gasket, spacer (if so equipped), and the lower gasket from the intake manifold.

4. Before installing the carburetor, clean the gasket mounting surfaces of the spacer and carburetor. Place the spacer between two new gaskets and position the spacer and the gaskets on the intake manifold. Position the carburetor on the spacer and gasket and secure it with the retaining nuts. To prevent leakage, distortion or damage to the carburetor body flange, snug the nuts, then alternately tighten each nut in a criss-cross pattern.

5. Connect the inline fuel line, throttle cable, transmission linkage and all electrical connections and vacuum lines on the carburetor.

6. Adjust the engine idle speed, the idle fuel mixture and install the air cleaner.

FLOAT AND FUEL LEVEL ADJUSTMENTS

Carter Model YFA & YFA Feedback 1-bbl (Dry Adjustment)

1. Remove the air cleaner

2. Disconnect the choke heat tube at the carburetor air horn. Disconnect the fuel inlet line at the filter.

3. Disconnect the electric choke wire at the connector.

4. Remove the wire clip retaining the link joining the fast idle choke lever to the fast idle cam and remove the link. Remove the air horn assembly attaching screws, dashpot and bracket assembly and air horn gasket. Discard the gasket.

5. Fabricate a float level gauge to the specified float level dimension. Refer to the Carburetor Specification chart for dimensions.

6. Invert the air horn assembly, and check the clearance from the float indentation on the top of the float to the bottom of the air horn with the float level gauge. Hold the air horn at eye level when gauging the float level. The float arm (lever) should be resting on the needle pin. **Do not load the needle when adjusting the float.** Bend the float arm as necessary to adjust the float level (clearance). **Do not bend the tab at the end of the float arm.** It prevents the float from striking the bottom of the fuel bowl when empty.

7. Install a new air horn to main body gasket. **Make sure all holes in the new gasket have been properly punched and that no foreign material has adhered to the gasket.** Install the air horn assembly, connect vent line to canister (if so equipped), and bracket assembly and air horn attaching screws and tighten to 27–37 in.lbs. Position the link and plastic bushing joining the fast idle cam to the fast idle choke lever and retain in place on the fast idle cam with the plastic bushing and wire clip. Make sure the mechanical fuel bowl vent rod is engaged with the forked actuating lever (if so equipped).

8. Connect the fuel inlet line to the fuel filter.

9. Connect the electric choke wire.

10. Install the air cleaner. Start the engine and run it until normal operating temperature is reached. Adjust the idle fuel mixture and idle speed.

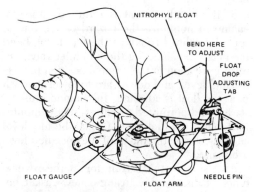

Float level adjustment for the Carter YFA & YFA Feedback carburetor

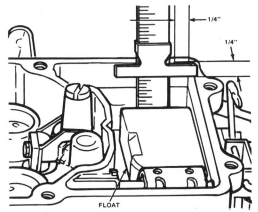

Float level adjustment for the Motorcraft 2150A 2-bbl. carburetor

Motorcraft Model 2150 2-bbl (Wet Adjustment)

1. Operate the engine until it reaches normal operating temperature. Place the vehicle on a level surface and stop the engine.

2. Remove the carburetor air cleaner assembly.

3. Remove the air horn attaching screws and the carburetor identification tag. Temporarily, leave the air horn and gasket in position on the carburetor main body and start the engine. Let the engine idle for a few minutes, then rotate the air horn out of the way and remove the air horn gasket to provide access to the float assembly.

4. While the engine is idling, use a scale to measure the vertical distance from the top machined surface of the carburetor main body to the level of the fuel in the fuel bowl. The measurement must be made at least ¼ in. away from any vertical surface to assure an accurate reading, because the surface of the fuel is concave—being higher at the edges than in the center. Care must be exercised to measure the fuel level at the point of contact with the float.

5. If any adjustment is required, stop the engine to minimize the hazard of fire due to spilled gasoline. To adjust the fuel level, bend the float tab contacting the fuel inlet valve upward in relation to the original position to raise the fuel level, and downward to lower it. Each time the float is adjusted, the engine must be started and permitted to idle for a few minutes to stabilize the fuel level. Check the fuel level after each adjustment, until the specified level is obtained.

6. Assemble the carburetor in the reverse order of disassembly, using a new gasket between the air horn and the main carburetor body.

FLOAT DROP ADJUSTMENT

Carter Model YFA & YFA Feedback 1-bbl

1. Remove the air cleaner

2. Disconnect the choke heat tube at the carburetor air horn. Disconnect the fuel inlet line at the filter.

3. Disconnect the electric choke wire at the connector.

4. Remove the wire clip retaining the link joining the fast idle choke lever to the fast idle cam and remove the link. Remove the air horn assembly attaching screws, dashpot and bracket assembly and air horn gasket. Discard the gasket.

5. Fabricate a float drop gauge to the specified dimension 38.1mm (1.5 inch) minimum.

6. Hold the air horn upright and let the float hang free. Measure the maximum clearance from the toe end of the float to the casting surface. Hold the air horn at eye level when gauging the dimension.

7. To adjust, bend the tab at the end of the float arm to obtain the specified setting.

8. Install a new air horn to main body gasket. **Make sure all holes in the new gasket have been properly punched and that no foreign material has adhered to the gasket.** Install the air horn assembly, connect vent line to canister (if so equipped), and bracket assembly and air horn attaching screws and tighten to 27–37 in.lbs. Position the link and plastic bushing joining the fast idle cam to the fast idle choke lever and retain in place on the fast idle cam with the plastic bushing and wire clip. Make sure the mechanical fuel bowl vent rod is engaged with the forked actuating lever (if so equipped).

9. Connect the fuel inlet line to the fuel filter.

10. Connect the electric choke wire.

11. Install the air cleaner. Start the engine and run it until normal operating temperature

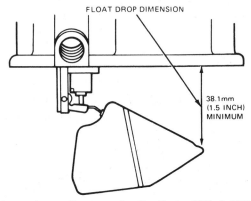

Float drop adjustment for the Carter YFA & YFA Feedback carburetor

is reached. Adjust the idle fuel mixture and idle speed.

FAST IDLE SPEED ADJUSTMENT

Carter YFA & YFA Feedback 1-bbl

1. Place the transmission in Neutral or Park.
2. Bring the engine to normal operating temperature.
3. Turn the ignition key to the Off position.
4. Put the air conditioner selector in the Off position.
5. Disconnect the vacuum hose at the EGR valve and plug.
6. Place the fast idle RPM adjusting screw on the specified step of the fast idle cam.
7. Start the engine without touching the accelerator pedal: Check/adjust fast idle RPM to specification. Refer to the under hood sticker for specifications.
8. Rev the engine momentarily, allowing the engine to return to idle and turn the ignition key to Off position.
9. Remove the plug from the EGR vacuum hose and reconnect.

Motorcraft Model 2150A 2-bbl

1. Place the transmission in park or neutral.
2. Bring the engine to normal operating temperature.
3. Disconnect and plug the vacuum hose at the EGR and purge valves.
4. Place the fast idle lever on the "V" step of the fast idle cam.
5. Adjust the fast idle rpm to specifications.
6. Reconnect the EGR and purge vacuum hoses.

ACCELERATING PUMP STROKE ADJUSTMENT

Motorcraft Model 2150A 2-bbl

The accelerating pump stroke has been factory set for a particular engine application and should not be readjusted. If the stroke has been changed from the specified hole reset to specifications by following these procedures.

1. Using a blunt-tipped punch, remove and retain the roll pin from the accelerator pump cover.
NOTE: *Support the area under the roll pin when removing the pin.*
2. Rotate the pump link and rod assembly until the keyed end of the assembly is aligned with the keyed hole in the pump over-travel lever.
3. Reposition the rod and swivel assembly in the specified hole and reinstall the pump link in the accelerator pump cover.
NOTE: *A service accelerator rod and swivel assembly is available (9F687) and must be used if replacement is necessary.*
Adjustment holes are not provided on the temperature-compensated accelerator pump carburetors.
4. Reinstall the rod pin.

CHOKE PULLDOWN ADJUSTMENT

Carter YFA & YFA Feedback

1. Remove the air cleaner assembly.
2. Hold the throttle plate fully open and close the choke plate as far as possible without forcing it. Use a drill of the proper diameter to check the clearance between the choke plate

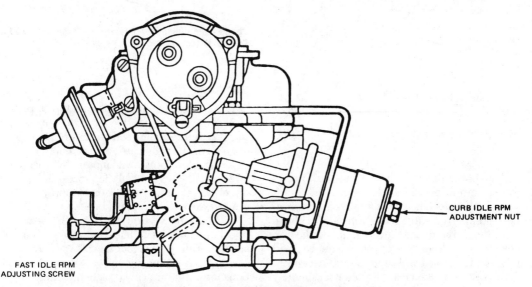

CURB IDLE RPM ADJUSTMENT NUT

FAST IDLE RPM ADJUSTING SCREW

4-122,140 engines—Carter YFA & YFA Feedback fast idle speed adjustment

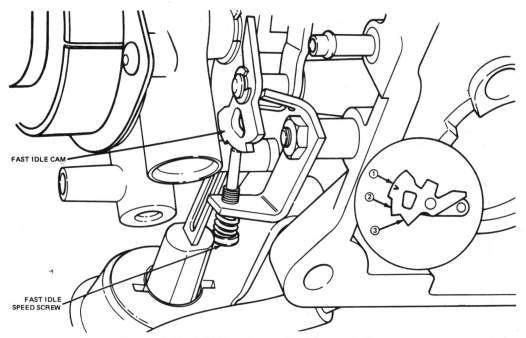

Motorcraft 2150A 2-bbl. carburetor fast idle speed adjustment

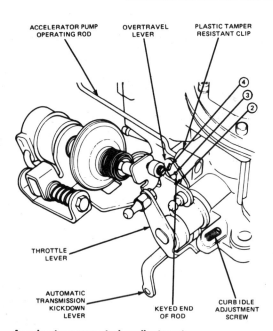

Accelerator pump stroke adjustment

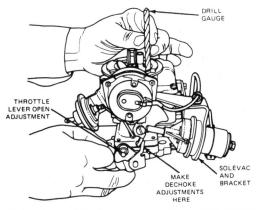

Choke plate pulldown adjustment—Carter YFA & YFA Feedback carburetor

Motorcraft 2150A

1. Set throttle on fast idle cam top step.
2. Note index position of choke bimetallic cap. Loosen retaining screws and rotate cap 90 degrees in the rich (closing) direction.
3. Activate pulldown motor by manually forcing pulldown control diaphragm link in the direction of applied vacuu or by applying vacuum to external vacuum tube.
4. Measure vertical hard gauge clearance between choke plate and center of carburetor air horn wall nearest fuel bowl.

Pulldown setting should be within specifications for minimum choke plate opening.

If choke plate pulldown is found to be out of

and air horn. Refer to the Carburetor Specification chart for specifications.

3. If the clearance is not within specification, adjust by bending the arm on the choke trip lever of the throttle lever. Bending the arm downward will decrease the clearance, and bending it upward will increase the clearance. Always recheck the clearance after making any adjustment.

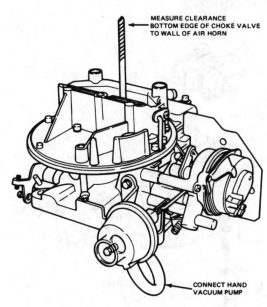

MEASURE CLEARANCE BOTTOM EDGE OF CHOKE VALVE TO WALL OF AIR HORN

CONNECT HAND VACUUM PUMP

Motorcraft 2150A choke plate pulldown adjustment

specification, reset by adjusting diaphragm stop on end of choke pulldown diaphragm.

If pulldown is reset, cam clearance should be checked and reset if required.

After pulldown check is completed, reset choke bimetallic cap to recommended index position as specified in the Carburetor Specifications Chart. Check and reset fast idle speed to specifications if necessary.

OVERHAUL

Efficient carburetion depends greatly on careful cleaning and inspection during overhaul since dirt, gum, water or varnish in or on the carburetor parts are often responsible for poor performance.

Overhaul the carburetor in a clean, dustfree area. Carefully disassemble the carburetor, reerring often to the exploded views. Keep all similar and look-alike parts segregated during disassembly and cleaning to avoid accidental interchange during assembly. Make a note of all jet sizes.

When the carburetor is disassembled, wash all parts (except diaphragms, electric choke unit, pump plunger and any other plastic, leather, fiber, or rubber parts) in clean carburetor solvent. Do not leave the parts in the solvent any longer than is necessary to sufficiently loosen the dirt and deposits. Excessive cleaning may remove the special finish from the float bowl and choke valve bodies, leaving hese parts unfit for service. Rinse all parts in clean solvent and blow them dry with compressed air or allow them to air dry, while resting on clean, lintless paper. Wipe clean all cork, plastic, leather and fiber parts with a clean, lint-free cloth.

Blow out all passages and jets with compressed air and be sure that there are no restrictions or blockages. Never use wire or similar tools to clean jets, fuel passages or air bleeds. Clean all jets and valves separately to avoid accidental interchange.

Examine all parts for wear or damage. If wear or damage is found, replace the defective parts. Especially, inspect the following:

1. Check the float needle and seat for wear. If wear is found, replace the complete assembly.

2. Check the float hinge pin for wear and the float(s) for dents or distortion. Replace the float if fuel has leaked into it.

3. Check the throttle and choke shaft bores for wear or an out-of-round condition. Damage or wear to the throttle arm, shaft or shaft bore will often require replacement of the throttle body. These parts require a close tolerance of fit; wear may allow air leakage, which could affect starting and idling.

NOTE: *Throttle shafts and bushings are not normally included in overhaul kits. They can be purchased separately.*

4. Inspect the idle mixture adjusting needles for burrs or grooves. Any such condition requires replacement of the needle, since you will not be able to obtain a satisfactory idle.

5. Test the accelerator pump check valves. They should pass air one way, but not the other. Test for proper seating by blowing and sucking on the valve. Replace the valve as necessary. If the valve is satisfactory, wash the valve again to remove moisture.

6. Check the bowl cover for warped surfaces with a straightedge.

7. Closely inspect the valves and seats for wear and damage, replacing as necessary.

8. After the carburetor is assembled, check the choke valve for freedom of operation.

Carburetor overhaul kits are recommended for each overhaul. These kits contain all gaskets and new parts to replace those which deteriorate most rapidly. Failure to replace all of the parts supplied with the kit (especially gaskets) can result in poor performance later.

NOTE: *Most carburetor rebuilding kits include specific procedures which should be followed during overhaul.*

Most carburetor manufacturers supply overhaul kits of these basic types: minor repair; major repair; and gasket kits. Basically, they contain the following:

Minor Repair Kits:
- All gaskets
- Float needle valve
- Mixture adjusting screws

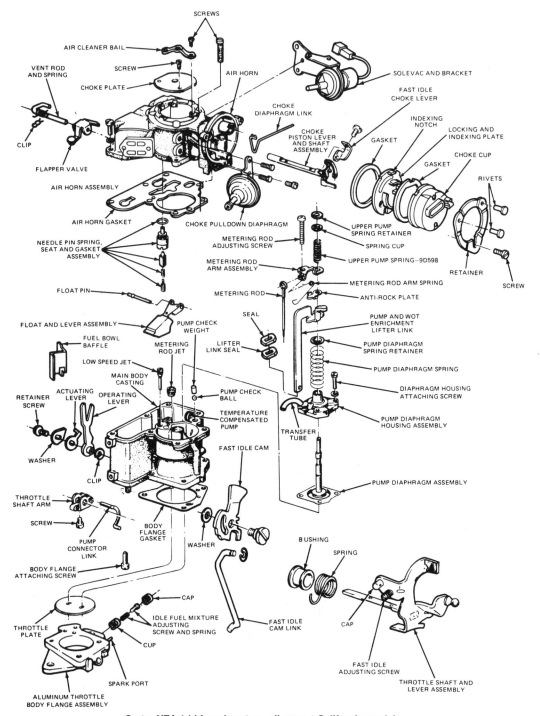

Carter YFA 1-bbl. carburetor—all except California models

- All diaphragms
- Spring for the pump diaphragm

Major Repair Kits:
- All jets and gaskets
- All diaphragms
- Float needle valve

- Mixture adjusting screws
- Pump ball valve
- Main jet carrier
- Float
- Some float bowl cover hold-down screws and washers

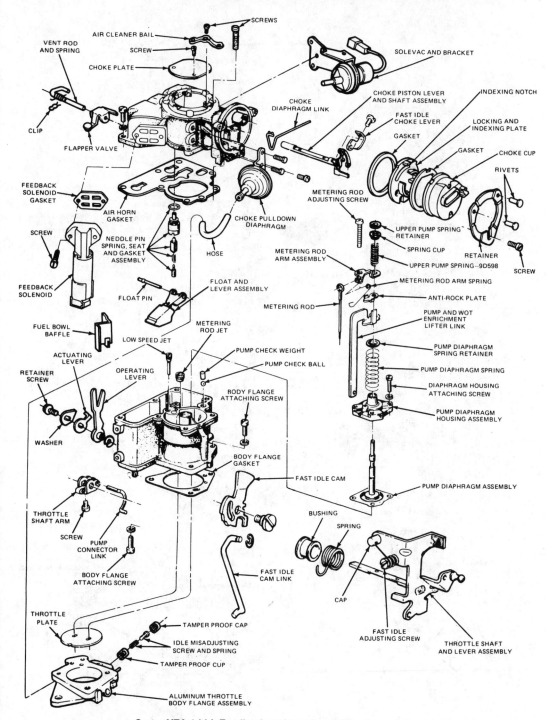

Carter YFA 1-bbl. Feedback carburetor—California models

Gasket Kits:
  • All gaskets

After cleaning and checking all components, reassemble the carburetor, using new parts and referring to the exploded view. When reassembling, make sure that all screws and jets are tight in their seats, but do not overtighten, as the tips will be distorted. Tighten all screws gradually, in rotation. Do not tighten needle valves into their seats; uneven jetting will result. Always use new gaskets. Be sure to adjust the float level.

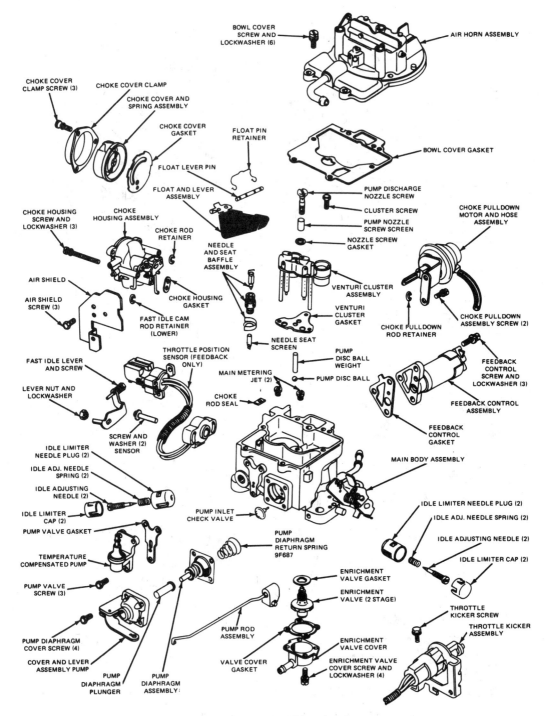

BOWL COVER SCREW AND LOCKWASHER (6)

AIR HORN ASSEMBLY

CHOKE COVER CLAMP SCREW (3)

CHOKE COVER CLAMP

CHOKE COVER AND SPRING ASSEMBLY

CHOKE COVER GASKET

FLOAT PIN RETAINER

BOWL COVER GASKET

FLOAT LEVER PIN

FLOAT AND LEVER ASSEMBLY

PUMP DISCHARGE NOZZLE SCREW

CLUSTER SCREW

CHOKE PULLDOWN MOTOR AND HOSE ASSEMBLY

CHOKE HOUSING SCREW AND LOCKWASHER (3)

CHOKE HOUSING ASSEMBLY

CHOKE ROD RETAINER

PUMP NOZZLE SCREW SCREEN

NOZZLE SCREW GASKET

NEEDLE AND SEAT BAFFLE ASSEMBLY

VENTURI CLUSTER ASSEMBLY

CHOKE PULLDOWN ASSEMBLY SCREW (2)

AIR SHIELD

CHOKE HOUSING GASKET

VENTURI CLUSTER GASKET

CHOKE PULLDOWN ROD RETAINER

CHOKE PULLDOWN ROD RETAINER

AIR SHIELD SCREW (3)

FAST IDLE CAM ROD RETAINER (LOWER)

NEEDLE SEAT SCREEN

THROTTLE POSITION SENSOR (FEEDBACK ONLY)

PUMP DISC BALL WEIGHT

FEEDBACK CONTROL SCREW AND LOCKWASHER (3)

FAST IDLE LEVER AND SCREW

MAIN METERING JET (2)

PUMP DISC BALL

LEVER NUT AND LOCKWASHER

CHOKE ROD SEAL

FEEDBACK CONTROL ASSEMBLY

SCREW AND WASHER (2) SENSOR

FEEDBACK CONTROL GASKET

IDLE LIMITER NEEDLE PLUG (2)

MAIN BODY ASSEMBLY

IDLE ADJ. NEEDLE SPRING (2)

IDLE ADJUSTING NEEDLE (2)

IDLE LIMITER NEEDLE PLUG (2)

IDLE LIMITER CAP (2)

PUMP INLET CHECK VALVE

IDLE ADJ. NEEDLE SPRING (2)

PUMP VALVE GASKET

IDLE ADJUSTING NEEDLE (2)

PUMP DIAPHRAGM RETURN SPRING 9F687

IDLE LIMITER CAP (2)

TEMPERATURE COMPENSATED PUMP

ENRICHMENT VALVE GASKET

PUMP VALVE SCREW (3)

ENRICHMENT VALVE (2 STAGE)

THROTTLE KICKER SCREW

PUMP DIAPHRAGM COVER SCREW (4)

THROTTLE KICKER ASSEMBLY

PUMP ROD ASSEMBLY

ENRICHMENT VALVE COVER

COVER AND LEVER ASSEMBLY PUMP

PUMP DIAPHRAGM PLUNGER

PUMP DIAPHRAGM ASSEMBLY

VALVE COVER GASKET

ENRICHMENT VALVE COVER SCREW AND LOCKWASHER (4)

Motorcraft 2150A 2-bbl. carburetor

1984 Carburetor Specifications

CARTER YFA

Check the carburetor part number tag to determine which specifications to use for your vehicle

Engine	Part Number	Choke Pulldown Setting	Fast Idle Cam Setting	Dechoke Setting	Float Setting (Dry)	Choke Cap Setting	Fast Idle
4-122(2000)	E37E-9510-EB	.320	.140	.270	.650	Orange	2000 ①
	E37E-9510-FB	.320	.140	.270	.650	Grey	2000 ①
4-140(2300)	E37E-9510-BB	.320	.140	.270	.650	Yellow	2000 ①
	E37E-9510-LB, NB,RB,TB	.320	.140	.270	.650	Grey	2000 ①

① 1900 rpm for vehicles with less than 100 miles.

MOTORCRAFT 2150A

Check the carburetor part number tag to determine which specifications to use for your vehicle

Engine	Part Number	Choke Pulldown Setting	Fast Idle Cam Setting	Dechoke Setting	Float Level (Wet)	Float Level (Dry)	Accelerator Pump Lever Location	Choke Cap Setting	Fast Idle
6-173(2800)	E37E-9510-AAA, ABA,ADA,AEA E47E-9510-TA, VA	.136	V-notch	.250	.810	7/16	#4	V-notch	3000 ②

② 2800 rpm for vehicles with les than 100 miles.

1983 Carburetor Specifications

CARTER YFA

Check the carburetor part number tag to determine which specifications to use for your vehicle.

Engine	Part Number	Choke Pulldown Setting	Fast Idle Cam Setting	Dechoke Setting	Float Setting (Dry)	Choke Cap Setting	Fast Idle
4-122(2000)	E27E-9510-CC	.320	.140	.220	.650	Orange	2000 ①
	E27E-9510-CB, GB	.320	.140	.220	.650	Yellow	2000 ①
	E37E-9510-EA	.320	.140	.270	.650	Orange	2000 ①
	E37E-9510-FA	.320	.140	.270	.650	Grey	2000 ①
4-140(2300)	E27E-9510-BB, FB E37E-9510-BA	.320	.140	.270	.650	Yellow	2000 ①
	E27E-9510-EB, HA,HB	.320	.140	.220	.650	Black	2000 ①
	E27E-9510-FA	.320	.140	.270	.650	Yellow	2000 ①
	E37E-9510-LA, LB,NA,NB,RA, RB,TA,TB	.320	.140	.270	.650	Grey	2000 ①

① 1900 rpm for vehicles with less than 100 miles.

1983 Carburetor Specifications (cont.)

MOTORCRAFT 2150A

Check the carburetor part number tag to determine which specifications to use for your vehicle

Engine	Part Number	Choke Pulldown Setting	Fast Idle Cam Setting	Dechoke Setting	Float Level (Wet)	Float Level (Dry)	Accelerator Pump Lever Location	Choke Cap Setting	Fast Idle
6-173(2800)	E37E-9510-AAA	.136	V-notch	.250	.810	$7/16''$	#4	V-notch	3000②
	E37E-9510-ABA	.136	V-notch	.250	.810	$7/16''$	#4	V-notch	3000②
	E37E-9510-ADA	.136	V-notch	.250	.810	$7/16''$	#4	V-notch	3000②

② 2800 rpm for vehicles with less than 100 miles.

Fuel Tank

REMOVAL AND INSTALLATION

Midship Fuel Tank

1. Drain the fuel from the fuel tank.
2. Loosen the fill pipe clamp.
3. Remove the bolts securing the skid plate and brackets to the frame, if so equipped. Remove the skid plate and brackets as an assembly.
4. Remove the bolt and nut from the rear strap and remove the rear strap.
5. Remove the nut from the front strap and remove the front strap.
6. Remove the clamp from the feed hose at the sender unit.
7. Remove the fuel hose from sender unit.
8. Remove the fuel vapor hose from the vapor valve.
9. Lower the tank from vehicle.
10. Remove the shield from tank.
11. Remove the front mounting bolt from the vehicle by drilling a hole in the cab floor over the bolt hole (drill dimple in floor pan).
12. Install the front mounting bolt to vehicle.
13. Attach the lower insulators to the front and rear straps using adhesive ESB-M2G115-A or equivalent.
14. Attach the rear strap to the vehicle.
15. Install the shield on tank.
16. Position the tank to the vehicle. Attach the front strap to vehicle.
17. Attach the fuel vapor hose to the vapor valve.
18. Attach the fuel hose to the sender unit.
19. Install the clamps to feed and return hoses at the sender unit.
20. Install the filler pipe in position. Tighten the fill pipe clamp.
21. Install the nut to the front mounting bolt and tighten to 18-20 ft. lbs.
22. Install the bolt to the rear strap and tighten.

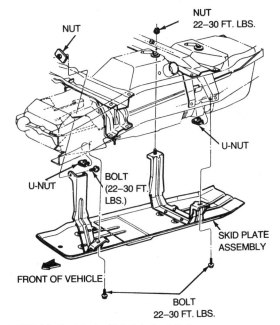

Midship fuel tank skid plate installation

23. Install the skid plate and bracket assembly, if so equipped. Tighten the screws to 25–30 ft. lbs.

Rear Fuel Tank (Dual Tanks)

1. Insert a siphon through the filler neck and drain the fuel into a suitable container.
2. Raise the rear of the vehicle. Remove the skid plate, if so equipped.
3. To avoid any chance of sparking at or near the tank, disconnect the ground cable from the vehicle battery. Disconnect the fuel gauge sending unit wire at the fuel tank.
4. Loosen the clamp on the fuel filler pipe hose at the filler pipe and disconnect the hose from the pipe.
5. Loosen the hose clamps, slide the clamps forward and disconnect the fuel line at the fuel gauge sending unit.

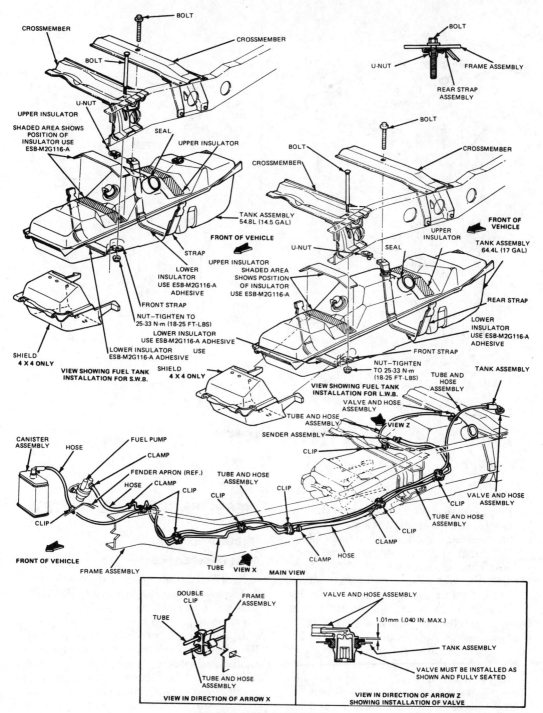

Midship fuel tank installation

6. If the fuel gauge sending unit is to be removed, turn the unit retaining ring, and gasket, and remove the unit from the tank.

7. Remove the strap attaching nut at each tank mounting strap, swing the strap down, and lower the tank enough to gain access to the tank vent hose.

8. Disconnect the fuel tank vent hose at the top of the tank. Disconnect the fuel tank-to-separator tank lines at the fuel tank.

9. Lower the fuel tank and remove it from under the vehicle.

To install the fuel tank:

10. Position the forward edge of the tank to

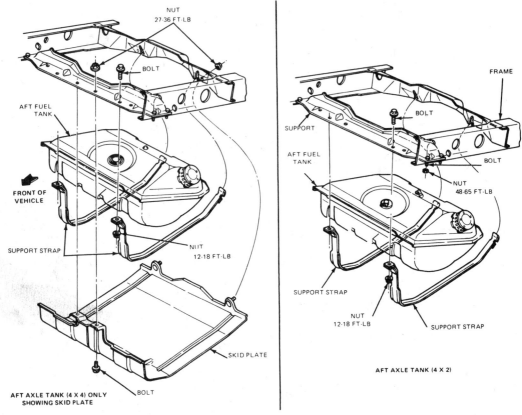

NUT
27-36 FT-LB

BOLT

FRAME

AFT FUEL
TANK

BOLT

SUPPORT

AFT FUEL
TANK

BOLT

FRONT OF
VEHICLE

NUT
48-65 FT-LB

SUPPORT STRAP

NUT
12-18 FT-LB

SUPPORT STRAP

NUT
12-18 FT-LB

SUPPORT STRAP

SKID PLATE

AFT AXLE TANK (4 X 2)

AFT AXLE TANK (4 X 4) ONLY
SHOWING SKID PLATE

BOLT

Rear fuel tank installation

the frame crossmember, and connect the vent hose to the top of the tank. Connect the fuel tank-to-separator tank lines at the fuel tank.

11. Position the tank and mounting straps, and install the attaching nuts and flat washers.

12. If the fuel gauge sending unit was removed, make sure that all of the old gasket material has been removed from the unit mounting surface on the fuel tank. Using a new gasket, position the fuel gauge sending unit to the fuel tank and secure it with the retaining ring.

13. Connect the fuel line at the fuel gauge sending unit and tighten the hose clamps securely. Install the drain plug, if so equipped.

14. Connect the fuel gauge sending unit wire to the sending unit.

15. Install the skid plate and tighten the mounting nuts, if so equipped.

16. Connect the filler pipe-to-tank hose at the filler pipe and install the hose clamp.

17. Connect the vehicle battery ground cable.

18. Fill the tank and check all connections for leaks.

19. Lower the vehicle.

DIESEL ENGINE FUEL SYSTEM

Injector Timing

4-134 Diesel Engine

NOTE: *Special tools Ford 14-0303, Static Timing Gauge Adapter and D82L4201A, Metric Dial Indicator, or the equivalents are necessary to set or check the injector timing.*

1. Disconnect both battery ground cables. Remove the air inlet hose from the air cleaner and intake manifold.

2. Remove the distributor head plug bolt and washer from the injection pump.

3. Install the Timing Gauge Adapter and Metric Dial Indicator so that the indicator pointer is in contact with the injector pump plunger and gauge reads approximately 2.0mm (0.08 inch).

4. Align the 2° ATDC (after top dead center) on the crankshaft pulley with the indicator on the timing case cover.

5. Slowly turn the engine counterclockwise until the dial indicator pointer stops moving (approximately 30°–50°).

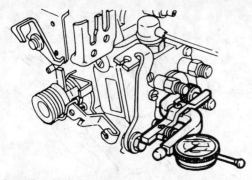

Installing the injection pump timing gauge

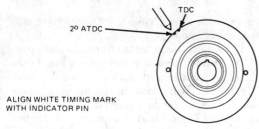

ALIGN WHITE TIMING MARK
WITH INDICATOR PIN

Aligning the timing mark

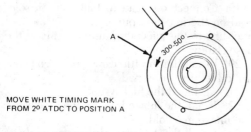

MOVE WHITE TIMING MARK
FROM 2° ATDC TO POSITION A

Moving the crankshaft pulley timing mark

6. Adjust the dial indicator to 0 (Zero). Confirm that the dial indicator does not move from Zero, by rotating the crankshaft slightly right and left.

7. Turn the crankshaft clockwise until the timing mark aligns with the cover indicator. The dial indicator should read 1, plus or minus 0.02mm (0.04, plus or minus 0.0008 inch). If the reading is not within specifications, adjust the timing as follows;

   a. Loosen the injection pump mounting nuts and bolts.

   b. Rotate the injection pump counterclockwise (reverse direction of engine rotation) past the correct timing position, then clockwise until the timing is correct. This procedure will eliminate gear backlash.

   c. Repeat Steps 5, 6, and 7 to check that the timing is properly adjusted.

8. Remove the dial indicator and adapter. Install the injector head gasket and plug. Install all removed parts.

9. Run engine, check and adjust idle RPM. Check for fuel leaks.

Fuel Filter and Priming Pump Assembly

REMOVAL AND INSTALLATION

1. Disconnect both battery ground cables.
2. Disconnect and cap the fuel filter inlet and outlet lines.
3. Remove the two bolts/nuts attaching the priming pump to the bracket an remove the pump.
4. Remove the two bolts attaching the bracket to the engine and remove the bracket.
5. Install the fuel filter mounting bracket on the engine.
6. Install the priming pump assembly on the bracket.
7. Install the fuel filter lines and clamps.
8. Connect both battery ground cables.
9. Run the engine and check for fuel leaks.

Injection Pump

REMOVAL AND INSTALLATION

1. Disconnect both battery ground cables.
2. Remove the radiator fan and shroud. Loosen and remove the A/C compressor/power steering pump drive belt and idler pulley, if so equipped. Remove the injection pump drive gear cover and gasket.
3. Rotate the engine until the injection pump drive gear keyway is at TDC.
4. Remove the large nut and washer attaching the drive gear to the injection pump.

   NOTE: *Care should be taken not to drop the washer into timing gear case.*

5. Disconnect the intake hose from the air cleaner and intake manifold.
6. Disconnect the throttle cable and the speed control cable, if so equipped.
7. Disconnect and cap the fuel inlet line at injection pump.
8. Disconnect the fuel shut-off solenoid lead at the injection pump.
9. Disconnect and remove the fuel injection lines from the nozzles and injection pump. Cap all the fuel lines and fittings.
10. Disconnect the lower fuel return line from the injection pump and the fuel hoses. Loosen the lower No. 3 intake port nut and remove the fuel return line.
11. Remove the two nuts attaching the injection pump to the front timing gear cover and one bolt attaching the pump to the rear support bracket.
12. Install a Gear and Hub Remover, Tool T83T-6306-A or equivalent, in the drive gear cover and attach to the injection pump drive

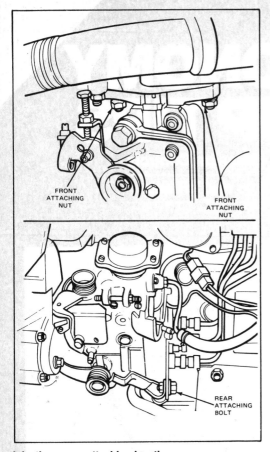

Injection pump attaching locations

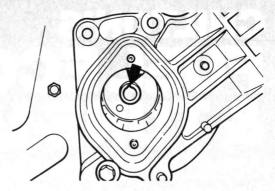

Aligning the key and keyway in the TDC position

gear. Rotate the screw clockwise until the injection pump disengages from the drive gear. Remove the injection pump.

NOTE: *Carefully remove the injection pump to avoid dropping the key into the timing gear case. Disconnect the cold start cable before removing the injection pump from the vehicle.*

NOTE: *Connect the cold start cable to pump before positioning the injection pump in the timing gear case.*

13. Install the injection pump in position in the timing gear case aligning the key with keyway in the drive gear in the TDC position.

NOTE: *Use care to avoid dropping the key in the timing gear case.*

14. Install the nuts and washers attaching the injection pump to the timing gear case and tighten to draw the injection pump into position.

NOTE: *Do not tighten at this time.*

15. Install the bolt attaching the injection pump to the rear support. Install the washer and nut attaching the injection drive gear to the injection pump and tighten.

16. Install the injection pump drive gear

cover, with a new gasket, on the timing gear case cover and tighten.

17. Adjust the injection timing at this time.

18. Install the lower fuel return line to the injection pump and intake manifold stud. Tighten the Banjo bolt on the injection pump and nut on the intake manifold. Install the connecting fuel hoses and clamps. Install the fuel injection lines to the injection pump and nozzles.

19. Connect the lead to fuel shut-off solenoid on the injection pump. Connect the fuel inlet line to the injection pump and install the hose clamp.

20. Install the throttle cable and speed control cable, if so equipped.

21. Air bleed the fuel system.

22. Install the intake hose on the air cleaner and intake manifold.

23. Install the A/C compressor/power steering pump drive belt and idler pulley, if so equipped.

24. Install the radiator shroud and radiator fan.

25. Connect both battery ground cables.

26. Run the engine and check for oil and fuel leaks.

Fuel Injectors

REMOVAL & INSTALLATION

1. Disconnect both battery ground cables.

2. Disconnect and remove the injection lines from the nozzles and injection pump. Cap all lines and fittings.

3. Remove the fuel return line and gaskets.

4. Remove the bolts attaching the fuel line heater clamp to the cylinder head and position the heater out of the way.

5. Remove the nozzles, using a 27mm deepwell socket.

6. Remove the nozzle washer (copper) and nozzle gasket (steel), using Tool T71-P-19703-C or equivalent.

CHILTON'S
FUEL ECONOMY & TUNE-UP TIPS

55 WAYS TO IMPROVE FUEL ECONOMY

Tune-up • Spark Plug Diagnosis • Emission Controls

Fuel System • Cooling System • Tires and Wheels

General Maintenance

CHILTON'S FUEL ECONOMY & TUNE-UP TIPS

Fuel economy is important to everyone, no matter what kind of vehicle you drive. The maintenance-minded motorist can save both money and fuel using these tips and the periodic maintenance and tune-up procedures in this Repair and Tune-Up Guide.

There are more than 130,000,000 cars and trucks registered for private use in the United States. Each travels an average of 10-12,000 miles per year, and, and in total they consume close to 70 billion gallons of fuel each year. This represents nearly ⅔ of the oil imported by the United States each year. The Federal government's goal is to reduce consumption 10% by 1985. A variety of methods are either already in use or under serious consideration, and they all affect you driving and the cars you will drive. In addition to "down-sizing", the auto industry is using or investigating the use of electronic fuel

delivery, electronic engine controls and alternative engines for use in smaller and lighter vehicles, among other alternatives to meet the federally mandated Corporate Average Fuel Economy (CAFE) of 27.5 mpg by 1985. The government, for its part, is considering rationing, mandatory driving curtailments and tax increases on motor vehicle fuel in an effort to reduce consumption. The government's goal of a 10% reduction could be realized — and further government regulation avoided — if every private vehicle could use just 1 less gallon of fuel per week.

How Much Can You Save?

Tests have proven that almost anyone can make at least a 10% reduction in fuel consumption through regular maintenance and tune-ups. When a major manufacturer of spark plugs sur-

TUNE-UP

1. Check the cylinder compression to be sure the engine will really benefit from a tune-up and that it is capable of producing good fuel economy. A tune-up will be wasted on an engine in poor mechanical condition.

2. Replace spark plugs regularly. New spark plugs alone can increase fuel economy 3%.

3. Be sure the spark plugs are the correct type (heat range) for your vehicle. See the Tune-Up Specifications.

Heat range refers to the spark plug's ability to conduct heat away from the firing end. It must conduct the heat away in an even pattern to avoid becoming a source of pre-ignition, yet it must also operate hot enough to burn off conductive deposits that could cause misfiring.

The heat range is usually indicated by a number on the spark plug, part of the manufacturer's designation for each individual spark plug. The numbers in bold-face indicate the heat range in each manufacturer's identification system.

Manufacturer	Typical Designation
AC	R **45** TS
Bosch (old)	WA **145** T30
Bosch (new)	HR **8** Y
Champion	RBL **15** Y
Fram/Autolite	4**15**
Mopar	P-**62** PR
Motorcraft	BRF-**42**
NGK	BP **5** ES-15
Nippondenso	W **16** EP
Prestolite	14GR **5** 2A

Periodically, check the spark plugs to be sure they are firing efficiently. They are excellent indicators of the internal condition of your engine.

On AC, Bosch (new), Champion, Fram/Autolite, Mopar, Motorcraft and Prestolite, a higher number indicates a hotter plug. On Bosch (old), NGK and Nippondenso, a higher number indicates a colder plug.

4. Make sure the spark plugs are properly gapped. See the Tune-Up Specifications in this book.

5. Be sure the spark plugs are firing efficiently. The illustrations on the next 2 pages show you how to "read" the firing end of the spark plug.

6. Check the ignition timing and set it to specifications. Tests show that almost all cars have incorrect ignition timing by more than 2°.

veyed over 6,000 cars nationwide, they found that a tune-up, on cars that needed one, increased fuel economy over 11%. Replacing worn plugs alone, accounted for a 3% increase. The same test also revealed that 8 out of every 10 vehicles will have some maintenance deficiency that will directly affect fuel economy, emissions or performance. Most of this mileage-robbing neglect could be prevented with regular maintenance.

Modern engines require that all of the functioning systems operate properly for maximum efficiency. A malfunction anywhere wastes fuel. You can keep your vehicle running as efficiently and economically as possible, by being aware of your vehicle's operating and performance characteristics. If your vehicle suddenly develops performance or fuel economy problems it could be due to one or more of the following:

PROBLEM	POSSIBLE CAUSE
Engine Idles Rough	Ignition timing, idle mixture, vacuum leak or something amiss in the emission control system.
Hesitates on Acceleration	Dirty carburetor or fuel filter, improper accelerator pump setting, ignition timing or fouled spark plugs.
Starts Hard or Fails to Start	Worn spark plugs, improperly set automatic choke, ice (or water) in fuel system.
Stalls Frequently	Automatic choke improperly adjusted and possible dirty air filter or fuel filter.
Performs Sluggishly	Worn spark plugs, dirty fuel or air filter, ignition timing or automatic choke out of adjustment.

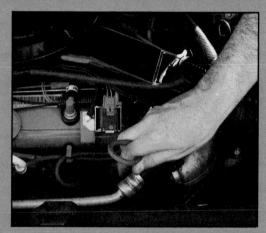

Check spark plug wires on conventional point type ignition for cracks by bending them in a loop around your finger.

Be sure that spark plug wires leading to adjacent cylinders do not run too close together. (Photo courtesy Champion Spark Plug Co.)

7. If your vehicle does not have electronic ignition, check the points, rotor and cap as specified.

8. Check the spark plug wires (used with conventional point-type ignitions) for cracks and burned or broken insulation by bending them in a loop around your finger. Cracked wires decrease fuel efficiency by failing to deliver full voltage to the spark plugs. One misfiring spark plug can cost you as much as 2 mpg.

9. Check the routing of the plug wires. Misfiring can be the result of spark plug leads to adjacent cylinders running parallel to each other and too close together. One wire tends to

pick up voltage from the other causing it to fire "out of time".

10. Check all electrical and ignition circuits for voltage drop and resistance.

11. Check the distributor mechanical and/or vacuum advance mechanisms for proper functioning. The vacuum advance can be checked by twisting the distributor plate in the opposite direction of rotation. It should spring back when released.

12. Check and adjust the valve clearance on engines with mechanical lifters. The clearance should be slightly loose rather than too tight.

SPARK PLUG DIAGNOSIS

Normal

APPEARANCE: This plug is typical of one operating normally. The insulator nose varies from a light tan to grayish color with slight electrode wear. The presence of slight deposits is normal on used plugs and will have no adverse effect on engine performance. The spark plug heat range is correct for the engine and the engine is running normally.

CAUSE: Properly running engine.

RECOMMENDATION: Before reinstalling this plug, the electrodes should be cleaned and filed square. Set the gap to specifications. If the plug has been in service for more than 10-12,000 miles, the entire set should probably be replaced with a fresh set of the same heat range.

Oil Deposits

APPEARANCE: The firing end of the plug is covered with a wet, oily coating.

CAUSE: The problem is poor oil control. On high mileage engines, oil is leaking past the rings or valve guides into the combustion chamber. A common cause is also a plugged PCV valve, and a ruptured fuel pump diaphragm can also cause this condition. Oil fouled plugs such as these are often found in new or recently overhauled engines, before normal oil control is achieved, and can be cleaned and reinstalled.

RECOMMENDATION: A hotter spark plug may temporarily relieve the problem, but the engine is probably in need of work.

Incorrect Heat Range

APPEARANCE: The effects of high temperature on a spark plug are indicated by clean white, often blistered insulator. This can also be accompanied by excessive wear of the electrode, and the absence of deposits.

CAUSE: Check for the correct spark plug heat range. A plug which is too hot for the engine can result in overheating. A car operated mostly at high speeds can require a colder plug. Also check ignition timing, cooling system level, fuel mixture and leaking intake manifold.

RECOMMENDATION: If all ignition and engine adjustments are known to be correct, and no other malfunction exists, install spark plugs one heat range colder.

Carbon Deposits

APPEARANCE: Carbon fouling is easily identified by the presence of dry, soft, black, sooty deposits.

CAUSE: Changing the heat range can often lead to carbon fouling, as can prolonged slow, stop-and-start driving. If the heat range is correct, carbon fouling can be attributed to a rich fuel mixture, sticking choke, clogged air cleaner, worn breaker points, retarded timing or low compression. If only one or two plugs are carbon fouled, check for corroded or cracked wires on the affected plugs. Also look for cracks in the distributor cap between the towers of affected cylinders.

RECOMMENDATION: After the problem is corrected, these plugs can be cleaned and reinstalled if not worn severely.

Photos Courtesy Fram Corporation

MMT Fouled

APPEARANCE: Spark plugs fouled by MMT (Methycyclopentadienyl Maganese Tricarbonyl) have reddish, rusty appearance on the insulator and side electrode.

CAUSE: MMT is an anti-knock additive in gasoline used to replace lead. During the combustion process, the MMT leaves a reddish deposit on the insulator and side electrode.

RECOMMENDATION: No engine malfunction is indicated and the deposits will not affect plug performance any more than lead deposits (see Ash Deposits). MMT fouled plugs can be cleaned, regapped and reinstalled.

High Speed Glazing

APPEARANCE: Glazing appears as shiny coating on the plug, either yellow or tan in color.

CAUSE: During hard, fast acceleration, plug temperatures rise suddenly. Deposits from normal combustion have no chance to fluff-off; instead, they melt on the insulator forming an electrically conductive coating which causes misfiring.

RECOMMENDATION: Glazed plugs are not easily cleaned. They should be replaced with a fresh set of plugs of the correct heat range. If the condition recurs, using plugs with a heat range one step colder may cure the problem.

Ash (Lead) Deposits

APPEARANCE: Ash deposits are characterized by light brown or white colored deposits crusted on the side or center electrodes. In some cases it may give the plug a rusty appearance.

CAUSE: Ash deposits are normally derived from oil or fuel additives burned during normal combustion. Normally they are harmless, though excessive amounts can cause misfiring. If deposits are excessive in short mileage, the valve guides may be worn.

RECOMMENDATION: Ash-fouled plugs can be cleaned, gapped and reinstalled.

Detonation

APPEARANCE: Detonation is usually characterized by a broken plug insulator.

CAUSE: A portion of the fuel charge will begin to burn spontaneously, from the increased heat following ignition. The explosion that results applies extreme pressure to engine components, frequently damaging spark plugs and pistons.

Detonation can result by over-advanced ignition timing, inferior gasoline (low octane) lean air/fuel mixture, poor carburetion, engine lugging or an increase in compression ratio due to combustion chamber deposits or engine modification.

RECOMMENDATION: Replace the plugs after correcting the problem.

Photos Courtesy Champion Spark Plug Co.

EMISSION CONTROLS

13. Be aware of the general condition of the emission control system. It contributes to reduced pollution and should be serviced regularly to maintain efficient engine operation.

14. Check all vacuum lines for dried, cracked or brittle conditions. Something as simple as a leaking vacuum hose can cause poor performance and loss of economy.

15. Avoid tampering with the emission control system. Attempting to improve fuel econ-

FUEL SYSTEM

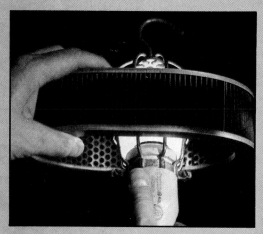

Check the air filter with a light behind it. If you can see light through the filter it can be reused.

Extremely clogged filters should be discarded and replaced with a new one.

18. Replace the air filter regularly. A dirty air filter richens the air/fuel mixture and can increase fuel consumption as much as 10%. Tests show that ⅓ of all vehicles have air filters in need of replacement.

19. Replace the fuel filter at least as often as recommended.

20. Set the idle speed and carburetor mixture to specifications.

21. Check the automatic choke. A sticking or malfunctioning choke wastes gas.

22. During the summer months, adjust the automatic choke for a leaner mixture which will produce faster engine warm-ups.

COOLING SYSTEM

29. Be sure all accessory drive belts are in good condition. Check for cracks or wear.

30. Adjust all accessory drive belts to proper tension.

31. Check all hoses for swollen areas, worn spots, or loose clamps.

32. Check coolant level in the radiator or expansion tank.

33. Be sure the thermostat is operating properly. A stuck thermostat delays engine warm-up and a cold engine uses nearly twice as much fuel as a warm engine.

34. Drain and replace the engine coolant at least as often as recommended. Rust and scale

TIRES & WHEELS

38. Check the tire pressure often with a pencil type gauge. Tests by a major tire manufacturer show that 90% of all vehicles have at least 1 tire improperly inflated. Better mileage can be achieved by over-inflating tires, but never exceed the maximum inflation pressure on the side of the tire.

39. If possible, install radial tires. Radial tires deliver as much as ½ mpg more than bias belted tires.

40. Avoid installing super-wide tires. They only create extra rolling resistance and decrease fuel mileage. Stick to the manufacturer's recommendations.

41. Have the wheels properly balanced.

omy by tampering with emission controls is more likely to worsen fuel economy than improve it. Emission control changes on modern engines are not readily reversible.

16. Clean (or replace) the EGR valve and lines as recommended.

17. Be sure that all vacuum lines and hoses are reconnected properly after working under the hood. An unconnected or misrouted vacuum line can wreak havoc with engine performance.

23. Check for fuel leaks at the carburetor, fuel pump, fuel lines and fuel tank. Be sure all lines and connections are tight.

24. Periodically check the tightness of the carburetor and intake manifold attaching nuts and bolts. These are a common place for vacuum leaks to occur.

25. Clean the carburetor periodically and lubricate the linkage.

26. The condition of the tailpipe can be an excellent indicator of proper engine combustion. After a long drive at highway speeds, the inside of the tailpipe should be a light grey in color. Black or soot on the insides indicates an overly rich mixture.

27. Check the fuel pump pressure. The fuel pump may be supplying more fuel than the engine needs.

28. Use the proper grade of gasoline for your engine. Don't try to compensate for knocking or "pinging" by advancing the ignition timing. This practice will only increase plug temperature and the chances of detonation or pre-ignition with relatively little performance gain.

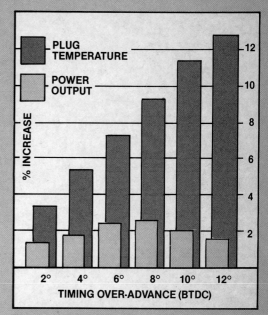

Increasing ignition timing past the specified setting results in a drastic increase in spark plug temperature with increased chance of detonation or preignition. Performance increase is considerably less. (Photo courtesy Champion Spark Plug Co.)

that form in the engine should be flushed out to allow the engine to operate at peak efficiency.

35. Clean the radiator of debris that can decrease cooling efficiency.

36. Install a flex-type or electric cooling fan, if you don't have a clutch type fan. Flex fans use curved plastic blades to push more air at low speeds when more cooling is needed; at high speeds the blades flatten out for less resistance. Electric fans only run when the engine temperature reaches a predetermined level.

37. Check the radiator cap for a worn or cracked gasket. If the cap does not seal properly, the cooling system will not function properly.

42. Be sure the front end is correctly aligned. A misaligned front end actually has wheels going in differed directions. The increased drag can reduce fuel economy by .3 mpg.

43. Correctly adjust the wheel bearings. Wheel bearings that are adjusted too tight increase rolling resistance.

Check tire pressures regularly with a reliable pocket type gauge. Be sure to check the pressure on a cold tire.

GENERAL MAINTENANCE

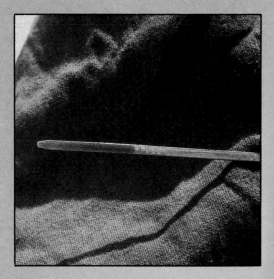

Check the fluid levels (particularly engine oil) on a regular basis. Be sure to check the oil for grit, water or other contamination.

A vacuum gauge is another excellent indicator of internal engine condition and can also be installed in the dash as a mileage indicator.

44. Periodically check the fluid levels in the engine, power steering pump, master cylinder, automatic transmission and drive axle.

45. Change the oil at the recommended interval and change the filter at every oil change. Dirty oil is thick and causes extra friction between moving parts, cutting efficiency and increasing wear. A worn engine requires more frequent tune-ups and gets progressively worse fuel economy. In general, use the lightest viscosity oil for the driving conditions you will encounter.

46. Use the recommended viscosity fluids in the transmission and axle.

47. Be sure the battery is fully charged for fast starts. A slow starting engine wastes fuel.

48. Be sure battery terminals are clean and tight.

49. Check the battery electrolyte level and add distilled water if necessary.

50. Check the exhaust system for crushed pipes, blockages and leaks.

51. Adjust the brakes. Dragging brakes or brakes that are not releasing create increased drag on the engine.

52. Install a vacuum gauge or miles-per-gallon gauge. These gauges visually indicate engine vacuum in the intake manifold. High vacuum = good mileage and low vacuum = poorer mileage. The gauge can also be an excellent indicator of internal engine conditions.

53. Be sure the clutch is properly adjusted. A slipping clutch wastes fuel.

54. Check and periodically lubricate the heat control valve in the exhaust manifold. A sticking or inoperative valve prevents engine warm-up and wastes gas.

55. Keep accurate records to check fuel economy over a period of time. A sudden drop in fuel economy may signal a need for tune-up or other maintenance.

© 1980 Chilton Book Company, Radnor, PA 19089

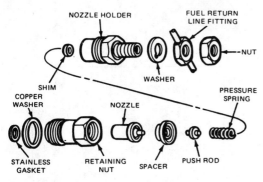

Fuel injection nozzle assembly components

7. Clean the nozzle assemblies with Nozzle Cleaning Kit, Rotunda 14-0301 or equivalent, and a suitable solvent, and dry thoroughly. Clean the nozzle seats in the cylinder head with Nozzle Seat Cleaner, T83T-9527-B or equivalent.

8. Position the new nozzle washers and gaskets in the nozzle seats, install the nozzles and tighten.

NOTE: *Install the nozzle gaskets with blue side face up (toward nozzle).*

9. Position the fuel line heater clamps and install attaching bolts.

10. Install the fuel return line wih new gaskets on nozzles.

11. Install the injection lines on the nozzles and injection pump and tighten the line nuts.

12. Connect both battery ground cables. Run the engine and check for fuel leaks.

Fuel Cut-Off Solenoid

REMOVAL AND INSTALLATION

1. Disconnect both battery ground cables.
2. Remove the connector from the fuel cut-off solenoid.
3. Remove the fuel cut-off solenoid assembly.
4. Install the fuel cut-off solenoid, with a new O-ring, and tighten.
5. Install the connector on the fuel cut-off solenoid.
6. Connect both battery ground cables. Run the engine and check for fuel leaks.

Glow Plug System

The "quick start; afterglow" system is used to enable the engine to start more quickly when the engine is cold. It consists of the four glow plugs, the control module, two relays, a glow plug resistor assembly, coolant temperature switch, clutch and neutral switches and connecting wiring. Relay power and feedback circuits are protected by fuse links in the wiring

harness. The control module is protected by a separate 10A fuse in the fuse panel.

When the ignition switch is turned to the ON position, a Wait-to-Start signal appears near the cold-start knob on the panel. When the signal appears, relay No. 1 also closes and full system voltage is applied to the glow plugs. If engine coolant temperature is below 30°C (86°F), relay No. 2 also closes at this time. After three seconds, the control module turns off the Wait-to-Start light indicating that the engine is ready for starting. If the ignition switch is left in the ON position about three seconds more without cranking, the control opens relay No. 1 and current to the plugs stops to prevent overheating. However, if coolant temperature is below 30°C (86°F) when relay No. 1 opens, relay No. 2 remains closed to apply reduced voltage to the plugs through the glow plug resistor until the ignition switch is turned off.

When the engine is cranked, the control module cycles relay No. 1 intermittently. Thus, glow plug voltage will alterante between 12 and four volts, during cranking, with relay No. 2 closed, or between 12 and zero volts with relay No. 2 open. After the engine starts, alternator output signals the control module to stop the No. 1 relay cycling and the afterglow function takes over.

If the engine coolant temperature is below 30°C (86°F), the No. 2 relay remains closed. This applies reduced (4.2 to 5.3) voltage to the glow plugs through the glow plug resistor. When the vehicle is under way (clutch and neutral switches closed), or coolant temperature is above 30°C (86°F), the control module opens relay No. 2, cutting off all current to the glow plugs.

TESTING THE GLOW PLUGS

1. Disconnect the leads from each glow plug. Connect one lead of the ohmmeter to the glow plug terminal and the other lead to a good ground. Set the ohmmeter on the X1 scale. Test each glow plug in the like manner.

2. If the meter indicates less than one ohm, the problem is not with the glow plug.

3. If the ohmmeter indicates one or more ohms, replace the glow plug and retest.

REMOVAL AND INSTALLATION

1. Disconnect both battery ground cables.
2. Disconnect the glow plug harness from the glow plugs.
3. Using a 12mm deepwell socket, remove the glow plugs.
4. Install the glow plugs, using a 12mm deepwell socket, and tighten to 11–15 ft. lbs.
5. Install the glow plug harness on the glow plugs.
6 Connect both battery ground cables.

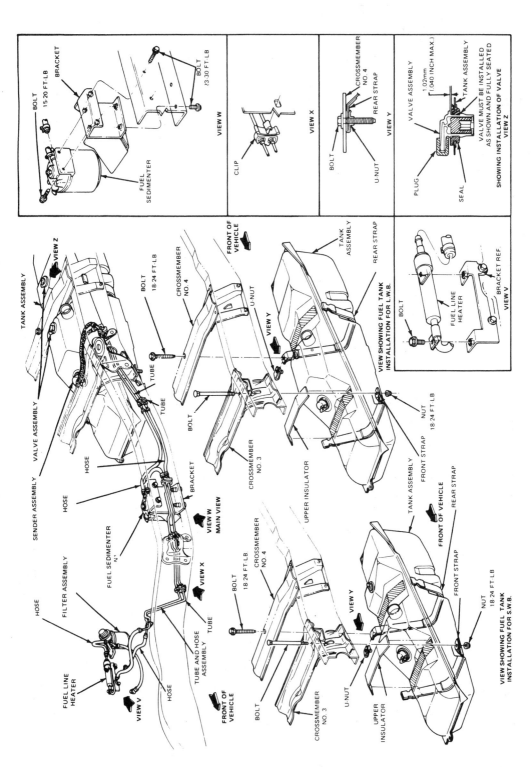

Midship fuel tank installation—diesel engine

Fuel Tank

REMOVAL AND INSTALLATION

Midship Fuel Tank

1. Drain the fuel tank.
2. Loosen the fill pipe clamp.
3. Remove the bolt and bushing from the rear strap and remove the rear strap. Remove the nut from the front strap and remove the front strap.

4. Remove the clamps from the feed and return hoses at the sender. Remove the fuel hoses from the sender unit.

5. Remove the fuel vapor hose from the vapor valve.

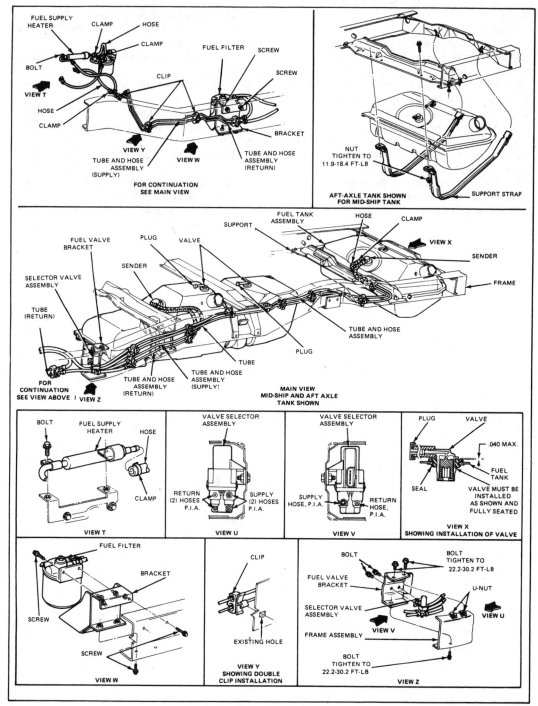

Dual fuel tank installation—diesel engine

6. Lower the tank from the vehicle and remove the front upper insulator from the tank.

7. Remove the rear upper insulator from the tank. Replace the front and rear lower insulators on the front and rear straps, if insulators are damaged.

8. Remove the front mounting bolt from vehicle (see drill dimple in cab floor behind seat), by drilling a 0.945 inch diameter hole in the cab floor over the bolt hole.

To install:

9. Install the front mounting bolt to the vehicle and insert a Ford No. W651014 plug in the cab floor hole.

10. Attach the lower insulators to the front and rear straps using Ford Adhesive ESB-M2G115-A or equivalent.

11. Attach the rear strap to the vehicle. Attach the upper front and rear insulators to the fuel tank using Ford Adhesive ESB-M2G115-A or equivalent.

12. Position the tank to the vehicle. Attach the front strap to the vehicle.

13. Attach the fuel hoses to sender units.

14. Install the clamps to the feed and return hoses at the sender unit.

15. Install the nut to the front mounting bolt and tighten to 18–25 ft. lbs.

16. Install the bolt and nut to the rear strap.

17. Install the filler pipe in position. Tighten the fill pipe clamp.

Aft Fuel Tank (Dual Tanks)

1. Drain the fuel from the fuel tank.

2. Remove the two bolts from the fuel tank support and straps.

3. Loosen the screw clamp from the fill pipe grommet.

4. Remove the clamps from the feed and return hoses at sender

5. Lower the fuel tank.

6. Remove the sender unit and the vapor valve tubes.

7. Raise the fuel tank and attach the sender unit.

8. Attach the two bolts to the fuel tank support and straps and tighten.

9. Install the clamps and attach the fuel feed and return hoses to the sender.

Chassis Electrical

5

UNDERSTANDING AND TROUBLESHOOTING ELECTRICAL SYSTEMS

For any electrical system to operate, it must make a complete circuit. This simply means that the power flow from the battery must make a complete circle. When an electrical component is operating, power flows from the battery to the component, passes through the component causing it to perform its function (lighting a light bulb, for example) and then returns to the battery through the ground of the circuit. This ground is usually (but not always) the metal part of the vehicle on which the electrical component is mounted.

Perhaps the easiest way to visualize this is to think of connecting a light bulb with two wires attached to it to your vehicle battery. The battery in your vehicle has two posts (negative and positive). If one of the two wires attached to the light bulb was attached to the negative post of the battery and the other wire was attached to the positive post of the battery, you would have a complete circuit. Current from the battery would flow out one post, through the wire attached to it and then to the light bulb, causing it to light. It would then leave the light bulb, travel through the other wire, and return to the other post of the battery.

The normal automotive circuit differs from this simple example in two ways. First, instead of having a return wire from the bulb to the battery, the light bulb returns the current to the battery through the chassis of the vehicle. Since the negative battery cable is attached to the chassis and the chassis is made of electrically conductive metal, the chassis of the vehicle can serve as a ground wire to complete the circuit. Secondly, most automotive circuits contain switches to turn components on and off as required.

There are many types o switches, but the most common simply serves to prevent the passage of current when it is turned off. Since the switch is a part of the circle necessary for a complete circuit, it operates to leave an opening in the circuit, and thus an incomplete or open circuit, when it is turned off.

Some electrical components which require a large amount of current to operate also have a relay in their circuit. Since these circuits carry a large amount of current, the thickness of the wire (gauge size) in the circuit is also greater. If this large wire were connected from the component to the control switch on the instrument panel, and thn back to the component, a voltage drop would occur in the circuit. To prevent this potential drop in voltage, an electromagnetic switch (relay) is used. The large wires in the circuit are connected from the vehicle battery to one side of the relay, and from the opposite side of the relay to the component. The relay is normally open, preventing current from passing through the circuit. An additional, smaller, wire is connected from the relay to the control switch for the circuit. When the control switch is turned on, it completes the circuit. This closes the relay and allows current to flow from the battery to the component. The horn, headlight, and starter circuits are three which use relays.

You have probably noticed how the vehicle's instrument panel lights get brighter the faster you rev the engine. This happens because your alternator (which supplies the battery) puts out more current at speeds above idle. This is normal. However, it is possible for larger surges of current to pass through the electrical system of your car. If this surge of current were to reach an electrical component, it could burn the component out. To prevent this from happening, fuses are connected into the current supply wires of most of the major electrical systems of your vehicle. The fuse serves to head off the surge at the pass. When an electrical current of excessive power passes through the component's fuse, the fuse blows out and breaks the circuit, saving it from destruction.

The fuse also protects the component from damage if the power supply wire to the component is grounded before the current reaches the component.

There is another important rule to the complete circle circuit. *Every complete circuit from a power source must include a component which is using the power from the power source.* If you were to disconnect the light bulb from the previous example of a light bulb being connected to the battery by two wires together (take our word for it—don't try it) the result would literally be shocking. A similar thing happens (on a smaller scale) when the power supply wire to a component or the electrical component itself becomes grounded before the normal ground connection for the circuit. To prevent damage to the system, the fuse for the circuit blows to interrupt the circuit—protecting the components from damage. Because grounding a wire from a power source makes a complete circuit—less the required component to use the power—this phenomenon is caled a short circuit. The most common causes of short circuits are: the rubber insulation on a wire breaking or rubbing through to expose the current carrying core of the wire to a metal part of the vehicle, or a short switch.

Some electrical systems on the vehicle are protected by a circuit breaker which is, basically, a self-repairing fuse. When either of the above-described events takes place in a system which is protected by a circuit breaker, the circuit breaker opens the circuit the sam way a fuse does. However, when either the short is removed from the cicuit or the surge subsides, the circuit breaker resets itself and does not have to be replaced as a fuse does.

The final protective device in the chassis electrical system is a fuse link. A fuse link is a wire that acts as a fuse. It is connected between the starter relay and the main wiring harness for the car. This connection is under the hood, very near a similar fuse link which protects all the chassis electrical components. It is the probable cause of trouble when none of the electrical components function, unless the battery is disconnected or dead.

Electrical problems generally fall into one of three areas:

1. The component that is not functioning is not receiving current.
2. The component itself is not functioning.
3. The component is not properly grounded.

Problems that fall into the first category are by far the most complicated. It is the current

supply system to the component which contains all the switches, relays, fuses, etc.

The electrical system can be checked with a test light and a jumper wire. A test light is a device that looks like a pointed screwdriver with a wire attached to it. It has a light bulb in its handle. A jumper wire is a piece of insulated wire with an alligator clip attached to each end.

If a light bulb is not working, you must follow a systematic plan to determine which of the three causes is the villain.

1. Turn on the switch that controls the inoperable bulb.
2. Disconnect the power suply wire from the bulb.
3. Attach the ground wire on the test light to a good metal ground.
4. Touch the probe end of the test light to the end of the power supply wire that was disconnected from the bulb. If the bulb is receiving current, the test light will go on.

NOTE: *If the bulb is one which works only when the ignition key is turned on (turn signal), make sure the key is turned on.*

If the test light does not go on, then the problem is in the circuit between the battery and the bulb. As mentioned before, this includes all the switches, fuses, and relays in the system. The problem is an open circuit between the battery and the bulb. If the fuse is blown and, when replaced, immediately blows again, there is a short circuit in the system which must be located and reapired. If there is a switch in the system, bypass it with a jumper wire. This is done by connecting one end of the jumper wire to the power supply wire into the switch, and the other end of the jumper wire to the wire coming out of the switch. If the test light lights with the jumper wire installed, the switch or whatever was bypassed is defective.

NOTE: *Never substitute the jumper wire for the bulb, as the bulb is the component required to use the power from the power source.*

5. If the bulb in the test light goes on, then the current is getting to the bulb that is not working in the vehicle. This eliminates the first of the three possible causes. Connect the power supply wire and connect a jumper wire from the bulb to a good metal ground. Do this with the switch which controls the bulb turned on, and also the ignition switch turned on if it is required for the light to work. If the bulb works with the jumper wire installed, then it has a bad ground. This is usually caused by the metal area on which the bulb mounts to the car being coated with some type of foreign matter or rust.

6. If neither test located the source of the trouble, then the light bulb itself is defective.

The above test procedure can be applied to

any of the components of the chassis electrical system by substituting the component that is not working for the light bulb. *Remember that for any electrical system to work, all connections must be clean and tight.*

HEATER

Blower

REMOVAL AND INSTALLATION

1. Disconnect the battery ground cable.
2. On California vehicles, remove the emission module forward of the blower motor.
3. Disconnect the wire harness connector from the blower motor by pushing down on the connector tabs and pulling the connector off the motor.
4. Disconnect the cooling tube at the blower motor.
5. Remove the three screws attaching the blower motor and wheel to the heater blower assembly.
6. Holding the cooling tube aside, pull the blower motor and wheel from the heater blower assembly and remove from the vehicle.
7. Remove the blower wheel hub clamp from

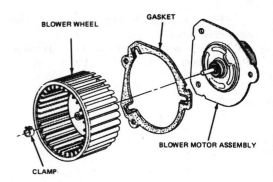

Blower wheel exploded view

the motor shaft. Then, pull the blower wheel from the motor shaft.
8. Installation is the reverse of the removal procedure.

Heater Core

REMOVAL AND INSTALLATION

1. Allow the engine to cool down. Using a thick cloth, turn the radiator cap slowly to the first stop. Step back while the pressure is released. When the pressure has been released, tighten the radiator cap on the radiator.

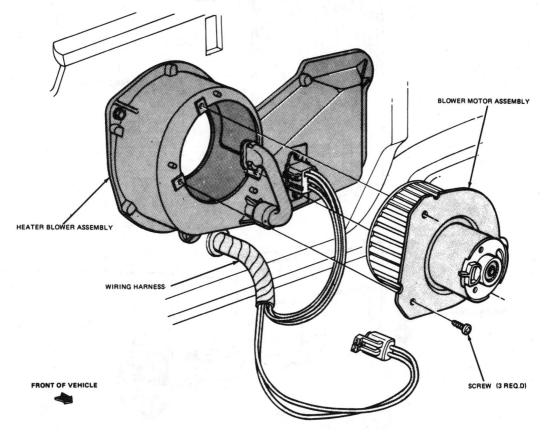

Blower motor assembly removal and installation

2. Disconnect the heater hoses from the heater core tubes and plug hoses.

3. In the passenger compartment, remove the five screws attaching the heater core access cover to the plenum assembly and remove the access cover.

4. Pull the heater core rearward and down, removing it from the plenum assembly.

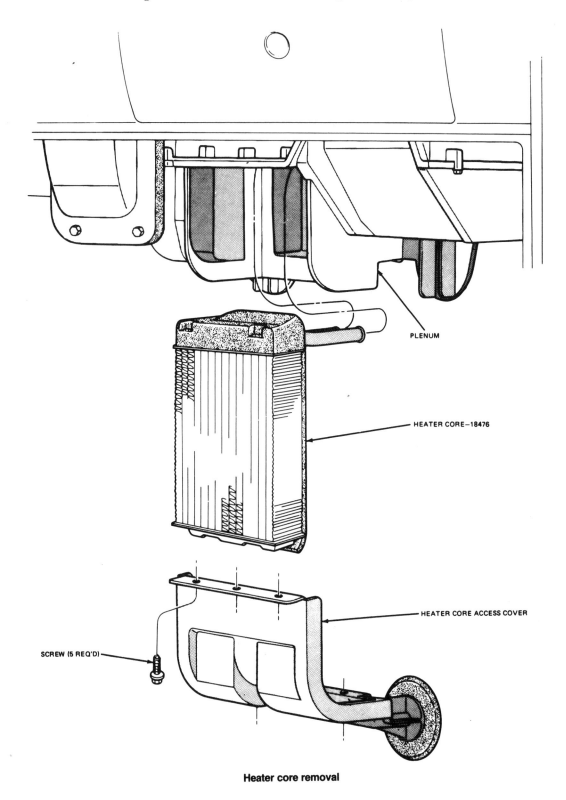

PLENUM

HEATER CORE—18476

HEATER CORE ACCESS COVER

SCREW (5 REQ'D)

Heater core removal

To install:

5. Position the heater core and seal in the plenum assembly.

6. Install the heater core access cover to the plenum assembly and secure with five screws.

7. Install the heater hoses to the heater core tubes at the dash panel in the engine compartment. Do not over-tighten hose clamps.

8. Check the coolant level and add coolant as required.

9. Start the engine and check the system for coolant leaks.

RADIO

REMOVAL AND INSTALLATION

1. Disconnect the battery ground cable.

2. Remove the knobs and discs from the radio control shafts.

3. Remove the two steering column shroud-to-panel retaining screws and remove the shroud.

4. Remove the lower instrument panel trim (no screws).

5. Detach the cluster trim cover or applique from the instrument panel by removing the eight screws.

6. Remove the four screws securing the mounting plate assembly to the instrument panel and remove the radio with the mounting plate and rear bracket.

7. Disconnect the antenna leadin cable, speaker wires and the radio (power) wire.

8. Remove the nut and washer assembly attaching the radio rear support.

9. Remove the nuts and washers from the radio control shafts and remove the mounting plate from the radio.

To install:

10. Install the radio rear support using the nut and washer assembly.

11. Install the mounting plate to the radio using the two lockwashers and two nuts.

12. Connect the wiring connectors to the radio and position the radio with the mounting plate to the instrument panel.

NOTE: *Make sure that the hair pin area of the rear bracket is engaged to the instrument panel support.*

13. Secure the mounting plate to the instrument panel with the four screws.

NOTE: *Make sure the mounting plate is fully seated on the instrument panel.*

14. Install the panel trim covers and steering column shroud.

15. Install the knobs and discs to the radio control shafts.

16. Connect the battery ground cable.

WINDSHIELD WIPERS

WIPER ARM AND BLADE REPLACEMENT

To remove the arm and blade assembly, raise the blade end of the arm off of the windshield and move the slide latch away from the pivot shaft. The wiper arm can now be removed from the shaft without the use of any tools. To install, push the main head over the pivot shaft. Be sure the wipers are in the parked position, and the blade assembly is in its correct position. Hold the main arm head onto the pivot shaft while raising the blade end of the wiper arm and push the slide latch into the lock under the pivot shaft head. Then, lower the blade to the windshield. If the blade does not lower to the windshield, the slide latch is not completely in place.

Wiper Switch
REPLACEMENT

NOTE: *The switch handle is an integral part of the switch and cannot be replaced separately.*

1. Disconnect the negative battery cable from the battery.

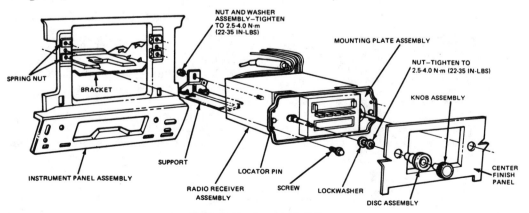

Radio removal and installation

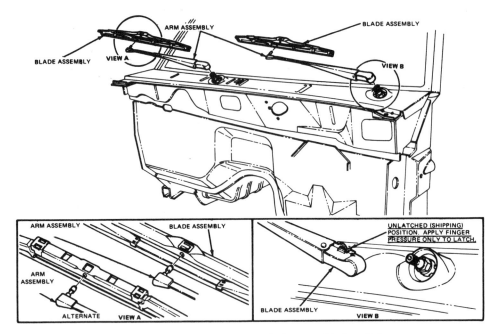

Windshield wiper arm and blade assembly installation

2. Remove the steering column trim shrouds.

3. Disconnect the quick connect electrical connector.

4. Peel back the foam sight shield, remove the two hex-head screws holding the switch, and remove the windshield wiper switch.

To install:

5. Position the switch on the column and install the two hexhead screws. Replace the foam sight shield over the switch.

6. Connect the quick connect electrical connector.

7. Install the upper and lower trim shrouds.

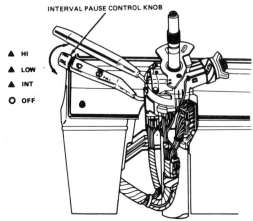

Windshield wiper switch

Motor

REMOVAL AND INSTALLATION

1. Turn the wiper switch on. Turn the ignition switch on until the blades are straight up and then turn ignition off to keep them there.

2. Remove the R.H. wiper arm and blade.

3. Remove the negative battery cable.

4. Remove the R.H. pivot nut and allow the linkage to drop into the cowl.

5. Remove the linkage access cover, located on the R.H. side of the dash panel near the wiper motor.

6. Reach through the access cover opening and unsnap the wiper motor clip.

7. Push the clip away from the linkage until it clears the nib on the crank pin. Then, push the clip off the linkage.

8. Remove the wiper linkage from motor crank pin.

9. Disconnect the wiper motor's wiring connector.

10. Remove the wiper motor's three attaching screws and remove the motor.

To install:

11. Install the motor and attach the three attaching screws.

12. Connect the wiper motor's wiring connector.

13. Install the clip completely on the R.H. linkage. Make sure the clip is completely on.

NOTE: *Do not put the linkage on the motor crank pin and then try to install the clip.*

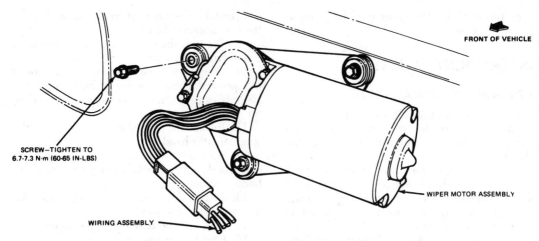

FRONT OF VEHICLE

SCREW—TIGHTEN TO
6.7-7.3 N·m (60-65 IN-LBS)

WIPER MOTOR ASSEMBLY

WIRING ASSEMBLY

Wiper motor installation

14. Install the L.H. linkage on the wiper motor crank pin.

15. Install the R.H. linkage on the wiper motor crank pin and pull the linkage on to the crank pin until it snaps.

NOTE: *The clip is properly installed if the nib is protruding through the center of the clip.*

16. Reinstall the R.H. wiper pivot shaft and nut.

17. Reconnect the battery and turn the ignition "ON." Turn the wiper switch off so the wiper motor will park, then turn the ignition "OFF." Replace the R.H. linkage access cover.

18. Install the R.H. wiper blade and arm.

19. Check the system for proper operation.

Pivot Shaft and Linkage

REMOVAL AND INSTALLATION

1. Perform steps 1 through 8 of the wiper motor removal procedure.

2. Slide the R.H. pivot shaft and linkage assembly out through the R.H. access opening.

3. If the L.H. linkage is to be serviced, remove the L.H. wiper arm and blade assembly.

4. Remove the L.H. linkage access cover.

5. Remove the L.H. pivot nut, lower the linkage and slide it out through the L.H. access opening.

NOTE: *The left and right pivot and linkage assemblies are serviced separately.*

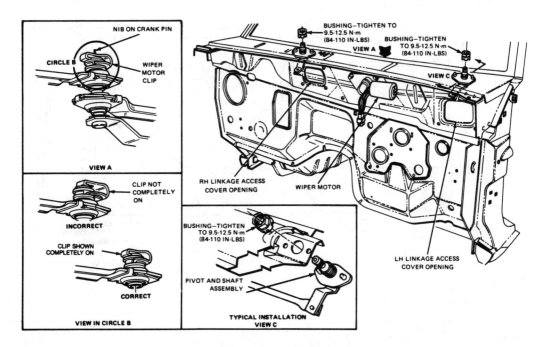

Windshield wiper pivot shaft and linkage assembly installation

6. Installation is the reverse of the removal procedure above.

INSTRUMENT CLUSTER

REMOVAL AND INSTALLATION

1. Disconnect the battery ground cable.

2. Remove the two steering column shroud-to-panel retaining screws and remove the shroud.

3. Remove the lower instrument panel trim.

4. Remove the cluster trim cover from the instrument panel by removing the eight screws.

5. Remove the four instrument cluster to panel retaining screws.

6. Position the cluster slightly away from the panel for access to the back of the cluster, to disconnect the speedometer.

NOTE: *If there is not sufficient access to disengage the speedometer cable from the speedometer, it may be necessary to remove the speedometer cable at the transmission and pull cable through cowl, to allow room to reach the speedometer quick disconnect.*

7. Disconnect the wiring harness connector from the printed circuit, and any bulb-and-socket assemblies from the wiring harness to the cluster assembly and remove the cluster assembly from the instrument panel.

To install:

8. Apply approximately ³⁄₁₆ inch diameter ball of D7AZ-19A331-A Silicone Dielectric compound or equivalent in the drive hole of the speedometer head.

9. Position the cluster near its opening in the instrument panel.

10. Connect the wiring harness connector to the printed circuit, and any bulb-and-socket assemblies from the wiring harness to the cluster assembly.

11. Install the speedometer cable to the speedometer head.

12. Position the cluster to the instrument panel and install the four cluster to panel retaining screws.

13. Install the panel trim covers and the steering column shroud.

14. Connect the battery ground cable.

15. Check operation of all gauges, lamps and signals.

Speedometer Cable Core
REMOVAL AND INSTALLATION

1. Reach up behind the cluster and disconnect the cable by depressing the quick disconnect tab and pulling the cable away.

2. Remove the cable from the casing. If the cable is broken, raise the vehicle on a hoist and disconnect the cable from the transmission.

3. Remove the cable from the casing.

4. To remove the casing from the vehicle, pull it through the floor pan.

5. To replace the cable, slide the new cable

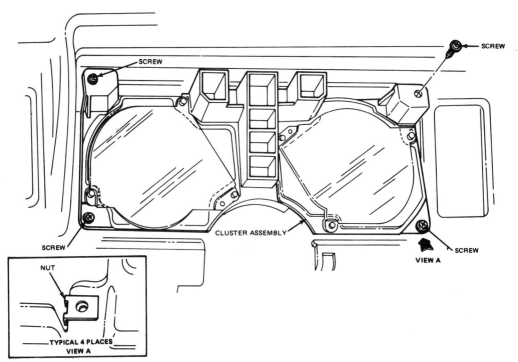

Instrument cluster assembly

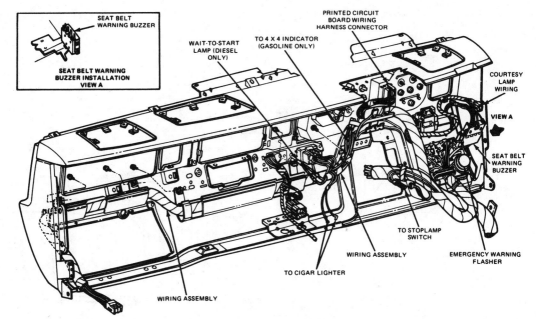

Rear view of the instrument panel

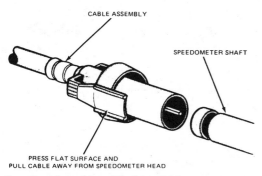

Speedometer cable quick-disconnect

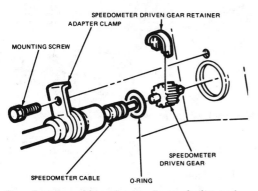

Speedometer cable and gear—transmission end

into the casing and connect it at the transmission.

6. Route the cable through the floor pan and position the grommet in its groove in the floor.

7. Push the cable onto the speedometer head.

Ignition Switch
REMOVAL AND INSTALLATION

NOTE: *The removal and installation procedure for the ignition switch will be found in Chapter 8 under steering for the steering column mounted ignition switch.*

LIGHTING

Headlights
REMOVAL AND INSTALLATION

1. Remove the headlamp door attaching screws and remove the headlamp door.

2. Remove the headlight retaining ring screws, and remove the retaining ring. Do not disturb the adjusting screw settings.

3. Pull the headlight bulb forward and disconnect the wiring assembly plug from the bulb.

4. Connect the wiring assembly plug to the new bulb. Place the bulb in position, making sure that the locating tabs of the bulb are fitted in the positioning slots.

5. Install the headlight retaining ring.

6. Place the headlight trim ring or door into position, and install the retaining screws.

Headlight Switch
REMOVAL AND INSTALLATION

1. Disconnect the battery ground cable.

2. Pull the headlight switch knob to the headlight on position.

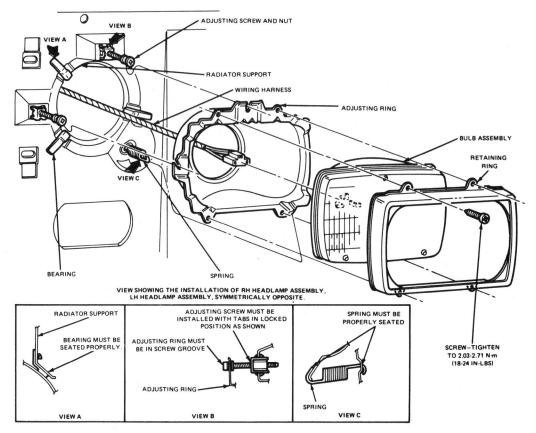

Headlight assembly

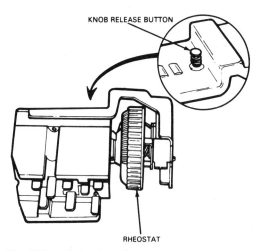

Headlight switch release button

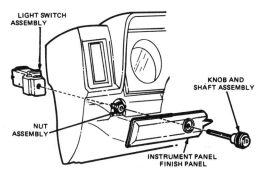

Headlight switch installation

3. Depress the shaft release button and remove the knob and shaft assembly.

4. Remove the instrument panel finish panel.

5. Unscrew the mounting nut and remove the switch from the instrument panel, then remove the wiring connector from the switch.

To install:

6. Connect the wiring connector to the headlamp switch, position the switch in the instrument panel and install the mounting nut.

7. Install the instrument panel finish panel.

8. Install the headlamp switch knob and shaft assembly by pushing the shaft into the switch until it locks into position.

9. Connect the battery ground cable, and check the operation of the headlight switch.

CIRCUIT PROTECTION

Fusible Links

The fusible link is a short length of special, Hypalon (high temperature) insulated wire, integral with the engine compartment wiring harness and should not be confused with standard wire. It is several wire gauges smaller than the circuit which it protects. Under no circumstances should a fuse link replacement repair be made using a length of standard wire cut from bulk stock or from another wiring harness.

REPLACEMENT

To repair any blown fusible link use the following procedure.

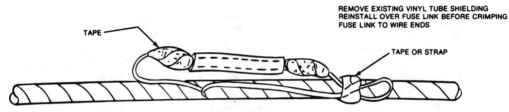

TYPICAL REPAIR USING THE SPECIAL #17 GA. (9.00" LONG-YELLOW) FUSE LINK REQUIRED FOR THE AIR/COND. CIRCUITS (2) #687E and #261A LOCATED IN THE ENGINE COMPARTMENT

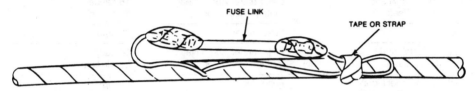

TYPICAL REPAIR FOR ANY IN-LINE FUSE LINK USING THE SPECIFIED GAUGE FUSE LINK FOR THE SPECIFIC CIRCUIT

TYPICAL REPAIR USING THE EYELET TERMINAL FUSE LINK OF THE SPECIFIED GAUGE FOR ATTACHMENT TO A CIRCUIT WIRE END

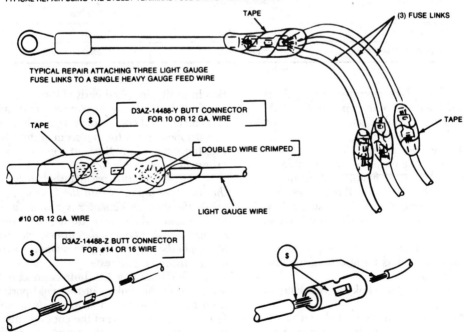

TYPICAL REPAIR ATTACHING THREE LIGHT GAUGE FUSE LINKS TO A SINGLE HEAVY GAUGE FEED WIRE

FUSIBLE LINK REPAIR PROCEDURE

General fuse link repair procedure

Fuses and Circuit Breakers

Circuit	Location	Type of Device
A/C Clutch	Fuse Panel	15 amp.
Air Conditioner and/ or Heater Comb.	Fuse Panel	30 amp.
Alternator	Starter Motor Relay	16 gauge fusible link
Alternator	Electric Choke	20 gauge fusible link
Back-up lamps and Turn Signals	Fuse Panel	15 amp.
Cigar Lighter, Horns	Fuse Panel	20 amp.
Dome, Courtesy, Clock and Glove Box Light	Fuse Panel	15 amp.
Headlights	Headlight Switch	18 amp. circuit breaker
Headlight Switch and Fuse Panel Feed	L.H. Fender Apron Near Voltage Regulator	16 gauge fusible link
Heater	Fuse Panel	30 amp.
Ignition Switch and Fuse Panel Feed	L.H. Fender Apron Near Voltage Regulator	16 gauge fusible link
Instrument Panel Lights, Auto. Trans., Floor Shift Illumination	Fuse Panel	5 amp.
Radio	Fuse Panel	10 amp.
Stop and Emergency Flasher Lamps	Fuse Panel	20 amp.
Tail, Parking, License Lamps	Fuse Panel	15 amp.
Trailer Tow	Starter Relay	16 guage fusible link
Warning Lights	Fuse Panel	15 amp.
Front Windshield Wiper	Fuse Panel	15 amp

1. Determine which circuit is damaged, its location and the cause of the open fusible link. If the damaged fuse link is one of three fed by a common No. 10 or 12 gauge feed wire, determine the specific affected circuit.

2. Disconnect the negative battery cable.

3. Cut the damaged fusible link from the wiring harness and discard it. If the fusible link is one of three circuits fed by a single feed wire, cut it out of the harness at each splice end and discard it.

4. Identify and procure the proper fusible link and butt connectors for attaching the fusible link to the harness.

5. To repair any fusible link in a 3-link group with one feed:

a. After cutting the open link out of the harness, cut each of the remaining undamaged fusible links close to the feed wire weld.

b. Strip approximately ½ inch of insula-tion from the detached ends of the two good fusible links. Then insert two wire ends into one end of a butt connector and carefully push one stripped end of the replacement fuse link into the same end of the butt connector and crimp all three firmly together.

NOTE: *Care must be taken when fitting the three fusible links into the butt connector as the internal diameter is a snug fit for three wires. Make sure to use a proper crimping tool. Pliers, side cutters, etc. will not apply the proper crimp to retain the wires and withstand a pull test.*

c. After crimping the butt connector to the three fusible links, cut the weld portion from the feed wire and strip approximately ½ inch of insulation from the cut end. Insert the stripped end into the open end of the butt connector and crimp very firmly.

d. To attach the remaining end of the replacement fusible link, strip approximately ½ inch of insulation from the wire end of the circuit from which the blow fusible link was removed, and firmly crimp a butt connector or equivalent to the stripped wire. Then, insert the end of the replacement link into the other end of the connector and crimp firmly.

e. Using rosin core solder with a consistency of 60 percent tin and 40 percent lead, solder the connectors and the wires at the repairs and insulate with electrical tape.

6. To replace any fusible link on a single circuit in a harness, cut out the damaged portion, strip approximately ½ inch of insulation from the two wire ends and attach the appropriate replacement fusible link to the stripped wire ends with two proper size butt connectors. Solder the connectors and wires and insulate with tape.

7. To repair any fusible link which has an eyelet terminal on one end such as the charging circuit, cut off the open fusible link behind the weld, strip approximately ½ inch of insulation from the cut end and attach the appropriate new eyelet fusible link to the cut stripped wire with an appropriate size butt connector. Solder the connectors and wires at the repair and insulate with tape.

8. Connect the negative battery cable to the battery and test the system for proper operation.

NOTE: *Do not mistake a resistor wire for a fusible link. The resistor wire is generally longer and has print stating, "Resistor-don't cut or splice."*

NOTE: *When attaching a single No. 16, 17, 18 or 20 gauge fusible link to a heavy gauge wire, always double the stripped wire end of the fusible link before inserting and crimping it into the butt connector for positive wire retention.*

Turn Signal and Hazard Flasher Locations

Both the turn signal flasher and the hazard warning flasher are mounted on the fuse panel on the truck. To gain access to the fuse panel,

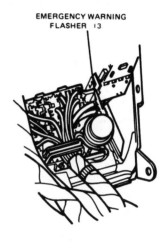

EMERGENCY WARNING
FLASHER 13

REAR VIEW OF FUSE PANEL

Hazard flasher location

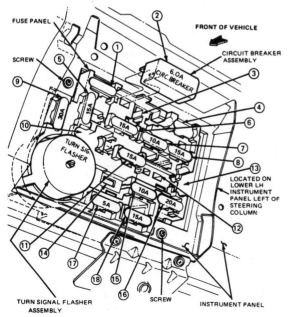

① 15 AMP. FUSE—STOP LAMPS, EMERGENCY WARNING FLASHER

② 6 AMP. C.B.—WINDSHIELD WIPER & WASHER

③ (NOT USED)

④ 15 AMP. FUSE—REAR LAMPS, PARK LAMPS, MARKER LAMPS, LICENSE LAMPS, INSTRUMENT ILLUMINATION, TRAILER LAMPS RELAY

⑤ 15 AMP. FUSE—T/S FLASHER, BACK—UP LAMPS

⑥ 15 AMP. FUSE—4 x 4 INDICATOR, CLOCK DISPLAY, SPEED CONTROL

⑦ 10 AMP. FUSE—DIESEL CONTROL MODULE

⑧ 15 AMP. FUSE—COURTESY LAMPS, DOME LAMP, CLOCK, GLOVE BOX LAMP, "HEAD LAMPS ON" INDICATOR

⑨ 30 AMP. FUSE—HEATER & A/C MOTOR BLOWER, A/C CLUTCH

⑩ (NOT USED)

⑪ 15 AMP. FUSE—RADIO/TAPE PLAYER

⑫ (NOT USED)

⑬ (NOT USED)

⑭ (NOT USED)

⑮ 10 AMP. FUSE—FUEL TANK SELECTOR

⑯ 20 AMP. FUSE—CIGAR LIGHTER, HORNS

⑰ 5 AMP. FUSE—INSTR. PANEL ILLUM. LAMPS, AUTO. TRANS. FLOOR SHIFT ILLUMINATION

⑱ 15 AMP. FUSE—WARNING LAMPS, SEAT BELT BUZZER, CARBURETOR CIRCUITS

Fuse panel

remove the cover from the lower edge of the instrument panel below the steering column. First remove the two fasteners from the lower edge of the cover. Then pull the cover downward until the spring clips disengage from the instrument panel.

The turn signal flasher unit is mounted on the front of the fuse panel, and the hazard warning flasher is mounted on the rear of the fuse panel.

WIRING DIAGRAMS

Wiring diagrams have been left out of this book. As trucks have become more complex, and available with longer and longer option lists, wiring diagrams have grown in size and complexity also. It has become virtually impossible to provide a readable reproduction in a reasonable number of pages. Information on ordering wiring diagrams from the vehicle manufacturer can be found in the owners manual.

MANUAL TRANSMISSION

Identification

There are two manual transmissions in the Ranger. They may appear to visually look the same, however one is a five speed and one is a four speed. They may be identified by checking the transmission code on the Safety Standard Certification Label. The four speed is code X and the five speed is code 5. Both transmissions also have a service identification tag located on the front right side of the transmission case.

SHIFTER AND LINKAGE ADJUSTMENTS

Both the four and five speed transmissions gearshift mechanism is a direct control with the floor shift. The floor shift mechanism is built into the transmission extension housing. There are no adjustments necessary on these transmissions.

REMOVAL AND INSTALLATION

4-Spd. and 5-Spd. Transmissions

1. Shift the gearshift lever in the neutral position.

2. Remove the shifter boot retainer screws. Remove the bolts attaching the retainer cover to the gearshift lever retainer.

3. Pull the gearshift lever assembly, shim and bushing straight up and away from the gearshift lever retainer.

4. Cover the shift tower opening in the extension housing with a cloth to avoid dropping dirt into the transmission.

5. Disconnect the clutch master cylinder push rod from the clutch pedal.

6. Open the hood and disconnect the negative battery cable from the battery terminal.

7. Raise the vehicle and support on jackstand.

8. Disconnect the driveshaft at the rear axle drive flange.

9. Pull the driveshaft rearward and disconnect from the transmission. Install a suitable plug in the extension housing to prevent lubricant leakage.

10. Remove the clutch housing dust shield and slave cylinder and hang it at one side.

11. Remove the speedometer cable from the extension housing.

12. Disconnect the starter motor and backup lamp switch wires.

13. Place a jack under the engine, protecting the oil pan with a wood block.

14. On 4 x 4 models, remove the Borg-Warner 1350 Transfer Case as described later in this chapter.

15. Remove the starter motor. Position a transmission jack under the transmission.

16. Remove the bolts, lockwashers and flat washers attaching the transmission to the engine rear plate.

17. Remove the nuts and bolts attaching the transmission mount and damper to the crossmember.

18. Remove the nuts attaching the crossmember to the frame side rails and remove the crossmember.

19. Lower the engine jack. Work the clutch housing off the locating dowels and slide the transmission rearward until the input shaft spline clears the clutch disc. Remove the transmission from the vehicle.

To Install:

20. Make sure that all the mating surfaces and the locating dowels on the engine rear plate and clutch housing are free of burrs, dirt or paint.

21. Mount the transmission on a transmission jack. Position it under the truck and start the input shaft into the clutch disc. Align the splines on the input shaft with the splines in the clutch disc. Move the transmission forward

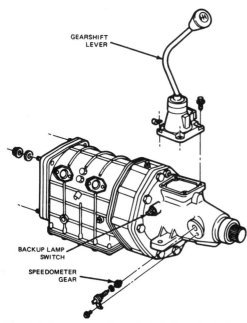

GEARSHIFT
LEVER

BACKUP LAMP
SWITCH

SPEEDOMETER
GEAR

Gearshift lever removal and installation—typical

and carefully seat the clutch housing on the locating dowels of the engine rear plate. The engine plate dowels must not bind in the clutch housing dowel holes.

22. Install the bolts and flat washers that attach the clutch housing to the engine rear plate and tighten to 28–38 ft. lbs. Remove the transmission jack.

23. Install the starter motor. Tighten the attaching nuts to 15–20 ft. lbs.

24. Raise the engine and install the rear crossmember, insulator and damper, and attaching nuts and washers.

25. Install the bolts, nuts and washers attaching the transmission mount to the crossmember. Remove the engine jack.

26. On 4 x 4 models, install the Borg Warner Transfer Case as described later in this chapter.

27. Insert the driveshaft into the transmission extension housing and install the center bearing attaching nuts, washers and lockwashers.

28. Connect the driveshaft to the rear axle

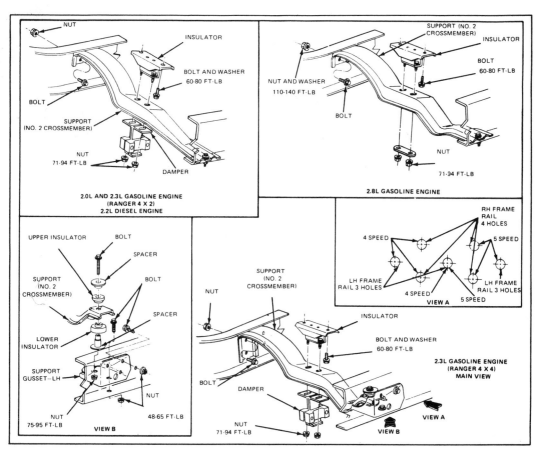

Crossmember removal and installation

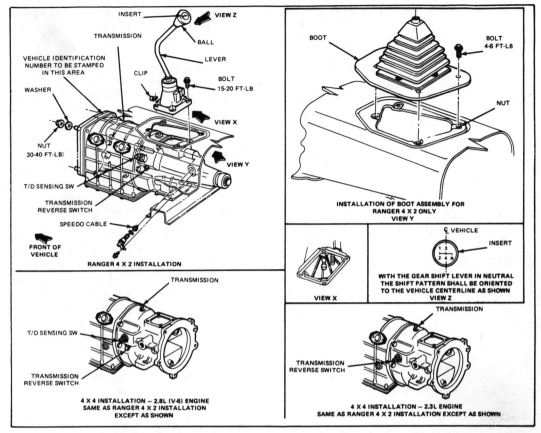

Transmission and gearshift lever assembly—gasoline engine shown, diesel similar

drive flange. Tighten the attaching bolts to 70–95 ft. lbs.

29. Connect the starter and back-up lamp switch wires.

30. Install the clutch slave cylinder and dust shield on the clutch housing.

31. Install the speedometer cable.

32. Check the transmission fluid level at both fill plugs. Fill with specified lubricant if necessary.

33. Remove the jackstands and lower the vehicle.

34. Open the hood and connect the negative battery cable.

35. Re-connect the clutch master cylinder push rod to the clutch pedal.

36. Remove the cloth from the shift tower opening in the extension housing.

37. Position the gearshift lever assembly straight up above the gearshift lever retainer, then insert the gearshift in the retainer. Install the bolts attaching the retainer cover to the gearshift lever retainer and tighten them to 15–20 ft. lbs.

38. Install the cover boot with the retainer screws.

CLUTCH

ADJUSTMENTS

NOTE: *The clutch system on this Ford vehicle is hydraulicly activated. The hydraulic clutch system locates the clutch pedal and provides automatic clutch adjustment. No adjustment of the clutch linkage or pedal position is required.*

REMOVAL AND INSTALLATION

1. Disconnect the clutch master cylinder from the clutch pedal.

2. Raise the vehicle on a hoist and support on jackstands.

3. Remove the dust shield from the clutch housing. Disconnect the hydraulic clutch linkage from the housing and release lever. Remove the starter.

4. Remove the bolts attaching the clutch housing to the engine block.

5. Mark the driveshaft to the companion flange so it may be installed in its original position and remove the driveshaft.

6. Remove the nuts attaching the trans-

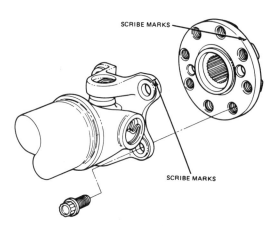

SCRIBE MARKS

SCRIBE MARKS

Marking the driveshaft and flange for correct installation

mission and insulator to the no. 2 crossmember support.

7. Raise the transmission with a transmission jack and remove the no. 2 crossmember support. Lower the transmission and clutch housing.

8. Remove the release lever, and hub and bearing.

9. Mark the assembled position of the pressure plate to the flywheel so it may be installed in its original position if it's not being replaced.

10. Loosen the pressure plate attaching bolts evenly until the pressure plate springs are expanded, and remove the bolts.

11. Remove the pressure plate and the clutch disc from the flywheel. Remove the pilot bearing only if it needs to be replaced.

To install:

12. Position the clutch disc on the flywheel so that the Clutch Alignment Shaft D79T-7550-A or equivalent can enter the clutch pilot bearing and align the disc.

13. When re-installing the original pressure plate and cover assembly, align the assembly and flywheel according to the marks made during the removal operations. Position the pressure plate and cover assembly on the flywheel, align the pressure plate and disc, and install the retaining bolts that fasten the assembly to the flywheel. Torque the bolts to 15–24 ft. lbs., and remove the clutch disc alignment tool.

14. Position the clutch release bearing and the bearing hub on the release lever. Install the release lever on the release lever seat in the flywheel housing. Apply a light film of lithium-base grease to the release lever fingers and to the lever pivot ball. Fill the groove of the release bearing hub with grease.

15. Raise the transmission and clutch housing assembly into position. Install the no. 2 crossmember support to the frame. Install connecting nuts, bolts and washers. Tighten to specified torque as shown in the illustration.

16. Lower the transmission and insulator into the support. Install and tighten nuts. Remove the transmission jack.

17. Install the driveshaft making sure the

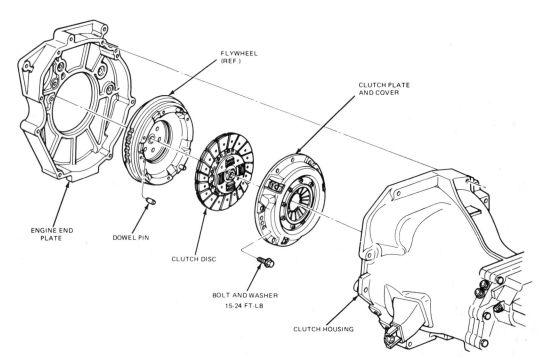

FLYWHEEL (REF.)

CLUTCH PLATE AND COVER

ENGINE END PLATE

DOWEL PIN

CLUTCH DISC

BOLT AND WASHER 15-24 FT-LB

CLUTCH HOUSING

Clutch, flywheel and clutch housing assembly—4-122,140 engines

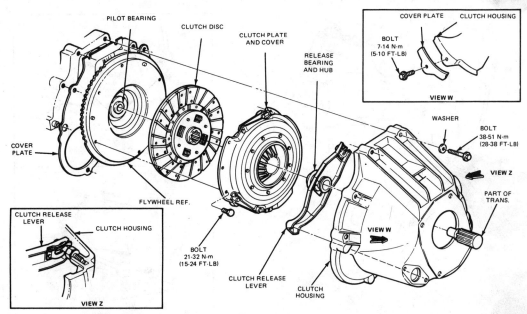

Clutch, flywheel and clutch housing assembly—6-173 engine

index marks on the driveshaft are aligned with the marks on the companion flange. Torque the nuts and bolts to 70–95 ft. lbs.

18. Install the bolts attaching the housing to the engine block in the correct position as removed. Torque the bolts to 28–38 ft. lbs.

19. Install the hydraulic clutch linkage on the housing in position with the release lever. Install the dust shield and install the starter.

20. Lower the truck and connect the clutch hydraulic system master cylinder to the clutch pedal. Check the clutch for proper operation.

Clutch Hydraulic Master and Slave Cylinder

REMOVAL AND INSTALLATION

NOTE: *The clutch hydraulic system is serviced as a complete unit; it has been bled of air and filled with fluid. Individual compo-*

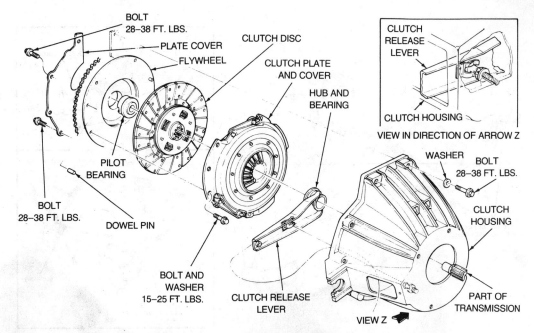

Clutch, flywheel and clutch housing assembly—4-134 diesel engine

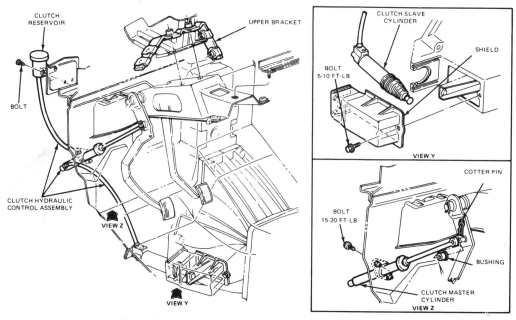

Hydraulic clutch system components—4-122,140 engines

nents of the system are not available separately.

1. Remove the lock pin and disconnect the master cylinder push rod from the clutch pedal.

2. 4-122,140 gasoline engines: Remove the bolt attaching the dust shield to the clutch housing and remove the dust shield. Push the slave cylinder rearward to disengage from the recess in the housing lugs, then slide outward to remove.

6-173 gasoline engine and 4-134 diesel engine: Remove the bolts attaching the slave cylinder to the clutch housing and remove the slave cylinder. Disengage the push rod from the re-

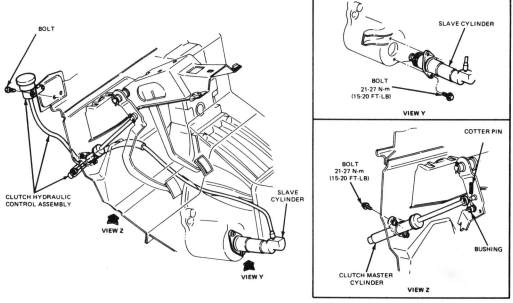

Hydraulic clutch system components—6-173 engine

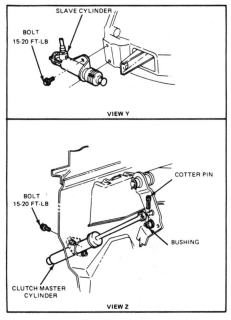

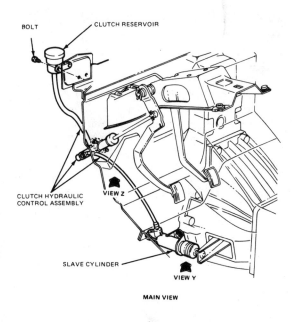

Hydraulic clutch system components—4-134 diesel engine

lease lever as the cylinder is removed. Retain the push rod to release lever plastic bearing inserts.

3. Remove the two bolts attaching the master cylinder to the firewall.

4. Remove the two bolts attaching the fluid reservoir to the cowl access cover.

5. Remove the master cylinder from the opening in the firewall and remove the hydraulic system assembly upward and out of the engine compartment.

To install:

6. Position the hydraulic system downward into the engine compartment. The slave to master cylinder tube routing is to be above the brake tubes and below the steering column shaft.

NOTE: *On 6-173 vehicles, the tube must lay on top of the clutch housing.*

7. Insert the master cylinder push rod through the opening in the firewall, position the master cylinder on the firewall, and install the attaching bolts. Torque the bolts to 15–20 ft. lbs.

8. Position the fluid reservoir on the cowl opening cover and install the attaching bolts. Torque the attaching bolts to 15–20 ft. lbs.

9. Install the slave cylinder by pushing the slave cylinder push rod into the cylinder, engage the push rod and plastic bearing inserts into the release lever, and attach the cylinder to the clutch housing.

NOTE: *With a new system, the slave cylinder contains a shipping strap that pre-posi-*

tions the push rod for installation, and also provides a bearing insert. Following installation of the slave cylinder, the first actuation of the clutch pedal will break the shipping strap and give normal system operation.

10. 4-122,140 engines: Snap the dust shield into position. Install the retaining bolt and tighten to 5–10 ft. lbs.

6-173 gasoline and 4-134 diesel engines: Install the bolts attaching the slave cylinder to the clutch housing and torque them to 15–20 ft. lbs.

11. Clean and apply a light film of oil to the master cylinder push rod bushing and install the bushing and push rod to the clutch pedal. Retain with the lock pin.

12. Depress the clutch pedal at least 10 times to verify smooth operation and proper clutch release.

AUTOMATIC TRANSMISSION

Identification

There are two optional automatic transmissions in the Ford Ranger. They may be identified by checking the transmission code on the Safety Standard Certification Label attached to the drivers side door post. The Ford C3 transmission is code V and the Ford C5 transmission is code W.

PAN REMOVAL AND FILTER SERVICE

NOTE: *For C5 Automatic Transmission (Code W) use fluid that meets Ford Specification ESP-M2C166-H (Type H) or equivalent. The C3 Automatic Transmission uses Dexron II® automatic transmission fluid.*

1. Loosen the transmission pan attaching bolts to drain the fluid from the transmission.

2. When all the fluid has drained from the transmission, remove and thoroughly clean the pan and screen. Discard the pan gasket.

3. Place a new gasket on the pan, and install the pan on the transmission.

4. Add 3 quarts of fluid to the transmission through the filler tube.

5. Check the fluid level.

If it is necessary to perform a complete drain and refill, it will be necessary to remove the remaining fluid from the torque converter and the cooler lines.

To drain the torque converter:

a. Remove the converter housing lower cover.

b. Rotate the torque converter until the drain plug comes into view.

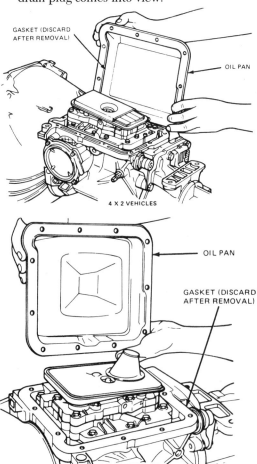

Pan and filter removal and installation

c. Remove the drain plug and allow the transmission fluid to drain.

d. Flush the cooler lines completely.

FRONT BAND ADJUSTMENT

C3

1. Remove the downshift rod from the transmission downshift lever. Clean all of the dirt away from the band adjusting nut and screw area. Remove and discard the locknut.

2. Tighten the adjusting screw to 10 ft. lbs. Back off the adjusting screw exactly two turns.

3. Install a new locknut, hold the adjusting screw in position and tighten the locknut 35–45 ft. lbs. Install the downshift rod.

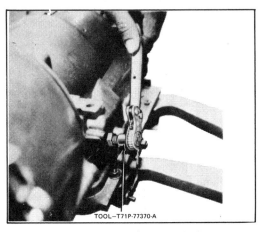

TOOL—T71P-77370-A

Adjusting the front band—C3 transmission

INTERMEDIATE BAND ADJUSTMENT

C5

1. Clean all dirt from the adjusting screw and remove and discard the locknut.

2. Install a new locknut on the adjusting screw. Using a torque wrench, tighten the adjusting screw to 10 ft. lbs.

3. Back off the adjusting screw EXACTLY 4¼ TURNS.

4. Hold the adjusting screw steady and tighten the locknut to 40 ft. lbs.

REAR BAND (LOW-REVERSE) ADJUSTMENT

C5

1. Clean all dirt from around the band adjusting screw and remove and discard the locknut.

2. Install a new locknut on the adjusting screw. Using a torque wrench, tightening the adjusting screw to 10 ft. lbs.

3. Back off the adjusting screw EXACTLY 3 FULL TURNS.

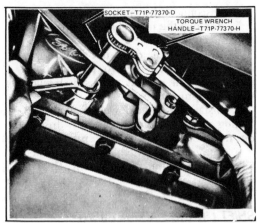

Adjusting the intermediate band—C5 transmission

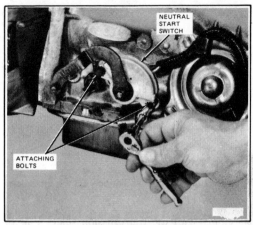

Neutral safety switch location—C5 transmission

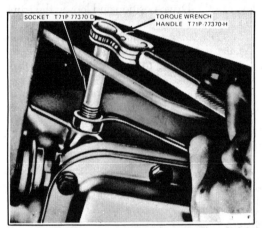

Adjusting the low-reverse band—C5 transmission

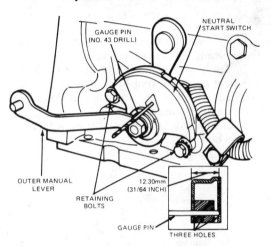

Adjusting the neutral safety switch—C5 transmission

4. Hold the adjusting screw steady and tighten the locknut to 40 ft. lbs.

NEUTRAL SAFETY SWITCH ADJUSTMENT

C5

1. With the automatic transmission linkage properly adjusted, loosen the two switch attaching bolts.

2. Place the transmission selector lever in neutral. Rotate the switch and insert the gauge pin (No. 43 $3/32$ inch drill shank end) fully into the gauge pin holes of the switch. The gauge pin has to be inserted a full $31/64$ inch into the three holes of the switch. Move the switch as necessary to allow the drill to rest against the case.

3. Tighten the two switch attaching bolts 55–75 in. lbs. Remove the drill from the switch.

4. Check the operation of the switch. The engine should start only with the transmission selector lever in "N" or "P".

NEUTRAL SAFETY SWITCH REMOVAL AND INSTALLATION

C3

1. Disconnect the negative cable from the battery.

2. Disconnect the neutral safety switch electrical harness from the neutral safety switch.

3. Remove the neutral safety switch and O-ring using the neutral safety switch socket tool (T74P-77247-A) or equivalent.

CAUTION: Other tools could crush or puncture the walls of the switch.

4. Install the neutral safety switch and O-ring using the neutral safety switch socket tool (T74P-77247-A).

5. Tighten the switch to 7–10 ft. lbs.

6. Connect the neutral safety switch electrical harness to the neutral safety switch.

7. Connect the negative cable to the battery post.

8. Check the operation of the switch with the parking brake engaged. The engine should

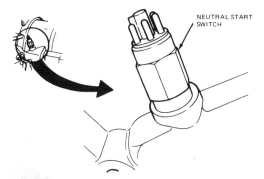

Neutral safety switch installation—C3 transmission

start only with the transmission selector lever in "N" or "P".

C5

1. Remove the downshift linkage rod from the transmission downshift lever.

2. Apply rust penetrant to the outer lever attaching nut to prevent breaking the inner lever shaft. Remove the transmission downshift outer lever attaching nut and lever.

3. Remove the two neutral start switch retaining bolts.

4. Disconnect the multiple wire connector.

5. Remove the neutral start switch from the transmission.

6. Install the neutral start switch on the transmission. Install the two retaining bolts.

7. Adjust the neutral safety switch following the above provedure.

8. Install the outer downshift lever and retaining nut, and tighten the nut. Install the downshift linkage rod with the retaining clips.

9. Connect the wire multiple connector. Check the operation of the switch. The engine should start only with the transmission selector lever in "N" or "P".

SHIFT LINKAGE ADJUSTMENT

1. Position the transmission selector control lever in the Drive position and loosen the trunnion bolt.

NOTE: *Make sure that the shift lever detent pawl is held against the rearward Drive detent stop during the linkage adjustment procedure.*

2. Position the transmission manual lever in the Drive range by moving the bellcrank lever all the way rearward, then forward three detents.

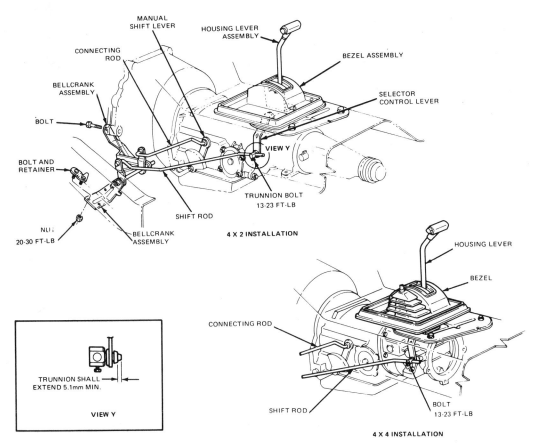

Shift control linkage assembly

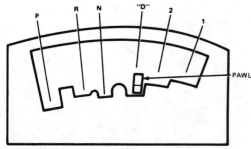

PAWL TO BE AGAINST REARWARD "D" (DRIVE) DETENT STOP

Pawl positioning for the linkage adjustment

3. With the transmission selector lever and manual lever in the Drive position, apply light forward pressure to the shifter control tower arm while tightening the trunnion bolt to 13–23 ft. lbs. Forward pressure on the shifter lower arm will ensure correct positioning within the Drive detent as noted in Step 1.

After adjustment, check for Park engagement. The control lever must move to the right when engaged in Park. Check the transmission control lever in all detent positions with the engine running to ensure correct detent/transmission action. Readjust if necessary.

KICKDOWN ROD

Adjustment

NOTE: *The engine should be at operating temperature whenever kickdown rod adjustments are made.*

1. Place a 6 lb. weight on the kickdown lever.

2. Rotate the throttle to the wide open position.

3. Insert a .060 inch feeler gauge between the throttle lever and the adjusting screw.

4. Rotate the adjusting screw until it makes contact with the feeler gauge. Remove the feeler gauge.

5. After the adjustment has been made a clearance of .001 to .008 inch is acceptable.

6. Remove the weight from the kickdown lever.

AUTOMATIC TRANSMISSION REMOVAL AND INSTALLATION

C3 Transmission

1. Raise the vehicle and safely support on jackstands. Place a drain pan under the trans-

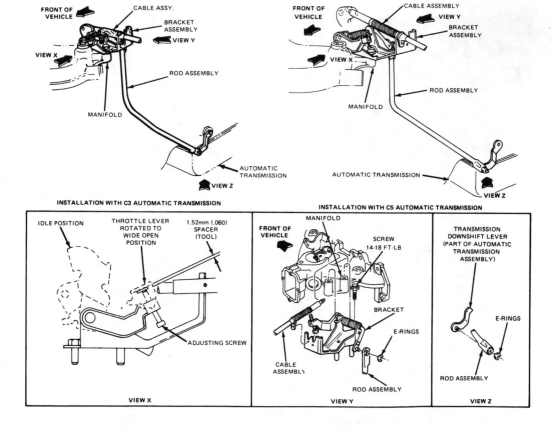

Kickdown rod installation and adjustment

mission fluid pan. Starting at the rear of the pan and working toward the front, loosen the attaching bolts and allow the fluid to drain. Then remove all of the pan attaching bolts except two at the front, to allow the fluid to further drain. After all the fluid has drained, install two bolts on the rear side of the pan to temporarily hold it in place.

2. Remove the converter drain plug access cover and adapter plate bolts from the lower end of the converter housing.

3. Remove the four flywheel to converter attaching nuts. Crank the engine to turn the converter to gain access to the nuts, using a wrench on the crankshaft pulley attaching bolt. *On belt driven overhead camshaft engines, never turn the engine backwards.*

4. Crank the engine until the converter drain plug is accessible and remove the plug. Place a drain pan under the converter to catch the fluid. After all the fluid has been drained from the converter, reinstall the plug and tighten to 20–30 ft. lbs. Remove the driveshaft. Install cover, plastic bag etc. over end of extension housing.

5. Remove the speedometer cable from the extension housing. Disconnect the shift rod at the transmission manual lever. Disconnect the

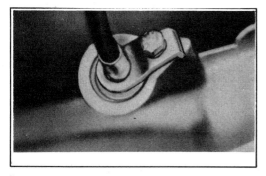

Speedometer cable removal point—C3 transmission

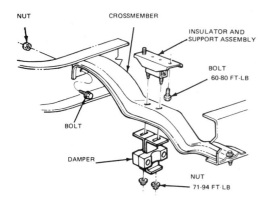

Crossmember removal and installation—C3 transmission

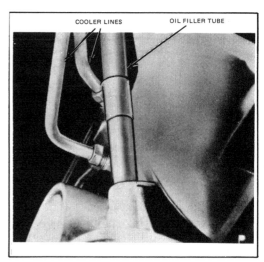

COOLER LINES   OIL FILLER TUBE

Disconnect locations of the oil cooler lines and oil filler tube

downshift rod at the transmission downshift lever.

6. Remove the starter-to-converter housing attaching bolts and position the starter out of the way.

7. Disconnect the neutral safety switch wires from the switch. Remove the vacuum line from the transmission vacuum modulator.

8. Position a suitable jack under the transmission and raise it slightly.

9. Remove the engine rear support-to-crossmember bolts. Remove the crossmember-to-frame side support attaching bolts and remove the crossmember insulator and support and damper.

10. Lower the jack under the transmission and allow the transmission to hang.

11. Position a jack to the front of the engine and raise the engine to gain access to the two upper converter housing-to-engine attaching bolts.

12. Disconnect the oil cooler lines at the transmission. Plug all openings to keep out dirt.

13. Remove the lower converter housing-to-engine attaching bolts. Remove the transmission filler tube.

14. Secure the transmission to the jack with a safety chain.

15. Remove the two upper converter housing-to-engine attaching bolts. Move the transmission to the rear and down to remove it from under the vehicle.

To install:

16. Position the converter to the transmission making sure the converter hub is fully engaged in the pump. With the converter properly installed, place the transmission on the jack and secure with safety chain.

17. Rotate the converter so the drive studs

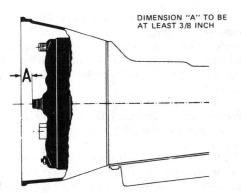

DIMENSION "A" TO BE
AT LEAST 3/8 INCH

Positioning of the converter hub to the bell housing flange—C3 transmission

and drain plug are in alignment with their holes in the flywheel. With the transmission mounted on a transmission jack, move the converter and transmission assembly forward into position being careful not to damage the flywheel and the converter pilot.

CAUTION: *During this move, to avoid damage, do not allow the transmission to get into a nosed down position as this will cause the converter to move forward and disengage from the pump gear. The converter must rest squarely against the flywheel. This indicates that the converter pilot is not binding in the engine crankshaft.*

18. Install the two upper converter housing-to-engine attaching bolts and tighten to 28–38 ft. lbs.

19. Remove the safety chain from the transmission. Insert the filler tube in the stub tube and secure it to the cylinder block with the attaching bolt. Tighten the bolt to 28–38 ft. lbs. If the stub tube is loosened or dislodged, it should be replaced. Install the oil cooler lines in the retaining clip at the cylinder block. Connect the lines to the transmission case.

20. Remove the jack supporting the front of the engine. Raise the transmission. Position the crossmember, insulator and support and damper to the frame side supports and install the attaching bolts. Tighten the bolts to 20–30 ft. lbs.

21. Lower the transmission and install the rear engine support-to-crossmember nut. Tighten the bolt to 60–80 ft. lbs.

22. Remove the transmission jack. Install the vacuum hose on the transmission vacuum unit. Install the vacuum line into the retaining clip.

23. Connect the neutral safety switch plug to the switch. Install the starter and tighten the attaching bolts to 15–20 ft. lbs.

24. Install the four flywheel-to-converter attaching nuts.

When assembling the flywheel to the con-

verter, first install the attaching nuts and tighten to 20–34 ft. lbs.

25. Install the converter drain plug access cover and adaptor plate bolts. Tighten the bolts to 12–16 ft. lbs.

26. Connect the muffler inlet pipe to the exhaust manifold.

27. Connect the transmission shift rod to the manual lever. Connect the downshift rod to the downshift lever.

28. Connect the speedometer cable to the extension housing. Install the driveshaft. Tighten the companion flange U-bolt attaching nuts to 70–95 ft. lbs.

29. Adjust the manual and downshift linkage as required.

30. Lower the vehicle. Fill the transmission to the correct level with the specified fluid. Refer to Chapter 1 under Fluids and Lubricants for the correct procedure. Start the engine and shift the transmission to all ranges, then recheck the fluid level.

C5 Transmission—4 x 2 Models

1. Raise the vehicle and safely support on jackstands. Place the drain pan under the transmission fluid pan. Starting at the rear of the pan and working toward the front, loosen the attaching bolts and allow the fluid to drain. Finally remove all of the pan attaching bolts except two at the front, to allow the fluid to further drain. With fluid drained, install two bolts on the rear side of the pan to temporarily hold it in place.

2. Remove the converter drain plug access cover from the lower end of the converter housing.

3. Remove the converter-to-flywheel attaching nuts. Place a wrench on the crankshaft pulley attaching bolt to turn the converter to gain access to the nuts.

4. Place a drain pan under the converter

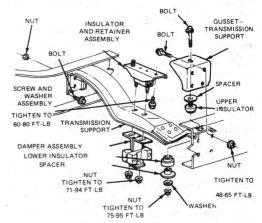

Transmission crossmember—removal and installation

to catch the fluid. With the wrench on the crankshaft pulley attaching bolt, turn the converter to gain access to the converter drain plug and remove the plug. After the fluid has been drained, reinstall the plug.

5. Disconnect the driveshaft from the rear axle and slide shaft rearward from the transmission. Install a suitable cover or plug in the extension housing to prevent fluid leakage. Mark the rear driveshaft yoke and axle flange so they can be installed in their original position.

6. Disconnect the cable from the terminal on the starter motor. Remove the three attaching bolts and remove the starter motor. Disconnect the neutral start switch wires at the plug connector.

7. Remove the rear mount-to-crossmember attaching nuts and the two crossmember-to-frame attaching bolts. Remove the right and left gusset.

8. Remove the two engine rear insulator-to-extension housing attaching bolts.

9. Disconnect the TV linkage rod from the transmission TV lever. Disconnect the manual rod from the transmission manual lever at the transmission.

10. Remove the two bolts securing the bellcrank bracket to the converter housing.

11. Raise the transmission with a suitable jack to provide clearance to remove the crossmember. Remove the rear mount from the crossmember and remove the crossmember from the side supports. Lower the transmission to gain access to the oil cooler lines. Disconnect each oil line from the fittings on the transmission.

12. Disconnect the speedometer cable from the extension housing.

13. Remove the bolt that secures the transmission fluid filler tube to the cylinder block. Lift the filler tube and the dipstick from the transmission.

14. Secure the transmission to the jack with the chain. Remove the converter housing-to-cylinder block attaching bolts.

15. Carefully move the transmission and converter assembly away from the engine and, at the same time, lower the jack to clear the underside of the vehicle.

To install:

16. Tighten the converter drain plug to specifications. Position the converter on the transmission, making sure the converter drive flats are fully engaged in the pump gear by rotating the converter.

17. With the converter properly installed, place the transmission on the jack. Secure the transmission to the jack with a chain.

18. Rotate the converter until the studs and drain plug are in alignment with the holes in the flywheel. Move the converter and transmission assembly forward into position, using care not to damage the flywheel and the converter pilot. The converter must rest squarely against the flywheel. This indicates that the converter pilot is not binding in the engine crankshaft.

19. Install and tighten the converter housing-to-engine attaching bolts to specification.

20. Remove the safety chain from around the transmission.

21. Install the new O-ring on the lower end of the transmission filler tube. Insert the tube in the transmission case and secure the tube to the engine with the attaching bolt.

22. Connect the speedometer cable to the extension housing.

23. Connect the oil cooler lines to the right side of transmission case.

24. Secure the engine rear support to the extension housing and tighten the bolts to specification.

25. Position the crossmember on the side supports. Lower the transmission and remove the jack. Secure the crossmember to the side supports with the attaching bolts.

26. Position the damper assembly over the engine rear support studs. (The painted face of the damper is facing forward when installed in the vehicle.) Secure the rear engine support to the crossmember.

27. Position the bellcrank to the converter housing and install the two attaching bolts.

28. Connect the TV linkage rod to the transmission TV lever. Connect the manual linkage rod to the manual lever at the transmission.

29. Secure the converter-to-flywheel attaching nuts and tighten them to specification.

30. Install the converter housing access cover and secure it with the attaching bolts.

31. Secure the starter motor in place with the attaching bolts. Connect the cable to the terminal on the starter. Connect the neutral start switch wires at the plug connector.

32. Connect the driveshaft to the rear axle so the index marks on the companion flange and the rear yoke are aligned. Lubricate the slip yoke with grease. Adjust the shift linkage as required.

33. Adjust throttle linkage.

34. Lower the vehicle. Fill the transmission to the correct level with the specified fluid. Refer to Chapter 1 under Fluids and Lubricants for the correct procedure. Start the engine and shift the transmission to all ranges, then recheck the fluid level.

C5 Transmission—4 x 4 Models

1. Remove the bolt securing the fluid filler tube to the engine valve cover bracket.

2. Raise the vehicle on a hoist and support with jackstands.

3. Place a drain pan under the transmission fluid pan.

4. Starting at the rear of the pan and working towards the front, loosen the attaching bolts and allow the fluid to drain. Finally, remove all of the pan attaching bolts except two at the front, to allow the fluid to drain further. With fluid drained, install two bolts on the rear side of the pan to temporarily hold it in place.

5. Remove the converter drain plug access cover from the lower end of the converter housing.

6. Remove the converter-to-flywheel attaching nuts.

7. Place a wrench on the crankshaft pulley attaching bolt to turn the converter to gain access to the nuts.

8. Place a drain pan under the converter to catch the fluid. With the wrench on the crankshaft pulley attaching bolt, turn the converter to gain access to the converter drain plug and remove the plug. After the fluid has been drained, reinstall the plug.

9. Disconnect the cable from the terminal at the starter motor. Remove the three attaching bolts and remove the starter motor. Disconnect the neutral safety switch wires at the plug connector.

Remove the rear mount-to-crossmember attaching nuts and the two crossmember-to-frame attaching bolts. Remove the right and left gusset.

10. Remove the two engine rear insulator-to-extension housing attaching bolts.

11. Disconnect the TV linkage rod from the transmission TV lever. Disconnect the manual rod from the transmission manual lever at the transmission. Disconnect the downshift and manual linkage rods from the levers on the transmission.

12. Remove the vacuum hose from the vacuum diaphragm unit. Remove the vacuum line from the retaining clip.

13. Remove the two bolts securing the bellcrank bracket to the converter housing.

14. Remove the transfer case. Refer to Transfer Case, in this chapter for the correct procedure.

15. Raise the transmission with a transmission jack to provide clearance to remove the crossmember. Remove the rear mount from the crossmember and remove the crossmember from the side supports.

16. Lower the transmission to gain access to the oil cooler lines.

17. Disconnect each oil line from the fittings on the transmission.

18. Disconnect the speedometer cable from the extension housing.

19. Secure the transmission to the jack with the chain.

20. Secure the converter housing-to-cylinder block attaching bolts.

21. Carefully move the transmission and converter assembly away from the engine and, at the same time, lower the jack to clear the underside of the vehicle.

22. Remove the converter and mount the transmission in a holding fixture.

To install:

23. Tighten the converter drain plug to 15–28 ft. lbs.

24. Position the converter on the transmission, making sure the converter drive flats are fully engaged in the pump gear by rotating the converter.

25. With the converter properly installed, place the transmission on the jack. Secure the transmission to the jack with a chain.

26. Rotate the converter until the studs and drain plug are in alignment with the holes in the flywheel.

27. Move the converter and transmission assembly forward into position using care not to damage the flywheel and the converter pilot. The converter must rest squarely against the flywheel. This indicates that the converter pilot is not binding in the engine crankshaft.

28. Install and tighten the converter housing-to-engine attaching bolts to 22–32 in. lbs.

29. Remove the safety chain from around the transmission.

30. Install a new O-ring on the lower end of the transmission filler tube. Insert the tube in the transmission case.

31. Connect the speedometer cable to the extension housing.

32. Connect the oil cooler lines to the right of the transmission case.

33. Position the crossmember on the side supports.

34. Position the rear mount insulator on the crossmember and install the attaching bolts and nuts.

35. Install the transfer case. Refer to Transfer Case, in this chapter.

36. Secure the engine rear support to the extension housing and tighten the bolts.

37. Lower the transmission and remove the jack.

38. Secure the crossmember to the side supports with the attaching bolts and tighten the bolts.

39. Position the bellcrank to the converter housing and install the two attaching bolts.

40. Connect the downshift and manual link-

age rods to their respective levers on the transmission.

41. Connect the vacuum line to the vacuum diaphragm making sure that the line is in the retaining clip.

42. Secure the converter-to-flywheel attaching nuts and tighten them to 20–34 ft. lbs.

43. Install the converter housing access cover and secure it with the attaching bolts.

44. Secure the starter motor in place with the attaching bolts. Connect the cable to the terminal on the starter. Connect the neutral safety switch wires at the plug connector.

45. Adjust the shift linkage as required. Refer to shift linkage adjustment, shown earlier in this chapter.

46. Remove the jackstands and lower the vehicle.

47. Position the transmission fluid filler tube to the valve cover bracket and secure with the attaching bolt.

48. Fill the transmission to the correct level with the specified fluid. Refer to Chapter 1 under Fluids and Lubricants for the correct procedure. Start the engine and shift the transmission to all ranges, then recheck the fluid level.

TRANSFER CASE

The transfer case used in the Ford Ranger is the Borg Warner 13-50. It is a two-speed part-time four wheel drive transfer case.

SHIFT LEVER ADJUSTMENT

NOTE: *The Borg Warner 13-50 does not require adjustment.*

REMOVAL AND INSTALLATION

1. Raise the vehicle on a hoist and support on jackstands.

2. Remove the skid plate from frame, if so equipped.

3. Place a drain pan under transfer case, remove the drain plug and drain the fluid from the transfer case.

4. Disconnect the four-wheel drive indicator switch wire connector at the transfer case.

5. Disconnect the front driveshaft from the axle input yoke.

6. Loosen the clamp retaining the front driveshaft boot to the transfer case, and pull the driveshaft and front boot assembly out of the transfer case front output shaft.

7. Disconnect the rear driveshaft from the transfer case output shaft yoke.

8. Disconnect the speedometer drive gear from the transfer case rear cover.

9. Disconnect the vent hose from the control lever.

10. Loosen or remove the large bolt and the small bolt retaining the shifter to the extension housing. Pull on the control lever until the bushing slides off the transfer case shift lever pin. If necessary, unscrew the shift lever from the control lever.

11. Remove the heat shield from the transfer case.

12. Support the transfer case with a transmission jack.

13. Remove the five bolts retaining the transfer case to the transmission and the extension housing.

14. Slide the transfer case rearward off the transmission output shaft and lower the transfer case from the vehicle. Remove the gasket from between the transfer case and extension housing.

To install:

15. Place a new gasket between the transfer case and the extension housing.

16. Raise the transfer case with the transmission jack so that the transmission output shaft aligns with the splined transfer case input shaft. Slide the transfer case forward onto the transmission output shaft and onto the dowel pin. Install the five bolts retaining the transfer case to the extension housing. Torque the bolts to 25–35 ft. lbs. in the sequence shown in the diagram.

17. Remove the transmission jack from the transfer case.

18. Install the heat shield on the transfer case. Torque the bolts to 27–37 ft. lbs.

19. Move the control lever until the bushing is in position over the transfer case shift lever pin. Install and hand start the attaching bolts. First, tighten the large bolt retaining the shifter to the extension housing to 70–90 ft. lbs., then the small bolt to 31–42 ft. lbs.

NOTE: *Always tighten the large bolt retaining the shifter to the extension housing before tightening the small bolt.*

20. Install the vent assembly so the white marking on the hose is in position in the notch in the shifter.

NOTE: *The upper end of the vent hose should be two inches above the top of the shifter and positioned inside of the shift lever boot.*

21. Connect the speedometer drive gear to the transfer case rear cover. Torque the screw to 20–25 in. lbs.

22. Connect the rear driveshaft to the transfer case output shaft yoke. Torque the bolts to 12–15 ft. lbs.

23. Clean the transfer case front output shaft female splines. Apply 5–8 grams of Lubriplate® equivalent to the splines. Insert the front driveshaft male spline.

24. Connect the front driveshaft to the axle

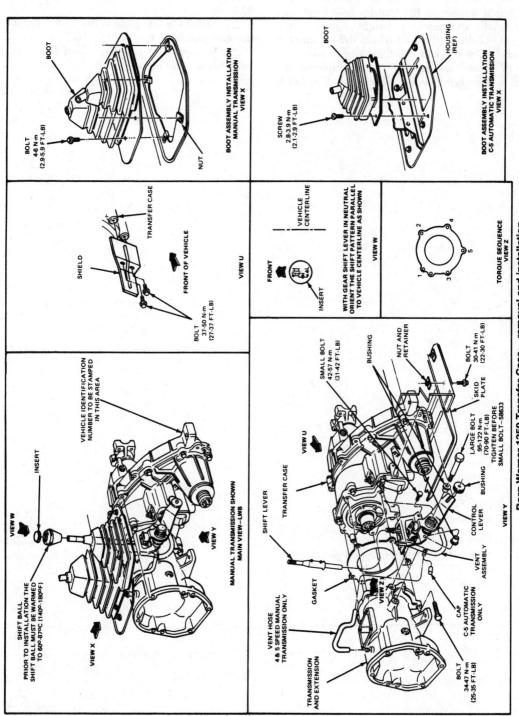

Borg Warner 1350 Transfer Case—removal and installation

input yoke. Torque the bolts to 12–15 ft. lbs.

25. Push the driveshaft boot to engage the external groove on the transfer case front output shaft. Secure with a clamp.

26. Connect the four-wheel drive indicator switch wire connector at the transfer case.

27. Install the drain plug and torque to 14–22 ft. lbs. Remove the fill plug and install 3 U.S. pints of DEXRON®-II, automatic transmission fluid. Install fill plug and torque to 14–22 ft. lbs.

28. Install the skid plate to the frame. Torque the nuts and bolts to 22–30 ft. lbs.

29. Remove the jackstands and lower the vehicle from the hoist.

DRIVE LINE

Front Driveshaft—4 x 4 Models

The driveshaft is a steel tube which is used to transfer torque from the engine, through the transmission output shaft, to the differential in the axle, which in turn transmits torque to the wheels.

Driveshafts differ in length, diameter, and type of slip yoke and axle attachment, to accommodate various wheelbase and powertrain combinations.

The front driveshaft connects the power flow from the transfer case to the front drive axle. It incorporates two single cardan universal joint assemblies, a tube assembly, an axle attachment flange, a slip yoke and a dust slinger/rubber boot assembly.

NOTE: *Every time the vehicle is raised on a hoist, inspect the rubber boot for rips and/or tears. Replace if required.*

REMOVAL AND INSTALLATION

NOTE: *All driveshafts are balanced. Mark the driveshaft in relation to the end yoke so that it may be installed in the original position.*

1. Pull back on the dust slinger to remove the boot from the transfer case slip yoke.

2. Remove the bolts and remove the straps that retain the driveshaft to the front driving axle yoke.

3. Remove the U-joint assembly from the front driving axle yoke.

NOTE: *Do not allow the driveshaft to hang free. Support the driveshaft during removal procedures.*

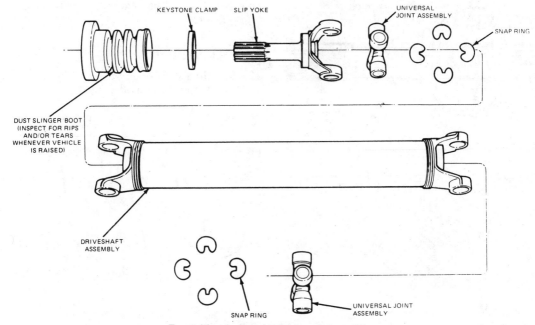

Front driveshaft and U-joints—4x4 models

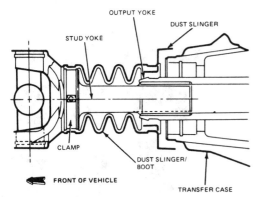

Dust slinger and boot assembly

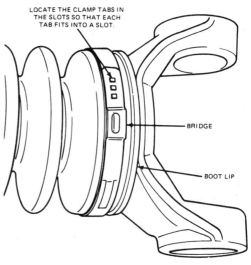

Keystone clamp installation

4. Slide the splined yoke assembly out of the transfer case and remove the driveshaft assembly.

5. Remove the Keystone clamp with end cutter pliers and discard the clamp. Remove the boot from the stud yoke. Inspect the boot and replace if there is any evidence of rips or tears.

6. Inspect the stud yoke splines for wear or damage. Replace if required.

To install:

7. Install the dust slinger/boot assembly on the stud yoke making sure the boot is seated in the groove in the yoke.

8. Install a new Keystone clamp on the boot. Locate the clamp tabs in the slots so each tab fits into a slot. Crimp the clamp securely using Keystone Clamp Pliers, T63P-9171-A or equivalent. Do not crimp to the point where the clamp bridge is cut or the boot is damaged.

9. Apply a light coating of Lubriplate® or equivalent to the yoke splines and the edge of the inner diameter of the rubber boot.

NOTE: *This step is important because it aids in proper dust slinger/boot to output yoke installation.*

10. Slide the driveshaft into the transfer case front output yoke assembly. Make sure the wide tooth splines on the slip yoke are indexed to the output yoke in the transfer case.

11. Position the U-joint assembly in the front drive axle yoke in its original position. Install the bolts and straps. Tighten the bolts to 10–15 ft. lbs.

12. Firmly press the dust slinger until the boot is felt to engage the output yoke in the transfer case.

Rear Driveshaft

The rear driveshaft assembly on all 4 x 2, and 4 x 4 long wheelbase models incorporates two

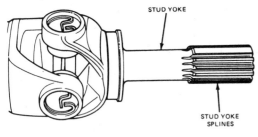

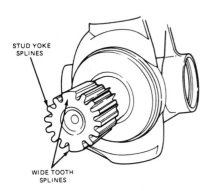

Inspection of the stud yoke assembly

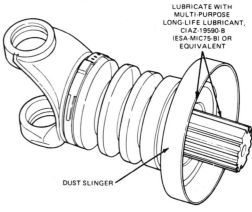

Boot and yoke lubrication points

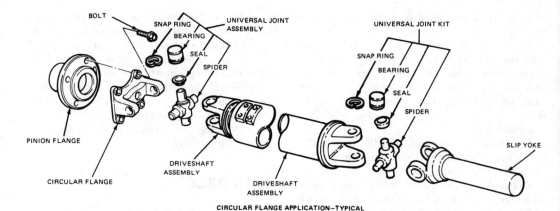

CIRCULAR FLANGE APPLICATION—TYPICAL

Rear driveshaft with single cardan U-joint—All 4x2, and 4x4 long wheelbase models

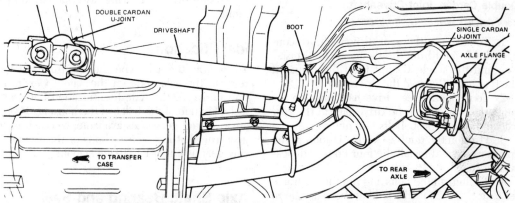

Rear driveshaft with double cardan U-joint—4x4 short wheelbase models

single cardan universal joints, a slip yoke, a tube assembly and axle attachment flange.

The splined slip yoke and transmission output shaft permit the driveshaft to move forward and rearward as the axle moves up and down. This provides smooth performance during vehicle operation.

The rear driveshaft assembly on the 4 x 4 short wheelbase model is of the double Cardan type which incorporates two U-joints, a centering socket yoke, and a center yoke at the transfer case end of each shaft. A single U-joint is used at the axle end of the shafts.

There is only one flush type fitting for the centering device.

All driveshafts are balanced. Therefore, if the vehicle is to be undercoated, cover the driveshaft to prevent undercoating material from getting on the shaft.

REMOVAL AND INSTALLATION
Single Cardan Joint Driveshaft

4 x 2 MODELS

1. To maintain driveshaft balance, mark the rear driveshaft yoke and axle companion flange

so they may be installed in their original positions.

2. Remove the attaching bolts and disconnect the driveshaft from the axle companion flange. Pull the driveshaft toward the rear of the vehicle until the slip yoke clears the transmission extension housing and seal. Install a plastic bag or plug in the extension housing to prevent lubricant leakage.

To install:

3. Lubricate the slip yoke splines with Lubriplate® or equivalent lubricant. Remove the plug from the transmission extension. Inspect the housing seal for damage; replace if required. Install the driveshaft assembly. Do not allow the slip yoke assembly to bottom on the output shaft with excessive force.

4. Install the driveshaft so the index mark on the rear yoke is in line with the index mark on the axle companion flange. This assures original driveline balance.

5. Tighten all circular flange bolts to 70–95 lb. ft.

4 x 4 LONG WHEELBASE MODELS

1. To maintain driveshaft balance, mark the rear driveshaft yoke and axle companion flange

so they may be installed in their original positions.

2. Remove the attaching bolts and disconnect the driveshaft from the axle companion flange. Remove the bolts and straps which attach the driveshaft to the rear of the transfer case. Discard the straps. Remove the driveshaft.

To install:

3. Install the driveshaft into the rear of the transfer case. Install new U-joint retaining straps. Install the bolts and tighten.

4. Install the driveshaft so the index mark on the rear yoke is in line with the index mark on the axle companion flange. This assures original driveshaft balance.

Double Cardan Joint Driveshaft

4 x 4 SHORT WHEELBASE MODELS

1. To remove the rear driveshaft, disconnect the U-joint from the flange at the transfer case and the single U-joint from the flange at the rear axle. Remove the driveshaft.

2. To install the rear driveshaft, position the single U-joint end of the driveshaft to the rear axle and install the U-bolts and nuts.

3. Position the double Cardan U-joint to the transfer case and install the four bolts and lockwashers.

4. Tighten all the bolts and nuts at the transfer case to 20–28 ft. lbs. and at the rear axle to 8–15 ft. lbs.

U-Joints

DISASSEMBLY AND ASSEMBLY

1. Mark the position of the spiders, the center yoke, and the centering socket as related to the stud yoke which is welded to the front of the driveshaft tube. The spiders must be assembled with the bosses in their original positions to provide proper clearance.

2. Remove the snap-rings that secure the bearings in the front of the center yoke.

3. Position the driveshaft in a vise so that the bearing caps that are pressed into the cen-

ter yoke can be pressed or driven out with a drift and hammer. Do this for all of the spiders.

4. Clean all the serviceable parts in cleaning solvent. If you are using a repair kit, install all of the parts supplied with the kit.

NOTE: *If the driveshaft is damaged in any way, replace the complete driveshaft to insure a balanced assembly.*

5. Assemble the U-joints in the reverse order of disassembly.

REAR AXLE

A Ford conventional, integral-carrier type rear axle is used on the Ford Ranger. A Traction-Lok differential is available as optional equipment.

Identification

To identify the axle type used on this vehicle, refer to the axle code on the Safety Certification Label, or the Axle Identification Label attached to one of the bolts on the housing. There are two ring gear sizes available; 6¾ inch ring gear axle that has 8 cover bolts or the 7½ inch ring gear axle that has 10 cover bolts.

Axle Shaft, Bearing and Seal
REMOVAL AND INSTALLATION

NOTE: *The following procedure requires the use of special tools, including a shop press.*

1. Jack up the vehicle and support it on jackstands.

2. Remove the wheel.

3. Working through the hole in the flange, remove the nuts that secure the wheel bearing retainer.

4. Pull the axle assembly out of the axle housing.

5. Whenever an axle shaft is removed the oil seal should be replaced. Install one nut to hold the brake backing plate in place and remove the oil seal with a slide hammer and adapter.

6. If the wheel bearing is to be replaced, the inner retaining ring must be loosened. Never use heat to do this.

7. Nick the retaining ring deeply with a cold chisel in several places. It will then slide off the axle.

8. The use of a shop press is necessary for the removal of the bearing.

To install:

9. Lightly coat the wheel bearing bores with axle lubricant.

10. Press the bearing and then the inner re-

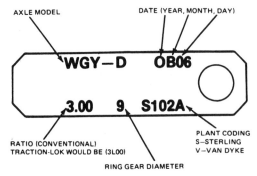

Axle identification tag

taining ring onto the shaft until the retainer seats against the bearing.

11. Install the oil seal with a seal installing tool.

12. Place a new gasket between the housing flange and the backing plate, then carefully slide the axle shaft into the housing so that the rough forging of the shaft will not damage the oil seal.

13. Start the axle splines into the side gear and push the shaft in until it bottoms in the housing.

14. Install the bearing retainer plate and nuts.

15. Install the brake drum and wheel.

FRONT DRIVE AXLE

The front axle installed in the Ford Ranger is a Dana model 28. The axle is equipped with manual or automatic locking hubs.

Identification

The cover on the front of the carrier housing is integral with the left hand axle arm assembly. A manufacturing date code and a complete Ford part number is stamped on the left carrier arm between the fill plug and the end of the axle.

Manual Locking Hubs
REMOVAL AND INSTALLATION

1. Raise the vehicle and install jackstands.
2. Remove the wheel and tire assembly.
3. Remove the retainer washers from the lug nut studs and remove the manual locking hub assembly.
4. To remove the internal hub lock assembly from the outer body assembly, remove the outer lock ring seated in the hub body groove.
5. The internal assembly, spring and clutch gear will now slide out of the hub body.

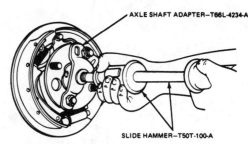

Removing the rear axle shaft

CAUTION: *Do not remove the screw from the plastic dial.*

6. Rebuild the hub assembly in the reverse order of disassembly.

To install:

7. Install the manual locking hub assembly over the spindle and place the retainer washers on the lug nut studs.

8. Install the wheel and tire assembly. Install the lug nuts and torque to 85–115 ft. lb.

FRONT WHEEL BEARING ADJUSTMENT

1. Raise the vehicle and install jackstands.
2. Remove the wheel and tire assembly.
3. Remove the retainer washers from the lug nut studs and remove the manual locking hub assembly from the spindle.
4. Remove the snap ring from the end of the spindle shaft.
5. Remove the axle shaft spacer, needle thrust bearing and the bearing spacer.
6. Remove the outer wheel bearing locknut from the spindle using four-prong spindle nut spanner wrench, T83T-1197-A or equivalent. Make sure the tabs on the tool engage the slots in the locknut.
7. Remove the locknut washer from the spindle.
8. Loosen the inner wheel bearing locknut

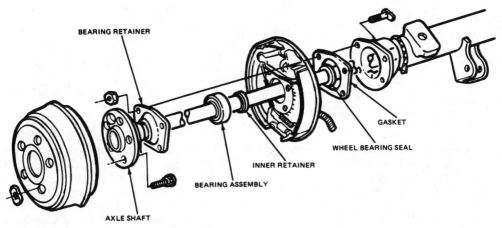

Rear axle shaft assembly

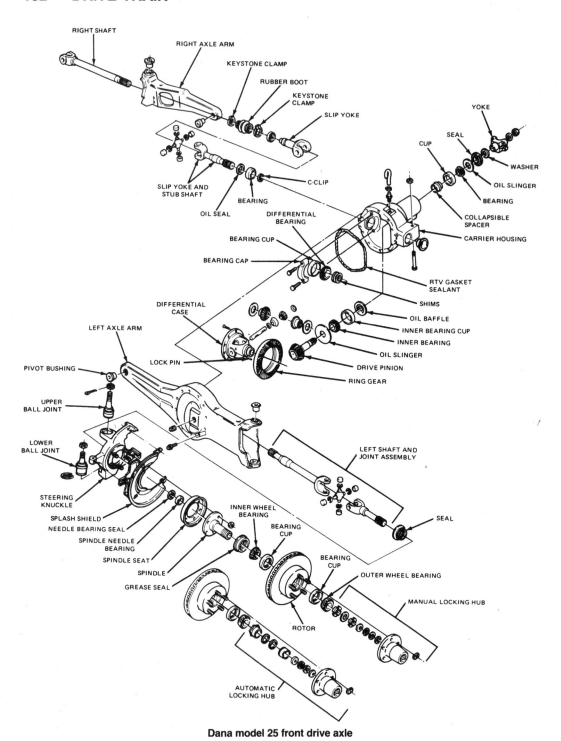

Dana model 25 front drive axle

using four prong spindle nut spanner wrench, T83T-1197-A. or equivalent. Make sure that the tabs on the tool engage the slots in the locknut and that the slot in the tool is over the pin on the locknut.

9. Tighten the inner locknut to 35 ft. lbs. to seat the bearings.

10. Spin the rotor and back off the inner locknut ¼ turn. Install the lockwasher on the spindle. It may be necessary to turn the inner locknut slightly so that the pin on the locknut aligns with the closest hole in the lockwasher.

11. Install the outer wheel bearing locknut using four-prong spindle nut spanner wrench,

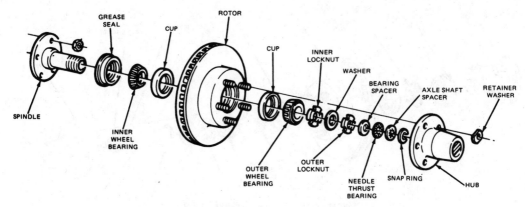

Manual locking hub—Exploded view

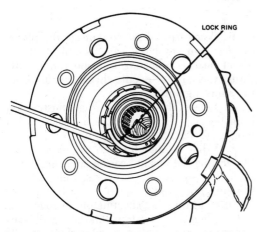

Removing the outer lock ring from the manual locking hub

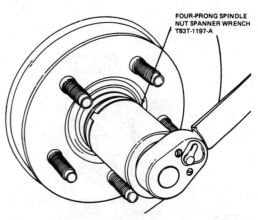

Removing and installing the outer or inner locknut

T83T-1197-A or equivalent. Tighten locknut to 150 ft. lbs.

12. Install the bearing thrust spacer, needle thrust bearing and axle shaft spacer.

13. Clip the snap ring onto the end of the spindle.

14. Install the manual hub assembly over the spindle. Install the retainer washers.

15. Install the wheel and tire assembly. Install and torque lugnuts to 85–115 ft. lbs.

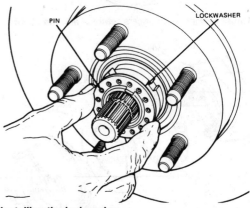

Installing the lockwasher

16. Check the end play of the wheel and tire assembly on the spindle. End play should be 0.001–0.003 inch.

Automatic Locking Hubs

HUB REMOVAL AND INSTALLATION AND FRONT WHEEL BEARING ADJUSTMENT

1. Raise the vehicle and install jackstands.
2. Remove the wheel and tire assembly.

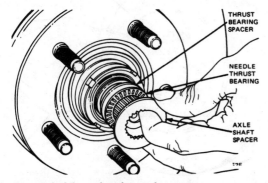

Removal of thrust bearing and spacers

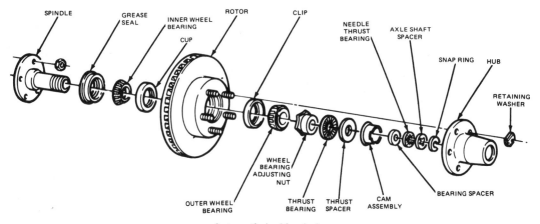

SPINDLE · GREASE SEAL · INNER WHEEL BEARING · CUP · ROTOR · CLIP · NEEDLE THRUST BEARING · AXLE SHAFT SPACER · SNAP RING · HUB · RETAINING WASHER · WHEEL BEARING ADJUSTING NUT · OUTER WHEEL BEARING · THRUST BEARING · THRUST SPACER · CAM ASSEMBLY · BEARING SPACER

Automatic locking hub

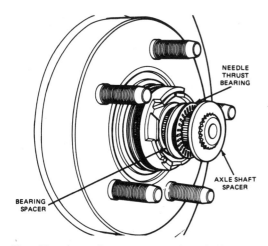

NEEDLE THRUST BEARING · AXLE SHAFT SPACER · BEARING SPACER

Thrust bearing and spacers removal and installation

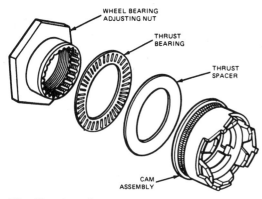

WHEEL BEARING ADJUSTING NUT · THRUST BEARING · THRUST SPACER · CAM ASSEMBLY

Wheel bearing adjustment

3. Remove the retainer washers from the lug nut studs and remove the automatic locking hub assembly from the spindle.

4. Remove the snap ring from the end of the spindle shaft.

5. Remove the axle shaft spacer, needle thrust bearing and the bearing spacer.

6. Being careful not to damage the plastic moving cam, pull the cam assembly off the wheel bearing adjusting nut and remove the thrust washer and needle thrust bearing from the adjusting nut.

7. Loosen the wheel bearing adjusting nut from the spindle using a 2⅜ inch hex socket tool, T70T-4252-B or equivalent.

8. While rotating the hub and rotor assembly, torque the wheel bearing adjusting nut to 35 ft. lbs. to seat the bearings, then back off the nut ¼ turn (90°).

9. Retorque the adjusting nut to 16 in. lbs.

10. Align the closest hole in the wheel bearing adjusting nut with the center of the spindle keyway slot. Advance the nut to the next hole if required.

11. Install the locknut needle bearing and thrust washer in the order of removal and push or press the cam assembly onto the locknut by lining up the key in the fixed cam with the spindle keyway.

12. Install the bearing thrust washer, needle thrust bearing and axle shaft spacer.

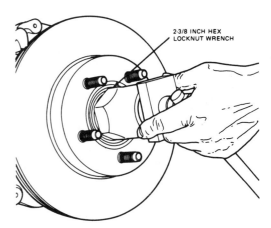

2-3/8 INCH HEX LOCKNUT WRENCH

Wheel bearing adjustment nut

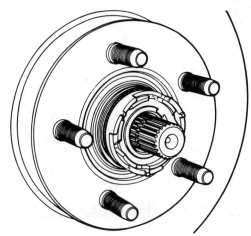

Installing the cam assembly

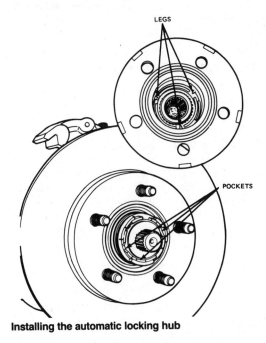

LEGS

POCKETS

Installing the automatic locking hub

13. Clip the snap ring onto the end of the spindle.

14. Install the automatic locking hub assembly over the spindle by lining up the three legs in the hub assembly with three pockets in the cam assembly. Install the retainer washers.

15. Install the wheel and tire assembly. Torque the lugnuts to 85–115 ft. lbs.

16. Final end play of the wheel on the spindle should be 0.001–0.003 inch.

Front Wheel Bearing and Grease Seal

REPACKING AND REPLACEMENT

NOTE: *The following procedure requires the use of several special tools.*

1. Raise the vehicle and install jackstands.
2. Remove the wheel and tire assembly.
3. Remove the retainer washers and remove the manual or automatic locking hub assembly.
4. Remove the brake caliper. Remove the snap ring, axle shaft spacer, needle thrust bearing and the bearing thrust washer from the spindle.
5. Refer to Manual Locking or Automatic Locking Hubs in this chapter for removal.
6. Remove the hub and rotor. Remove the outer wheel bearing cone.
7. Remove the grease seal from the rotor with Seal Remover Tool-1175-AC and Slide Hammer T50T-100-A or equivalent. Discard seal and replace with a new one upon assembly.
8. Remove the inner wheel bearing.
9. Inspect the bearing cups for pits or cracks. If necessary, remove them with Internal Puller D80L-943-A and Slide Hammer, T50T-100-A. or equivalent.

NOTE: *If new cups are installed, install new cone and roller assemblies.*

10. Lubricate the bearings with Disc Brake wheel bearing grease, Ford Specification, ESA-M1C75-B or equivalent. Clean all old grease from the hub. Pack the cones and rollers. If a bearing packer is not available, work as much lubricant as possible between the rollers and the cages.

11. If bearing cups are to be installed, position cups in rotor and drive in place with Bearing Cup Replacer T73T-4222-B and Driver Handle, T80T-4000-W.

12. Position the inner bearing in the inner cup in the rotor. Install the grease seal by driving in place with Hub Seal Replacer, T83T-1175-B and Driver Handle, T80T-4000-W.

13. Carefully install the rotor onto the spindle.

14. Install the outer wheel bearing in the rotor.

15. Refer to Manual Locking or Automatic Locking Hubs—Front Wheel Bearing Adjustment in this chapter for the remainder of installation.

Suspension and Steering

2WD FRONT SUSPENSION

The 2wd suspension is the coil spring, twin I-beam type. It is composed of coil springs, I-beam axle arms, radius arms, upper and lower ball joints, spindles, tie rods, shock absorbers and optional stabilizer bar.

Ranger 2wd suspensions use two I-beam type front axles (one for each wheel). One end of each axle is attached to the spindle and radius arm assembly and the other is attached to a frame pivot bracket on the opposite side of the vehicle.

Each spindle is connected to the axle by upper and lower ball joints. The ball joints have a special bearing material which never requires lubrication.

Spindle movement is controlled by tie rods and the steering linkage.

Springs
REMOVAL AND INSTALLATION

1. Raise the front of the vehicle and place jackstands under the frame and a jack under the axle.

NOTE: *The axle must not be permitted to hang by the brake hose. If the length of the brake hose is not sufficient to provide adequate clearance for removal and installation of the spring, the disc brake caliper must be removed from the spindle according to the procedures specified in Chapter 9 or a Strut Spring Compressor, T81P-5310-A or equiv-*

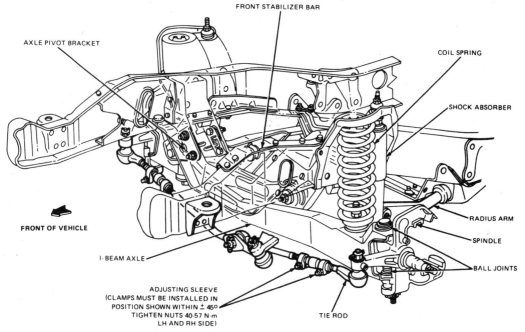

Front suspension assembly—2WD models

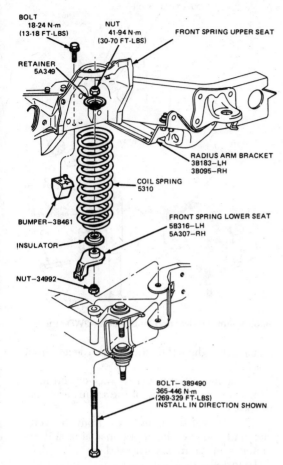

Coil spring removal and installation—2WD models

through the lower spring seat. Rotate the spring so the built-in retainer on the upper spring seat is cleared. Remove the spring.

To install:

5. If removed, install the bolt in the axle arm and install the nut all the way down. Install the spring lower seat and lower insulator.

6. With the axle in the lowest position, install the top of the spring in the upper seat. Rotate the spring into position.

7. Raise the axle slowly until the spring is seated in the lower spring upper seat. Install the lower retainer and nut.

8. Remove the jack and jackstands and lower vehicle.

Shock Absorbers

TESTING

1. Visually check the shock absorbers for the presence of fluid leakage. A thin film of fluid is acceptable. Anything more than that means that the shock absorber must be replaced.

2. Disconnect the lower end of the shock absorber. Compress and extend the shock fully as fast as possible. If the action is not smooth in both directions, or there is no pressure resistance, replace the shock absorber. Shock ab-

alent may be used to compress the spring sufficiently, so that the caliper does not have to be removed. After removal, the caliper must be placed on the frame or otherwise supported to prevent suspending the caliper from the caliper hose. These precautions are absolutely necessary to prevent serious damage to the tube portion of the caliper hose assembly.

2. Remove the nut securing the lower retainer to spring slot. Remove the lower retainer.

3. Lower the axle as far as it will go without stretching the brake hose and tube assembly. The axle should now be unsupported without hanging by the brake hose. If not, then either remove the caliper or use Strut Spring Compressor Tool, T81P-5310-A or equivalent to avoid placing damaging tension.

4. If sufficient slack exists in the brake hose and tube assembly, a long pry bar may be used to remove the coil spring. Insert the pry bar between the two axles and force the appropriate I-beam axle down far enough so that the spring may be lifted over the bolt that passes

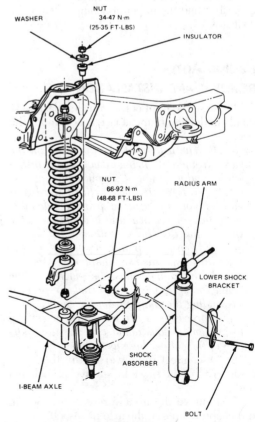

Front shock absorber installation—2WD models

sorbers should be replaced in pairs if they have accumulated more than 20,000 miles of wear. In the case of relatively new shock absorbers, where one has failed, that one, alone, may be replaced.

REMOVAL AND INSTALLATION

NOTE: *Prior to installing a new shock absorber, hold it upright and extend it fully. Invert it and fully compress and extend it at least three times. This will bleed trapped air.*

1. Raise the vehicle to provide additional access and remove the bolt and nut attaching the shock absorber to the lower bracket on the radius arm.

2. Remove the nut, washer and insulator from the shock absorber at the frame bracket and remove the shock absorber.

To install the front shock absorber:

3. Position the washer and insulator on the shock absorber rod and position the shock absorber to the frame bracket.

4. Position the insulator and washer on the shock absorber rod and install the attaching nut loosely.

5. Position the shock absorber to the lower bracket and install the attaching bolt and nut loosely.

6. Tighten the lower attaching bolts to 48–68 ft. lbs., and the upper attaching bolts to 25–35 ft. lbs.

Radius Arm
REMOVAL AND INSTALLATION

1. Raise the front of the vehicle, place jack-stands under the frame. Place a jack under the axle.

NOTE: *The axle must be supported on the jack throughout spring removal and installation, and must not be permitted to hang by the brake hose. If the length of the brake hose is not sufficient to provide adequate clearance for removal and installation of the spring, the disc brake caliper must be removed from the spindle according to the procedures specified in Chapter 9. After removal, the caliper must be placed on the frame or otherwise supported to prevent suspending the caliper from the caliper hose. These precautions are absolutely necessary to prevent serious damage to the tube portion of the caliper hose assembly.*

2. Disconnect the lower end of the shock absorber from the shock lower bracket (bolt and nut).

3. Remove the front spring as outlined in this chapter. Loosen the axle pivot bolt.

4. Remove the spring lower seat from the radius arm, and then remove the bolt and nut

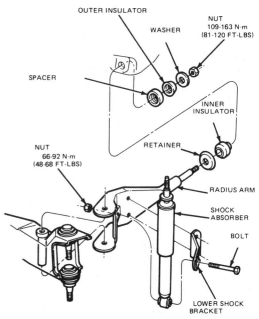

Radius arm removal and installation—2WD models

that attaches the radius arm to the axle and front bracket.

5. Remove the nut, rear washer and insulator from the rear side of the radius arm rear bracket.

6. Remove the radius arm from the vehicle, and remove the inner insulator and retainer from the radius arm stud.

To install:

7. Position the front end of the radius arm to the axle. Install the attaching bolt from underneath, and install the nut finger tight.

8. Install the retainer and inner insulator on the radius arm stud and insert the stud through the radius arm rear bracket.

9. Install the rear washer, insulator and nut on the arm stud at the rear side of the arm rear bracket. Tighten the nut to 81–120 ft. lbs.

10. Tighten the nut on the radius arm-to-axle bolt to 160–220 ft. lbs.

11. Install the spring lower seat and spring insulator on the radius arm so that the hole in the seat goes over the arm-to-axle bolt. Tighten the axle pivot bolt to 120–150 ft. lbs.

12. Install the front spring as outlined in the foregoing procedures.

13. Connect the lower end of the shock absorber to the lower bracket on the radius arm with the attaching bolt and nut with the bolt head installed towards tire, tighten the nut to 48–68 ft. lbs.

Ball Joints and Spindle Assembly
REMOVAL AND INSTALLATION

1. Raise the front of the vehicle and install jackstands.

2. Remove the wheel and tire assembly.

3. Remove the caliper assembly from the rotor and hold it out of the way with wire. Refer to Chapter 9 for this procedure.

4. Remove the dust cap, cotter pin, nut, nut retainer, washer, and outer bearing, and remove the rotor from the spindle.

5. Remove inner bearing cone and seal. Discard the seal.

6. Remove brake dust shield.

7. Disconnect the steering linkage from the spindle and spindle arm by removing the cotter pin and nut.

8. Remove the cotter pin from the lower ball joint stud. Remove the nut from the upper and lower ball joint stud.

9. Strike the lower side of the spindle to pop the ball joints loose from the spindle.

CAUTION: *Do not use a ball joint fork to separate the ball joint from the spindle, as this will damage the seal and the ball joint socket.*

10. Remove the spindle.

11. Remove the snap ring from the ball joints. Assemble C-Frame assembly (T74P-4635-C) or equivalent and receiving cup (D81T-3010-A) or equivalent. Turn the forcing screw clockwise until the ball joint is removed from axle.

12. Assemble the C-Frame assembly and receiving cup on the lower ball joint and turn the forcing screw clockwise until the ball joint is removed.

NOTE: *Always remove upper ball joint first.*
CAUTION: *Do not heat the ball joint or the axle to aid in removal.*
To install:
NOTE: *Lower ball joint must be installed first.*

13. To install the lower ball joint, assemble C-Frame assembly, ball joint receiver cup (D81T-3010-A5) or equivalent and installation cup (D81T-3010-A1) or equivalent inside cup (D81T-3010-A4) or equivalent. Turn the forc-

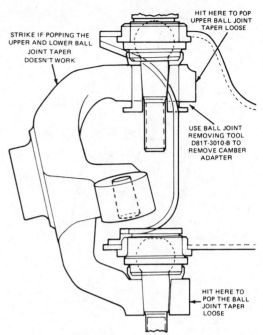

Spindle assembly—removal and installation—2WD models

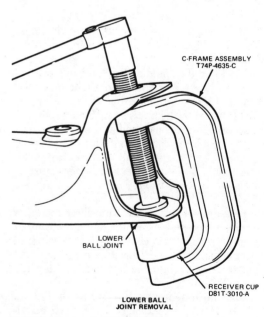

Ball joint removal—2WD models

ing screw clockwise until the ball joint is seated.

CAUTION: *Do not heat the ball joint or axle to aid in installation.*

14. Install the snap ring onto the upper ball joint.

15. To install the upper ball joint, assemble the C-frame and repeat Steps 13 and 14.

NOTE: *A three-step sequence for tightening ball stud nuts must be followed to avoid excessive turning effort of spindle about axle.*

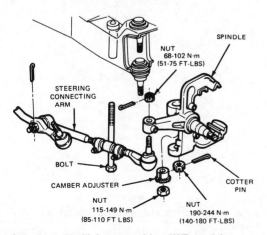

Spindle and balljoint assembly—2WD models

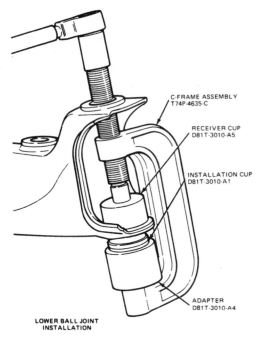

Ball joint installation—2WD models

the cotter pin and dust cap as described in Chapter 9.

25. Install the caliper as described in Chapter 9.

26. Connect the steering linkage to the spindle. Tighten the nut to 51–75 ft. lbs. and advance the nut as required for installation of the cotter pin.

27. Install the wheel and tire assembly. Lower the vehicle. Check, and if necessary, adjust the toe setting. Refer to Front End Alignment in this chapter.

Stabilizer Bar

REMOVAL AND INSTALLATION

1. Remove the nuts and U-bolts retaining the lower shock bracket/stabilizer bar bushing to radius arm.

2. Remove retainers and remove the stabilizer bar and bushing.

To install:

3. Place stabilizer bar in position on the radius arm and bracket.

4. Install retainers and U-bolts. Tighten re-

16. Prior to assembly of the spindle, make sure the upper and lower ball joints seals are in place.

17. Place the spindle over the ball joints. Apply Loctite® or equivalent to the lower ball stud and tighten to 30 ft. lbs. If the lower ball stud turns while the nut is being tightened, push the spindle up against the ball stud.

18. Install the camber adjuster in the upper spindle over the upper ball joint. If camber adjustment is necessary, special adapters must be installed. Refer to Front End Alignment in this chapter.

19. Apply Loctite® or equivalent to upper ball joint stud and install nut. Hold the camber adapter with a wrench to keep the ball stud from turning. If the ball stud turns, tap the adapter deeper into the spindle. Tighten the nut to 85–110 ft. lbs.

20. Finish tightening the lower ball stud nut to 104–106 ft. lbs. Advance nut to next castellation and install cotter pin.

21. Install the dust shield.

22. Pack the inner and outer bearing cones with high temperature wheel bearing grease. Use a bearing packer. If a bearing packer is unavailable, pack the bearing cone by hand working the grease through the cage behind the rollers.

23. Install the inner bearing cone and seal. Install the hub and rotor on the spindle.

24. Install the outer bearing cone, washer, and nut. Adjust bearing end play and install

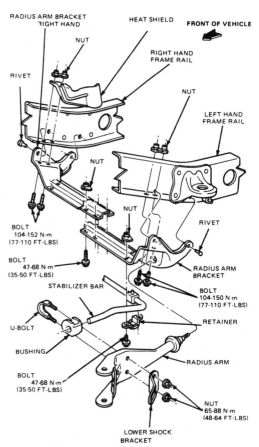

Front stabilizer bar removal and installation—2WD models

tainer bolts to 35–50 ft. lbs. Tighten U-bolt nuts to 48–64 ft. lbs.

Front I-Beam Axle

REMOVAL AND INSTALLATION

1. Remove the front wheel spindle and the front spring, as outlined in the foregoing procedures.

2. Remove the spring lower seat from the radius arm, and then remove the bolt and nut that attaches the radius arm to the (I-Beam) front axle.

3. Remove the axle-to-frame pivot bracket bolt and nut.

4. To install, position the axle to the frame pivot bracket and install the bolt and nut finger tight.

5. Position the opposite end of the axle to the radius arm, install the attaching bolt from underneath through the bracket, the radius arm, and the axle. Install the nut and tighten to 120–150 ft. lbs.

6. Position the axle up against the jounce bumper to place the pivot bushing in proper orientation. Tighten the axle-to-frame pivot bracket bolt to specifications.

7. Install the spring lower seat on the radius arm so that the hole in the seat indexes over the arm-to-axle bolt.

8. Install the front spring as outlined in this chapter.

9. Tighten the axle-to-frame pivot bracket bolt to specified torque.

10. Install the front wheel spindle as outlined in this chapter.

Camber Adapter

REMOVAL AND INSTALLATION

NOTE: *Use the Camber Adjuster Removal Tool, (D81T-3010-B) or equivalent only after the ball joint tapers have been popped loose.*

1. Remove the nut from the upper ball joint stud.

2. Strike the inside of the spindle, to pop the upper ball joint taper loose from the spindle.

3. If the upper ball joint does not pop loose, back the lower ball joint nut about half way down the lower ball joint stud, and strike the side of the lower spindle.

4. Remove the camber adjusting sleeve, us-

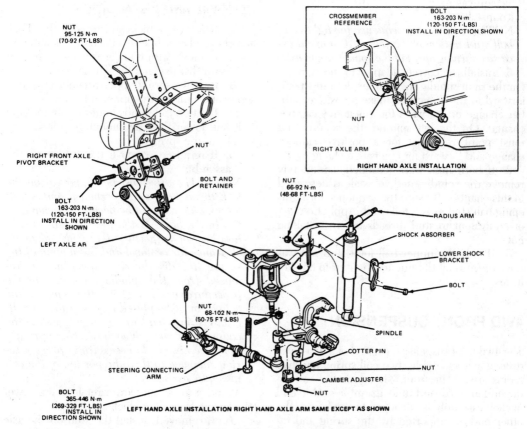

I-Beam axle assembly—removal and installation

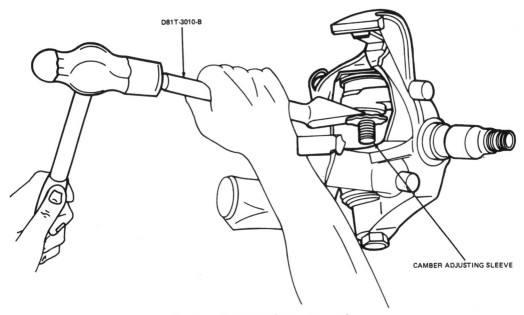

Camber adjustment sleeve—removal

ing Camber Adjuster Removal Tool (D81T-3010-B) or equivalent.

To install:

NOTE: *A three-step sequence for tightening ball stud nuts must be followed to avoid excessive turning effort of the spindle about axle.*

5. Install the correct adapter in the spindle. On the right spindle the adapter slot must point forward in the vehicle to make a positive camber change or rearward for a negative camber change. On the left spindle, the adapter slot must point rearward for a positive camber change and forward for a negative change.

2. If both nuts were loosened, completely remove the spindle, and reinstall as described in this chapter. Be sure the sequence for tightening ball stud nuts is followed. Apply Loctite® or equivalent to stud threads before installing nut.

3. If only the upper ball joint stud nut was removed, install the nut and tighten to 85–110 ft. lbs.

4WD FRONT SUSPENSION

The 4wd front suspension consists of a two-piece driving axle assembly, two coil spring and two radius arms. The front axle consists of two independent yoke and tube assemblies. One end of each assembly is anchored to the frame, the other end is supported by the spring and radius arm.

Springs
REMOVAL AND INSTALLATION

1. Raise the vehicle and remove the shock absorber-to-lower bracket attaching bolt and nut.

2. Remove spring lower retainer attaching nuts from the inside of the spring coil.

3. Remove spring upper retainer attaching screw and remove the upper retainer.

4. Position jackstands under the frame side rails and lower the axle enough to relieve tension from the spring.

5. If required, remove the stud from the axle assembly.

NOTE: *The axle must be supported on the jack throughout spring removal and installation, and must not be permitted to hang by the brake hose. If the length of the brake hose is not sufficient to provide adequate clearance for removal and installation of the spring, the disc brake caliper must be removed from the spindle according to the procedures in Chapter 9. After removal, the caliper must be placed on the frame or otherwise supported to prevent suspending the caliper from the caliper hose. These precautions are absolutely necessary to prevent serious damage to the tube portion of the caliper hose assembly.*

Remove the spring, lower retainer, and lower the spring from the vehicle.

6. If removed, install the stud on the axle and torque to 160–220 ft. lbs.

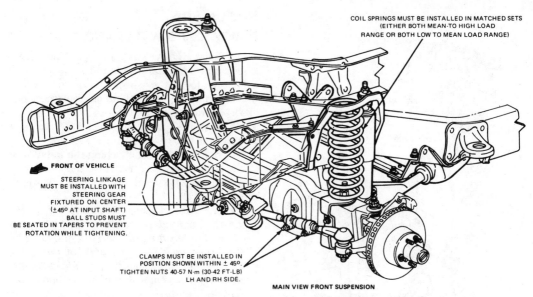

COIL SPRINGS MUST BE INSTALLED IN MATCHED SETS
(EITHER BOTH MEAN-TO HIGH LOAD
RANGE OR BOTH LOW TO MEAN LOAD RANGE)

FRONT OF VEHICLE

STEERING LINKAGE
MUST BE INSTALLED WITH
STEERING GEAR
FIXTURED ON CENTER
(±45° AT INPUT SHAFT)
BALL STUDS MUST
BE SEATED IN TAPERS TO PREVENT
ROTATION WHILE TIGHTENING.

CLAMPS MUST BE INSTALLED IN
POSITION SHOWN WITHIN ± 45°.
TIGHTEN NUTS 40-57 N·m (30-42 FT-LB)
LH AND RH SIDE.

MAIN VIEW FRONT SUSPENSION

Front suspension assembly—4WD models

7. Install the lower seat and spacer over the stud.

8. Place the spring in position and slowly raise the front axle. Ensure springs are positioned correctly in the upper spring seats.

9. Position the spring lower retainer over the stud and lower seat and torque the attaching nut to 70–100 ft. lbs.

10. Position the shock absorber to the lower bracket and install the attaching bolt and nut.

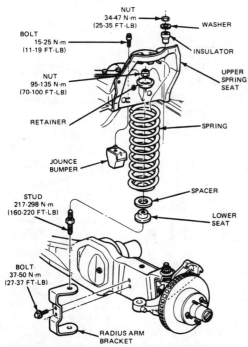

NUT
34-47 N·m
(25-35 FT-LB)

WASHER

BOLT
15-25 N·m
(11-19 FT-LB)

INSULATOR

NUT
95-135 N·m
(70-100 FT-LB)

UPPER
SPRING
SEAT

RETAINER

SPRING

JOUNCE
BUMPER

SPACER

STUD
217-298 N·m
(160-220 FT-LB)

LOWER
SEAT

BOLT
37-50 N·m
(27-37 FT-LB)

RADIUS ARM
BRACKET

Coil spring removal and installation—4WD models

Tighten the bolt and nut to 42–72 ft. lbs. Remove safety stands and lower the vehicle.

Shock Absorbers

TESTING

1. Visually check the shock absorbers for the presence of fluid leakage. A thin film of fluid is acceptable. Anything more than that means that the shock absorber must be replaed.

2. Disconnect the lower end of the shock absorber. Compress and extend the shock fully as fast as possible. If the action is not smooth in both directions, or there is no pressure resistance, replace the shock absorber. Shock absorbers should be replaced in pairs if they have accumulated more than 20,000 miles of wear. In the case of relatively new shock absorbers, where one has failed, that one, alone, may be replaced.

REMOVAL AND INSTALLATION

NOTE: *Prior to installing a new shock absorber, hold it upright and extend it fully. Invert it and fully compress and extend it at least three times. This will bleed trapped air.*

1. Raise the vehicle to provide additional access and remove the bolt and nut attaching the shock absorber to the lower bracket on the radius arm.

2. Remove the nut, washer and insulator from the shock absorber at the frame bracket and remove the shock absorber.

To install the front shock absorber:

3. Position the washer and insulator on the shock absorber rod and position the shock absorber to the frame bracket.

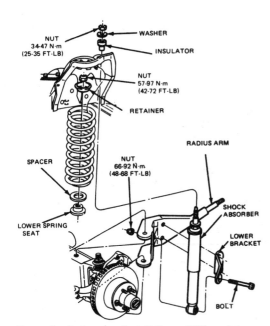

NUT
34-47 N·m
(25-35 FT-LB)

WASHER

INSULATOR

NUT
57-97 N·m
(42-72 FT-LB)

RETAINER

RADIUS ARM

SPACER

NUT
66-92 N·m
(48-68 FT-LB)

LOWER SPRING
SEAT

SHOCK
ABSORBER

LOWER
BRACKET

BOLT

Front shock absorber installation—4WD models

4. Position the insulator and washer on the shock absorber rod and install the attaching nut loosely.

5. Position the shock absorber the lower bracket and install the attaching bolt and nut loosely.

6. Tighten the lower attaching bolts to 48–68 ft. lbs., and the upper attaching bolts to 25–35 ft. lbs.

Radius Arm

REMOVAL AND INSTALLATION

1. Raise the vehicle and position safety stands under the frame side rails.

2. Remove the shock absorber-to-lower bracket attaching bolt and nut and pull the shock absorber free of the radius arm.

3. Remove spring lower retainer attaching bolt from inside of the spring coil.

4. Remove the nut attaching the radius arm to the frame bracket and remove the radius arm rear insulator. Lower the axle and allow axle to move forward.

NOTE: *The axle must be supported on the jack throughout spring removal and installation, and must not be permitted to hang by the brake hose. If the length of the brake hose is not sufficient to provide adequate clearance for removal and installation of the spring, the disc brake caliper must be removed from the spindle according to the procedures specified in Chapter 9. After removal, the caliper must be placed on the frame or otherwise supported to prevent suspending the caliper from the caliper hose. These precautions are absolutely necessary to prevent serious damage to the tube portion of the caliper hose assembly.*

5. Remove the bolt and stud attaching radius arm to axle.

6. Move the axle forward and remove the radius arm from the axle. Then, pull the radius arm from the frame bracket.

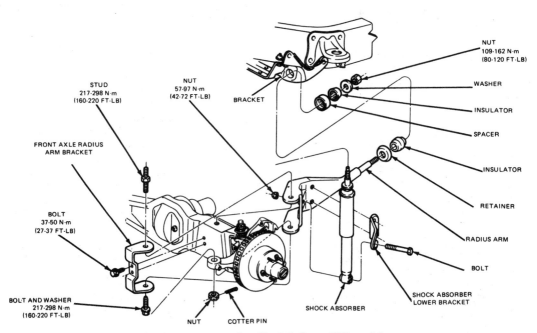

STUD
217-298 N·m
(160-220 FT-LB)

NUT
57-97 N·m
(42-72 FT-LB)

BRACKET

NUT
109-162 N·m
(80-120 FT-LB)

WASHER

INSULATOR

SPACER

INSULATOR

RETAINER

RADIUS ARM

FRONT AXLE RADIUS
ARM BRACKET

BOLT
37-50 N·m
(27-37 FT-LB)

BOLT

BOLT AND WASHER
217-298 N·m
(160-220 FT-LB)

NUT

COTTER PIN

SHOCK ABSORBER

SHOCK ABSORBER
LOWER BRACKET

Radius arm removal and installation—4WD models

7. Position the washer and insulator on the rear of the radius arm and insert the radius arm to the frame bracket.

8. Position the rear insulator and washer on the radius arm and loosely install the attaching nut.

9. Position the radius arm to the axle.

10. Install lower bolt and upper stud-type bolt attaching radius arm bracket to axle. Tighten to 160–220 ft. lb. Install and tighten front bracket bolts to 27–37 ft. lbs.

11. Position the spring lower seat, spring insulator and retainer to the spring and axle. Install the two attaching bolts. Tighten the axle pivot bolt to 120–150 ft. lbs.

12. Tighten the radius rod rear attaching nut to 80–120 ft. lbs.

13. Position the shock absorber to the lower bracket and install the attaching bolt and nut. Tighten the nut to 40–60 ft. lbs. Remove safety stands and lower the vehicle.

Steering Knuckle and Ball Joints
REMOVAL AND INSTALLATION

1. Raise the vehicle and support on jackstands.

2. Remove the wheel and tire assembly.

3. Remove the caliper as described in Chapter 9.

4. Remove hub locks, wheel bearings, and lock nuts.

5. Remove the hub and rotor. Remove the outer wheel bearing cone.

6. Remove the grease seal from the rotor with Seal Remover Tool-1175-AC and Slide Hammer T50T-100-A or equivalent. Discard seal and replace with a new one upon assembly.

7. Remove the inner wheel bearing.

8. Remove the inner and outer bearing cups from the rotor with Bearing Cup Puller, D78P-1225-B or equivalent.

9. Remove the nuts retaining the spindle to the steering knuckle. Tap the spindle with a plastic or rawhide hammer to jar the spindle from the knuckle. Remove the splash shield.

10. On the right side of the vehicle remove the shaft and joint assembly by pulling the assembly out of the carrier.

11. On the right side of the carrier, remove and discard the keystone clamp from the shaft and joint assembly and the stub shaft. Slide the rubber boot onto the stub shaft and pull the shaft and joint assembly from the splines of the stub shaft.

12. Place the spindle in a vise on the second step of the spindle. Wrap a shop towel around the spindle or use a brass-jawed vise to protect the spindle.

13. Remove the oil seal and needle bearing from the spindle with slide Hammer T50T-100-A and Seal Remover, Tool-1175-AC or equivalent.

14. If required, remove the seal from the shaft, by driving off with a hammer.

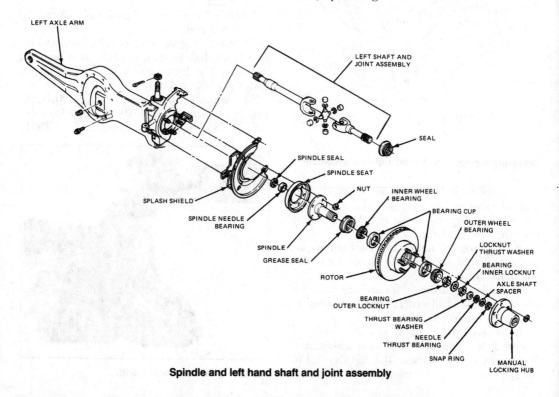

Spindle and left hand shaft and joint assembly

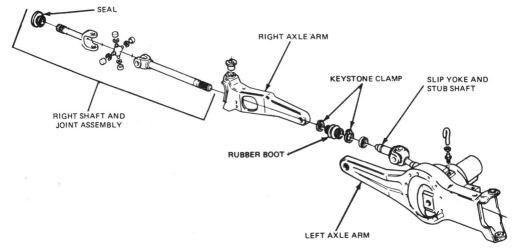

Right hand shaft and joint assembly

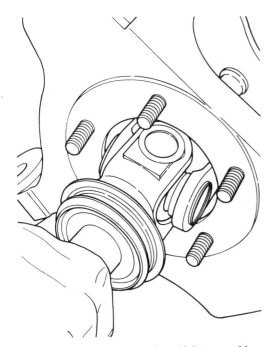

Removing the right hand shaft and joint assembly

15. If the tie rod has not been removed, then remove cotter pin from the tie rod nut and then remove nut. Tap on the tie rod stud to free it from the steering arm.

16. Remove the upper ball joint cotter pin and nut. Loosen the lower ball joint nut to the end of the stud.

17. Strike the inside of the spindle near the upper and lower ball joints to break the spindle loose from the ball joint studs.

18 Remove the camber adjuster sleeve. If required, use Pitman Arm Puller, T64P-3590-F or equivalent to remove the adjuster out of the spindle.

19. Place knuckle in vise and remove snap ring from bottom ball joint socket if so equipped.

20. Assemble the C-Frame, D79T-3010-AA, Forcing Screw, D79T-3010-AE and Ball Joint Remover T83T-3050-A or equivalent on the lower ball joint.

21. Turn forcing screw clockwise until the lower ball joint is removed from the steering knuckle.

22. Repeat steps 20 and 21 for the upper ball joint.

NOTE: *Always remove lower ball joint first.*
To install:
NOTE: *The lower ball joint must always be installed first.*

23. Clean the steering knuckle bore and insert lower ball joint in knuckle as straight as possible. The lower ball joint doesn't have a cotter pin hole in the stud.

24. Assemble the C-Frame, D79T-3010-AA, Forcing Screw, D79T-3010-AE, Ball Joint Installer, T83T-3050-A and Receiver Cup T80T-

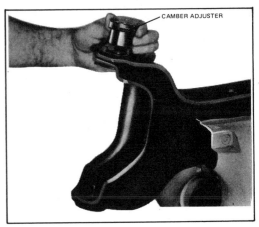

Removing the camber bushing

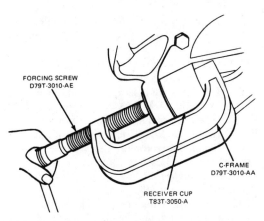

Ball joint removal—4WD models

3010-A3 or equivalent tools, to install the lower ball joint.

25. Turn the forcing screw clockwise until the lower ball joint is firmly seated. Install the snap ring on the lower ball joint.

NOTE: *If the ball joint cannot be installed to the proper depth, realignment of the receiver cup and ball joint installer will be necessary.*

26. Repeat steps 24 and 25 for the upper ball joint.

27. Assemble the knuckle to the axle arm assembly. Install the camber adjuster on the top ball joint stud with the arrow pointing outboard for 'positive camber' and the arrow pointing inboard for 'negative camber' 'Zero' camber bushings will not have an arrow and

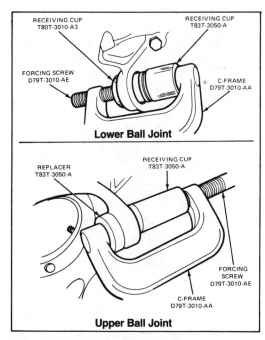

Lower Ball Joint

Upper Ball Joint

Ball joint installation—4WD models

may be rotated in either direction as long as the lugs on the yoke engage the slots in the bushing.

CAUTION: *The following torque sequence must be followed exactly when securing the spindle. Excessive spindle turning effort may result in reduced steering returnability if this procedure is not followed.*

28. Install a new nut on the bottom ball joint stud and tighten to 40 ft. lbs.

29. Install a new nut on the top ball stud and tighten to 85–100 ft. lbs., then advance nut until castellation aligns with cotter pin hole and install cotter pin.

30. Finish tightening the lower nut to 95–110 ft. lbs.

NOTE: *The camber adjuster will seat itself into the spindle at a predetermined position during the tightening sequence. DO NOT attempt to adjust this position.*

31. Clean all dirt and grease from the spindle bearing bore. Bearing bores must be free from nicks and burrs.

32. Place the bearing in the bore with the manufacturer's identification facing outward. Drive the bearing into the bore using Spindle Bearing Replacer, T83T-3123-A and Driver Handle T80T-4000-W or equivalent.

33. Install the grease seal in the bearing bore with the lip side of the seal facing towards the tool. Drive the seal in the bore with Spindle Bearing Replacer, T83T-3123-A and Driver Handle T80-4000-W or equivalent. Coat the bearing seal lip with Lubriplate®.

34. If removed, install a new shaft seal. Place the shaft in a press, and install the seal with Spindle/Axle Seal Installer, T83T-3132-A, or equivalent.

35. On the right side of the carrier, install the rubber boot and new keystone clamps on

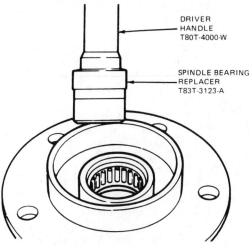

Spindle bearing installation

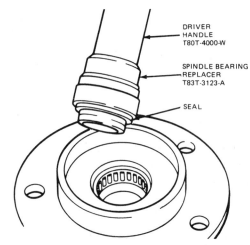

Spindle seal installation

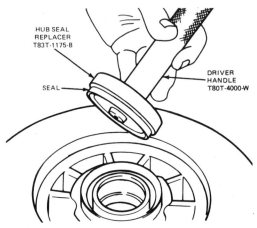

Shaft seal installation

the stub shaft slip yoke. Since the splines on the shaft are phased, there is only one way to assemble the right shaft and joint assembly into the slip yoke. Align the missing spline in the slip yoke barrel with the gapless male spline on the shaft and joint assembly. Slide the right shaft and joint assembly into the slip yoke making sure the splines are fully engaged. Slide the boot over the assembly and crimp the keystone clamp using Keystone Clamp Pliers, T63P-9171-A or equivalent.

36. On the left side of the carrier slide the shaft and joint assembly through the knuckle and engage the splines on the shaft in the carrier.

37. Install the splash shield and spindle onto the steering knuckle. Install and tighten the spindle nuts to 35–45 ft. lbs.

38. Drive the bearing cups into the rotor using bearing cup replacer T73T-4222-B and Driver Handle, T80T-4000-W or equivalent.

39. Pack the inner and outer wheel bearings

and the lip of the oil seal with Multi-Purpose Long-Life Lubricant, C1AZ-19590-B or equivalent.

40. Place te inner wheel bearing in the inner cup. Drive the grease seal into the bore with Hub Seal Replacer, T83T-1175-B and Driver Handle, T80T-4000-W or equivalent. Coat the bearing seal lip with multipurpose long life lubricant, C1AZ-19590-B or equivalent.

41. Install the rotor on the spindle. Install the outer wheel bearing into cup.

NOTE: *Verify that the grease seal lip totally encircles the spindle.*

42. Install the wheel bearing, locknut, thrust bearing, snap ring, and locking hubs.

Stabilizer Bar

REMOVAL AND INSTALLATION

1. Remove the nuts and U-bolts retaining the lower shock bracket/stabilizer bar bushing to the radius arm.

2. Remove the retainers and remove the stabilizer bar and bushing.

3. Place the stabilizer bar in position on the radius arm and bracket.

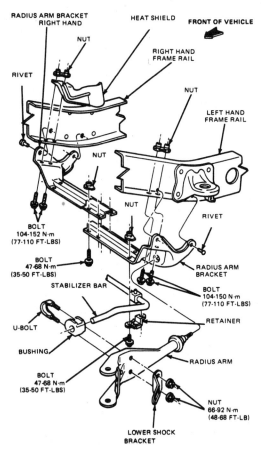

Front stabilizer bar removal and installation—4WD models

4. Install the retainers and U-bolts. Tighten the retainer bolts to 35–50 ft. lbs. Tighten the U-bolt nuts to 48–68 ft. lbs.

FRONT END ALIGNMENT

If you should start to notice abnormal tire wear patterns and handling (steering wheel is hard to return to straight ahead position after negotiating a turn on pavement in 2WD), and misalignment of caster and camber are suspected, make the following checks:

1. Check the air pressure in all the tires. Make sure that the pressures agree with those specified for the tires and vehicle model being checked.

2. Raise the front of the vehicle off the ground. Grasp each front tire at the front and rear, and push the wheel inward and outward. If any free-play is noticed adjust the wheel bearings.

NOTE: *There is supposed to be a very, very small amount of free-play present where the wheel bearings are concerned. Replace the bearings if they are worn or damaged.*

3. Check all steering linkage for wear or maladjustment. Adjust and/or replace all worn parts.

4. Check the steering gear mounting bolts and tighten if necessary.

5. Rotate each front wheel slowly, and observe the amount of lateral or side runout. If the wheel runout exceeds ⅛ in., replace the wheel or install the wheel on the rear.

6. Inspect the radius arms to be sure they are not bent or damaged. Inspect the bushings at the radius arm-to-axle attachment and radius arm-to-frame attachment points for wear or looseness. Repair or replace parts as required.

2WD and 4WD Models

CHECKING CASTER AND CAMBER ANGLES

Caster angles are built into the front axles and cannot be adjusted. On 4x2 models, camber is adjusted by replacing a camber adjuster in the upper ball joint socket. Camber adjusters are available in 0°, ½°, 1° and 1½° increments. On 4x4 models, camber adjustment is provided by means of a series of interchangeable mounting sleeves (camber adjusters) for the upper ball joint stud. Four sleeves are available in ½° camber increments, providing a 3° range of adjustment (from 1½° negative to 1½° positive).

Caster is the number of degrees of backward (positive) or forward (negative) tilt of the spindle (king) pin or the line connecting the ball joint centers. Camber is the number of degrees the top of the wheel tilts outward (positive) or inward (negative) from a vertical plane.

Before checking caster or camber, perform the toe alignment check. Using alignment equipment known to be accurate and following the equipment manufacturer's instructions,

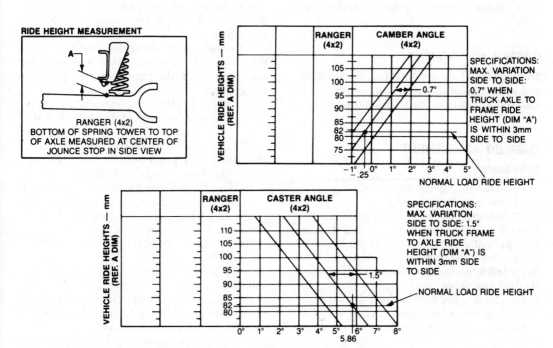

2WD Model—alignment specifications

RIDE HEIGHT MEASUREMENT

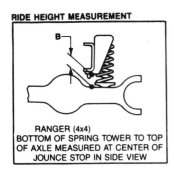

RANGER (4x4)
BOTTOM OF SPRING TOWER TO TOP
OF AXLE MEASURED AT CENTER OF
JOUNCE STOP IN SIDE VIEW

CAMBER ANGLE

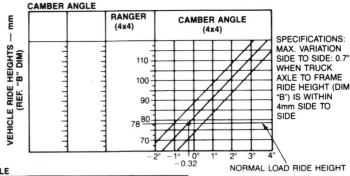

CASTER ANGLE

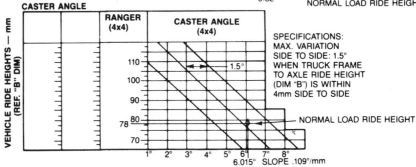

4WD Model—alignment specifications

measure and record the caster angle and the camber angle of both front wheels. Refer to the front wheel alignment charts for specifications.

If the caster and camber measurements exceed the maximum variances, inspect for damaged front suspension components. Replace as required.

NOTE: *Twin-I-Beam axles are not to be bent or twisted to correct caster or camber readings.*

CASTER ADJUSTMENT

The caster angle is designed into the front axle and cannot be adjusted on vehicles equipped with coil spring type front suspensions.

CAMBER ADJUSTMENT

2WD Models

1. Raise the vehicle on a hoist.
2. Remove the front wheels.
3. Remove the upper ball joint nut. Remove the cotter pin on the lower ball stud, and back the nut down to the end of the stud.
4. Strike the spindle near the upper and lower ball joints to break the spindle loose from the ball joint studs.

NOTE: *Be sure to pop the ball joint tapers loose as described above before using the Camber Adjustment Removal Tool, D81T-3010-B.*

5. Use Camber Adjuster Removing Tool,

D81T-3010-B to wedge the camber adjuster out of the spindle.

6. Replace the adjuster with the desired camber adjuster.

• Camber adjusters are available in 0°, ½°, 1° and 1½°.

• To increase camber (more positive), align the slot as follows: on the driver side, point the slot to the rear of the vehicle. On the passenger side, point the slot rearward to the front of the vehicle.

• To decrease camber (more negative), align the slot as follows: on the driver side, point the slot forward. On the passenger side, point the slot rearward.

7. Apply Loctite® or equivalent to the upper ball stud and hand start the upper ball stud nut.

8. Remove the lower ball stud nut and apply Loctite® or equivalent to the lower ball stud.

9. Hand start the lower ball stud nut.

NOTE: *The following torque sequence must be followed exactly when securing the spindle. Improper tightening may result in excessive spindle turning efforts.*

10. Partially tighten the lower ball stud nut to 35 ft. lbs.

11. Tighten the upper ball stud nut to 85–110 ft. lbs.

12. Finsih tightening the lower ball stud nut to 104–146 ft. lbs. Advance the nut to the next castellation and install cotter pin.

13. Install the front wheels and lower the vehicle.

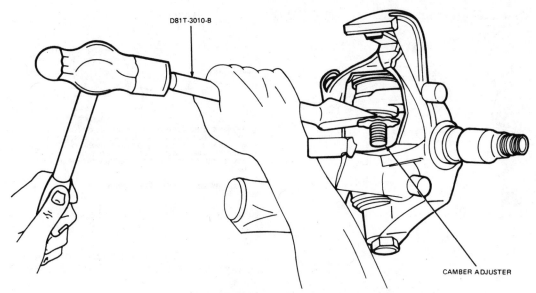

D81T-3010-B

CAMBER ADJUSTER

Removing the camber adjusting sleeve—2WD models

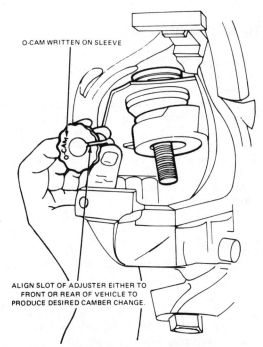

O-CAM WRITTEN ON SLEEVE

ALIGN SLOT OF ADJUSTER EITHER TO FRONT OR REAR OF VEHICLE TO PRODUCE DESIRED CAMBER CHANGE.

Installing the camber adjusting sleeve

4WD Models

1. Raise the vehicle on a hoist and remove the front wheels.

2. Remove the upper ball joint cotter pin and nut.

3. Loosen the lower ball joint nut and back off nut to the end of the stud.

4. Strike the inside of the spindle near the upper and lower ball joints to break the spindle loose from the ball joint studs.

5. Remove the camber adjuster sleeve. If required, use Pitman Arm Puller, T64P-3590-F, to remove the adjuster from the spindle.

6. Install the camber adjuster on the top ball joint stud with the arrow pointing outboard for 'positive camber' and the arrow pointing inboard for negative camber 'Zero' camber bushings will not have an arrow and may be rotated in either direction as long as the lugs on the yoke engage the slots in the bushing.

NOTE: *Excessive spindle turning effort, causing poor steering returnability may result if the fastener tightening sequence described in steps are not followed.*

7. Remove the lower ball joint stud nut and discard.

8. Install a new lower ball joint stud nut and tighten to 40 ft. lbs.

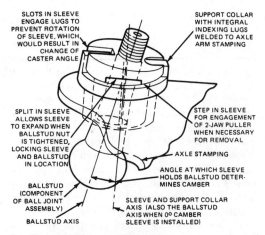

SLOTS IN SLEEVE ENGAGE LUGS TO PREVENT ROTATION OF SLEEVE, WHICH WOULD RESULT IN CHANGE OF CASTER ANGLE

SUPPORT COLLAR WITH INTEGRAL INDEXING LUGS WELDED TO AXLE ARM STAMPING

SPLIT IN SLEEVE ALLOWS SLEEVE TO EXPAND WHEN BALLSTUD NUT IS TIGHTENED, LOCKING SLEEVE AND BALLSTUD IN LOCATION

STEP IN SLEEVE FOR ENGAGEMENT OF 2-JAW PULLER WHEN NECESSARY FOR REMOVAL

AXLE STAMPING

ANGLE AT WHICH SLEEVE HOLDS BALLSTUD DETERMINES CAMBER

BALLSTUD (COMPONENT OF BALL JOINT ASSEMBLY)

SLEEVE AND SUPPORT COLLAR AXIS (ALSO THE BALLSTUD AXIS WHEN 0° CAMBER SLEEVE IS INSTALLED)

BALLSTUD AXIS

Camber adjustment—4WD models

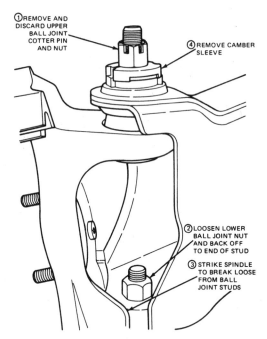

① REMOVE AND DISCARD UPPER BALL JOINT COTTER PIN AND NUT

④ REMOVE CAMBER SLEEVE

② LOOSEN LOWER BALL JOINT NUT AND BACK OFF TO END OF STUD

③ STRIKE SPINDLE TO BREAK LOOSE FROM BALL JOINT STUDS

Camber adjusting sleeve removal—4WD models

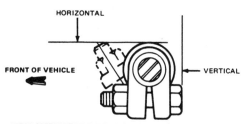

HORIZONTAL

FRONT OF VEHICLE

VERTICAL

AFTER SETTING TOE, THE TWO CLAMP BOLTS/NUTS ON EACH ADJUSTING SLEEVE MUST BE POSITIONED WITHIN A LIMIT OF ± 45 DEGREES AS SHOWN WITH THE THREADED END OF THE BOLTS ON BOTH ADJUSTING SLEEVES POINTING TOWARDS THE FRONT OF THE VEHICLE.

Toe alignment clamp positioning

Rotate the connecting rod tube until the correct toe-in is obtained, then tighten the clamp bolts.

2. Recheck the toe-in to make sure that no changes occurred when the bolts were tightened.

3. Normal toe setting is $\frac{1}{32}$ in. Range is $\frac{3}{32}$ out—$\frac{5}{32}$ inch in.

REAR SUSPENSION

Semi-elliptic leaf springs are used on the rear axle suspension. The springs are mounted outside the frame members, and are attached to the axle with two U-bolts. The front end of each spring is attached to a hanger, which is part of the frame side member, with a bolt and nut. The rear end of the spring is attached to a shackle assembly with a bolt and nut and the shackle assembly is attached to a hanger.

The shock absorbers are attached to a bracket which is part of the axle tube and extend up to an upper bracket at a slight rearward angle.

Springs

REMOVAL AND INSTALLATION

1. Raise the vehicle and install jackstands under the frame. The vehicle must be supported in such a way that the rear axle hangs free with the tire a few inches off the ground. Place a hydraulic floor jack under the center of the axle housing.

2. Disconnect the shock absorber from the axle.

3. Remove the U-bolt attaching nuts and remove the two U-bolts and the spring clip plate.

4. Lower the axle to relieve the spring tension and remove the nut from the spring front attaching bolt.

5. Remove the spring front attaching bolt from the spring and hanger with a drift.

6. Remove the nut from the shackle-to-hanger attaching bolt and drive the bolt from

9. Install a new nut on the top ball joint stud and tighten to 85–100 ft. lbs., then advance nut until castellation aligns with cotter pin hole and install cotter pin.

10. Finish tightening the lower nut to 95–110 ft. lbs.

NOTE: *The camber adjuster will seat itself in the spindle at a pre-determined position during the tightening sequence. Do not attempt to adjust this position.*

11. Reinstall the wheels and lower the vehicle.

12. Recheck the camber and adjust toe-in as described in this chapter.

TOE-IN ADJUSTMENT

Toe-in can be measured by either a front end alignment machine or by the following method:

With the front wheels in the straight ahead position, measure the distance between the extreme front and the extreme rear of the front wheels. In other words, measure the distance across the undercarriage of the vehicle between the two front edges and the two rear edges of the two front wheels. Both of these measurements (front and rear of the two wheels) must be taken at an equal distance from the floor and at the approximate centerline of the spindle. The difference between these two distances is the amount that the wheels toe-in or toe-out. The wheels should always be adjusted to toe-in according to specifications.

1. Loosen the clamp bolts at each end of the left tie-rod, seen from the front of the vehicle.

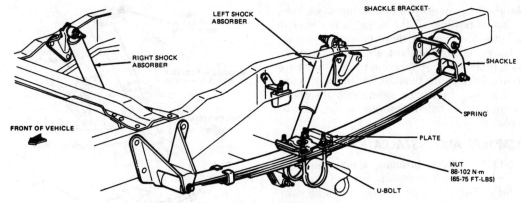

Rear suspension assembly

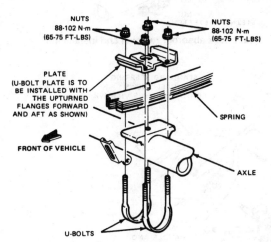

U-bolt and spring plate assembly

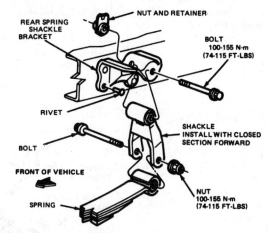

Spring to rear shackle assembly

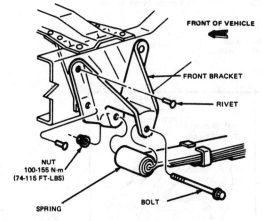

Spring to front bracket assembly

the shackle and hanger with a drift and remove the spring from the vehicle.

7. Remove the nut from the spring rear attaching bolt. Drive the bolt out of the spring and shackle with a drift.

To install the rear spring:

8. Position the shackle to the spring rear eye and install the bolt and nut.

9. Position the spring front eye and bushing to the spring front hanger, and install the attaching bolt and nut.

10. Position the spring rear eye and bushing to the shackle, and install the attaching bolt and nut.

11. Raise the axle to the spring and install the U-bolts and spring clip plate.

12. Remove the jackstands and lower the vehicle.

13. Torque the spring U-bolt nuts to 65–75 ft. lbs. Torque the front spring bolt and nut to 75–115 ft. lbs. and the rear shackle bolts and nuts to 75–115 ft. lbs.

Shock Absorbers

TESTING

1. Visually check the shock absorbers for the presence of fluid leakage. A thin film of fluid is acceptable. Anything more than that means that the shock absorber must be replaced.

2. Disconnect the lower end of the shock

absorber. Compress and extend the shock fully, as fast as possible. If the action is not smooth in both directions, or there is no pressure resistance, replace the shock absorber. Shock absorbers should be replaced in pairs if they have accumulated more than 20,000 miles of wear. In the case of relatively new shock absorbers, where one has failed, that one, alone, may be replaced.

REMOVAL AND INSTALLATION

NOTE: *Prior to installing a new shock absorber, hold it right side up and extend it fully. Turn it upside down and fully compress and extend it at least three times. This will bleed any trapped air.*

1. Raise the vehicle and place jackstands under the axle.

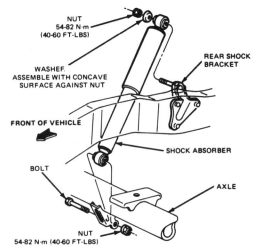

Rear shock absorber removal and installation

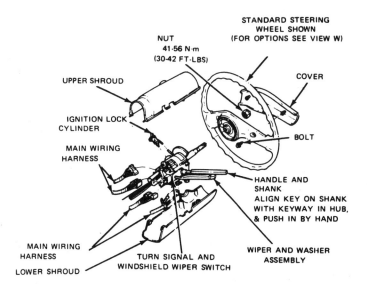

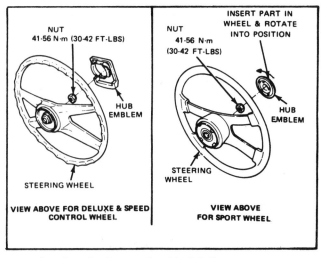

Steering wheel removal and installation

2. Remove the shock absorber-to-upper bracket attaching nut and washers, and bushing from the shock absorber rod.

3. Remove the shock absorber-to-axle attaching bolt. Drive the bolts from the axle bracket and shock absorber with a brass drift and remove the shock absorber.

4. Position the washers and bushing on the shock absorber rod and position the shock absorber at the upper bracket.

5. Position the bushing and washers on the shock absorber rod and install the attaching nut loosely.

6. Position the shock absorber at the axle housing bracket and install the attaching bolt and nut. Tighten the upper and lower nuts to 40–60 ft. lbs.

STEERING

Steering Wheel
REMOVAL AND INSTALLATION

1. Remove the steering wheel hub cover by removing the screws from the spokes and lifting the steering wheel hub cover. On the deluxe wheel, pop the hub emblem off. On sport wheels, unscrew the hub emblem.

2. Disconnect the horn switch wires by pulling the spoke terminal from the blade connectors. On vehicles equipped with speed control, squeeze or pinch the "J" clip ground wire terminal firmly and pull it out of the hole in the steering wheel. Do not pull the ground terminal out of the threaded hole without squeezing the terminal clip to relieve the spring retention of the terminal in the threaded hole.

3. Remove the horn switch assembly and disconnect the horn and speed control wire (if so equipped).

4. Remove the steering wheel attaching nut.

5. Using a steering wheel puller, remove the steering wheel from the upper steering shaft. Do not use a knock-off type steering wheel puller or strike the end of the steering column upper shaft with a hammer. This could cause damage to the steering shaft bearing.

To install:

6. Position the steering wheel on the end of the steering wheel shaft. Align the mark and the flats on the steering wheel with the mark and the flats on the shaft, assuring that the straight ahead steering wheel position corresponds to the straight ahead position of the front wheels.

7. Install the wheel nut. Tighten the nut to 30–40 ft. lbs.

8. Install the horn switch assembly and connect the horn and speed control wire (if so equipped).

9. Install the cover or trim emblem.

10. Check the steering column for proper operation.

Turn Signal/Hazard Flasher Switch Assembly

CAUTION: *The corrugated outer tube steering shaft column uper support bracket assembly and shrouds affect energy absorption on impact. It is absolutely necessary to handle these components with care when performing any service operation.*

REMOVAL AND INSTALLATION

1. For tilt column only, remove the upper extension shroud by squeezing it at the six and twelve o'clock positions and popping it free of the retaining plate at the three o'clock position.

2. Remove the two trim shroud havles by removing the two attaching screws.

3. Remove the turn signal switch lever by grasping the lever and by using a pulling and twisting motion of the hand while pulling the lever straight out from the switch.

4. Peel back the foam sight shield from the turn signal switch.

5. Disconnect the two turn signal switch electrical connectors.

6. Remove the two self-tapping screws attaching the turn signal switch to the lock cylinder housing. Disengage the switch from the housing.

To install:

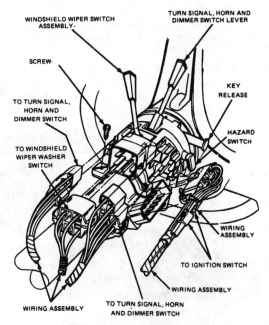

Column mounted switch wiring connections

7. Align the turn signal switch mounting holes with the corresponding holes in the lock cylinder housing, and install two self-tapping screws.

8. Stick the foam sight shield to the turn signal switch.

9. Install the turn signal switch lever into the switch manually, by aligning the key on the lever with the keyway in the switch and by pushing the lever toward the switch to full engagement.

10. Install the two turn signal switch electrical connectors to full engagement.

11. Install the steering column trim shrouds.

Ignition Switch

REMOVAL AND INSTALLATION

1. Rotate the lock cylinder key to the Lock position. Disconnect the negative battery cable from the battery.

2. For tilt column only, remove the upper extension shroud by squeezing it at the six and twelve o'clock positions and popping it free of the retaining plate at the three o'clock position.

3. Remove the two trim shroud havles by removing the two attaching screws.

4. Disconnect the ignition switch electrical connector.

5. Drill out the break-off head bolts connecting the switch to the lock cylinder housing by using a ⅛ inch drill.

6. Remove the two bolts, using an Ex-3 "easy-out" tool or equivalent.

7. Disengage the ignition switch from the actuator pin.

To install:

8. Rotate the ignition key to the RUN position (approximately 90 degrees clockwise from Lock).

9. Install the replacement switch by aligning the holes on the switch casting base with the holes in the lock cylinder housing. Note that the replacement switch is provided in the Run position. Minor movement of the lock cylinder to align the actuator pin with the "U" shaped slot in the switch carrier may be required.

10. Install the new break-off-head bolts and tighten until heads shear off (approximately 35–50 in. lbs.).

11. Connect the electrical connector to the ignition switch.

12. Connect the negative battery cable to the battery terminal. Check the ignition switch for proper operation in all modes.

13. Install the steering column trim shrouds.

Ignition Lock Cylinder Assembly

NOTE: *The following procedure pertains to vehicles that have functional lock cylinders. Ignition keys are available for these vehicles, or the ignition key numbers are known and the proper key can be made.*

If the ignition lock is inoperative, and the lock cylinder cannot be rotated, the repair should be refered to a competent mechanic.

REMOVAL AND INSTALLATION

1. Disconnect the battery ground cable.

2. Remove the trim shroud. Remove the electrical connector from the key warning switch.

3. Turn the lock cylinder to the RUN position.

4. Place a ⅛ inch diameter pin or small drift punch in the hole located at 4 o'clock and 1¼ inch from the outer edge of the lock cylinder

Lock cylinder assembly removal and installation

housing. Depress the retaining pin, and pull out the lock cylinder.

To install:

5. Prior to installation of the lock cylinder, lubricate the cylinder cavity, including the drive gear, with Lubriplate® or equivalent.

6. To install the lock cylinder, turn the lock cylinder to the RUN position, depress the retaining pin, and insert it into the lock cylinder housing. Assure that the cylinder is fully seated and aligned into the inter-locking washer before turning the key to the OFF position. This action will permit the cylinder retaining pin to extend into the hole in the lock cylinder housing.

7. Using the ignition key, rotate the lock cylinder to ensure correct mechanical operation in all positions. Install the electrical connector onto the key warning switch.

8. Connect the battery ground cable.

9. Check for proper ignition functions and verify that the column is locked in the LOCK position.

10. Install the trim shrouds.

Steering Linkage Connecting Rods

Replace the drag link if a ball stud is excessively loose or if the drag link is bent. Do not attempt to straighten a drag link.

Replace the connecting rod if the ball stud is excessively loose, if the connecting rod is bent or if the threads are stripped. Do not attempt to straighten connecting rod. Always check to insure that the adjustment sleeve and clamp stops are correctly installed on the truck.

REMOVAL AND INSTALLATION

1. Remove the cotter pins and nuts from the drag link, ball studs and from the right connecting the rod ball studs.

2. Remove the right connecting rod ball stud from the right spindle assembly and pitman arm.

3. Remove the drag link ball studs from the spindle and the connecting rod assembly.

4. Loosen the clamp bolt and turn the rod out of the adjustment sleeve.

5. Lubricate the threads of the new connecting rod, and turn it into the adjustment sleeve to about the same distance the old rods were installed. This will provide an approximate toe-in setting. Position the connecting rod ball studs in the spindle arms.

6. Position the new drag link, ball studs in the spindle, and connecting rod assembly and install nuts.

7. Position the right connecting rod ball stud in the drag link and install nut.

8. Tighten all the nuts to 50–75 ft. lbs. and install the cotter pins.

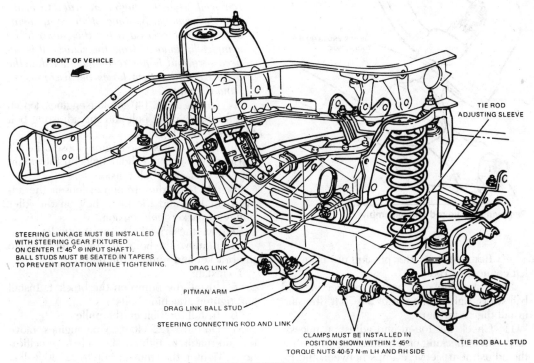

FRONT OF VEHICLE

TIE ROD ADJUSTING SLEEVE

STEERING LINKAGE MUST BE INSTALLED WITH STEERING GEAR FIXTURED ON CENTER (± 45° @ INPUT SHAFT). BALL STUDS MUST BE SEATED IN TAPERS TO PREVENT ROTATION WHILE TIGHTENING.

DRAG LINK

PITMAN ARM

DRAG LINK BALL STUD

STEERING CONNECTING ROD AND LINK

CLAMPS MUST BE INSTALLED IN POSITION SHOWN WITHIN ± 45° TORQUE NUTS 40-57 N·m LH AND RH SIDE

TIE ROD BALL STUD

MAIN VIEW FRONT SUSPENSION

Steering linkage assembly—2WD models

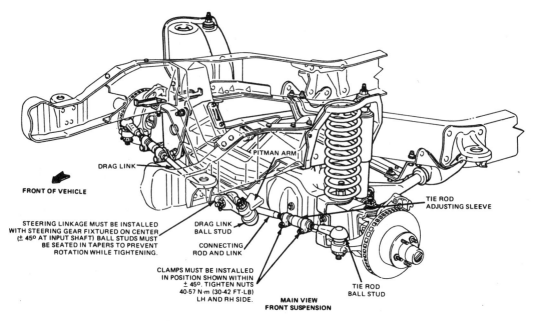

DRAG LINK

FRONT OF VEHICLE

PITMAN ARM

STEERING LINKAGE MUST BE INSTALLED
WITH STEERING GEAR FIXTURED ON CENTER
(± 45º AT INPUT SHAFT) BALL STUDS MUST
BE SEATED IN TAPERS TO PREVENT
ROTATION WHILE TIGHTENING.

DRAG LINK
BALL STUD

CONNECTING
ROD AND LINK

CLAMPS MUST BE INSTALLED
IN POSITION SHOWN WITHIN
± 45º. TIGHTEN NUTS
40-57 N·m (30-42 FT-LB)
LH AND RH SIDE.

TIE ROD
ADJUSTING SLEEVE

TIE ROD
BALL STUD

MAIN VIEW
FRONT SUSPENSION

Steering linkage assembly—4WD models

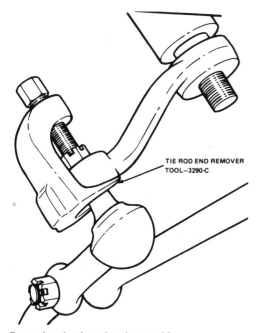

TIE ROD END REMOVER
TOOL–3290-C

Removing the tie rod end assembly

9. Remove the cotter pin and nut from the left connecting rod.

10. Install the nuts on the connecting rod ball studs, tighten the nut to 50–75 ft. lbs. and install the cotter pin.

11. Check the toe-in and adjust, if necessary. After checking or adjusting toe-in, center the adjustment sleeve clamps between the locating nibbs, position the clamps and tighten the nuts to 29–41 ft. lbs.

Power Steering Pump
REMOVAL AND INSTALLATION

1. Position a drain pan under the power steering pump.

2. Disconnect the pressure and return lines at the pump.

NOTE: *If the power steering pump is being removed from the engine in order to facilitate the removal of some other component, and it is not necessary for the pump to be completely removed from the vehicle, it is not necessary and is not recommended that the pressure and return hoses be disconnected from the pump.*

3. On the 4-122,140 gasoline engines, loosen the alternator pivot bolt and the adjusting bolt to slacken belt tension.

On the 6-173 gasoline engine, loosen the adjustment nut and the slider bolts on the pump support to slacken belt tension.

On the 4-134 diesel engine, loosen the adjustment bolt and the pivot bolt on the idler pulley to slacken belt tension.

Remove the drive belt from the pulley.

4. Remove the bolts attaching the pump to the bracket and remove the pump.

To install:

5. Install the pump on the bracket. Install and tighten attaching bolts.

6. Install the belt on the pulley.

7. On the 4-122,140 gasoline engines, move the alternator to tighten the belt to specifications. Tighten the adjuster bolt to 22–40 ft. lbs. and the alternator pivot bolt to 40–50 ft. lbs.

On the 6-173 gasoline engine, tighten the

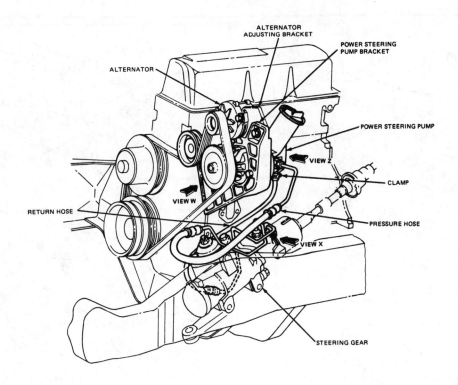

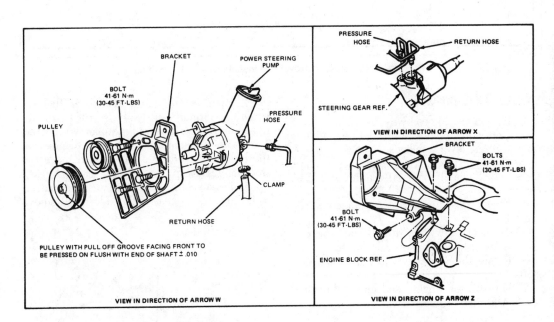

Power steering pump removal and installation—4-122,140 engines

adjustment nut to tighten the belt to specification. Tighten the slider bolts to 35–47 ft. lbs.

On the 4-134 diesel engine, insert a ½ inch drive breaker bar or ratchet into the slot in the idler pulley. Slide the pulley over to obtain the correct belt tension. Tighten the pivot bolt and the adjustment bolt to 30–45 ft. lbs.

8. Install the pressure hose to the pump fitting.

9. Connect the return hose to the pump, and tighten the clamp.

10. Fill the reservoir with the proper type of power steering fluid. Perform the system bleeding operation shown below.

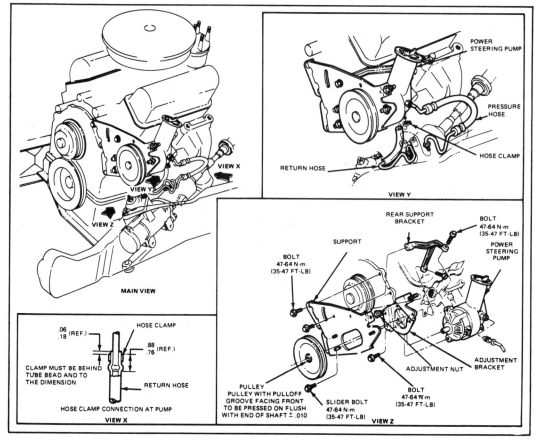

Power steering pump removal and installation—6-173 engine

SYSTEM BLEEDING

1. Disconnect the coil wire.
2. Crank the engine and continue adding fluid until the level stabilizes.
3. Continue to crank the engine and rotate the steering wheel about 30° to either side of center.
4. Check the fluid level and add as required.
5. Connect the coil wire and start the engine. Allow it to run for several minutes.
6. Rotate the steering wheel from stop to stop.
7. Shut off the engine and check the fluid level. Add fluid as necessary.

Manual Steering Gear

REMOVAL AND INSTALLATION

1. Disengage the flex coupling shield from the steering gear input shaft shield and slide it up the intermediate shaft.
2. Remove the bolt that retains the flex coupling to the steering gear.
3. Remove the steering gear input shaft shield.

4. Remove the nut and washer that secures the Pitman arm to the sector shaft. Remove the Pitman arm using Pitman Arm Puller, T64P-3590-F or equivalent. Do not hammer on the end of the puller as this can damage the steering gear.
5. Remove the bolts and washers that attach the steering gear to the side rail. Remove the gear.

To install:

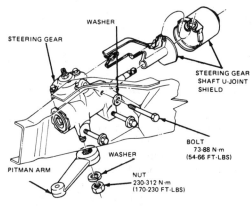

Manual steering gear removal and installation

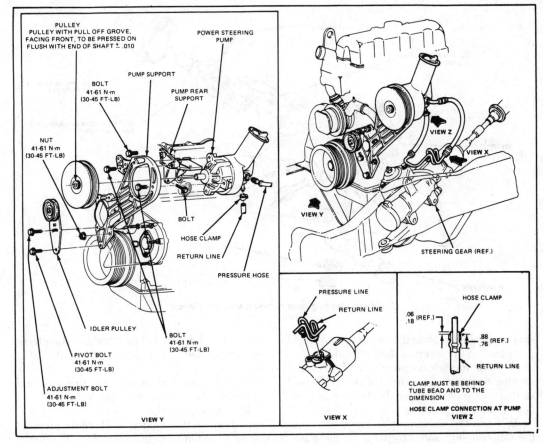

Power steering pump removal and installation—4-134 diesel engine

6. Rotate the gear input shaft (wormshaft) from stop to stop, counting the total number of turns. Then turn back exactly half-way, placing the gear on center.

7. Slide the steering gear input shaft shield on the steering gear input shaft.

8. Position the flex coupling on the steering gear input shaft. Ensure that the flat on the gear input shaft is facing straight up and aligns with the flat on the flex coupling. Install the steering gear to side rail with bolts and washers. Torque the bolts to 66 ft. lbs.

9. Place the Pitman arm on the sector shaft and install the attaching washer and nut. Align the two blocked teeth on the Pitman arm with four missing teeth on the steering gear sector shaft. Tighten the nut to 230 ft. lbs.

10. Install the flex coupling to steering gear input shaft attaching bolt and tighten to 35 ft. lbs.

11. Snap the flex coupling shield to the steering gear input shield.

12. Check the system to ensure equal turns from center to each lock position.

Power Steering Gear
REMOVAL AND INSTALLATION

1. Disconnect the pressure and return lines from the steering gear. Plug the lines and the ports in the gear to prevent entry of dirt.

2. Remove the upper and lower steering gear shaft u-joint shield from the flex coupling. Remove the bolts that secure the flex coupling to the steering gear and to the column steering shaft assembly.

3. Raise the vehicle and remove the Pitman arm attaching nut, and washer.

4. Remove the Pitman arm from the sector shaft using Tool T64P-3590-F. Remove the tool from the Pitman arm. Do not damage the seals.

5. Support the steering gear, and remove the steering gear attaching bolts.

6. Work the steering gear free of the flex coupling. Remove the steering gear from the vehicle.

To install:

7. Install the lower u-joint shield onto the

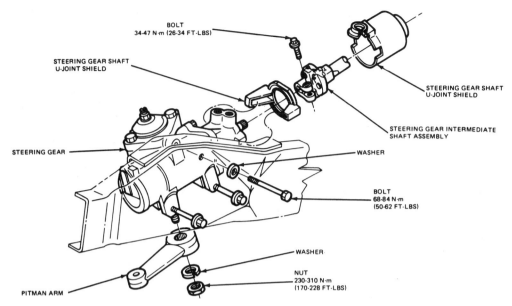

BOLT
34-47 N·m (26-34 FT-LBS)

STEERING GEAR SHAFT
U-JOINT SHIELD

STEERING GEAR SHAFT
U-JOINT SHIELD

STEERING GEAR INTERMEDIATE
SHAFT ASSEMBLY

STEERING GEAR

WASHER

BOLT
68-84 N·m
(50-62 FT-LBS)

WASHER

NUT
230-310 N·m
(170-228 FT-LBS)

PITMAN ARM

Power steering gear removal and installation

steering gear lugs. Slide the upper u-joint shield into place on the steering shaft assembly.

8. Slide the flex coupling into place on the steering shaft assembly. Turn the steering wheel so that the spokes are in the horizontal position. Center the steering gear input shaft.

9. Slide the steering gear input shaft into the flex coupling and into place on the frame side rail. Install the attaching bolts and tighten to 50–62 ft. lbs.

10. Be sure the wheels are in the straight ahead position, then install the Pitman arm on the sector shaft. Install the Pitman arm attaching washer and nut. Tighten nut to 170–230 ft. lb.

11. Connect and tighten the pressure and the return lines to the steering gear.

12. Disconnect the coil wire. Fill the reservoir. Turn on the ignition and turn the steering wheel from left to right to distribute the fluid.

13. Re-check fluid level and add fluid, if necessary. Connect the coil wire, start the engine and turn the steering wheel from side to side. Inspect for fluid leaks.

BRAKE SYSTEM

Adjustment

The drum brakes are self-adjusting and require a manual adjustment only after the brake
shoes have been relined or replaced.

NOTE: *Disc brakes are not adjustable.*

To adjust the brakes, follow the procedure
given below:

1. Raise the vehicle and support it with safety
stands.

2. Remove the rubber plug from the adjusting slot on the backing plate.

3. Insert a small screwdriver or piece of firm
wire (coathanger wire) into the adjusting slot
and push the automatic adjusting lever out and
free of the starwheel on the adjusting screw and
hold it there.

4. Engage the topmost tooth possible on the
starwheel with the brake adjusting spoon. Move
the end of the adjusting spoon upward to move
the adjusting screw starwheel downward and
contract the adjusting screw. Back off the adjusting screw starwheel until the wheel spins

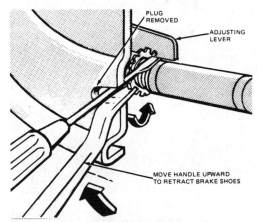

PLUG
REMOVED

ADJUSTING
LEVER

MOVE HANDLE UPWARD
TO RETRACT BRAKE SHOES

**Cutaway of the position and operation of the brake
adjusting tools during adjustment**

freely with a minimum of drag. Keep track of
the number of turns that the starwheel is backed
off, or the number of strokes taken with the
brake adjusting spoon.

5. Repeat this operation for the other side.
When backing off the brakes on the other side,
the starwheel adjuster must be backed off the
same number of turns to prevent side-to-side
brake pull.

6. When all drum brakes are adjusted, make
several stops while backing the vehicle, to
equalize the brakes at all of the wheels.

7. Remove the safety stands and lower the
vehicle. Road test the vehicle.

HYDRAULIC SYSTEM

Master Cylinder
REMOVAL AND INSTALLATION
Manual Brakes

1. Working from inside the cab below the
instrument panel, disconnect the wires from the
stop lamp switch.

2. Remove the retaining nut, shoulder bolt
and spacers, securing the master cylinder push
rod to the brake pedal assembly. Remove the
stop lamp switch from the pedal.

3. Disconnect the brake hydraulic system
lines from the master cylinder.

4. Remove the master cylinder-to-dash panel
retaining nuts, and remove the master cylinder.

5. Remove the boot from the master cylinder push rod.

To install:

6. Place the master cylinder assembly on the
dash panel in the engine compartment and install the retaining bolts. Tighten the bolts to
13–25 ft. lbs.

7. Loosely connect the hydraulic brake system lines to the master cylinder.

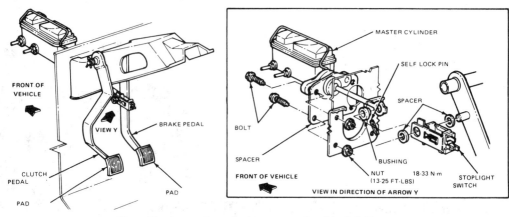

Manual brake master cylinder—removal and installation

8. Secure the push rod to the brake pedal assembly using the shoulder bolt. Make sure the bushings and spacers are installed properly. Install self-locking nut.

9. Connect the wires to the stop lamp switch. Bleed the brake system as described in this chapter. Centralize the differential valve. Fill the dual master cylinder reservoirs with DOT 3 brake fluid to within ¼ inch of the top. Install the gasket and reservoir cover.

Power Brakes

1. With the engine turned off, push the brake pedal down to expel vacuum from the brake booster system.

2. Disconnect the hydraulic lines from the brake master cylinder.

3. Remove the brake booster-to-master cylinder retaining nuts and lock washers. Remove the master cylinder from the brake booster.

4. Before installing the master cylinder, check the distance from the outer end of the booster assembly push rod to the front face of the brake booster assembly. Turn the push rod adjusting screw in or out as required to obtain the length shown.

5. Position the master cylinder assembly over the booster push rod and onto the two studs on the booster asembly. Install the attaching nuts and lockwashers and tighten to 13–25.

6. Loosely connect the hydraulic brake system lines to the master cylinder.

7. Bleed the hydraulic brake system. Centralize the differential valve. Then, fill the dual

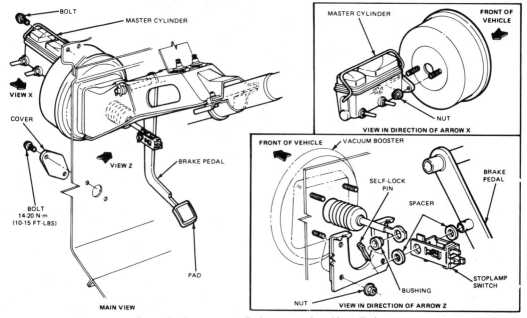

Power brake master cylinder removal and installation

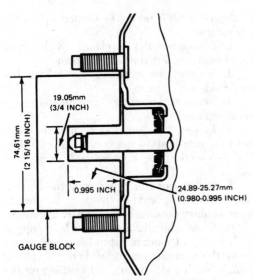

Bendix booster push rod gauge, dimensions and adjustment

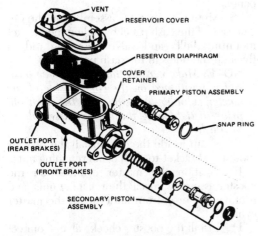

Exploded view of the master cylinder

master cylinder reservoirs with DOT 3 brake fluid to within ¼ inch of the top. Install the gasket and reservoir cover.

OVERHAUL

The most important thing to remember when rebuilding the master cylinder is cleanliness. Work in clean surroundings with clean tools and clean cloths or paper for drying purposes. Have plenty of clean alcohol and brake fluid on hand to clean and lubricate the internal components. There are service repair kits available for overhauling the master cylinder.

1. Clean the outside of the master cylinder and remove the filler cap and gasket (diaphragm). Pour out any fluid that remains in the cylinder reservoir. Do not use any fluids other than brake fluid or alcohol to clean the master cylinder.

2. Unscrew the piston stop from the bottom of the cylinder body. Remove the O-ring seal from the piston stop. Discard the seal.

3. Remove the pushrod boot, if so equipped, from the groove at the rear of the master cylinder.

4. Remove the snap-ring retaining the primary and secondary piston assemblies within the cylinder body.

5. Remove the pushrod (if so equipped) and primary piston assembly from the master cylinder. Discard the piston assembly, including the boot (if so equipped).

6. Apply an air hose to the rear brake outlet port of the cylinder body and carefully blow the secondary piston out of the cylinder body.

7. Remove the return spring, spring retainer, cup protector, and cups from the secondary piston. Discard the cup protector and cups.

8. Clean all of the remaining parts in clean isopropyl alcohol and inspect the parts for chipping, excessive wear or damage. Replace them as required.

NOTE: *When using a master cylinder repair kit, install all the parts supplied in the kit.*

9. Check all recesses, reopenings and internal passages to be sure they are open and free from foreign matter. Use compressed air to blow out dirt and cleaning solvent remaining after the parts have been cleaned in the alcohol. Place all the parts on a clean pan, lint-free cloth, or paper to dry.

10. Dip all the parts, except the cylinder body, in clean brake fluid.

11. Assemble the two secondary cups, back-to-back, in the grooves near the end of the secondary piston.

12. Install the secondary piston assembly in the master cylinder.

13. Install a new O-ring on the piston stop, and start the stop into the cylinder body.

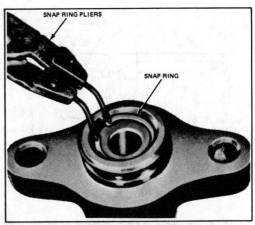

Snap ring removal from the master cylinder

14. Position the boot, snap-ring and push-rod retainer on the pushrod. Make sure the pushrod retainer is seated securely on the ball end of the rod. Seat the pushrod in the primary piston assembly.

15. Install the primary piston assembly in the master cylinder. Push the primary piston inward and tighten the secondary piston stop to retain the secondary piston in the bore.

16. Press the pushrod and pistons inward and install the snap-ring in the cylinder body.

17. Before the master cylinder is installed on the vehicle, the unit must be bled: support the master cylinder body in a vise, and fill both fluid reservoirs with brake fluid.

18. Loosely install plugs in the front and rear brake outlet bores. Depress the primary piston several times until air bubbles cease to appear in the brake fluid.

19. Tighten the plugs and attempt to depress the piston. The piston travel should be restricted after all air is expelled.

20. Remove the plugs. Install the cover and gasket (diaphragm) assembly, and make sure the cover retainer is tightened securely.

21. Install the master cylinder in the vehicle and bleed the hydraulic system.

Booster

REMOVAL AND INSTALLATION

NOTE: *Make sure that the booster rubber reaction disc is properly installed if the master cylinder push rod is removed or accidentally pulled out. A dislodedged disc may cause excessive pedal travel and extreme operation sensitivity. The disc is black compared to the silver colored valve plunger that will be exposed after the push rod and front seal is removed. The booster unit is serviced as an assembly and must be replaced if the reaction disc cannot be properly installed and aligned, or if it cannot be located within the unit itself.*

1. Disconnect the stop lamp switch wiring to prevent running the battery down.

2. Support the master cylinder from the underside with a prop.

3. Remove the master cylinder-to-booster retaining nuts.

4. Loosen the clamp that secures the manifold vacuum hose to the booster check valve, and remove the hose. Remove the booster check valve.

5. Pull the master cylinder off the booster and leave it supported by the prop, far enough away to allow removal of the booster assembly.

6. From inside the cab on vehicles equipped with push rod mounted stop lamp switch, remove the retaining pin and slide the stop lamp switch, push rod, spacers and bushing off the brake pedal arm.

7. From the engine compartment remove the bolts that attach the booster to the dash panel.

8. Mount the booster assembly on the engine side of the dash panel by sliding the bracket mounting bolts and valve operating rod in through the holes in the dash panel.

NOTE: *Make certain that the booster push rod is positioned on the correct side of the master cylinder to install onto the push pin prior to tightening the booster assembly to the dash.*

9. From inside the cab, install the booster mounting bracket-to-dash panel retaining nuts.

10. Position the master cylinder on the booster assembly, install the retaining nuts, and remove the prop from underneath the master cylinder.

11. Install the booster check valve. Connect the manifold vacuum hose to the booster check valve and secure with the clamp.

12. From inside the cab on vehicles equipped with push rod mounted stop lamp switch, install the bushing and position the switch on the end of the push rod. Then install the switch and rod on the pedal arm, along with spacers on each side, and secure with the retaining pin.

13. Connect the stop lamp switch wiring.

14. Start the engine and check brake operation.

Vacuum Pump—4-134 Diesel Engine

REMOVAL AND INSTALLATION

1. Loosen the vacuum pump adjustment bolt and the pivot bolt. Slide the pump downward and remove the drive belt from the pulley.

NOTE: *If the vacuum pump drive belt is to*

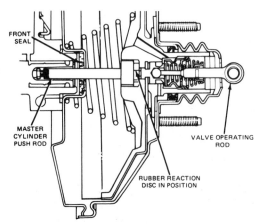

FRONT SEAL

MASTER CYLINDER PUSH ROD

VALVE OPERATING ROD

RUBBER REACTION DISC IN POSITION

Checking the reaction disc installation in the vacuum booster

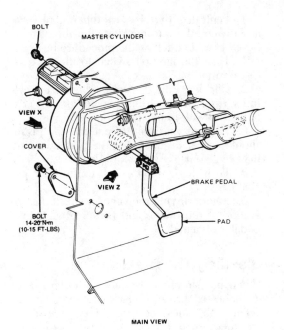

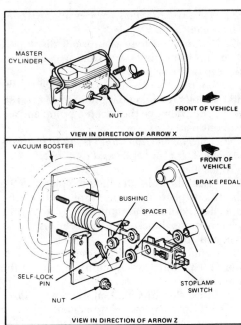

MAIN VIEW

Vacuum booster removal and installation

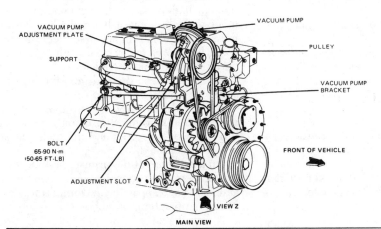

MAIN VIEW

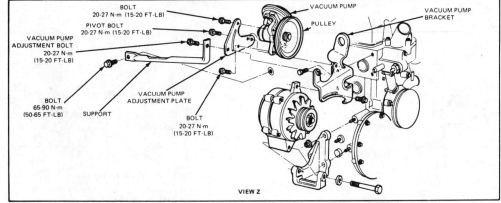

VIEW Z

Vacuum pump removal and installation—4-134 diesel engine

be replaced, the alternator drive belt must be removed.

2. Remove the hose clamp and disconnect the pump from the hose on the manifold vacuum outlet fitting.

3. Remove the pivot and adjustment bolts and the bolts retaining the pump to the adjustment plate. Remove the vacuum pump and adjustment plate.

NOTE: *The vacuum pump is not to be disassembled. It is only serviced as a unit.*

To install:

4. Install the bolts attaching the pump to the adjustment plate and tighten the bolts to 15–20 ft. lbs. Position the pump and plate on the vacuum pump bracket and loosely install the pivot and adjustment bolts.

5. Connect the hose from the manifold vacuum outlet fitting to the pump and install the hose clamp.

6. Install the drive belt on the pulley. Place a ⅜ inch drive breaker bar or ratchet into the slot on the vacuum pump adjustment plate. Lift up on the assembly until the specified belt tension is obtained. Tighten the pivot and adjustment bolts to 15–20 ft. lbs.

NOTE: *The alternator belt tension must be adjusted prior to adjusting the vacuum pump belt tension.*

7. Start the engine and verify proper operation of the brake system.

NOTE: *The BRAKE light will glow until vacuum builds up to the normal level.*

Centralizing the Pressure Differential Valve

After any repair or bleeding of the primary (front brake) or secondary (rear brake) system, the dual-brake system warning light will usually remain illuminated due to the pressure differential valve remaining in the off-center position.

To centralize the pressure differential valve and turn off the warning light after the systems have been bled, follow the procedure below.

1. Turn the ignition switch to the ACC or ON position.

2. Check the fluid level in the master cylinder reservoirs and fill them to within ¼ in. of the top with brake fluid, if necessary.

3. Depress the brake pedal and the piston should center itself causing the brake warning light to go out.

4. Turn the ignition switch to the OFF position.

5. Before driving the vehicle, check the operation of the brakes and be sure that a firm pedal is obtained.

Bleeding The Brakes

When any part of the hydraulic system has been disconnected for repair or replacement, air may get into the lines and cause spongy pedal action (because air can be compressed and brake fluid cannot). To correct this condition, it is necessary to bleed the hydraulic system after it has been properly connected to be sure all air is expelled from the brake cylinders and lines.

When bleeding the brake system, bleed one brake cylinder at a time, beginning at the cylinder with the longest hydraulic line (farthest from the master cylinder) first. Keep the master cylinder reservoir filled with brake fluid during the bleeding operation. Never use brake fluid that has been drained from the hydraulic system, no matter how clean it is.

It will be necessary to centralize the pressure differential value after a brake system failure has been corrected and the hydraulic system has been bled.

On the Bronco II the primary and secondary hydraulic brake systems are individual systems and are bled separately. During the entire bleeding operation, do not allow the reservoir

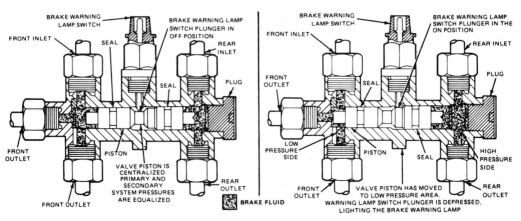

Cutaway view of a typical pressure differential valve

to run dry. Keep the master cylinder reservoir filled with brake fluid.

1. Clean all dirt from around the master cylinder fill cap, remove the cap and fill the master cylinder with brake fluid until the level is within ¼ in. of the top edge of the reservoir.

2. Clean off the bleeder screws at all 4 wheels. The bleeder screws are located on the inside of the brake backing plate, on the backside of the wheel cylinders and on the front brake calipers.

3. Attach a length of rubber hose over the nozzle of the bleeder screw at the wheel to be done first. Place the other end of the hose in a glass jar, submerged in brake fluid.

4. Open the bleeder screw valve ½–¾ turn.

5. Have an assistant slowly depress the brake pedal. Close the bleeder screw valve and tell your assistant to allow the brake pedal to return slowly. Continue this pumping action to force any air out of the system. When bubbles cease to appear at the end of the bleeder hose, close the bleeder valve and remove the hose.

6. Check the master cylinder fluid level and add fluid accordingly. Do this after bleeding each wheel.

7. Repeat the bleeding operation at the remaining 3 wheels, ending with the one closest to the master cylinder. Fill the master cylinder reservoir.

FRONT DISC BRAKES

Pads

INSPECTION

Replace the front pads when the pad thickness is at the minimum thickness recommended by Ford Motor Co. (⅟₃₂″), or at the minimum allowed by the applicable state or local motor vehicle inspection code. Pad thickness may be checked by removing the wheel and looking through the inspection port in the caliper assembly.

Front Caliper and Disc Brake Pads

REMOVAL AND INSTALLATION

NOTE: *Always replace all disc pad assemblies on an axle. Never service one wheel only.*

1. To avoid fluid overflow when the caliper piston is pressed into the caliper cylinder bores,

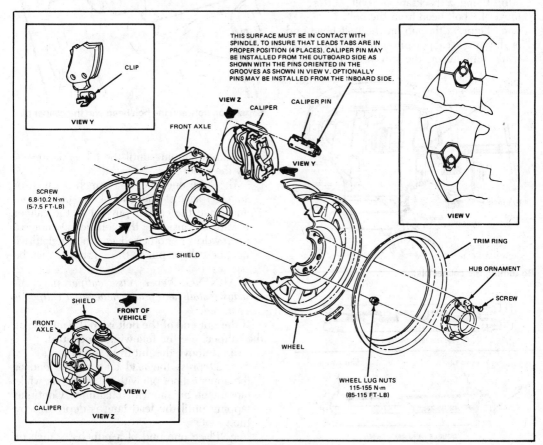

Front disc brake assembly

siphon or dip part of the brake fluid out of the larger master cylinder reservoir (connected to the front disc brakes). Discard the removed fluid.

2. Raise the vehicle and install jackstands. Remove a front wheel and tire assembly.

3. Place an eight-inch C-clamp on the caliper and tighten the clamp to bottom the caliper piston in the cylinder bore. Remove the clamp.

NOTE: *Do not use a screwdriver or similar tool to pry piston away from the rotor.*

4. There are three types of caliper pins used: a single tang type, a double tang type and a split-shell type. The pin removal process is dependent upon how the pin is installed (bolt head direction). Remove the upper caliper pin first.

NOTE: *On some applications, the pin may be retained by a nut and torx-head bolt (except the split-shell type).*

If the bolt head is on the outside of the caliper, use the following procedure:

a. From the inner side of the caliper, tap the bolt within the caliper pin until the bolt head on the outer side of the caliper shows a separation between the bolt head and the caliper pin.

b. Using a hacksaw or bolt cutter, remove the bolt head from the bolt.

c. Depress the tab on the bolt head end of the upper caliper pin with a screwdriver, while tapping on the pin with a hammer.

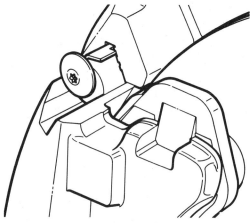

Caliper pin with the bolt head on the outside of the caliper

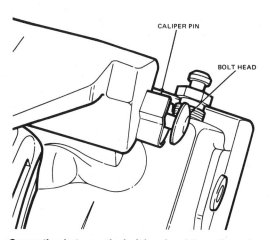

Separation between the bolt head and the caliper pin

Continue tapping until the tab is depressed by the v-slot.

d. Place one end of a punch (½ inch or smaller) against the end of the caliper pin and drive the caliper pin out of the caliper toward the inside of the vehicle. Do not use a screwdriver or other edged tool to help drive out the caliper pin as the v-grooves may be damaged.

WARNING: *Never reuse caliper pins. Always install new pins whenever a caliper is removed.*

If the nut end of the bolt is on the outside of the caliper, use the following procedure:

a. Remove the nut from the bolt.

b. Depress the lead tang on the end of the upper caliper pin with a screwdriver while tapping on the pin with a hammer. Continue tapping until the lead tang is depressed by the v-slot.

c. Place one end of a punch (½ inch or smaller) against the end of the caliper pin

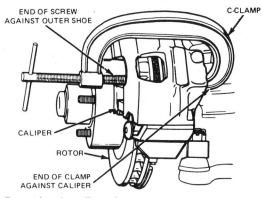

Bottoming the caliper piston

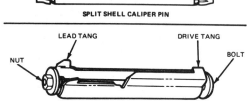

Caliper pins

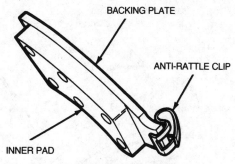

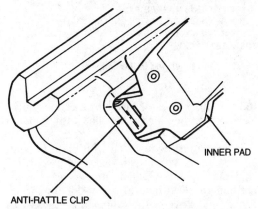

Anti-rattle clip installed on the inner pad

INNER PAD

ANTI-RATTLE CLIP

Installing the inner pad and the anti-rattle clip into the caliper

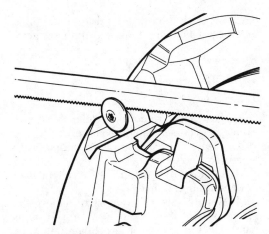

Removing the bolt head

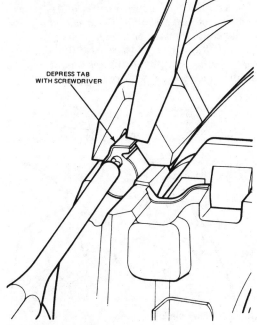

Removing the caliper pin

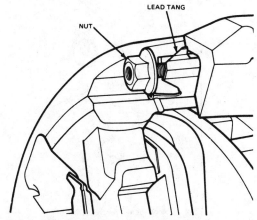

Caliper pin with a nut on the outside

and drive the caliper pin out of the caliper toward the inside of the vehicle. Do not use a screwdriver or other edged tool to help drive out the caliper pin as the v-grooves may be damaged.

5. Repeat the procedure in step 4 for the lower caliper pin.

6. Remove the caliper from the rotor. If the caliper is to be removed for service, remove the brake hose from the caliper.

7. Remove the outer pad. Remove the anti-rattle clips and remove the inner pad.

To install:

8. Place a new anti-rattle clip on the lower end of the inner pad. Be sure the tabs on the clip are positioned properly and the clip is fully seated.

9. Position the inner pad and anti-rattle clip in the abutment with the anti-rattle clip tab against the pad abutment and the loop-type spring away from the rotor. Compress the anti-rattle clip and slide the upper end of the pad in position.

10. Install the outer pad, making sure the torque buttons on the pad spring clip are seated solidly in the matching holes in the caliper.

11. Install the caliper on the spindle, making sure the mounting surfaces are free of dirt and lubricate the caliper grooves with Disc

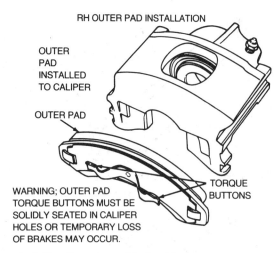

RH OUTER PAD INSTALLATION

OUTER
PAD
INSTALLED
TO CALIPER

OUTER PAD

WARNING; OUTER PAD
TORQUE BUTTONS MUST BE
SOLIDLY SEATED IN CALIPER
HOLES OR TEMPORARY LOSS
OF BRAKES MAY OCCUR.

TORQUE
BUTTONS

Installing the outer pad in the caliper

Brake Caliper Grease. Install new caliper pins, making sure the pins are installed with the fang in position as shown.

The pin must be installed with the lead tang in first, the bolt head facing outward (if equipped) and the pin positioned as shown. Position the lead tang in the v-slot mounting surface and drive in the caliper until the drive tang is flush with the caliper assembly. Install the nut (if equipped) and tighten to 32–47 in. lbs.

WARNING: *Never reuse caliper pins. Always install new pins whenever a caliper is removed.*

12. If removed, install the brake hose to the caliper.

13. Bleed the brakes as described earlier in this chapter.

14. Install the wheel and tire assembly. Torque the lug nuts to 85–115 ft. lbs.

15. Remove the jackstands and lower the vehicle. Check the brake fluid level and fill as necessary. Check the brakes for proper operation.

Calipers
OVERHAUL

1. For caliper removal, see the above procedure. Disconnect the brake hose.

2. Clean the exterior of the caliper with denatured alcohol.

3. Remove the plug from the caliper inlet port and drain the fluid.

4. Air pressure is necessary to remove the piston. When a source of compressed air is found, such as a shop or gas station, apply air to the inlet port slowly and carefully until the piston pops out of its bore.

WARNING: *If high pressure air is applied the piston will pop out with considerable force and cause damage or injury.*

5. If the piston jams, release the air pressure and tap sharply on the piston end with a soft hammer. Reapply air pressure.

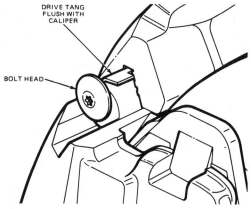

DRIVE TANG
FLUSH WITH
CALIPER

BOLT HEAD

Correct caliper pin installation

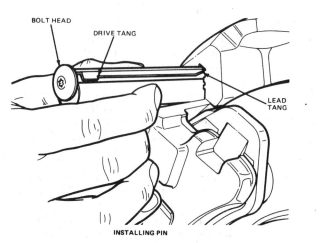

BOLT HEAD

DRIVE TANG

LEAD
TANG

INSTALLING PIN

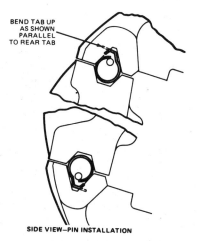

BEND TAB UP
AS SHOWN
PARALLEL
TO REAR TAB

SIDE VIEW—PIN INSTALLATION

Installing the caliper pin

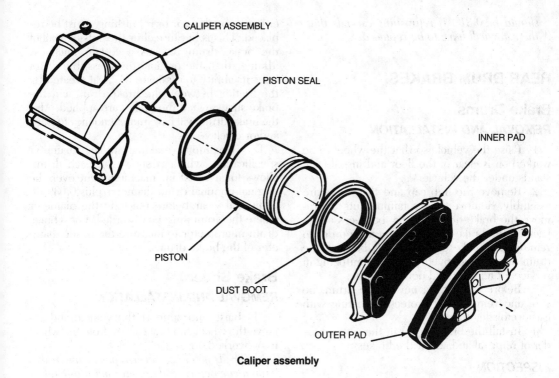

Caliper assembly

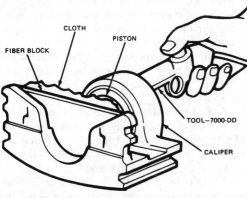

Caliper piston removal

6. When the piston is out, remove the boot from the piston and the seal from the bore.

7. Clean the housing and piston with denatured alcohol. Dry with compressed air.

8. Lubricate the new piston seal, boot and piston with clean brake fluid, and assemble them in the caliper.

9. The dust boot can be worked in with the fingers and the piston should be pressed straight in until it bottoms. Be careful to avoid cocking the piston in the bore.

10. A C-clamp may be necessary to bottom the piston.

11. Install the caliper using the procedure given in the pad and caliper replacement procedure above.

Rotor (Disc)
REMOVAL AND INSTALLATION

1. Jack up the front of the vehicle and support on jackstands.

2. Remove the wheel and tire.

3. Remove the caliper assembly as described earlier in this chapter.

4. Follow the procedure given under hub and wheel bearing removal in Chapter 7 for models with manual and automatic locking hubs.

NOTE: *New rotor assemblies come protected with an anti-rust coating which should be removed with denatured alcohol or degreaser. New hubs must be packed with EP wheel bearing grease. If the old rotors are to be reused, check them for cracks, grooves or wavyness. Rotors that aren't too badly scored or grooved can be resurfaced by most automotive shops. Minimum rotor thickness*

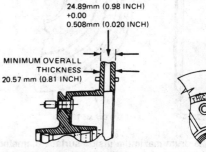

Disc brake service limits

should be 0.81". If refinishing exceeds that, the rotor will have to be replaced.

REAR DRUM BRAKES

Brake Drums
REMOVAL AND INSTALLATION

1. Raise the vehicle so that the wheel to be worked on is clear of the floor and install jackstands under the vehicle.

2. Remove the hub cap and the wheel/tire assembly. Remove the 3 retaining nuts and remove the brake drum. It may be necessary to back off the brake shoe adjustment in order to remove the brake drum. This is because the drum might be grooved or worn from being in service for an extended period of time.

3. Before installing a new brake drum, be sure and remove any protective coating with carburetor degreaser.

4. Install the brake drum in the reverse order of removal and adjust the brakes.

INSPECTION

After the brake drum has been removed from the vehicle, it should be inspected for runout, severe scoring, cracks, and the proper inside diameter.

Minor scores on a brake drum can be removed with fine emery cloth, provided that all grit is removed from the drum before it is installed on the vehicle.

A badly scored, rough, or out-of-round (runout) drum can be ground or turned on a brake drum lathe. Do not remove any more material from the drum than is necessary to provide a smooth surface for the brake shoe to contact. The maximum diameter of the braking surface is shown on the inside of each brake drum. Brake drums that exceed the maximum braking surface diameter shown on the brake drum,

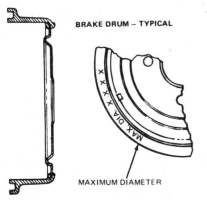

BRAKE DRUM – TYPICAL

MAXIMUM DIAMETER

Rear brake drum maximum inside surface diameter marking location

either through wear or refinishing, must be replaced. This is because after the outside wall of the brake drum reaches a certain thickness (thinner than the original thickness) the drum loses its ability to dissipate the heat created by the friction between the brake drum and the brake shoes, when the brakes are applied. Also the brake drum will have more tendency to warp and/or crack.

The maximum braking surface diameter specification, which is shown on each drum, allows for a 0.060 in. machining cut over the original nominal drum diameter plus 0.030 in. additional wear before reaching the diameter where the drum must be discarded. Use a brake drum micrometer to measure the inside diameter of the brake drums.

Brake Shoes
REMOVAL AND INSTALLATION

1. Raise and support the vehicle and remove the wheel and brake drum from the wheel to be worked on.

NOTE: *If you have never replaced the brakes on a car before and you are not too familiar with the procedures involved, only disassemble and assemble one side at a time, leaving the other side intact as a reference during reassembly.*

2. Install a clamp over the ends of the wheel cylinder to prevent the pistons of the wheel cylinder from coming out, causing loss of fluid and much grief.

3. Contract the brake shoes by pulling the self-adjusting lever away from the starwheel adjustment screw and turn the starwheel up and back until the pivot nut is drawn onto the starwheel as far as it will come.

4. Pull the adjusting lever, cable and automatic adjuster spring down and toward the rear to unhook the pivot hook from the large hole in the secondary shoe web. Do not attempt to pry the pivot hook from the hole.

5. Remove the automatic adjuster spring and the adjusting lever.

6. Remove the secondary shoe-to-anchor spring with a brake tool. (Brake tools are very common implements and are available at auto parts stores.) Remove the primary shoe-to-anchor spring and unhook the cable anchor. Remove the anchor pin plate.

7. Remove the cable guide from the secondary shoe.

8. Remove the shoe hold-down springs, shoes, adjusting screw, pivot nut, and socket. Note the color of each hold-down spring for assembly. To remove the hold-down springs, reach being the brake backing plate and place one finger on the end of one of the brake hold-

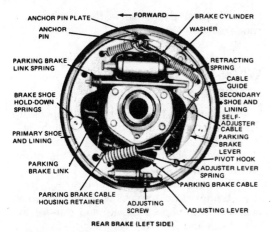

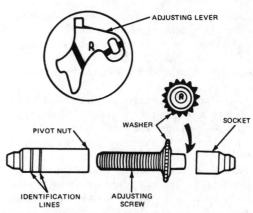

The adjusting screw starwheel and components and the self-adjusting lever identification

Rear brake assembly

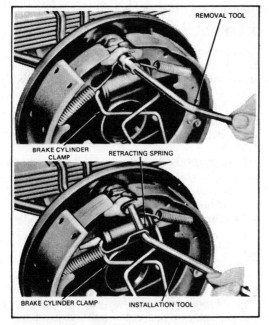

Removing and installing rear brake springs

down spring mounting pins. Using a pair of pliers, grasp the washer-type retainer on top of the hold-down spring that corresponds to the pin that you are holding. Push down on the pliers and turn them 90° to align the slot in the washer with the head on the spring mounting pin. Remove the spring and washer retainer and repeat this operation on the hold-down spring on the other shoe.

9. Remove the parking brake link and spring. Disconnect the parking brake cable from the parking brake lever.

10. After removing the rear brake secondary shoe, disassemble the parking brake lever from the shoe by removing the retaining clip and spring washer.

To assemble and install the brake shoes:

11. Assemble the parking brake lever to the secondary shoe and secure it with the spring washer and retaining clip.

12. Apply a *light* coating of Lubriplate® at the points where the brake shoes contact the backing plate.

13. Position the brake shoes on the backing plate, and install the hold-down spring pins, springs, and spring washer-type retainers. Install the parking brake link, spring and washer. Connect the parking brake cable to the parking brake lever.

14. Install the anchor pin plate, and place the cable anchor over the anchor pin with the crimped side toward the backing plate.

15. Install the primary shoe-to-anchor spring with the brake tool.

16. Install the cable guide on the secondary shoe web with the flanged holes fitted into the hole in the secondary shoe web. Thread the cable around the cable guide groove.

17. Install the secondary shoe-to-anchor (long) spring. Be sure that the cable end is not cocked or binding on the anchor pin when installed. All of the parts should be flat on the anchor pin. Remove the wheel cylinder piston clamp.

18. Apply Lubriplate® to the threads and the socket end of the adjusting starwheel screw. Turn the adjusting screw into the adjusting pivot nut to the limit of the threads and then back off ½ turn.

NOTE: *Interchanging the brake shoe adjusting screw assemblies from one side of the vehicle to the other would cause the brake shoes to retract rather than expand each time the automatic adjusting mechanism operated. To prevent this, the socket end of the adjusting screw is stamped with an "R" or an "L" for RIGHT or LEFT. The adjusting pivot nuts can be distinguished by the number of lines machined around the body of the nut; one line indicates left-hand nut and two lines indicates a right-hand nut.*

19. Place the adjusting socket on the screw and install this assembly between the shoe ends with the adjusting screw nearest to the secondary shoe.

20. Place the cable hook into the hole in the adjusting lever from the backing plate side. The adjusting levers are stamped with an "R" (right) or an "L" (left) to indicate their installation on the right or left hand brake assembly.

21. Position the hooked end of the adjuster spring in the primary shoe web and connect the loop end of the spring to the adjuster lever hole.

22. Pull the adjuster lever, cable and automatic adjuster spring down toward the rear to engage the pivot hook in the large hole in the secondary shoe web.

23. After installation, check the action of the adjuster by pulling the section of the cable between the cable guide and the adjusting lever toward the secondary shoe web far enough to lift the lever past a tooth on the adjusting screw starwheel. The lever should snap into position behind the next tooth, and release of the cable should cause the adjuster spring to return the lever to its original position. This return action of the lever will turn the adjusting screw starwheel one tooth. The lever should contact the adjusting screw starwheel one tooth above the center line of the adjusting screw.

If the automatic adjusting mechanism does not perform properly, check the following:

1. Check the cable end fittings. The cable ends should fill or extend slightly beyond the crimped section of the fittings. If this is not the case, replace the cable.

2. Check the cable guide for damage. The cable groove should be parallel to the shoe web, and the body of the guide should lie flat against the web. Replace the cable guide if this is not so.

3. Check the pivot hook on the lever. The hook surfaces should be square with the body on the lever for proper pivoting. Repair or replace the hook as necessary.

4. Make sure that the adjusting screw star-

wheel is properly seated in the notch in the shoe web.

Wheel Cylinders
REMOVAL AND INSTALLATION

1. To remove the wheel cylinder, jack up the vehicle and remove the wheel, hub, and drum.

2. Disconnect the brake line at the fitting on the brake backing plate.

3. Remove the brake assemblies.

4. Remove the screws that hold the wheel cylinder to the backing plate and remove the wheel cylinder from the vehicle.

5. Installation is the reverse of the above removal procedure. After installation adjust the brakes as described earlier in this chapter.

OVERHAUL

Wheel cylinder rebuilding kits are available for reconditioning wheel cylinders. The kits usually contain new cup springs, cylinder cups, and in some, new boots. The most important factor to keep in mind when rebuilding wheel cylinders is cleanliness. Keep all dirt away from the wheel cylinders when you are reassembling them.

1. Remove the wheel cylinder as described earlier.

2. Remove the rubber dust covers on the ends of the cylinder. Remove the pistons and piston cups and the spring. Remove the bleeder screw and make sure that it is not plugged.

3. Discard all of the parts that the rebuilding kit will replace.

4. Examine the inside of the cylinder. If it is severely rusted, pitted or scratched, then the cylinder must be replaced as the piston cups won't be able to seal against the walls of the cylinder.

5. Using a wheel cylinder hone or emery cloth and crocus cloth, polish the inside of the cylinder. The purpose of this is to put a new surface on the inside of the cylinder. Keep the inside of the cylinder coated with brake fluid while honing.

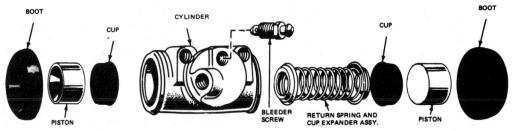

Rear wheel cylinder assembly

6. Wash out the cylinder with clean brake fluid after honing.

7. When reassembling the cylinder, dip all of the parts in clean brake fluid. Assemble the wheel cylinder in the reverse order of removal and disassembly.

PARKING BRAKE

Cable

ADJUSTMENT

Pre-Tension Procedure

NOTE: *This procedure is to be used when a new Tension Limiter has been installed.*

1. Depress the parking brake pedal.

2. Grip the Tension Limiter Bracket to prevent it from spinning and tighten the equalizer nut 2½" up the rod.

3. Check to make sure the cinch strap has slipped less than 1⅜" remaining.

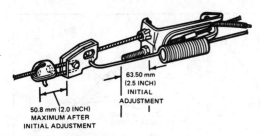

63.50 mm (2.5 INCH) INITIAL ADJUSTMENT

50.8 mm (2.0 INCH) MAXIMUM AFTER INITIAL ADJUSTMENT

Pre-tension adjustment

Final Adjustment

NOTE: *This procedure is to be used to remove the slack from the system if a new Tension Limiter has not been installed.*

1. Make sure the brake drums are cold for correct adjustment.

2. Position the parking brake pedal to the fully depressed position.

3. Grip the threaded rod to prevent it from spinning and tighten the equalizer nut 6 full turns past its original position on the threaded rod.

4. Attach an appropriate cable tension gauge (Rotunda Model 21-0018 or equivalent) behind the equalizer assembly either toward the right or left rear drum assembly and measure cable tension. Cable tension should be 400–600 lbs. with the parking brake pedal fully in the last detent position. If tension is low, repeat steps 2 and 3.

5. Release parking brake and check for rear wheel drag.

The cables should be tight enough to provide full application of the rear brake shoes, when the parking brake lever or foot pedal is placed in the fully applied position, yet loose enough to ensure complete release of the brake shoes when the lever is in the released position.

NOTE: *The Tension Limiter will reset the parking brake tension any time the system is disconnected provided the distance between the bracket and the cinch strap hook is reduced during adjustment. When the cinch strap contacts the bracket, the system tension will increase significantly and over tensioning may result. If all available adjustment travel has been used, the tension limiter must be replaced.*

REMOVAL AND INSTALLATION

Equalizer-To-Control Cable

1. Raise the vehicle on a hoist and support on jackstands. Back off the equalizer nut and remove slug of front cable from the tension limiter.

2. Remove the parking brake cable from the bracket.

3. Remove the jackstands and lower the vehicle. Remove the forward ball end of the parking brake cable from the control assembly clevis.

4. Remove the cable from the control assembly.

5. Using a fish wire or cord attached to the control lever end of the cable, remove the cable from the vehicle.

To install:

6. Transfer the fish wire or cord to the new cable. Position the cable in the vehicle, routing the cable through the dash panel. Remove the fish wire and secure the cable to the control.

7. Connect the forward ball end of the brake cable to the clevis of the control assembly. Raise the vehicle on a hoist.

8. Route the cable through the bracket.

9. Connect the slug of the cable to the Tension Limiter connector. Adjust the parking brake cable at the equalizer using the appropriate procedure shown above.

10. Rotate both rear wheels to be sure that the parking brakes are not dragging.

Equalizer-To-Rear Wheel Cables

1. Raise the vehicle and remove the hub cap, wheel, Tension Limiter and brake drum. Remove the locknut on the threaded rod and disconnect the cable from the equalizer.

2. Compress the prongs that retain the cable housing to the frame bracket, and pull the cable and housing out of the bracket.

3. Working on the wheel side, compress the prongs on the cable retainer so they can pass

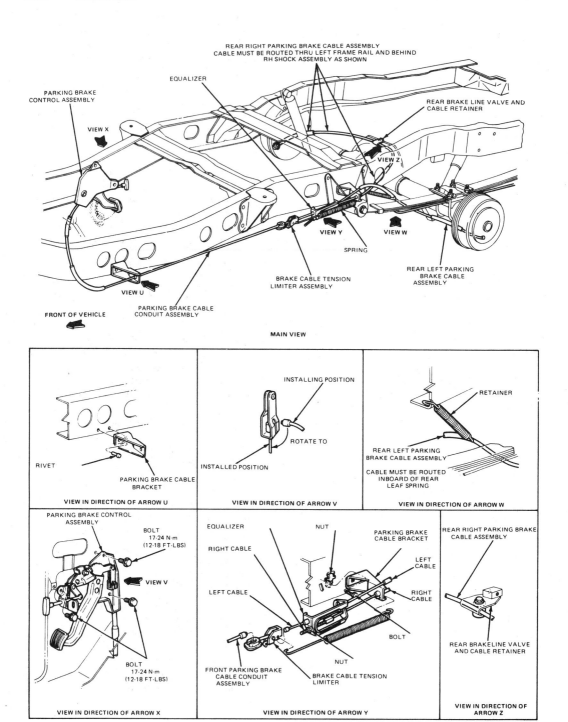

REAR RIGHT PARKING BRAKE CABLE ASSEMBLY
CABLE MUST BE ROUTED THRU LEFT FRAME RAIL AND BEHIND
RH SHOCK ASSEMBLY AS SHOWN

EQUALIZER

PARKING BRAKE
CONTROL ASSEMBLY

VIEW X

REAR BRAKE LINE VALVE AND
CABLE RETAINER

VIEW Z

VIEW Y   VIEW W

SPRING

REAR LEFT PARKING
BRAKE CABLE
ASSEMBLY

BRAKE CABLE TENSION
LIMITER ASSEMBLY

VIEW U

FRONT OF VEHICLE

PARKING BRAKE CABLE
CONDUIT ASSEMBLY

MAIN VIEW

RIVET

PARKING BRAKE CABLE
BRACKET

VIEW IN DIRECTION OF ARROW U

INSTALLING POSITION

ROTATE TO

INSTALLED POSITION

VIEW IN DIRECTION OF ARROW V

RETAINER

REAR LEFT PARKING
BRAKE CABLE ASSEMBLY

CABLE MUST BE ROUTED
INBOARD OF REAR
LEAF SPRING

VIEW IN DIRECTION OF ARROW W

PARKING BRAKE CONTROL
ASSEMBLY

BOLT
17-24 N·m
(12-18 FT·LBS)

VIEW V

BOLT
17-24 N·m
(12-18 FT·LBS)

VIEW IN DIRECTION OF ARROW X

EQUALIZER   NUT

RIGHT CABLE

PARKING BRAKE
CABLE BRACKET

LEFT
CABLE

RIGHT
CABLE

LEFT CABLE

BOLT

NUT

FRONT PARKING BRAKE
CABLE CONDUIT
ASSEMBLY

BRAKE CABLE TENSION
LIMITER

VIEW IN DIRECTION OF ARROW Y

REAR RIGHT PARKING BRAKE
CABLE ASSEMBLY

REAR BRAKELINE VALVE
AND CABLE RETAINER

VIEW IN DIRECTION OF
ARROW Z

Ranger parking brake system

Brake Specifications
All measurements in inches

Year	Master Cylinder Bore	Caliper Bore	Wheel Cylinder Bore		Rotor Diameter	Rotor Minimum Thickness	Rotor Maximum Run-out	Brake Drum Diameter		Machined Oversize	
			Front	Rear				Front	Rear	Front	Rear
1983–84	.9375	2.597	—	.750	10.28 ①	0.81	.003	—	9.00	—	9.06

① 4x4: 10.86

through the hole in the brake backing plate. Draw the cable retainer out of the hole.

4. With the spring tension off the parking brake lever, lift the cable out of the slot in the lever, and remove the cable through the brake backing plate hole.

To install:

5. Route the right cable behind the right shock and through the hole in the left frame side rail. Route the left cable inboard of the leaf spring. Pull the cable through the brake backing plate until the end of the cable is inserted over the slot in the parking brake lever. Pull the excess slack from the cable and insert the cable housing into the brake backing plate access hole until the retainer prongs expand.

6. Insert the front of the cable housing through the frame crossmember bracket until the prong expands. Insert the ball end of the cable into the key hole slots on the equalizer, rotate the equalizer 90° and recouple the Tension Limiter threaded rod to the equalizer.

7. Install the rear brake drum, wheel, and hub cap, and adjust the rear brake shoes.

8. Adjust the parking brake tension using the appropriate procedure shown above.

9. Rotate both rear wheels to be sure that the parking brakes are not dragging.

Troubleshooting

This section is designed to aid in the quick, accurate diagnosis of automotive problems. While automotive repairs can be made by many people, accurate troubleshooting is a rare skill for the amateur and professional alike.

In its simplest state, troubleshooting is an exercise in logic. It is essential to realize that an automobile is really composed of a series of systems. Some of these systems are interrelated; others are not. Automobiles operate within a framework of logical rules and physical laws, and the key to troubleshooting is a good understanding of all the automotive systems.

This section breaks the car or truck down into its component systems, allowing the problem to be isolated. The charts and diagnostic road maps list the most common problems and the most probable causes of trouble. Obviously it would be impossible to list every possible problem that could happen along with every possible cause, but it will locate MOST problems and eliminate a lot of unnecessary guesswork. The systematic format will locate problems within a given system, but, because many automotive systems are interrelated, the solution to your particular problem may be found in a number of systems on the car or truck.

USING THE TROUBLESHOOTING CHARTS

This book contains all of the specific information that the average do-it-yourself mechanic needs to repair and maintain his or her car or truck. The troubleshooting charts are designed to be used in conjunction with the specific procedures and information in the text. For instance, troubleshooting a point-type ignition system is fairly standard for all models, but you may be directed to the text to find procedures for troubleshooting an individual type of electronic ignition. You will also have to refer to the specification charts throughout the book for specifications applicable to your car or truck.

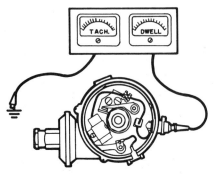

Tach-dwell hooked-up to distributor

TOOLS AND EQUIPMENT

The tools illustrated in Chapter 1 (plus two more diagnostic pieces) will be adequate to troubleshoot most problems. The two other tools needed are a voltmeter and an ohmmeter. These can be purchased separately or in combination, known as a VOM meter.

In the event that other tools are required, they will be noted in the procedures.

Troubleshooting Engine Problems

See Chapters 2, 3, 4 for more information and service procedures.

Index to Systems

System	To Test	Group
Battery	Engine need not be running	1
Starting system	Engine need not be running	2
Primary electrical system	Engine need not be running	3
Secondary electrical system	Engine need not be running	4
Fuel system	Engine need not be running	5
Engine compression	Engine need not be running	6
Engine vacuum	Engine must be running	7
Secondary electrical system	Engine must be running	8
Valve train	Engine must be running	9
Exhaust system	Engine must be running	10
Cooling system	Engine must be running	11
Engine lubrication	Engine must be running	12

Index to Problems

Problem: Symptom	Begin at Specific Diagnosis, Number ___
Engine Won't Start:	
Starter doesn't turn	1.1, 2.1
Starter turns, engine doesn't	2.1
Starter turns engine very slowly	1.1, 2.4
Starter turns engine normally	3.1, 4.1
Starter turns engine very quickly	6.1
Engine fires intermittently	4.1
Engine fires consistently	5.1, 6.1
Engine Runs Poorly:	
Hard starting	3.1, 4.1, 5.1, 8.1
Rough idle	4.1, 5.1, 8.1
Stalling	3.1, 4.1, 5.1, 8.1
Engine dies at high speeds	4.1, 5.1
Hesitation (on acceleration from standing stop)	5.1, 8.1
Poor pickup	4.1, 5.1, 8.1
Lack of power	3.1, 4.1, 5.1, 8.1
Backfire through the carburetor	4.1, 8.1, 9.1
Backfire through the exhaust	4.1, 8.1, 9.1
Blue exhaust gases	6.1, 7.1
Black exhaust gases	5.1
Running on (after the ignition is shut off)	3.1, 8.1
Susceptible to moisture	4.1
Engine misfires under load	4.1, 7.1, 8.4, 9.1
Engine misfires at speed	4.1, 8.4
Engine misfires at idle	3.1, 4.1, 5.1, 7.1, 8.4

Sample Section

Test and Procedure	Results and Indications	Proceed to
4.1—Check for spark: Hold each spark plug wire approximately ¼" from ground with gloves or a heavy, dry rag. Crank the engine and observe the spark.	→ If no spark is evident:	→ 4.2
	→ If spark is good in some cases:	→ 4.3
	→ If spark is good in all cases:	→ 4.6

Specific Diagnosis

This section is arranged so that following each test, instructions are given to proceed to another, until a problem is diagnosed.

Section 1—Battery

Test and Procedure	Results and Indications	Proceed to
1.1—Inspect the battery visually for case condition (corrosion, cracks) and water level.	If case is cracked, replace battery:	**1.4**
	If the case is intact, remove corrosion with a solution of baking soda and water (**CAUTION:** *do not get the solution into the battery*), and fill with water:	**1.2**

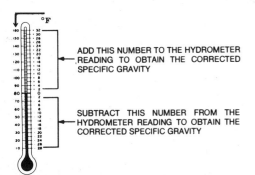

DIRT ON TOP OF BATTERY PLUGGED VENT
CORROSION
LOOSE CABLE OR POSTS
CRACKS
LOW WATER LEVEL   **Inspect the battery case**

Test and Procedure	Results and Indications	Proceed to
1.2—Check the battery cable connections: Insert a screwdriver between the battery post and the cable clamp. Turn the headlights on high beam, and observe them as the screwdriver is gently twisted to ensure good metal to metal contact.	If the lights brighten, remove and clean the clamp and post; coat the post with petroleum jelly, install and tighten the clamp:	**1.4**
	If no improvement is noted:	**1.3**

TESTING BATTERY CABLE CONNECTIONS USING A SCREWDRIVER

Test and Procedure	Results and Indications	Proceed to
1.3—Test the state of charge of the battery using an individual cell tester or hydrometer.	If indicated, charge the battery. **NOTE:** *If no obvious reason exists for the low state of charge (i.e., battery age, prolonged storage), proceed to:*	**1.4**

°F

ADD THIS NUMBER TO THE HYDROMETER READING TO OBTAIN THE CORRECTED SPECIFIC GRAVITY

SUBTRACT THIS NUMBER FROM THE HYDROMETER READING TO OBTAIN THE CORRECTED SPECIFIC GRAVITY

Specific Gravity (@ 80° F.)

Minimum	Battery Charge
1.260	100% Charged
1.230	75% Charged
1.200	50% Charged
1.170	25% Charged
1.140	Very Little Power Left
1.110	Completely Discharged

The effects of temperature on battery specific gravity (left) and amount of battery charge in relation to specific gravity (right)

Test and Procedure	Results and Indications	Proceed to
1.4—Visually inspect battery cables for cracking, bad connection to ground, or bad connection to starter.	If necessary, tighten connections or replace the cables:	**2.1**

Section 2—Starting System
See Chapter 3 for service procedures

Test and Procedure	Results and Indications	Proceed to

Note: Tests in Group 2 are performed with coil high tension lead disconnected to prevent accidental starting.

2.1—Test the starter motor and solenoid: Connect a jumper from the battery post of the solenoid (or relay) to the starter post of the solenoid (or relay).	If starter turns the engine normally:	2.2
	If the starter buzzes, or turns the engine very slowly:	2.4
	If no response, replace the solenoid (or relay).	3.1
	If the starter turns, but the engine doesn't, ensure that the flywheel ring gear is intact. If the gear is undamaged, replace the starter drive.	3.1
2.2—Determine whether ignition override switches are functioning properly (clutch start switch, neutral safety switch), by connecting a jumper across the switch(es), and turning the ignition switch to "start".	If starter operates, adjust or replace switch:	3.1
	If the starter doesn't operate:	2.3
2.3—Check the ignition switch "start" position: Connect a 12V test lamp or voltmeter between the starter post of the solenoid (or relay) and ground. Turn the ignition switch to the "start" position, and jiggle the key.	If the lamp doesn't light or the meter needle doesn't move when the switch is turned, check the ignition switch for loose connections, cracked insulation, or broken wires. Repair or replace as necessary:	3.1
	If the lamp flickers or needle moves when the key is jiggled, replace the ignition switch.	3.3

Checking the ignition switch "start" position

STARTER RELAY (IF EQUIPPED)

2.4—Remove and bench test the starter, according to specifications in the engine electrical section.	If the starter does not meet specifications, repair or replace as needed:	3.1
	If the starter is operating properly:	2.5
2.5—Determine whether the engine can turn freely: Remove the spark plugs, and check for water in the cylinders. Check for water on the dipstick, or oil in the radiator. Attempt to turn the engine using an 18″ flex drive and socket on the crankshaft pulley nut or bolt.	If the engine will turn freely only with the spark plugs out, and hydrostatic lock (water in the cylinders) is ruled out, check valve timing:	9.2
	If engine will not turn freely, and it is known that the clutch and transmission are free, the engine must be disassembled for further evaluation:	Chapter 3

Section 3—Primary Electrical System

Test and Procedure	Results and Indications	Proceed to
3.1—Check the ignition switch "on" position: Connect a jumper wire between the distributor side of the coil and ground, and a 12V test lamp between the switch side of the coil and ground. Remove the high tension lead from the coil. Turn the ignition switch on and jiggle the key.	If the lamp lights:	**3.2**
	If the lamp flickers when the key is jiggled, replace the ignition switch:	**3.3**
	If the lamp doesn't light, check for loose or open connections. If none are found, remove the ignition switch and check for continuity. If the switch is faulty, replace it:	**3.3**

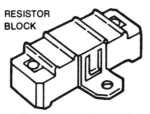

Checking the ignition switch "on" position

3.2—Check the ballast resistor or resistance wire for an open circuit, using an ohmmeter. See Chapter 3 for specific tests.	Replace the resistor or resistance wire if the resistance is zero. **NOTE:** *Some ignition systems have no ballast resistor.*	**3.3**

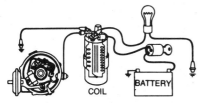

RESISTOR BLOCK

CALIBRATED RESISTANCE LEAD

Two types of resistors

3.3—On point-type ignition systems, visually inspect the breaker points for burning, pitting or excessive wear. Gray coloring of the point contact surfaces is normal. Rotate the crankshaft until the contact heel rests on a high point of the distributor cam and adjust the point gap to specifications. On electronic ignition models, remove the distributor cap and visually inspect the armature. Ensure that the armature pin is in place, and that the armature is on tight and rotates when the engine is cranked. Make sure there are no cracks, chips or rounded edges on the armature.	If the breaker points are intact, clean the contact surfaces with fine emery cloth, and adjust the point gap to specifications. If the points are worn, replace them. On electronic systems, replace any parts which appear defective. If condition persists:	**3.4**

Test and Procedure	Results and Indications	Proceed to
3.4—On point-type ignition systems, connect a dwell-meter between the distributor primary lead and ground. Crank the engine and observe the point dwell angle. On electronic ignition systems, conduct a stator (magnetic pickup assembly) test. See Chapter 3.	On point-type systems, adjust the dwell angle if necessary. **NOTE:** *Increasing the point gap decreases the dwell angle and vice-versa.*	**3.6**
	If the dwell meter shows little or no reading;	**3.5**
	On electronic ignition systems, if the stator is bad, replace the stator. If the stator is good, proceed to the other tests in Chapter 3.	

Dwell is a function of point gap

3.5—On the point-type ignition systems, check the condenser for short: connect an ohmmeter across the condenser body and the pigtail lead.	If any reading other than infinite is noted, replace the condenser	**3.6**

Checking the condenser for short

3.6—Test the coil primary resistance: On point-type ignition systems, connect an ohmmeter across the coil primary terminals, and read the resistance on the low scale. Note whether an external ballast resistor or resistance wire is used. On electronic ignition systems, test the coil primary resistance as in Chapter 3.	Point-type ignition coils utilizing ballast resistors or resistance wires should have approximately 1.0 ohms resistance. Coils with internal resistors should have approximately 4.0 ohms resistance. If values far from the above are noted, replace the coil.	**4.1**

Check the coil primary resistance

Section 4—Secondary Electrical System
See Chapters 2–3 for service procedures

Test and Procedure	Results and Indications	Proceed to
4.1—Check for spark: Hold each spark plug wire approximately ¼" from ground with gloves or a heavy, dry rag. Crank the engine, and observe the spark.	If no spark is evident:	**4.2**
	If spark is good in some cylinders:	**4.3**
	If spark is good in all cylinders:	**4.6**

Check for spark at the plugs

4.2—Check for spark at the coil high tension lead: Remove the coil high tension lead from the distributor and position it approximately ¼" from ground. Crank the engine and observe spark. **CAUTION:** *This test should not be performed on engines equipped with electronic ignition.*	If the spark is good and consistent:	**4.3**
	If the spark is good but intermittent, test the primary electrical system starting at 3.3:	**3.3**
	If the spark is weak or non-existent, replace the coil high tension lead, clean and tighten all connections and retest. If no improvement is noted:	**4.4**
4.3—Visually inspect the distributor cap and rotor for burned or corroded contacts, cracks, carbon tracks, or moisture. Also check the fit of the rotor on the distributor shaft (where applicable).	If moisture is present, dry thoroughly, and retest per 4.1:	**4.1**
	If burned or excessively corroded contacts, cracks, or carbon tracks are noted, replace the defective part(s) and retest per 4.1:	**4.1**
	If the rotor and cap appear intact, or are only slightly corroded, clean the contacts thoroughly (including the cap towers and spark plug wire ends) and retest per 4.1:	
	If the spark is good in all cases:	**4.6**
	If the spark is poor in all cases:	**4.5**

Inspect the distributor cap and rotor

CHILTON'S
AUTO BODY REPAIR TIPS

Tools and Materials • Step-by-Step Illustrated Procedures
How To Repair Dents, Scratches and Rust Holes
Spray Painting and Refinishing Tips

EASY
STEP-BY-STEP
TIPS FROM PROS

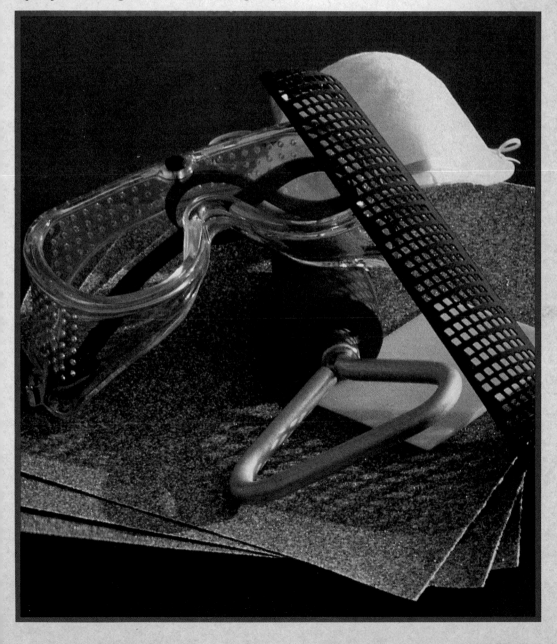

With a little practice, basic body repair procedures can be mastered by any do-it-yourself mechanic. The step-by-step repairs shown here can be applied to almost any type of auto body repair.

TOOLS & MATERIALS

You may already have basic tools, such as hammers and electric drills. Other tools unique to body repair — body hammers, grinding attachments, sanding blocks, dent puller, half-round plastic file and plastic spreaders — are relatively inexpensive and can be obtained wherever auto parts or auto body repair parts are sold. Portable air compressors and paint spray guns can be purchased or rented.

Auto Body Repair Kits

The best and most often used products are available to the do-it-yourselfer in kit form, from major manufacturers of auto body repair products. The same manufacturers also merchandise the individual products for use by pros.

Kits are available to make a wide variety of repairs, including holes, dents and scratches and fiberglass, and offer the advantage of buying the materials you'll need for the job. There is little waste or chance of materials going bad from not being used. Many kits may also contain basic body-working tools such as body files, sanding blocks and spreaders. Check the contents of the kit before buying your tools.

BODY REPAIR TIPS

Safety

Many of the products associated with auto body repair and refinishing contain toxic chemicals. Read all labels before opening containers and store them in a safe place and manner.

• Wear eye protection (safety goggles) when using power tools or when performing any operation that involves the removal of any type of material.

• Wear lung protection (disposable mask or respirator) when grinding, sanding or painting.

Sanding

1 Sand off paint before using a dent puller. When using a non-adhesive sanding disc, cover the back of the disc with an overlapping layer or two of masking tape and trim the edges. The disc will last considerably longer.

2 Use the circular motion of the sanding disc to grind *into* the edge of the repair. Grinding or sanding away from the jagged edge will only tear the sandpaper.

3 Use the palm of your hand flat on the panel to detect high and low spots. Do not use your fingertips. Slide your hand slowly back and forth.

WORKING WITH BODY FILLER

Mixing The Filler

Cleanliness and proper mixing and application are extremely important. Use a clean piece of plastic or glass or a disposable artist's palette to mix body filler.

1 Allow plenty of time and follow directions. No useful purpose will be served by adding more hardener to make it cure (set-up) faster. Less hardener means more curing time, but the mixture dries harder; more hardener means less curing time but a softer mixture.

2 Both the hardener and the filler should be thoroughly kneaded or stirred before mixing. Hardener should be a solid paste and dispense like thin toothpaste. Body filler should be smooth, and free of lumps or thick spots.

Getting the proper amount of hardener in the filler is the trickiest part of preparing the filler. Use the same amount of hardener in cold or warm weather. For contour filler (thick coats), a bead of hardener twice the diameter of the filler is about right. There's about a 15% margin on either side, but, if in doubt use less hardener.

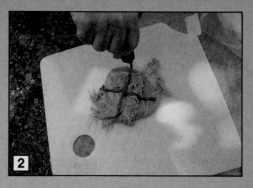

3 Mix the body filler and hardener by wiping across the mixing surface, picking the mixture up and wiping it again. Colder weather requires longer mixing times. Do not mix in a circular motion; this will trap air bubbles which will become holes in the cured filler.

Applying The Filler

1 For best results, filler should not be applied over 1/4" thick.

Apply the filler in several coats. Build it up to above the level of the repair surface so that it can be sanded or grated down.

The first coat of filler must be pressed on with a firm wiping motion.

Apply the filler in one direction only. Working the filler back and forth will either pull it off the metal or trap air bubbles.

REPAIRING DENTS

Before you start, take a few minutes to study the damaged area. Try to visualize the shape of the panel before it was damaged. If the damage is on the left fender, look at the right fender and use it as a guide. If there is access to the panel from behind, you can reshape it with a body hammer. If not, you'll have to use a dent puller. Go slowly and work the metal a little at a time. Get the panel as straight as possible before applying filler.

1 This dent is typical of one that can be pulled out or hammered out from behind. Remove the headlight cover, headlight assembly and turn signal housing.

2 Drill a series of holes ½ the size of the end of the dent puller along the stress line. Make some trial pulls and assess the results. If necessary, drill more holes and try again. Do not hurry.

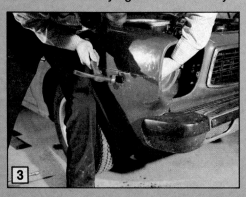

3 If possible, use a body hammer and block to shape the metal back to its original contours. Get the metal back as close to its original shape as possible. Don't depend on body filler to fill dents.

4 Using an 80-grit grinding disc on an electric drill, grind the paint from the surrounding area down to bare metal. Use a new grinding pad to prevent heat buildup that will warp metal.

5 The area should look like this when you're finished grinding. Knock the drill holes in and tape over small openings to keep plastic filler out.

6 Mix the body filler (see Body Repair Tips). Spread the body filler evenly over the entire area (see Body Repair Tips). Be sure to cover the area completely.

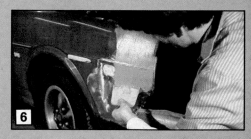

7 Let the body filler dry until the surface can just be scratched with your fingernail. Knock the high spots from the body filler with a body file ("Cheese-grater"). Check frequently with the palm of your hand for high and low spots.

8 Check to be sure that trim pieces that will be installed later will fit exactly. Sand the area with 40-grit paper.

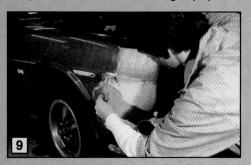

9 If you wind up with low spots, you may have to apply another layer of filler.

10 Knock the high spots off with 40-grit paper. When you are satisfied with the contours of the repair, apply a thin coat of filler to cover pin holes and scratches.

11 Block sand the area with 40-grit paper to a smooth finish. Pay particular attention to body lines and ridges that must be well-defined.

12 Sand the area with 400 paper and then finish with a scuff pad. The finished repair is ready for priming and painting (see Painting Tips).

Materials and photos courtesy of Ritt Jones Auto Body, Prospect Park, PA.

REPAIRING RUST HOLES

There are many ways to repair rust holes. The fiberglass cloth kit shown here is one of the most cost efficient for the owner because it provides a strong repair that resists cracking and moisture and is relatively easy to use. It can be used on large and small holes (with or without backing) and can be applied over contoured areas. Remember, however, that short of replacing an entire panel, no repair is a guarantee that the rust will not return.

1 Remove any trim that will be in the way. Clean away all loose debris. Cut away all the rusted metal. But be sure to leave enough metal to retain the contour or body shape.

2 Grind away all traces of rust with a 24-grit grinding disc. Be sure to grind back 3-4 inches from the edge of the hole down to bare metal and be sure all traces of paint, primer and rust are removed.

3 Block sand the area with 80 or 100 grit sandpaper to get a clear, shiny surface and feathered paint edge. Tap the edges of the hole inward with a ball peen hammer.

4 If you are going to use release film, cut a piece about 2-3″ larger than the area you have sanded. Place the film over the repair and mark the sanded area on the film. Avoid any unnecessary wrinkling of the film.

5 Cut 2 pieces of fiberglass matte to match the shape of the repair. One piece should be about 1″ smaller than the sanded area and the second piece should be 1″ smaller than the first. Mix enough filler and hardener to saturate the fiberglass material (see Body Repair Tips).

6 Lay the release sheet on a flat surface and spread an even layer of filler, large enough to cover the repair. Lay the smaller piece of fiberglass cloth in the center of the sheet and spread another layer of filler over the fiberglass cloth. Repeat the operation for the larger piece of cloth.

7 Place the repair material over the repair area, with the release film facing outward. Use a spreader and work from the center outward to smooth the material, following the body contours. Be sure to remove all air bubbles.

8 Wait until the repair has dried tack-free and peel off the release sheet. The ideal working temperature is 60°-90° F. Cooler or warmer temperatures or high humidity may require additional curing time. Wait longer, if in doubt.

9 Sand and feather-edge the entire area. The initial sanding can be done with a sanding disc on an electric drill if care is used. Finish the sanding with a block sander. Low spots can be filled with body filler; this may require several applications.

10 When the filler can just be scratched with a fingernail, knock the high spots down with a body file and smooth the entire area with 80-grit. Feather the filled areas into the surrounding areas.

11 When the area is sanded smooth, mix some topcoat and hardener and apply it directly with a spreader. This will give a smooth finish and prevent the glass matte from showing through the paint.

12 Block sand the topcoat smooth with finishing sandpaper (200 grit), and 400 grit. The repair is ready for masking, priming and painting (see Painting Tips).

Materials and photos courtesy Marson Corporation, Chelsea, Massachusetts

PAINTING TIPS

Preparation

1 SANDING — Use a 400 or 600 grit wet or dry sandpaper. Wet-sand the area with a ¼ sheet of sandpaper soaked in clean water. Keep the paper wet while sanding. Sand the area until the repaired area tapers into the original finish.

2 CLEANING — Wash the area to be painted thoroughly with water and a clean rag. Rinse it thoroughly and wipe the surface dry until you're sure it's completely free of dirt, dust, fingerprints, wax, detergent or other foreign matter.

3 MASKING — Protect any areas you don't want to overspray by covering them with masking tape and newspaper. Be careful not get fingerprints on the area to be painted.

4 PRIMING — All exposed metal should be primed before painting. Primer protects the metal and provides an excellent surface for paint adhesion. When the primer is dry, wet-sand the area again with 600 grit wet-sandpaper. Clean the area again after sanding.

Painting Techniques

P aint applied from either a spray gun or a spray can (for small areas) will provide good results. Experiment on an old piece of metal to get the right combination before you begin painting.

SPRAYING VISCOSITY (SPRAY GUN ONLY) — Paint should be thinned to spraying viscosity according to the directions on the can. Use only the recommended thinner or reducer and the same amount of reduction regardless of temperature.

AIR PRESSURE (SPRAY GUN ONLY) — This is extremely important. Be sure you are using the proper recommended pressure.

TEMPERATURE — The surface to be painted should be approximately the same temperature as the surrounding air. Applying warm paint to a cold surface, or vice versa, will completely upset the paint characteristics.

THICKNESS — Spray with smooth strokes. In general, the thicker the coat of paint, the longer the drying time. Apply several thin coats about 30 seconds apart. The paint should remain wet long enough to flow out and no longer; heavier coats will only produce sags or wrinkles. Spray a light (fog) coat, followed by heavier color coats.

DISTANCE — The ideal spraying distance is 8″-12″ from the gun or can to the surface. Shorter distances will produce ripples, while greater distances will result in orange peel, dry film and poor color match and loss of material due to overspray.

OVERLAPPING — The gun or can should be kept at right angles to the surface at all times. Work to a wet edge at an even speed, using a 50% overlap and direct the center of the spray at the lower or nearest edge of the previous stroke.

RUBBING OUT (BLENDING) FRESH PAINT — Let the paint dry thoroughly. Runs or imperfections can be sanded out, primed and repainted.

Don't be in too big a hurry to remove the masking. This only produces paint ridges. When the finish has dried for at least a week, apply a small amount of fine grade rubbing compound with a clean, wet cloth. Use lots of water and blend the new paint with the surrounding area.

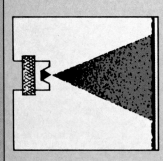

WRONG

Thin coat. Stroke too fast, not enough overlap, gun too far away.

CORRECT

Medium coat. Proper distance, good stroke, proper overlap.

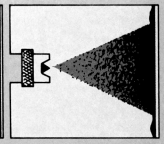

WRONG

Heavy coat. Stroke too slow, too much overlap, gun too close.

Test and Procedure	Results and Indications	Proceed to
4.4—Check the coil secondary resistance: On point-type systems connect an ohmmeter across the distributor side of the coil and the coil tower. Read the resistance on the high scale of the ohmmeter. On electronic ignition systems, see Chapter 3 for specific tests.	The resistance of a satisfactory coil should be between 4,000 and 10,000 ohms. If resistance is considerably higher (i.e., 40,000 ohms) replace the coil and retest per 4.1. **NOTE:** *This does not apply to high performance coils.*	

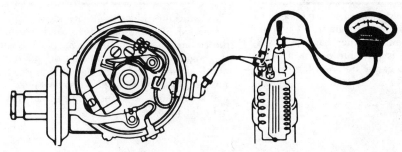

Testing the coil secondary resistance

Test and Procedure	Results and Indications	Proceed to
4.5—Visually inspect the spark plug wires for cracking or brittleness. Ensure that no two wires are positioned so as to cause induction firing (adjacent and parallel). Remove each wire, one by one, and check resistance with an ohmmeter.	Replace any cracked or brittle wires. If any of the wires are defective, replace the entire set. Replace any wires with excessive resistance (over $8000\,\Omega$ per foot for suppression wire), and separate any wires that might cause induction firing.	**4.6**

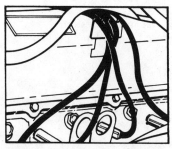 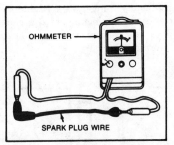 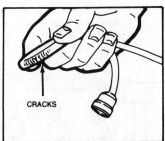

Misfiring can be the result of spark plug leads to adjacent, consecutively firing cylinders running parallel and too close together	On point-type ignition systems, check the spark plug wires as shown. On electronic ignitions, do not remove the wire from the distributor cap terminal; instead, test through the cap	Spark plug wires can be checked visually by bending them in a loop over your finger. This will reveal any cracks, burned or broken insulation. Any wire with cracked insulation should be replaced

Test and Procedure	Results and Indications	Proceed to
4.6—Remove the spark plugs, noting the cylinders from which they were removed, and evaluate according to the color photos in the middle of this book.	See following.	**See following.**

Test and Procedure	Results and Indications	Proceed to
4.7—Examine the location of all the plugs.	The following diagrams illustrate some of the conditions that the location of plugs will reveal.	**4.8**

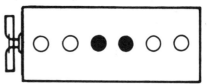

Two adjacent plugs are fouled in a 6-cylinder engine, 4-cylinder engine or either bank of a V-8. This is probably due to a blown head gasket between the two cylinders

The two center plugs in a 6-cylinder engine are fouled. Raw fuel may be "boiled" out of the carburetor into the intake manifold after the engine is shut-off. Stop-start driving can also foul the center plugs, due to overly rich mixture. Proper float level, a new float needle and seat or use of an insulating spacer may help this problem

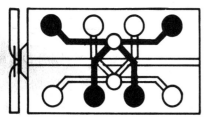

An unbalanced carburetor is indicated. Following the fuel flow on this particular design shows that the cylinders fed by the right-hand barrel are fouled from overly rich mixture, while the cylinders fed by the left-hand barrel are normal

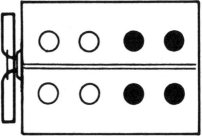

If the four rear plugs are overheated, a cooling system problem is suggested. A thorough cleaning of the cooling system may restore coolant circulation and cure the problem

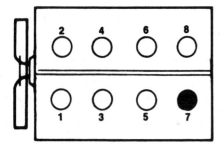

Finding one plug overheated may indicate an intake manifold leak near the affected cylinder. If the overheated plug is the second of two adjacent, consecutively firing plugs, it could be the result of ignition cross-firing. Separating the leads to these two plugs will eliminate cross-fire

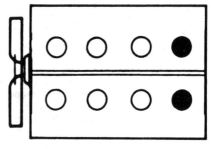

Occasionally, the two rear plugs in large, lightly used V-8's will become oil fouled. High oil consumption and smoky exhaust may also be noticed. It is probably due to plugged oil drain holes in the rear of the cylinder head, causing oil to be sucked in around the valve stems. This usually occurs in the rear cylinders first, because the engine slants that way

Test and Procedure	Results and Indications	Proceed to
4.8—Determine the static ignition timing. Using the crankshaft pulley timing marks as a guide, locate top dead center on the compression stroke of the number one cylinder.	The rotor should be pointing toward the No. 1 tower in the distributor cap, and, on electronic ignitions, the armature spoke for that cylinder should be lined up with the stator.	**4.8**
4.9—Check coil polarity: Connect a voltmeter negative lead to the coil high tension lead, and the positive lead to ground (**NOTE:** *Reverse the hook-up for positive ground systems*). Crank the engine momentarily. **Checking coil polarity**	If the voltmeter reads up-scale, the polarity is correct: If the voltmeter reads down-scale, reverse the coil polarity (switch the primary leads):	**5.1** **5.1**

Section 5—Fuel System
See Chapter 4 for service procedures

Test and Procedure	Results and Indications	Proceed to
5.1—Determine that the air filter is functioning efficiently: Hold paper elements up to a strong light, and attempt to see light through the filter.	Clean permanent air filters in solvent (or manufacturer's recommendation), and allow to dry. Replace paper elements through which light cannot be seen:	**5.2**
5.2—Determine whether a flooding condition exists: Flooding is identified by a strong gasoline odor, and excessive gasoline present in the throttle bore(s) of the carburetor.	If flooding is not evident: If flooding is evident, permit the gasoline to dry for a few moments and restart. If flooding doesn't recur: If flooding is persistent:	**5.3** **5.7** **5.5**

If the engine floods repeatedly, check the choke butterfly flap

Test and Procedure	Results and Indications	Proceed to
5.3—Check that fuel is reaching the carburetor: Detach the fuel line at the carburetor inlet. Hold the end of the line in a cup (not styrofoam), and crank the engine.	If fuel flows smoothly: If fuel doesn't flow (**NOTE:** *Make sure that there is fuel in the tank*), or flows erratically:	**5.7** **5.4**

Check the fuel pump by disconnecting the output line (fuel pump-to-carburetor) at the carburetor and operating the starter briefly

Test and Procedure	Results and Indications	Proceed to
5.4—Test the fuel pump: Disconnect all fuel lines from the fuel pump. Hold a finger over the input fitting, crank the engine (with electric pump, turn the ignition or pump on); and feel for suction.	If suction is evident, blow out the fuel line to the tank with low pressure compressed air until bubbling is heard from the fuel filler neck. Also blow out the carburetor fuel line (both ends disconnected):	**5.7**
	If no suction is evident, replace or repair the fuel pump: NOTE: *Repeated oil fouling of the spark plugs, or a no-start condition, could be the result of a ruptured vacuum booster pump diaphragm, through which oil or gasoline is being drawn into the intake manifold (where applicable).*	**5.7**
5.5—Occasionally, small specks of dirt will clog the small jets and orifices in the carburetor. With the engine cold, hold a flat piece of wood or similar material over the carburetor, where possible, and crank the engine.	If the engine starts, but runs roughly the engine is probably not run enough. If the engine won't start:	**5.9**
5.6—Check the needle and seat: Tap the carburetor in the area of the needle and seat.	If flooding stops, a gasoline additive (e.g., Gumout) will often cure the problem:	**5.7**
	If flooding continues, check the fuel pump for excessive pressure at the carburetor (according to specifications). If the pressure is normal, the needle and seat must be removed and checked, and/or the float level adjusted:	**5.7**
5.7—Test the accelerator pump by looking into the throttle bores while operating the throttle. **Check for gas at the carburetor by looking down the carburetor throat while someone moves the accelerator**	If the accelerator pump appears to be operating normally:	**5.8**
	If the accelerator pump is not operating, the pump must be reconditioned. Where possible, service the pump with the carburetor(s) installed on the engine. If necessary, remove the carburetor. Prior to removal:	**5.8**
5.8—Determine whether the carburetor main fuel system is functioning: Spray a commercial starting fluid into the carburetor while attempting to start the engine.	If the engine starts, runs for a few seconds, and dies:	**5.9**
	If the engine doesn't start:	**6.1**

Test and Procedure	Results and Indications	Proceed to
5.9—Uncommon fuel system malfunctions: See below:	If the problem is solved:	6.1
	If the problem remains, remove and recondition the carburetor.	

Condition	Indication	Test	Prevailing Weather Conditions	Remedy
Vapor lock	Engine will not restart shortly after running.	Cool the components of the fuel system until the engine starts. Vapor lock can be cured faster by draping a wet cloth over a mechanical fuel pump.	Hot to very hot	Ensure that the exhaust manifold heat control valve is operating. Check with the vehicle manufacturer for the recommended solution to vapor lock on the model in question.
Carburetor icing	Engine will not idle, stalls at low speeds.	Visually inspect the throttle plate area of the throttle bores for frost.	High humidity, 32–40° F.	Ensure that the exhaust manifold heat control valve is operating, and that the intake manifold heat riser is not blocked.
Water in the fuel	Engine sputters and stalls; may not start.	Pump a small amount of fuel into a glass jar. Allow to stand, and inspect for droplets or a layer of water.	High humidity, extreme temperature changes.	For droplets, use one or two cans of commercial gas line anti-freeze. For a layer of water, the tank must be drained, and the fuel lines blown out with compressed air.

Section 6—Engine Compression

See Chapter 3 for service procedures

6.1—Test engine compression: Remove all spark plugs. Block the throttle wide open. Insert a compression gauge into a spark plug port, crank the engine to obtain the maximum reading, and record.	If compression is within limits on all cylinders:	7.1
	If gauge reading is extremely low on all cylinders:	6.2
	If gauge reading is low on one or two cylinders: (If gauge readings are identical and low on two or more adjacent cylinders, the head gasket must be replaced.)	6.2

Checking compression

6.2—Test engine compression (wet): Squirt approximately 30 cc. of engine oil into each cylinder, and retest per 6.1.	If the readings improve, worn or cracked rings or broken pistons are indicated:	See Chapter 3
	If the readings do not improve, burned or excessively carboned valves or a jumped timing chain are indicated:	7.1
	NOTE: *A jumped timing chain is often indicated by difficult cranking.*	

Section 7—Engine Vacuum
See Chapter 3 for service procedures

Test and Procedure	Results and Indications	Proceed to
7.1—Attach a vacuum gauge to the intake manifold beyond the throttle plate. Start the engine, and observe the action of the needle over the range of engine speeds.	See below.	**See below**

INDICATION: normal engine in good condition

Proceed to: 8.1

Normal engine
Gauge reading: steady, from 17–22 in./Hg.

INDICATION: sticking valves or ignition miss

Proceed to: 9.1, 8.3

Sticking valves
Gauge reading: intermittent fluctuation at idle

INDICATION: late ignition or valve timing, low compression, stuck throttle valve, leaking carburetor or manifold gasket

Proceed to: 6.1

Incorrect valve timing
Gauge reading: low (10–15 in./Hg) but steady

INDICATION: improper carburetor adjustment or minor intake leak.

Proceed to: 7.2

Carburetor requires adjustment
Gauge reading: drifting needle

INDICATION: ignition miss, blown cylinder head gasket, leaking valve or weak valve spring

Proceed to: 8.3, 6.1

Blown head gasket
Gauge reading: needle fluctuates as engine speed increases

INDICATION: burnt valve or faulty valve clearance. Needle will fall when defective valve operates

Proceed to: 9.1

Burnt or leaking valves
Gauge reading: steady needle, but drops regularly

INDICATION: choked muffler, excessive back pressure in system

Proceed to: 10.1

Clogged exhaust system
Gauge reading: gradual drop in reading at idle

INDICATION: worn valve guides

Proceed to: 9.1

Worn valve guides
Gauge reading: needle vibrates excessively at idle, but steadies as engine speed increases

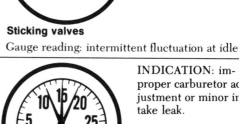

White pointer = steady gauge hand   Black pointer = fluctuating gauge hand

Test and Procedure	Results and Indications	Proceed to
7.2—Attach a vacuum gauge per 7.1, and test for an intake manifold leak. Squirt a small amount of oil around the intake manifold gaskets, carburetor gaskets, plugs and fittings. Observe the action of the vacuum gauge.	If the reading improves, replace the indicated gasket, or seal the indicated fitting or plug:	**8.1**
	If the reading remains low:	**7.3**
7.3—Test all vacuum hoses and accessories for leaks as described in 7.2. Also check the carburetor body (dashpots, automatic choke mechanism, throttle shafts) for leaks in the same manner.	If the reading improves, service or replace the offending part(s):	**8.1**
	If the reading remains low:	**6.1**

Section 8—Secondary Electrical System
See Chapter 2 for service procedures

Test and Procedure	Results and Indications	Proceed to
8.1—Remove the distributor cap and check to make sure that the rotor turns when the engine is cranked. Visually inspect the distributor components.	Clean, tighten or replace any components which appear defective.	**8.2**
8.2—Connect a timing light (per manufacturer's recommendation) and check the dynamic ignition timing. Disconnect and plug the vacuum hose(s) to the distributor if specified, start the engine, and observe the timing marks at the specified engine speed.	If the timing is not correct, adjust to specifications by rotating the distributor in the engine: (Advance timing by rotating distributor opposite normal direction of rotor rotation, retard timing by rotating distributor in same direction as rotor rotation.)	**8.3**
8.3—Check the operation of the distributor advance mechanism(s): To test the mechanical advance, disconnect the vacuum lines from the distributor advance unit and observe the timing marks with a timing light as the engine speed is increased from idle. If the mark moves smoothly, without hesitation, it may be assumed that the mechanical advance is functioning properly. To test vacuum advance and/or retard systems, alternately crimp and release the vacuum line, and observe the timing mark for movement. If movement is noted, the system is operating.	If the systems are functioning:	**8.4**
	If the systems are not functioning, remove the distributor, and test on a distributor tester:	**8.4**
8.4—Locate an ignition miss: With the engine running, remove each spark plug wire, one at a time, until one is found that doesn't cause the engine to roughen and slow down.	When the missing cylinder is identified:	**4.1**

Section 9—Valve Train
See Chapter 3 for service procedures

Test and Procedure	Results and Indications	Proceed to
9.1—Evaluate the valve train: Remove the valve cover, and ensure that the valves are adjusted to specifications. A mechanic's stethoscope may be used to aid in the diagnosis of the valve train. By pushing the probe on or near push rods or rockers, valve noise often can be isolated. A timing light also may be used to diagnose valve problems. Connect the light according to manufacturer's recommendations, and start the engine. Vary the firing moment of the light by increasing the engine speed (and therefore the ignition advance), and moving the trigger from cylinder to cylinder. Observe the movement of each valve.	Sticking valves or erratic valve train motion can be observed with the timing light. The cylinder head must be disassembled for repairs.	**See Chapter 3**
9.2—Check the valve timing: Locate top dead center of the No. 1 piston, and install a degree wheel or tape on the crankshaft pulley or damper with zero corresponding to an index mark on the engine. Rotate the crankshaft in its direction of rotation, and observe the opening of the No. 1 cylinder intake valve. The opening should correspond with the correct mark on the degree wheel according to specifications.	If the timing is not correct, the timing cover must be removed for further investigation.	**See Chapter 3**

Section 10—Exhaust System

Test and Procedure	Results and Indications	Proceed to
10.1—Determine whether the exhaust manifold heat control valve is operating: Operate the valve by hand to determine whether it is free to move. If the valve is free, run the engine to operating temperature and observe the action of the valve, to ensure that it is opening.	If the valve sticks, spray it with a suitable solvent, open and close the valve to free it, and retest. If the valve functions properly: If the valve does not free, or does not operate, replace the valve:	**10.2** **10.2**
10.2—Ensure that there are no exhaust restrictions: Visually inspect the exhaust system for kinks, dents, or crushing. Also note that gases are flowing freely from the tailpipe at all engine speeds, indicating no restriction in the muffler or resonator.	Replace any damaged portion of the system:	**11.1**

Section 11—Cooling System
See Chapter 3 for service procedures

Test and Procedure	Results and Indications	Proceed to
11.1—Visually inspect the fan belt for glazing, cracks, and fraying, and replace if necessary. Tighten the belt so that the longest span has approximately ½″ play at its mid-point under thumb pressure (see Chapter 1).	Replace or tighten the fan belt as necessary:	**11.2**

Checking belt tension

Test and Procedure	Results and Indications	Proceed to
11.2—Check the fluid level of the cooling system.	If full or slightly low, fill as necessary:	**11.5**
	If extremely low:	**11.3**
11.3—Visually inspect the external portions of the cooling system (radiator, radiator hoses, thermostat elbow, water pump seals, heater hoses, etc.) for leaks. If none are found, pressurize the cooling system to 14–15 psi.	If cooling system holds the pressure:	**11.5**
	If cooling system loses pressure rapidly, reinspect external parts of the system for leaks under pressure. If none are found, check dipstick for coolant in crankcase. If no coolant is present, but pressure loss continues:	**11.4**
	If coolant is evident in crankcase, remove cylinder head(s), and check gasket(s). If gaskets are intact, block and cylinder head(s) should be checked for cracks or holes.	
	If the gasket(s) is blown, replace, and purge the crankcase of coolant:	**12.6**
	NOTE: *Occasionally, due to atmospheric and driving conditions, condensation of water can occur in the crankcase. This causes the oil to appear milky white. To remedy, run the engine until hot, and change the oil and oil filter.*	
11.4—Check for combustion leaks into the cooling system: Pressurize the cooling system as above. Start the engine, and observe the pressure gauge. If the needle fluctuates, remove each spark plug wire, one at a time, noting which cylinder(s) reduce or eliminate the fluctuation.	Cylinders which reduce or eliminate the fluctuation, when the spark plug wire is removed, are leaking into the cooling system. Replace the head gasket on the affected cylinder bank(s).	

Pressurizing the cooling system

Test and Procedure	Results and Indications	Proceed to
11.5—Check the radiator pressure cap: Attach a radiator pressure tester to the radiator cap (wet the seal prior to installation). Quickly pump up the pressure, noting the point at which the cap releases.	If the cap releases within ± 1 psi of the specified rating, it is operating properly:	**11.6**
	If the cap releases at more than ± 1 psi of the specified rating, it should be replaced:	**11.6**

Checking radiator pressure cap

Test and Procedure	Results and Indications	Proceed to
11.6—Test the thermostat: Start the engine cold, remove the radiator cap, and insert a thermometer into the radiator. Allow the engine to idle. After a short while, there will be a sudden, rapid increase in coolant temperature. The temperature at which this sharp rise stops is the thermostat opening temperature.	If the thermostat opens at or about the specified temperature:	**11.7**
	If the temperature doesn't increase: (If the temperature increases slowly and gradually, replace the thermostat.)	**11.7**
11.7—Check the water pump: Remove the thermostat elbow and the thermostat, disconnect the coil high tension lead (to prevent starting), and crank the engine momentarily.	If coolant flows, replace the thermostat and retest per 11.6:	**11.6**
	If coolant doesn't flow, reverse flush the cooling system to alleviate any blockage that might exist. If system is not blocked, and coolant will not flow, replace the water pump.	

Section 12—Lubrication
See Chapter 3 for service procedures

Test and Procedure	Results and Indications	Proceed to
12.1—Check the oil pressure gauge or warning light: If the gauge shows low pressure, or the light is on for no obvious reason, remove the oil pressure sender. Install an accurate oil pressure gauge and run the engine momentarily.	If oil pressure builds normally, run engine for a few moments to determine that it is functioning normally, and replace the sender.	—
	If the pressure remains low:	**12.2**
	If the pressure surges:	**12.3**
	If the oil pressure is zero:	**12.3**
12.2—Visually inspect the oil: If the oil is watery or very thin, milky, or foamy, replace the oil and oil filter.	If the oil is normal:	**12.3**
	If after replacing oil the pressure remains low:	**12.3**
	If after replacing oil the pressure becomes normal:	—

Test and Procedure	Results and Indications	Proceed to
12.3—Inspect the oil pressure relief valve and spring, to ensure that it is not sticking or stuck. Remove and thoroughly clean the valve, spring, and the valve body.	If the oil pressure improves: If no improvement is noted:	— **12.4**
12.4—Check to ensure that the oil pump is not cavitating (sucking air instead of oil): See that the crankcase is neither over nor underfull, and that the pickup in the sump is in the proper position and free from sludge.	Fill or drain the crankcase to the proper capacity, and clean the pickup screen in solvent if necessary. If no improvement is noted:	**12.5**
12.5—Inspect the oil pump drive and the oil pump:	If the pump drive or the oil pump appear to be defective, service as necessary and retest per 12.1: If the pump drive and pump appear to be operating normally, the engine should be disassembled to determine where blockage exists:	**12.1** **See Chapter 3**
12.6—Purge the engine of ethylene glycol coolant: Completely drain the crankcase and the oil filter. Obtain a commercial butyl cellosolve base solvent, designated for this purpose, and follow the instructions precisely. Following this, install a new oil filter and refill the crankcase with the proper weight oil. The next oil and filter change should follow shortly thereafter (1000 miles).		

TROUBLESHOOTING EMISSION CONTROL SYSTEMS

See Chapter 4 for procedures applicable to individual emission control systems used on specific combinations of engine/transmission/model.

TROUBLESHOOTING THE CARBURETOR

See Chapter 4 for service procedures

Carburetor problems cannot be effectively isolated unless all other engine systems (particularly ignition and emission) are functioning properly and the engine is properly tuned.

Condition	Possible Cause
Engine cranks, but does not start	1. Improper starting procedure 2. No fuel in tank 3. Clogged fuel line or filter 4. Defective fuel pump 5. Choke valve not closing properly 6. Engine flooded 7. Choke valve not unloading 8. Throttle linkage not making full travel 9. Stuck needle or float 10. Leaking float needle or seat 11. Improper float adjustment
Engine stalls	1. Improperly adjusted idle speed or mixture **Engine hot** 2. Improperly adjusted dashpot 3. Defective or improperly adjusted solenoid 4. Incorrect fuel level in fuel bowl 5. Fuel pump pressure too high 6. Leaking float needle seat 7. Secondary throttle valve stuck open 8. Air or fuel leaks 9. Idle air bleeds plugged or missing 10. Idle passages plugged **Engine Cold** 11. Incorrectly adjusted choke 12. Improperly adjusted fast idle speed 13. Air leaks 14. Plugged idle or idle air passages 15. Stuck choke valve or binding linkage 16. Stuck secondary throttle valves 17. Engine flooding—high fuel level 18. Leaking or misaligned float
Engine hesitates on acceleration	1. Clogged fuel filter 2. Leaking fuel pump diaphragm 3. Low fuel pump pressure 4. Secondary throttle valves stuck, bent or misadjusted 5. Sticking or binding air valve 6. Defective accelerator pump 7. Vacuum leaks 8. Clogged air filter 9. Incorrect choke adjustment (engine cold)
Engine feels sluggish or flat on acceleration	1. Improperly adjusted idle speed or mixture 2. Clogged fuel filter 3. Defective accelerator pump 4. Dirty, plugged or incorrect main metering jets 5. Bent or sticking main metering rods 6. Sticking throttle valves 7. Stuck heat riser 8. Binding or stuck air valve 9. Dirty, plugged or incorrect secondary jets 10. Bent or sticking secondary metering rods. 11. Throttle body or manifold heat passages plugged 12. Improperly adjusted choke or choke vacuum break.
Carburetor floods	1. Defective fuel pump. Pressure too high. 2. Stuck choke valve 3. Dirty, worn or damaged float or needle valve/seat 4. Incorrect float/fuel level 5. Leaking float bowl

Condition	Possible Cause
Engine idles roughly and stalls	1. Incorrect idle speed 2. Clogged fuel filter 3. Dirt in fuel system or carburetor 4. Loose carburetor screws or attaching bolts 5. Broken carburetor gaskets 6. Air leaks 7. Dirty carburetor 8. Worn idle mixture needles 9. Throttle valves stuck open 10. Incorrectly adjusted float or fuel level 11. Clogged air filter
Engine runs unevenly or surges	1. Defective fuel pump 2. Dirty or clogged fuel filter 3. Plugged, loose or incorrect main metering jets or rods 4. Air leaks 5. Bent or sticking main metering rods 6. Stuck power piston 7. Incorrect float adjustment 8. Incorrect idle speed or mixture 9. Dirty or plugged idle system passages 10. Hard, brittle or broken gaskets 11. Loose attaching or mounting screws 12. Stuck or misaligned secondary throttle valves
Poor fuel economy	1. Poor driving habits 2. Stuck choke valve 3. Binding choke linkage 4. Stuck heat riser 5. Incorrect idle mixture 6. Defective accelerator pump 7. Air leaks 8. Plugged, loose or incorrect main metering jets 9. Improperly adjusted float or fuel level 10. Bent, misaligned or fuel-clogged float 11. Leaking float needle seat 12. Fuel leak 13. Accelerator pump discharge ball not seating properly 14. Incorrect main jets
Engine lacks high speed performance or power	1. Incorrect throttle linkage adjustment 2. Stuck or binding power piston 3. Defective accelerator pump 4. Air leaks 5. Incorrect float setting or fuel level 6. Dirty, plugged, worn or incorrect main metering jets or rods 7. Binding or sticking air valve 8. Brittle or cracked gaskets 9. Bent, incorrect or improperly adjusted secondary metering rods 10. Clogged fuel filter 11. Clogged air filter 12. Defective fuel pump

TROUBLESHOOTING FUEL INJECTION PROBLEMS

Each fuel injection system has its own unique components and test procedures, for which it is impossible to generalize. Refer to Chapter 4 of this Repair & Tune-Up Guide for specific test and repair procedures, if the vehicle is equipped with fuel injection.

TROUBLESHOOTING ELECTRICAL PROBLEMS

See Chapter 5 for service procedures

For any electrical system to operate, it must make a complete circuit. This simply means that the power flow from the battery must make a complete circle. When an electrical component is operating, power flows from the battery to the component, passes through the component causing it to perform its function (lighting a light bulb), and then returns to the battery through the ground of the circuit. This ground is usually (but not always) the metal part of the car or truck on which the electrical component is mounted.

Perhaps the easiest way to visualize this is to think of connecting a light bulb with two wires attached to it to the battery. If one of the two wires attached to the light bulb were attached to the negative post of the battery and the other were attached to the positive post of the battery, you would have a complete circuit. Current from the battery would flow to the light bulb, causing it to light, and return to the negative post of the battery.

The normal automotive circuit differs from this simple example in two ways. First, instead of having a return wire from the bulb to the battery, the light bulb returns the current to the battery through the chassis of the vehicle. Since the negative battery cable is attached to the chassis and the chassis is made of electrically conductive metal, the chassis of the vehicle can serve as a ground wire to complete the circuit. Secondly, most automotive circuits contain switches to turn components on and off as required.

Every complete circuit from a power source must include a component which is using the power from the power source. If you were to disconnect the light bulb from the wires and touch the two wires together (don't do this) the power supply wire to the component would be grounded before the normal ground connection for the circuit.

Because grounding a wire from a power source makes a complete circuit—less the required component to use the power—this phenomenon is called a short circuit. Common causes are: broken insulation (exposing the metal wire to a metal part of the car or truck), or a shorted switch.

Some electrical components which require a large amount of current to operate also have a relay in their circuit. Since these circuits carry a large amount of current, the thickness of the wire in the circuit (gauge size) is also greater. If this large wire were connected from the component to the control switch on the instrument panel, and then back to the component, a voltage drop would occur in the circuit. To prevent this potential drop in voltage, an electromagnetic switch (relay) is used. The large wires in the circuit are connected from the battery to one side of the relay, and from the opposite side of the relay to the component. The relay is normally open, preventing current from passing through the circuit. An additional, smaller, wire is connected from the relay to the control switch for the circuit. When the control switch is turned on, it grounds the smaller wire from the relay and completes the circuit. This closes the relay and allows current to flow from the battery to the component. The horn, headlight, and starter circuits are three which use relays.

It is possible for larger surges of current to pass through the electrical system of your car or truck. If this surge of current were to reach an electrical component, it could burn it out. To prevent this, fuses, circuit breakers or fusible links are connected into the current supply wires of most of the major electrical systems. When an electrical current of excessive power passes through the component's fuse, the fuse blows out and breaks the circuit, saving the component from destruction.

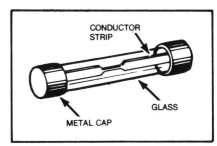

Typical automotive fuse

A circuit breaker is basically a self-repairing fuse. The circuit breaker opens the circuit the same way a fuse does. However, when either the short is removed from the circuit or the surge subsides, the circuit breaker resets itself and does not have to be replaced as a fuse does.

A fuse link is a wire that acts as a fuse. It is normally connected between the starter relay and the main wiring harness. This connection is usually under the hood. The fuse link (if installed) protects all the

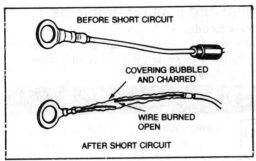

Most fusible links show a charred, melted insulation when they burn out

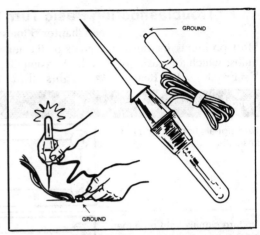

The test light will show the presence of current when touched to a hot wire and grounded at the other end

chassis electrical components, and is the probable cause of trouble when none of the electrical components function, unless the battery is disconnected or dead.

Electrical problems generally fall into one of three areas:

1. The component that is not functioning is not receiving current.

2. The component itself is not functioning.

3. The component is not properly grounded.

The electrical system can be checked with a test light and a jumper wire. A test light is a device that looks like a pointed screwdriver with a wire attached to it and has a light bulb in its handle. A jumper wire is a piece of insulated wire with an alligator clip attached to each end.

If a component is not working, you must follow a systematic plan to determine which of the three causes is the villain.

1. Turn on the switch that controls the inoperable component.

2. Disconnect the power supply wire from the component.

3. Attach the ground wire on the test light to a good metal ground.

4. Touch the probe end of the test light to the end of the power supply wire that was disconnected from the component. If the component is receiving current, the test light will go on.

NOTE: *Some components work only when the ignition switch is turned on.*

If the test light does not go on, then the problem is in the circuit between the battery and the component. This includes all the switches, fuses, and relays in the system. Follow the wire that runs back to the battery. The problem is an open circuit between the

battery and the component. If the fuse is blown and, when replaced, immediately blows again, there is a short circuit in the system which must be located and repaired. If there is a switch in the system, bypass it with a jumper wire. This is done by connecting one end of the jumper wire to the power supply wire into the switch and the other end of the jumper wire to the wire coming out of the switch. If the test light lights with the jumper wire installed, the switch or whatever was bypassed is defective.

NOTE: *Never substitute the jumper wire for the component, since it is required to use the power from the power source.*

5. If the bulb in the test light goes on, then the current is getting to the component that is not working. This eliminates the first of the three possible causes. Connect the power supply wire and connect a jumper wire from the component to a good metal ground. Do this with the switch which controls the component turned on, and also the ignition switch turned on if it is required for the component to work. If the component works with the jumper wire installed, then it has a bad ground. This is usually caused by the metal area on which the component mounts to the chassis being coated with some type of foreign matter.

6. If neither test located the source of the trouble, then the component itself is defective. Remember that for any electrical system to work, all connections must be clean and tight.

Troubleshooting Basic Turn Signal and Flasher Problems
See Chapter 5 for service procedures

Most problems in the turn signals or flasher system can be reduced to defective flashers or bulbs, which are easily replaced. Occasionally, the turn signal switch will prove defective.

F = Front   R = Rear   ● = Lights off   ○ = Lights on

Condition		Possible Cause
Turn signals light, but do not flash	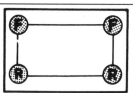	Defective flasher
No turn signals light on either side	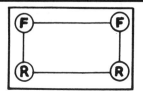	Blown fuse. Replace if defective. Defective flasher. Check by substitution. Open circuit, short circuit or poor ground.
Both turn signals on one side don't work	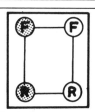	Bad bulbs. Bad ground in both (or either) housings.
One turn signal light on one side doesn't work	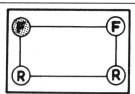	Defective bulb. Corrosion in socket. Clean contacts. Poor ground at socket.
Turn signal flashes too fast or too slowly	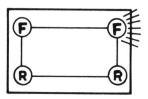	Check any bulb on the side flashing too fast. A heavy-duty bulb is probably installed in place of a regular bulb. Check the bulb flashing too slowly. A standard bulb was probably installed in place of a heavy-duty bulb. Loose connections or corrosion at the bulb socket.
Indicator lights don't work in either direction		Check if the turn signals are working. Check the dash indicator lights. Check the flasher by substitution.
One indicator light doesn't light		On systems with one dash indicator: See if the lights work on the same side. Often the filaments have been reversed in systems combining stoplights with taillights and turn signals. Check the flasher by substitution. On systems with two indicators: Check the bulbs on the same side. Check the indicator light bulb. Check the flasher by substitution.

Troubleshooting Lighting Problems
See Chapter 5 for service procedures

Condition	Possible Cause
One or more lights don't work, but others do	1. Defective bulb(s) 2. Blown fuse(s) 3. Dirty fuse clips or light sockets 4. Poor ground circuit
Lights burn out quickly	1. Incorrect voltage regulator setting or defective regulator 2. Poor battery/alternator connections
Lights go dim	1. Low/discharged battery 2. Alternator not charging 3. Corroded sockets or connections 4. Low voltage output
Lights flicker	1. Loose connection 2. Poor ground. (Run ground wire from light housing to frame) 3. Circuit breaker operating (short circuit)
Lights "flare"—Some flare is normal on acceleration—If excessive, see "Lights Burn Out Quickly"	High voltage setting
Lights glare—approaching drivers are blinded	1. Lights adjusted too high 2. Rear springs or shocks sagging 3. Rear tires soft

Troubleshooting Dash Gauge Problems
Most problems can be traced to a defective sending unit or faulty wiring. Occasionally, the gauge itself is at fault. See Chapter 5 for service procedures.

Condition	Possible Cause
COOLANT TEMPERATURE GAUGE	
Gauge reads erratically or not at all	1. Loose or dirty connections 2. Defective sending unit. 3. Defective gauge. To test a bi-metal gauge, remove the wire from the sending unit. Ground the wire for an instant. If the gauge registers, replace the sending unit. To test a magnetic gauge, disconnect the wire at the sending unit. With ignition ON gauge should register COLD. Ground the wire; gauge should register HOT.

AMMETER GAUGE—TURN HEADLIGHTS ON (DO NOT START ENGINE). NOTE REACTION

Ammeter shows charge Ammeter shows discharge Ammeter does not move	1. Connections reversed on gauge 2. Ammeter is OK 3. Loose connections or faulty wiring 4. Defective gauge

Condition	Possible Cause

OIL PRESSURE GAUGE

Condition	Possible Cause
Gauge does not register or is inaccurate	1. On mechanical gauge, Bourdon tube may be bent or kinked. 2. Low oil pressure. Remove sending unit. Idle the engine briefly. If no oil flows from sending unit hole, problem is in engine. 3. Defective gauge. Remove the wire from the sending unit and ground it for an instant with the ignition ON. A good gauge will go to the top of the scale. 4. Defective wiring. Check the wiring to the gauge. If it's OK and the gauge doesn't register when grounded, replace the gauge. 5. Defective sending unit.

ALL GAUGES

Condition	Possible Cause
All gauges do not operate All gauges read low or erratically All gauges pegged	1. Blown fuse 2. Defective instrument regulator 3. Defective or dirty instrument voltage regulator 4. Loss of ground between instrument voltage regulator and frame 5. Defective instrument regulator

WARNING LIGHTS

Condition	Possible Cause
Light(s) do not come on when ignition is ON, but engine is not started Light comes on with engine running	1. Defective bulb 2. Defective wire 3. Defective sending unit. Disconnect the wire from the sending unit and ground it. Replace the sending unit if the light comes on with the ignition ON. 4. Problem in individual system 5. Defective sending unit

Troubleshooting Clutch Problems

It is false economy to replace individual clutch components. The pressure plate, clutch plate and throwout bearing should be replaced as a set, and the flywheel face inspected, whenever the clutch is overhauled. See Chapter 6 for service procedures.

Condition	Possible Cause
Clutch chatter	1. Grease on driven plate (disc) facing 2. Binding clutch linkage or cable 3. Loose, damaged facings on driven plate (disc) 4. Engine mounts loose 5. Incorrect height adjustment of pressure plate release levers 6. Clutch housing or housing to transmission adapter misalignment 7. Loose driven plate hub
Clutch grabbing	1. Oil, grease on driven plate (disc) facing 2. Broken pressure plate 3. Warped or binding driven plate. Driven plate binding on clutch shaft
Clutch slips	1. Lack of lubrication in clutch linkage or cable (linkage or cable binds, causes incomplete engagement) 2. Incorrect pedal, or linkage adjustment 3. Broken pressure plate springs 4. Weak pressure plate springs 5. Grease on driven plate facings (disc)

Troubleshooting Clutch Problems (cont.)

Condition	Possible Cause
Incomplete clutch release	1. Incorrect pedal or linkage adjustment or linkage or cable binding 2. Incorrect height adjustment on pressure plate release levers 3. Loose, broken facings on driven plate (disc) 4. Bent, dished, warped driven plate caused by overheating
Grinding, whirring grating noise when pedal is depressed	1. Worn or defective throwout bearing 2. Starter drive teeth contacting flywheel ring gear teeth. Look for milled or polished teeth on ring gear.
Squeal, howl, trumpeting noise when pedal is being released (occurs during first inch to inch and one-half of pedal travel)	Pilot bushing worn or lack of lubricant. If bushing appears OK, polish bushing with emery cloth, soak lube wick in oil, lube bushing with oil, apply film of chassis grease to clutch shaft pilot hub, reassemble. NOTE: Bushing wear may be due to misalignment of clutch housing or housing to transmission adapter
Vibration or clutch pedal pulsation with clutch disengaged (pedal fully depressed)	1. Worn or defective engine transmission mounts 2. Flywheel run out. (Flywheel run out at face not to exceed 0.005") 3. Damaged or defective clutch components

Troubleshooting Manual Transmission Problems
See Chapter 6 for service procedures

Condition	Possible Cause
Transmission jumps out of gear	1. Misalignment of transmission case or clutch housing. 2. Worn pilot bearing in crankshaft. 3. Bent transmission shaft. 4. Worn high speed sliding gear. 5. Worn teeth or end-play in clutch shaft. 6. Insufficient spring tension on shifter rail plunger. 7. Bent or loose shifter fork. 8. Gears not engaging completely. 9. Loose or worn bearings on clutch shaft or mainshaft. 10. Worn gear teeth. 11. Worn or damaged detent balls.
Transmission sticks in gear	1. Clutch not releasing fully. 2. Burred or battered teeth on clutch shaft, or sliding sleeve. 3. Burred or battered transmission mainshaft. 4. Frozen synchronizing clutch. 5. Stuck shifter rail plunger. 6. Gearshift lever twisting and binding shifter rail. 7. Battered teeth on high speed sliding gear or on sleeve. 8. Improper lubrication, or lack of lubrication. 9. Corroded transmission parts. 10. Defective mainshaft pilot bearing. 11. Locked gear bearings will give same effect as stuck in gear.
Transmission gears will not synchronize	1. Binding pilot bearing on mainshaft, will synchronize in high gear only. 2. Clutch not releasing fully. 3. Detent spring weak or broken. 4. Weak or broken springs under balls in sliding gear sleeve. 5. Binding bearing on clutch shaft, or binding countershaft. 6. Binding pilot bearing in crankshaft. 7. Badly worn gear teeth. 8. Improper lubrication. 9. Constant mesh gear not turning freely on transmission mainshaft. Will synchronize in that gear only.

Condition	Possible Cause
Gears spinning when shifting into gear from neutral	1. Clutch not releasing fully. 2. In some cases an extremely light lubricant in transmission will cause gears to continue to spin for a short time after clutch is released. 3. Binding pilot bearing in crankshaft.
Transmission noisy in all gears	1. Insufficient lubricant, or improper lubricant. 2. Worn countergear bearings. 3. Worn or damaged main drive gear or countergear. 4. Damaged main drive gear or mainshaft bearings. 5. Worn or damaged countergear anti-lash plate.
Transmission noisy in neutral only	1. Damaged main drive gear bearing. 2. Damaged or loose mainshaft pilot bearing. 3. Worn or damaged countergear anti-lash plate. 4. Worn countergear bearings.
Transmission noisy in one gear only	1. Damaged or worn constant mesh gears. 2. Worn or damaged countergear bearings. 3. Damaged or worn synchronizer.
Transmission noisy in reverse only	1. Worn or damaged reverse idler gear or idler bushing. 2. Worn or damaged mainshaft reverse gear. 3. Worn or damaged reverse countergear. 4. Damaged shift mechanism.

TROUBLESHOOTING AUTOMATIC TRANSMISSION PROBLEMS

Keeping alert to changes in the operating characteristics of the transmission (changing shift points, noises, etc.) can prevent small problems from becoming large ones. If the problem cannot be traced to loose bolts, fluid level, misadjusted linkage, clogged filters or similar problems, you should probably seek professional service.

Transmission Fluid Indications

The appearance and odor of the transmission fluid can give valuable clues to the overall condition of the transmission. Always note the appearance of the fluid when you check the fluid level or change the fluid. Rub a small amount of fluid between your fingers to feel for grit and smell the fluid on the dipstick.

If the fluid appears:	It indicates:
Clear and red colored	Normal operation
Discolored (extremely dark red or brownish) or smells burned	Band or clutch pack failure, usually caused by an overheated transmission. Hauling very heavy loads with insufficient power or failure to change the fluid often result in overheating. Do not confuse this appearance with newer fluids that have a darker red color and a strong odor (though not a burned odor).
Foamy or aerated (light in color and full of bubbles)	1. The level is too high (gear train is churning oil) 2. An internal air leak (air is mixing with the fluid). Have the transmission checked professionally.
Solid residue in the fluid	Defective bands, clutch pack or bearings. Bits of band material or metal abrasives are clinging to the dipstick. Have the transmission checked professionally.
Varnish coating on the dipstick	The transmission fluid is overheating

TROUBLESHOOTING DRIVE AXLE PROBLEMS

First, determine when the noise is most noticeable.

Drive Noise: Produced under vehicle acceleration.

Coast Noise: Produced while coasting with a closed throttle.

Float Noise: Occurs while maintaining constant speed (just enough to keep speed constant) on a level road.

External Noise Elimination

It is advisable to make a thorough road test to determine whether the noise originates in the rear axle or whether it originates from the tires, engine, transmission, wheel bearings or road surface. Noise originating from other places cannot be corrected by servicing the rear axle.

ROAD NOISE

Brick or rough surfaced concrete roads produce noises that seem to come from the rear axle. Road noise is usually identical in Drive or Coast and driving on a different type of road will tell whether the road is the problem.

TIRE NOISE

Tire noise can be mistaken as rear axle noise, even though the tires on the front are at fault. Snow tread and mud tread tires or tires worn unevenly will frequently cause vibrations which seem to originate elsewhere; *temporarily, and for test purposes only,* inflate the tires to 40–50 lbs. This will significantly alter the noise produced by the tires, but will not alter noise from the rear axle. Noises from the rear axle will normally cease at speeds below 30 mph on coast, while tire noise will continue at lower tone as speed is decreased. The rear axle noise will usually change from drive conditions to coast conditions, while tire noise will not. Do not forget to lower the tire pressure to normal after the test is complete.

ENGINE/TRANSMISSION NOISE

Determine at what speed the noise is most pronounced, then stop in a quiet place. With the transmission in Neutral, run the engine through speeds corresponding to road speeds where the noise was noticed. Noises produced with the vehicle standing still are coming from the engine or transmission.

FRONT WHEEL BEARINGS

Front wheel bearing noises, sometimes confused with rear axle noises, will not change when comparing drive and coast conditions. While holding the speed steady, lightly apply the footbrake. This will often cause wheel bearing noise to lessen, as some of the weight is taken off the bearing. Front wheel bearings are easily checked by jacking up the wheels and spinning the wheels. Shaking the wheels will also determine if the wheel bearings are excessively loose.

REAR AXLE NOISES

Eliminating other possible sources can narrow the cause to the rear axle, which normally produces noise from worn gears or bearings. Gear noises tend to peak in a narrow speed range, while bearing noises will usually vary in pitch with engine speeds.

Noise Diagnosis

The Noise Is:	Most Probably Produced By:
1. Identical under Drive or Coast	Road surface, tires or front wheel bearings
2. Different depending on road surface	Road surface or tires
3. Lower as speed is lowered	Tires
4. Similar when standing or moving	Engine or transmission
5. A vibration	Unbalanced tires, rear wheel bearing, unbalanced driveshaft or worn U-joint
6. A knock or click about every two tire revolutions	Rear wheel bearing
7. Most pronounced on turns	Damaged differential gears
8. A steady low-pitched whirring or scraping, starting at low speeds	Damaged or worn pinion bearing
9. A chattering vibration on turns	Wrong differential lubricant or worn clutch plates (limited slip rear axle)
10. Noticed only in Drive, Coast or Float conditions	Worn ring gear and/or pinion gear

Troubleshooting Steering & Suspension Problems

Condition	Possible Cause
Hard steering (wheel is hard to turn)	1. Improper tire pressure 2. Loose or glazed pump drive belt 3. Low or incorrect fluid 4. Loose, bent or poorly lubricated front end parts 5. Improper front end alignment (excessive caster) 6. Bind in steering column or linkage 7. Kinked hydraulic hose 8. Air in hydraulic system 9. Low pump output or leaks in system 10. Obstruction in lines 11. Pump valves sticking or out of adjustment 12. Incorrect wheel alignment
Loose steering (too much play in steering wheel)	1. Loose wheel bearings 2. Faulty shocks 3. Worn linkage or suspension components 4. Loose steering gear mounting or linkage points 5. Steering mechanism worn or improperly adjusted 6. Valve spool improperly adjusted 7. Worn ball joints, tie-rod ends, etc.
Veers or wanders (pulls to one side with hands off steering wheel)	1. Improper tire pressure 2. Improper front end alignment 3. Dragging or improperly adjusted brakes 4. Bent frame 5. Improper rear end alignment 6. Faulty shocks or springs 7. Loose or bent front end components 8. Play in Pitman arm 9. Steering gear mountings loose 10. Loose wheel bearings 11. Binding Pitman arm 12. Spool valve sticking or improperly adjusted 13. Worn ball joints
Wheel oscillation or vibration transmitted through steering wheel	1. Low or uneven tire pressure 2. Loose wheel bearings 3. Improper front end alignment 4. Bent spindle 5. Worn, bent or broken front end components 6. Tires out of round or out of balance 7. Excessive lateral runout in disc brake rotor 8. Loose or bent shock absorber or strut
Noises (see also "Troubleshooting Drive Axle Problems")	1. Loose belts 2. Low fluid, air in system 3. Foreign matter in system 4. Improper lubrication 5. Interference or chafing in linkage 6. Steering gear mountings loose 7. Incorrect adjustment or wear in gear box 8. Faulty valves or wear in pump 9. Kinked hydraulic lines 10. Worn wheel bearings
Poor return of steering	1. Over-inflated tires 2. Improperly aligned front end (excessive caster) 3. Binding in steering column 4. No lubrication in front end 5. Steering gear adjusted too tight
Uneven tire wear (see "How To Read Tire Wear")	1. Incorrect tire pressure 2. Improperly aligned front end 3. Tires out-of-balance 4. Bent or worn suspension parts

HOW TO READ TIRE WEAR

The way your tires wear is a good indicator of other parts of the suspension. Abnormal wear patterns are often caused by the need for simple tire maintenance, or for front end alignment.

Excessive wear at the center of the tread indicates that the air pressure in the tire is consistently too high. The tire is riding on the center of the tread and wearing it prematurely. Occasionally, this wear pattern can result from outrageously wide tires on narrow rims. The cure for this is to replace either the tires or the wheels.

This type of wear usually results from consistent under-inflation. When a tire is under-inflated, there is too much contact with the road by the outer treads, which wear prematurely. When this type of wear occurs, and the tire pressure is known to be consistently correct, a bent or worn steering component or the need for wheel alignment could be indicated.

Feathering is a condition when the edge of each tread rib develops a slightly rounded edge on one side and a sharp edge on the other. By running your hand over the tire, you can usually feel the sharper edges before you'll be able to see them. The most common causes of feathering are incorrect toe-in setting or deteriorated bushings in the front suspension.

When an inner or outer rib wears faster than the rest of the tire, the need for wheel alignment is indicated. There is excessive camber in the front suspension, causing the wheel to lean too much putting excessive load on one side of the tire. Misalignment could also be due to sagging springs, worn ball joints, or worn control arm bushings. Be sure the vehicle is loaded the way it's normally driven when you have the wheels aligned.

Cups or scalloped dips appearing around the edge of the tread almost always indicate worn (sometimes bent) suspension parts. Adjustment of wheel alignment alone will seldom cure the problem. Any worn component that connects the wheel to the suspension can cause this type of wear. Occasionally, wheels that are out of balance will wear like this, but wheel imbalance usually shows up as bald spots between the outside edges and center of the tread.

Second-rib wear is usually found only in radial tires, and appears where the steel belts end in relation to the tread. It can be kept to a minimum by paying careful attention to tire pressure and frequently rotating the tires. This is often considered normal wear but excessive amounts indicate that the tires are too wide for the wheels.

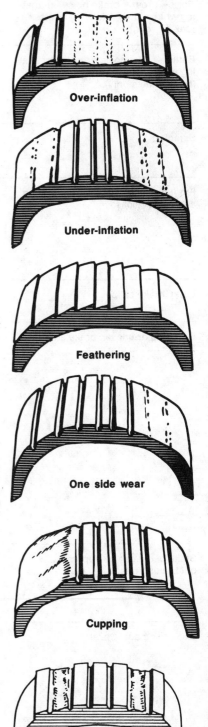

Over-inflation

Under-inflation

Feathering

One side wear

Cupping

Second-rib wear

Troubleshooting Disc Brake Problems

Condition	Possible Cause
Noise—groan—brake noise emanating when slowly releasing brakes (creep-groan)	Not detrimental to function of disc brakes—no corrective action required. (This noise may be eliminated by slightly increasing or decreasing brake pedal efforts.)
Rattle—brake noise or rattle emanating at low speeds on rough roads, (front wheels only).	1. Shoe anti-rattle spring missing or not properly positioned. 2. Excessive clearance between shoe and caliper. 3. Soft or broken caliper seals. 4. Deformed or misaligned disc. 5. Loose caliper.
Scraping	1. Mounting bolts too long. 2. Loose wheel bearings. 3. Bent, loose, or misaligned splash shield.
Front brakes heat up during driving and fail to release	1. Operator riding brake pedal. 2. Stop light switch improperly adjusted. 3. Sticking pedal linkage. 4. Frozen or seized piston. 5. Residual pressure valve in master cylinder. 6. Power brake malfunction. 7. Proportioning valve malfunction.
Leaky brake caliper	1. Damaged or worn caliper piston seal. 2. Scores or corrosion on surface of cylinder bore.
Grabbing or uneven brake action—Brakes pull to one side	1. Causes listed under "Brakes Pull". 2. Power brake malfunction. 3. Low fluid level in master cylinder. 4. Air in hydraulic system. 5. Brake fluid, oil or grease on linings. 6. Unmatched linings. 7. Distorted brake pads. 8. Frozen or seized pistons. 9. Incorrect tire pressure. 10. Front end out of alignment. 11. Broken rear spring. 12. Brake caliper pistons sticking. 13. Restricted hose or line. 14. Caliper not in proper alignment to braking disc. 15. Stuck or malfunctioning metering valve. 16. Soft or broken caliper seals. 17. Loose caliper.
Brake pedal can be depressed without braking effect	1. Air in hydraulic system or improper bleeding procedure. 2. Leak past primary cup in master cylinder. 3. Leak in system. 4. Rear brakes out of adjustment. 5. Bleeder screw open.
Excessive pedal travel	1. Air, leak, or insufficient fluid in system or caliper. 2. Warped or excessively tapered shoe and lining assembly. 3. Excessive disc runout. 4. Rear brake adjustment required. 5. Loose wheel bearing adjustment. 6. Damaged caliper piston seal. 7. Improper brake fluid (boil). 8. Power brake malfunction. 9. Weak or soft hoses.

Troubleshooting Disc Brake Problems (cont.)

Condition	Possible Cause
Brake roughness or chatter (pedal pumping)	1. Excessive thickness variation of braking disc. 2. Excessive lateral runout of braking disc. 3. Rear brake drums out-of-round. 4. Excessive front bearing clearance.
Excessive pedal effort	1. Brake fluid, oil or grease on linings. 2. Incorrect lining. 3. Frozen or seized pistons. 4. Power brake malfunction. 5. Kinked or collapsed hose or line. 6. Stuck metering valve. 7. Scored caliper or master cylinder bore. 8. Seized caliper pistons.
Brake pedal fades (pedal travel increases with foot on brake)	1. Rough master cylinder or caliper bore. 2. Loose or broken hydraulic lines/connections. 3. Air in hydraulic system. 4. Fluid level low. 5. Weak or soft hoses. 6. Inferior quality brake shoes or fluid. 7. Worn master cylinder piston cups or seals.

Troubleshooting Drum Brakes

Condition	Possible Cause
Pedal goes to floor	1. Fluid low in reservoir. 2. Air in hydraulic system. 3. Improperly adjusted brake. 4. Leaking wheel cylinders. 5. Loose or broken brake lines. 6. Leaking or worn master cylinder. 7. Excessively worn brake lining.
Spongy brake pedal	1. Air in hydraulic system. 2. Improper brake fluid (low boiling point). 3. Excessively worn or cracked brake drums. 4. Broken pedal pivot bushing.
Brakes pulling	1. Contaminated lining. 2. Front end out of alignment. 3. Incorrect brake adjustment. 4. Unmatched brake lining. 5. Brake drums out of round. 6. Brake shoes distorted. 7. Restricted brake hose or line. 8. Broken rear spring. 9. Worn brake linings. 10. Uneven lining wear. 11. Glazed brake lining. 12. Excessive brake lining dust. 13. Heat spotted brake drums. 14. Weak brake return springs. 15. Faulty automatic adjusters. 16. Low or incorrect tire pressure.

Condition	Possible Cause
Squealing brakes	1. Glazed brake lining. 2. Saturated brake lining. 3. Weak or broken brake shoe retaining spring. 4. Broken or weak brake shoe return spring. 5. Incorrect brake lining. 6. Distorted brake shoes. 7. Bent support plate. 8. Dust in brakes or scored brake drums. 9. Linings worn below limit. 10. Uneven brake lining wear. 11. Heat spotted brake drums.
Chirping brakes	1. Out of round drum or eccentric axle flange pilot.
Dragging brakes	1. Incorrect wheel or parking brake adjustment. 2. Parking brakes engaged or improperly adjusted. 3. Weak or broken brake shoe return spring. 4. Brake pedal binding. 5. Master cylinder cup sticking. 6. Obstructed master cylinder relief port. 7. Saturated brake lining. 8. Bent or out of round brake drum. 9. Contaminated or improper brake fluid. 10. Sticking wheel cylinder pistons. 11. Driver riding brake pedal. 12. Defective proportioning valve. 13. Insufficient brake shoe lubricant.
Hard pedal	1. Brake booster inoperative. 2. Incorrect brake lining. 3. Restricted brake line or hose. 4. Frozen brake pedal linkage. 5. Stuck wheel cylinder. 6. Binding pedal linkage. 7. Faulty proportioning valve.
Wheel locks	1. Contaminated brake lining. 2. Loose or torn brake lining. 3. Wheel cylinder cups sticking. 4. Incorrect wheel bearing adjustment. 5. Faulty proportioning valve.
Brakes fade (high speed)	1. Incorrect lining. 2. Overheated brake drums. 3. Incorrect brake fluid (low boiling temperature). 4. Saturated brake lining. 5. Leak in hydraulic system. 6. Faulty automatic adjusters.
Pedal pulsates	1. Bent or out of round brake drum.
Brake chatter and shoe knock	1. Out of round brake drum. 2. Loose support plate. 3. Bent support plate. 4. Distorted brake shoes. 5. Machine grooves in contact face of brake drum (Shoe Knock). 6. Contaminated brake lining. 7. Missing or loose components. 8. Incorrect lining material. 9. Out-of-round brake drums. 10. Heat spotted or scored brake drums. 11. Out-of-balance wheels.

Troubleshooting Drum Brakes (cont.)

Condition	*Possible Cause*
Brakes do not self adjust	1. Adjuster screw frozen in thread. 2. Adjuster screw corroded at thrust washer. 3. Adjuster lever does not engage star wheel. 4. Adjuster installed on wrong wheel.
Brake light glows	1. Leak in the hydraulic system. 2. Air in the system. 3. Improperly adjusted master cylinder pushrod. 4. Uneven lining wear. 5. Failure to center combination valve or proportioning valve.

Mechanic's Data

General Conversion Table

Multiply By	To Convert	To	
		LENGTH	
2.54	Inches	Centimeters	.3937
25.4	Inches	Millimeters	.03937
30.48	Feet	Centimeters	.0328
.304	Feet	Meters	3.28
.914	Yards	Meters	1.094
1.609	Miles	Kilometers	.621
		VOLUME	
.473	Pints	Liters	2.11
.946	Quarts	Liters	1.06
3.785	Gallons	Liters	.264
.016	Cubic inches	Liters	61.02
16.39	Cubic inches	Cubic cms.	.061
28.3	Cubic feet	Liters	.0353
		MASS (Weight)	
28.35	Ounces	Grams	.035
.4536	Pounds	Kilograms	2.20
—	To obtain	From	Multiply by

Multiply By	To Convert	To	
		AREA	
.645	Square inches	Square cms.	.155
.836	Square yds.	Square meters	1.196
		FORCE	
4.448	Pounds	Newtons	.225
.138	Ft./lbs.	Kilogram/meters	7.23
1.36	Ft./lbs.	Newton-meters	.737
.112	In./lbs.	Newton-meters	8.844
		PRESSURE	
.068	Psi	Atmospheres	14.7
6.89	Psi	Kilopascals	.145
		OTHER	
1.104	Horsepower (DIN)	Horsepower (SAE)	.9861
.746	Horsepower (SAE)	Kilowatts (KW)	1.34
1.60	Mph	Km/h	.625
.425	Mpg	Km/1	2.35
—	To obtain	From	Multiply by

Tap Drill Sizes

National Coarse or U.S.S.

Screw & Tap Size	Threads Per Inch	Use Drill Number
No. 5	40	39
No. 6	32	36
No. 8	32	29
No. 10	24	25
No. 12	24	17
1/4	20	8
5/16	18	F
3/8	16	5/16
7/16	14	U
1/2	13	27/64
9/16	12	31/64
5/8	11	17/32
3/4	10	21/32
7/8	9	49/64

National Coarse or U.S.S.

Screw & Tap Size	Threads Per Inch	Use Drill Number
1	8	7/8
1 1/8	7	63/64
1 1/4	7	1 7/64
1 1/2	6	1 11/32

National Fine or S.A.E.

Screw & Tap Size	Threads Per Inch	Use Drill Number
No. 5	44	37
No. 6	40	33
No. 8	36	29
No. 10	32	21

National Fine or S.A.E.

Screw & Tap Size	Threads Per Inch	Use Drill Number
No. 12	28	15
1/4	28	3
6/16	24	1
3/8	24	Q
7/16	20	W
1/2	20	29/64
9/16	18	33/64
5/8	18	37/64
3/4	16	11/16
7/8	14	13/16
1 1/8	12	1 3/64
1 1/4	12	1 11/64
1 1/2	12	1 27/64

Drill Sizes In Decimal Equivalents

Inch	Decimal	Wire	mm	Inch	Decimal	Wire	mm	Inch	Decimal	Wire & Letter	mm	Inch	Decimal	Letter	mm	Inch	Decimal	mm
1/64	.0156		.39		.0730	49			.1614		4.1		.2717		6.9		.4331	11.0
	.0157		.4		.0748		1.9		.1654		4.2		.2720	I		7/16	.4375	11.11
	.0160	78			.0760	48			.1660	19			.2756		7.0		.4528	11.5
	.0165		.42		.0768		1.95		.1673		4.25		.2770	J		29/64	.4531	11.51
	.0173		.44	5/64	.0781		1.98		.1693		4.3		.2795		7.1	15/32	.4688	11.90
	.0177		.45		.0785	47			.1695	18			.2810	K			.4724	12.0
	.0180	77			.0787		2.0	11/64	.1719		4.36	9/32	.2812		7.14	31/64	.4844	12.30
	.0181		.46		.0807		2.05		.1730	17			.2835		7.2		.4921	12.5
	.0189		.48		.0810	46			.1732		4.4		.2854		7.25	1/2	.5000	12.70
	.0197		.5		.0820	45			.1770	16			.2874		7.3		.5118	13.0
	.0200	76			.0827		2.1		.1772		4.5		.2900	L		33/64	.5156	13.09
	.0210	75			.0846		2.15		.1800	15			.2913		7.4	17/32	.5312	13.49
	.0217		.55		.0860	44			.1811		4.6		.2950	M			.5315	13.5
	.0225	74			.0866		2.2		.1820	14			.2953		7.5	35/64	.5469	13.89
	.0236		.6		.0886		2.25		.1850	13		19/64	.2969		7.54		.5512	14.0
	.0240	73			.0890	43			.1850		4.7		.2992		7.6	9/16	.5625	14.28
	.0250	72			.0906		2.3		.1870		4.75		.3020	N			.5709	14.5
	.0256		.65		.0925		2.35	3/16	.1875		4.76		.3031		7.7	37/64	.5781	14.68
	.0260	71			.0935	42			.1890		4.8		.3051		7.75		.5906	15.0
	.0276		.7	3/32	.0938		2.38		.1890	12			.3071		7.8	19/32	.5938	15.08
	.0280	70			.0945		2.4		.1910	11			.3110		7.9	39/64	.6094	15.47
	.0292	69			.0960	41			.1929		4.9	5/16	.3125		7.93		.6102	15.5
	.0295		.75		.0965		2.45		.1935	10			.3150		8.0	5/8	.6250	15.87
	.0310	68			.0980	40			.1960	9			.3160	O			.6299	16.0
1/32	.0312		.79		.0981		2.5		.1969		5.0		.3189		8.1	41/64	.6406	16.27
	.0315		.8		.0995	39			.1990	8			.3228		8.2		.6496	16.5
	.0320	67			.1015	38			.2008		5.1		.3230	P		21/32	.6562	16.66
	.0330	66			.1024		2.6		.2010	7			.3248		8.25		.6693	17.0
	.0335		.85		.1040	37		13/64	.2031		5.16		.3268		8.3	43/64	.6719	17.06
	.0350	65			.1063		2.7		.2040	6		21/64	.3281		8.33	11/16	.6875	17.46
	.0354		.9		.1065	36			.2047		5.2		.3307		8.4		.6890	17.5
	.0360	64			.1083		2.75		.2055	5			.3320	Q		45/64	.7031	17.85
	.0370	63		7/64	.1094		2.77		.2067		5.25		.3346		8.5		.7087	18.0
	.0374		.95		.1100	35			.2087		5.3		.3386		8.6	23/32	.7188	18.25
	.0380	62			.1102		2.8		.2090	4			.3390	R			.7283	18.5
	.0390	61			.1110	34			.2126		5.4		.3425		8.7	47/64	.7344	18.65
	.0394		1.0		.1130	33			.2130	3		11/32	.3438		8.73		.7480	19.0
	.0400	60			.1142		2.9		.2165		5.5		.3445		8.75	3/4	.7500	19.05
	.0410	59			.1160	32		7/32	2188		5.55		.3465		8.8	49/64	.7656	19.44
	.0413		1.05		.1181		3.0		.2205		5.6		.3480	S			.7677	19.5
	.0420	58			.1200	31			.2210	2			.3504		8.9	25/32	.7812	19.84
	.0430	57			.1220		3.1		.2244		5.7		.3543		9.0		.7874	20.0
	.0433		1.1	1/8	.1250		3.17		.2264		5.75		.3580	T		51/64	.7969	20.24
	.0453		1.15		.1260		3.2		.2280	1			.3583		9.1		.8071	20.5
	.0465	56			.1280		3.25		.2283		5.8	23/64	.3594		9.12	13/16	.8125	20.63
3/64	.0469		1.19		.1285	30			.2323		5.9		.3622		9.2		.8268	21.0
	.0472		1.2		.1299		3.3		.2340	A			.3642		9.25	53/64	.8281	21.03
	.0492		1.25		.1339		3.4	15/64	.2344		5.95		.3661		9.3	27/32	.8438	21.43
	.0512		1.3		.1360	29			.2362		6.0		.3680	U			.8465	21.5
	.0520	55			.1378		3.5		.2380	B			.3701		9.4	55/64	.8594	21.82
	.0531		1.35		.1405	28			.2402		6.1		.3740		9.5		.8661	22.0
	.0550	54		9/64	.1406		3.57		.2420	C		3/8	.3750		9.52	7/8	.8750	22.22
	.0551		1.4		.1417		3.6		.2441		6.2		.3770	V			.8858	22.5
	.0571		1.45		.1440	27			.2460	D			.3780		9.6	57/64	.8906	22.62
	.0591		1.5		.1457		3.7		.2461		6.25		.3819		9.7		.9055	23.0
	.0595	53			.1470	26			.2480		6.3		.3839		9.75	29/32	.9062	23.01
	.0610		1.55		.1476		3.75	1/4	.2500	E	6.35		.3858		9.8	59/64	.9219	23.41
1/16	.0625		1.59		.1495	25			.2520		6.		.3860	W			.9252	23.5
	.0630		1.6		.1496		3.8		.2559		6.5		.3898		9.9	15/16	.9375	23.81
	.0635	52			.1520	24			.2570	F		25/64	.3906		9.92		.9449	24.0
	.0650		1.65		.1535		3.9		.2598		6.6		.3937		10.0	61/64	.9531	24.2
	.0669		1.7		.1540	23			.2610	G			.3970	X			.9646	24.5
	.0670	51		5/32	.1562		3.96		.2638		6.7		.4040	Y		31/32	.9688	24.6
	.0689		1.75		.1570	22		17/64	.2656		6.74	13/32	.4062		10.31		.9843	25.0
	.0700	50			.1575		4.0		.2657		6.75		.4130	Z		63/64	.9844	25.0
	.0709		1.8		.1590	21			.2660	H			.4134		10.5	1	1.0000	25.4
	.0728		1.85		.1610	20			.2677		6.8	27/64	.4219		10.71			

Index